Springer Geography

The Springer Geography series seeks to publish a broad portfolio of scientific books, aiming at researchers, students, and everyone interested in geographical research. The series includes peer-reviewed monographs, edited volumes, textbooks, and conference proceedings. It covers the entire research area of geography including, but not limited to, Economic Geography, Physical Geography, Quantitative Geography, and Regional/Urban Planning.

More information about this series at http://www.springer.com/series/10180

Joseph Strasser

Bangladesh's Leather Industry

Local Production Networks in the Global Economy

Springer

Joseph Strasser
Humboldt-Universität zu Berlin
Berlin
Germany

ISSN 2194-315X ISSN 2194-3168 (electronic)
Springer Geography
ISBN 978-3-319-22547-0 ISBN 978-3-319-22548-7 (eBook)
DOI 10.1007/978-3-319-22548-7

Library of Congress Control Number: 2015946776

Springer Cham Heidelberg New York Dordrecht London

Printed on acid-free paper

Springer International Publishing AG Switzerland is part of Springer Science+Business Media (www.springer.com)

To Shumon
Deceased on February 2, 2014

Acknowledgments

When I started the endeavour of a research project on Bangladesh's leather industry, I was unaware of the challenges posed by collecting information in the tanning estate. The language barrier, the pitfalls of intercultural communication, or the complexity of technical processes made the research process sometimes a daunting task. "Hazaribagh is not easy to fathom", I was told. Securing a livelihood there is even less so, as I learned in the course of my fieldwork. There are no words to describe my gratitude for all those people who engaged in either brief conversations or long-winded interviews, providing me with valuable insights into the leather sector while they put their own work on hold. Many of them I met several times, with some of them a relationship grew. One young man in his late twenties I witnessed physically deteriorate from early 2011, when he drove me on his motorbike through the tanning estate to his factory where he processed leather offcuts as inputs into fish and poultry feed, to late 2012 when he was already struggling with an inexplicable disease that had left him paralysed half a year ago. In February 2014, he was dead. It is pointless to speculate whether the daily exposure to highly toxic chemicals had a lethal impact on his health. This tragedy, however, gives reason to demand responsibility from decision-makers to finally commit to improving production conditions and reducing the vulnerability of all workers, entrepreneurs, and residents. Hazaribagh is due for change. This book is therefore dedicated to Shumon.

Given these circumstances, support of any kind was all the more important. I would like to express my gratitude to my supervisor Prof. Dr. Elmar Kulke, whose help, understanding, and patience contributed considerably to me completing my doctoral degree. It was under his guidance that I developed a focus in value chain research. I would like to thank the other reviewers Prof. Dr. Boris Braun and Prof. Dr. Peter Dannenberg for the assistance they provided at all levels of the research project. I very much appreciate their contributions in the form of regional and conceptual expertise.

I owe special thanks to my former colleagues from Dhaka INNOVATE Dr. Katrin Burkart and Dr. Oliver Grübner for their encouragement, inspirational discussions, and support at times of critical need. I am also thankful to the other project members Dr. Md. Mobarak Hossain Khan, Prof. Dr. Wilfried Endlicher, Prof. Dr. Patrick Hostert, and Prof. Dr. Alexander Krämer for their successful cooperation. The priority programme "Megacities-Megachallenge: Informal Dynamics of Global Change", of which Dhaka INNOVATE was a part, contributed immensely to my personal and professional development. I am especially grateful to Harald Sterly and Christine Hobelsberger for insightful and encouraging discussions. I appreciated the guidance, support, and hospitality of Dr. Md. Humayun Kabir and Dr. Roxana Hafiz at our partner institutions, University of Dhaka and Bangladesh University of Engineering and Technology (BUET).

I particularly owe my gratitude to my research assistants in Dhaka who were provided by the Department of Geography of the University of Dhaka and by the Department of Urban and Regional Planning of BUET without whose language skills and locational knowledge I would have been literally lost. I am indebted to Yasin Wahid Rabby for his time, accuracy, and loyalty particularly towards the end of the project. For their knowledge of the local area, their transcription, and translation work, I am grateful to Rabiul Islam, Reaid Alam, Yousuf Mahid, Al Emran, Shahanaz Aktar, Tazrina Habib Ananya, Md. Muhib Kabir, Mahbub Hasan, Muhammad Mahbubul Huq, Sohel Rana, Mehedi Hasan, Afia Sutana Shanta, Shuvangkor Shusmoy Roy, Md. Arif Hasan, Nishat Sharmin, Sobhana Nowshin, Mosharaf Hossain, Nabila Nur, and Shahadat Hossain Shakil.

I thank my former colleagues from the Economic Geography Division for their support and helpful discussions on my research work: Torsten Schmidt, Eva Fraedrich, Robert Kitzmann, Dr. Lech Suwala, Maria Caterina Velte, Juhl Jörgensen, Wolf-Dietrich Peiker, Sascha Brinkhoff, Sylvana Jahre, Janina Dobrowski, Marc Steinke, Mattias Romberg, Sabine Freigang, and Kathrin Klementz. I am especially obliged to Dr. Karsten Lehmann for the time, interest, and insightful comments he gave during my research as well as on the review of my final draft. I also would like to acknowledge Uta Schneider for her research assistance in the project. I am grateful to Lindsay Jane Munro who checked the final draft of the thesis for spelling and grammar.

I gratefully acknowledge the funding sources that made my doctoral research possible. I received funding from the German Research Foundation (DFG) within the priority programme (SPP 1233) "Megacities-Megachallenge: Informal Dynamics of Global Change" under Grant KU 884/16-3.

My time in Dhaka was made enjoyable in large part due to the company of Harald Sterly, Christine Hobelsberger, Annika Salingré, Silke Christiansen, Timm Boeken, Iris Schultz, Nils Jahn, and Lena Oppitz, with whom I shared both apartment and office, and emotional highs and lows in the process. Thank you for the many cups of tea you shared with me and your understanding that helped make sense of all of this.

Last, I would like to thank my closest friends and family for the motivation, encouragement, and support they provided me to complete this work. I acknowledge that this has not been just a taxing experience for me. Thank you.

March 2015 Joseph Strasser

Contents

Abbreviations and Acronyms

BCSIC	Bangladesh Cottage and Small Industries Corporation
BFLLFEA	Bangladesh Finished Leather, Leather goods and Footwear Exporters Association
BHSMA	Bangladesh Hide and Skin Merchants Association
BLSC	Bangladesh Leather Service Centre
BOI	Board of Investment
BPC	Business Promotion Council
BSCI	Business Social Compliance Initiative
BTA	Bangladesh Tannery Association
CETP	Central Effluent Treatment Plant
CF	Cost and Freight
COD	Chemical Oxygen Demand
COEL	Center of Excellence for Leather Skill Bangladesh Limited
CSR	Corporate Social Responsibility
DA	Documents against Acceptance
DCCI	Dhaka Chamber of Commerce and Industry
DLS	Department of Livestock Services
DE	Department of Environment
EC	European Commission
EPA	Environmental Protection Agency
EPB	Export Promotion Bureau
EPZ	Export Processing Zone
ETI	Ethical Trading Initiative
EU	European Union
FAO	Food and Agriculture Organization of the United Nations
FDI	Foreign Direct Investment
FOB	Freight on Board
GCC	Global Commodity Chain
GPN	Global Production Network
GVC	Global Value Chain
ILO	International Labour Organization

ISO	International Organization for Standardization
ITC	International Trade Centre
LC	Letter of Credit
LFMEAB	Leather Goods and Footwear Manufacturers and Exporters Association of Bangladesh
LGF	Leather goods and footwear
LSBPC	Leather Sector Business Promotion Council
LTSE	Leather Technologist SME Entrepreneurs
MDG	Millennium Development Goals
MSM	Micro-, Small-, and Medium-sized
MSME	Micro-, Small-, and Medium-sized Enterprises
NBR	National Board of Revenue
NGO	Non-governmental Organisation
NIE	New Institutional Economics
OHS	Occupational Health and Safety
PRICE	Poverty Reduction by Increasing the Competitiveness of Enterprises
RHS	Raw hides and skins
SCPR	Social Compliance and Producer relations
SEHD	Society for Environment and Human Development
SME	Small- and Medium-sized Enterprises
TT	Telegraphic Transfer
UN-DESA	United Nations, Department of Economic and Social Affairs
UNDP	United Nations Development Programme
UNIDO	United Nations Industrial Development Organization
USAID	United States Agency for International Development
US CPSC	United States Consumer Product Safety Commission
WFTO	World Fair Trade Organization

Chapter 1
Introduction

Abstract This section introduces into the dynamics of global production networks from the perspective of Bangladesh's little diversified economy. It puts recent disasters such as the collapse of Rana Plaza in April 2013 into a larger perspective of low-cost sourcing strategies of northern multinational companies. Against the backdrop of the garment industry being the central driver of Bangladesh's economy, the leather sector has been picked as a case study to showcase the coordination of inter-firm linkages in a marginalised but globally integrated industry. This work identifies institutional limitations that constrain competitiveness, points to adaptation strategies of local producers and presents the potential for improvement along the supply chain. Questions are raised as to what enterprises are actively involved in the global leather production network. Different from studies examining trade flows from the Global South to northern consumption markets, this book focuses on power relationships between local lead firms and micro, small and medium-sized enterprises (MSME) supplying and being subcontracted within local production networks. In particular, the conditions under which local MSMEs achieve exports are often overlooked and will be subject to analysis.

1.1 Rationale of the Study

Since the 1990s, Bangladesh's economy has experienced striking growth. Global division of labour, trade liberalisation and western consumer demands have boosted the labour-intensive garment industry in the South Asian low-cost nation to over 80 % of national export earnings (ITC 2014). Other export industries like jute, leather or fish and crustacean have been outshone in Bangladesh's little-diversified economy. Remarkably, economic growth has been accompanied by substantial improvements in other sectors. Bangladesh has already met several targets of the Millennium Development Goals (MDG) such as gender parity in primary and secondary education, under-five mortality and others (UNDP 2014). It has also made major progress in reducing the population living below $1 a day, although

J. Strasser, *Bangladesh's Leather Industry*,
Springer Geography, DOI 10.1007/978-3-319-22548-7_1

numbers have been stable in absolute terms (UNDP 2014). Despite promising development in the last decades, neoliberal policies have engulfed progress in social and environmental sustainability. Rampant economic growth symbolised by factories mushrooming at the urban fringe and urban sprawl driven by massive in-migration prompted the destruction of eco-systems by illegal land filling and development projects particularly around Bangladesh's capital (e.g. Jahangir Alam 2014; Islam 2005; SEHD 2002). Today, Dhaka ranks among the largest megacities in the world (UN-DESA 2014). However, housing facilities, public services and livelihood opportunities are lacking for a large part of the population (Hossain 2011).

With the garment industry growing at record rates, Bangladesh became the second largest clothes exporter after China. In particular, female labourers have benefited from employment opportunities in large export-oriented factories. A series of fatal disasters (e.g. Spectrum collapse in 2005; KTS textile fire in 2006; Tazreen fire in 2012; see Clean Clothes Campaign 2014) revealed the vulnerability of a thriving but unregulated industry embedded in global dynamics. The collapse of Rana Plaza in April 2013 epitomises the cynical excrescences of a globalising economy that connects labour-intensive low-cost industries in the South to northern markets at the expense of the most vulnerable. With 1,139 dead workers (and more than 2,500 injured), most of them female, the highest death toll ever registered in the history of manufacturing called worldwide attention to inhumane conditions at the lowest end of global production chains or networks (Clean Clothes Campaign 2014). A calamitous alliance of negligent factory owners, corrupt politicians and profit-seeking multinational companies was held to account for lax compliance with and enforcement of safety standards (e.g. building and fire standards). Non-governmental organisations (NGO) in consumer countries have been pressuring large global brands and retailers (e.g. Aldi, Benetton, Lidl, Mango, Primark, Zara) to meet social and production standards in low-cost countries (Clean Clothes Campaign 2014).[1] Irrespective of the responsibility of local elites infringing upon laws and regulations, Bangladesh's history of deadly industrial accidents is inextricably tied to the North's sourcing strategies and its insatiable demand for cheap consumer goods.

Trade is globally organised, but what matters is how it is organised (Sturgeon 2006). Labour-intensive manufacturing industries tend to be embedded in global production and distribution networks or chains respectively, where the position in the latter defines the value-added of the activity. It is generally agreed that global buying companies at the top end of the chain coordinate a sequence of economic activities from least productive activities in low-cost countries (e.g. assembly) to more value-added functions such as research and development (R&D), design or marketing concentrated in northern headquarters (e.g. Sturgeon 2009; Gereffi et al.

[1]One year after that, 155 global brands and retailers signed the Accord on Fire and Building Safety for their more than 1,000 supplying factories (of approximately 4,500) in Bangladesh (Clean Clothes Campaign 2013).

2005; Humphrey and Schmitz 2002; Gereffi 1994). However, tragedies such as Rana Plaza highlight a failure of governance as a result of changing coordination and control schemes within those chains: large global retailers either source directly from large producers in developing countries or in recent times increasingly from brokering intermediaries (Silva 2013). In either case, the final producer is often unknown and excluded from the global lead firm's control. Although this sourcing strategy has become a globalised practice, what is frequently overlooked is that large buyers tend to purchase from factories that are able to deliver equivalent quantities. The large supply base in low-cost countries, however, is constituted by micro, small and medium-sized enterprises (MSME), and the conditions under which they achieve exports often remain unnoticed.

In a low-cost sourcing strategy price determines competition. The current pressure on global brands and retailers testifies to the complex reality of labour-intensive, with often-polluting industries from developing countries being unfairly incorporated in global markets. The gains and strains of the corresponding economic activities are unevenly distributed at both global and local level. While NGOs raise awareness of poor production conditions and insufficient wages in large export factories, the conditions under which MSMEs cater to the international market generally escape public attention. Power asymmetries in local production networks and their impact on cross-border customer-producer relations are often missed; particularly, when it comes to industries that play a minor role in a country's export structure. Bangladesh's leather sector is not just a small national export earner and weakly integrated in the world market (see Sect. 1.2); the complexity of leather processing, for instance, encompasses a few intermediate products and the producers of each cannot be traced. Hence, the leather goods or footwear manufacturers might use finished leather as a raw material that has been processed by different tanneries, sometimes even in different countries. Such complexity leads to questions as to who is actively involved in global production networks and chains respectively, and under what circumstances.

Central to understanding global value chains is that spatially disperse buyer-supplier relations underlie an uneven distribution of information and knowledge. Such asymmetries at global level demand weaker actors at the lower end of the supply chain to adapt, often by means of informal practices. With power being asymmetrically distributed in local production networks, the competitiveness and market integration of SMEs is assumed to be affected, too. Such dynamics are strikingly visible in Bangladesh's leather industry, which consists of an export-oriented but ailing tanning industry and a leather goods and footwear sub-sector the export performance of which is picking up dynamically. This study aims to reveal power asymmetries in market integration and resulting (informal) adaptation strategies that serve for market entry. It advocates a holistic view of the local production network embedded in the global economy, analysing structures, processes and power asymmetries at the local level as a result of interdependencies with global dynamics.

1.2 Definition and Objectives of the Study

Bangladesh's remarkable economic growth has had little impact on the leather industry yet. Despite a notable effect on employment[2] and a favourable endowment of natural resources,[3] leather products in Bangladesh account for just 2 % of national exports compared to 83 % in garments and rank fifth in Bangladesh's scarcely diversified export economy (ITC 2014). The subsectoral export performance reflects an uneven development however, with the higher value-added leather goods and footwear sectors closing in on the more volatile leather processing industry (see Sect. 5.2.3.2). Despite a quick recovery after the global economic downturn in 2008 and constant improvements since, Bangladesh's leather industry lacks the competitiveness to keep up with some of its dynamically growing South and Southeast Asian neighbours (e.g. India, Vietnam). Its share of leather products in the world market accounts for only 0.36 % (ITC 2014), placing it 29th, one ahead of Pakistan (Fig. 1.1).

The major drawbacks in the leather processing industry in Bangladesh are homemade. Insufficiently developed backward linkages cause chronic shortages of raw hides and skins (see Strasser et al. 2013), or make leather processors reliant on importing machinery and inputs such as chemicals. When it comes to exporting leather, Bangladeshi producers have limited capabilities to acquire international buyers. Thus, tanners and commercial leather exporters[4] need to rely on the services of powerful brokers (buying agents). These agents carry out important functions to link up buyers and suppliers but also concentrate knowledge and information, preventing leather processors from moving on to more value-added functions.

In contrast, Bangladesh's leather manufacturing industry has experienced dynamic export growth since the beginning of the millennium, though from a very low level. Few large leather goods and footwear producers cater to international buyers, while micro, small and medium-sized manufacturers (MSMEs) lack the capabilities to export on a regular basis. MSMEs represent the large supply base serving the domestic market. However, they do not have direct access to their major source of income as the market is controlled by few local lead firms which integrate MSMEs selectively into their supply chain by subcontracting. Power inequalities in both markets appear to impede a better integration of MSMEs.

In addition to uneven inter-firm linkages, the institutional environment in Bangladesh has not kept pace with the changing requirements of international markets that have started demanding improvements in social, environmental and economic terms (e.g. Human Rights Watch 2012). According to expert interviews

---

[2]In 2006, it was estimated that 741,000 people were employed directly or indirectly in leather-related industries (GTZ 2006).

[3]Bangladesh ranks tenth in livestock (cattle, buffalo, goat, sheep) population (FAO 2014).

[4]Commercial leather exporters do not have their own tanneries but rent facilities to produce leather. Low overhead costs have turned them into serious competitors for tanneries providing the full range of tanning to finishing operations.

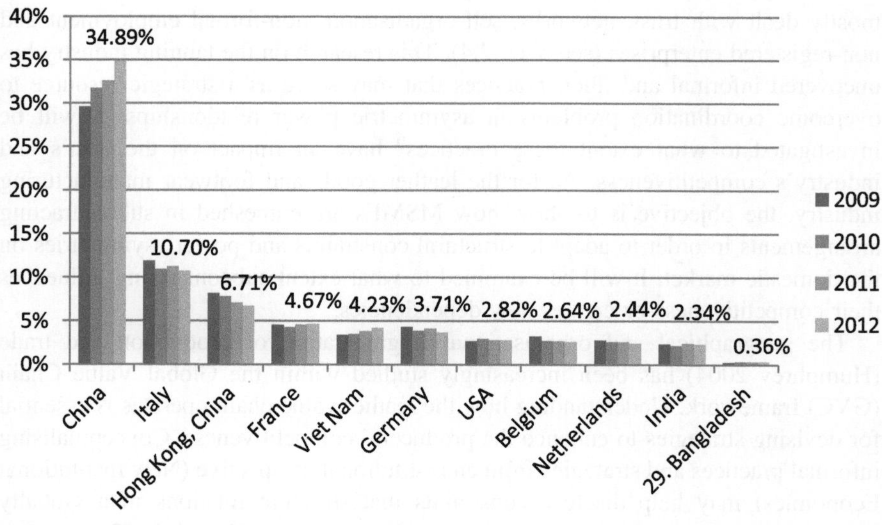

Fig. 1.1 Share of leather product exports in the world market, top ten countries plus Bangladesh, 2009–2012. *Source* ITC 2014; Own illustration

and Human Rights Watch (2012), large international buyers are wary of sourcing (directly) from Bangladesh and prefer to avoid negative publicity. Yet lax enforcement of environmental regulations and comparative advantages in labour costs seemed to have given Bangladesh's leather suppliers scope in the low-end market as interviews with producers and buying agents suggest. Missing investments in production technology, waste management or R&D on key supply industries (chemicals) constrain the industry's competitiveness on the world market. In response to these institutional limitations causing coordination problems, producers have learned to adapt, often informally, complementing or even substituting formally set procedures.

Research on global value chain dynamics in the leather industry has been mostly confined to environmental regulation and compliance (e.g. Dietsche 2011; Tewari and Pillai 2005; Lund-Thomson 2009; Hesselberg and Knutsen 2002). As opposed to case studies from Pakistan—and India, which ranks among the top ten leather exporting nations—Bangladesh lacks both a chemical input industry and a central effluent treatment plant (CETP), so global environmental standards have not been able to gain ground yet.[5] In view of the abovementioned coordination problems, it was considered to be more appropriate to investigate the informal dynamics understood as practices, routines and strategies within a local production network struggling for global market integration. To the author's knowledge, studies conceptualising informality within a continuum of informal-formal practices have

[5]The functionality of effluent treatment plants in India and Pakistan has been criticised as insufficient, while environmental regulation is weakly enforced (Dietsche 2011; Lund-Thomson 2009).

mostly dealt with trust, networks, self-organisation, non-formal employment and non-registered enterprises (see Sect. 2.4). This research on the tanning industry has uncovered informal and illicit practices that may serve as a strategic resource to overcome coordination problems in asymmetric power relationships. It will be investigated to what extent these practices[6] have an impact on the firm's and industry's competitiveness. As for the leather goods and footwear manufacturing industry, the objective is to show how MSMEs are enmeshed in subcontracting arrangements in order to adapt to structural constraints and power asymmetries on the domestic market. It will be examined to what extent subcontracting influences their competitiveness or creates new dependencies.

The geographical and organisational fragmentation of production and trade (Humphrey 2004) has been increasingly studied within the Global Value Chain (GVC) framework. Understanding how the leather value chain operates is essential for devising strategies to enhance the producers' competitiveness. Conceptualising informal practices and strategies from an institutional perspective (New Institutional Economics) may help disclose constraints that structure relations in a globally embedded low-cost industry. By linking the GVC (see Gereffi et al. 2005) approach with the New Institutional Economics (see North 1990) and informality (Etzold et al. 2009; Li 2007; Misztal 2000), informal institutionalised practices are analysed in relation to the opportunities they provide for producers in developing countries and in terms of their ability to modify power relations in GVC governance. Considerations of economic upgrading (Bettiol et al. 2011; Ponte and Ewert 2009; Humphrey 2004; Humphrey and Schmitz 2000/2002; Gereffi 1999) highlight the potential for acquiring capabilities that contribute to improving the position within the value chain. Given this framework, the objectives are to:

- Provide an overview of how the Bangladeshi leather value chain is organised and governed.
- Analyse how the Bangladeshi leather industry consisting of the leather processing and leather goods/footwear subsectors is integrated into the global market and to what extent informal arrangements including illicit practices are conducive to global market entry.
- Dissect the power relations along the value chain and analyse how local producers (tanners, leather goods/footwear producers) adapt to uphold competitiveness.
- Emphasise the need to devise upgrading strategies which pay heed to the reality of informal dynamics in a GVC to improve the local producers' competitiveness.
- Put the case study of the Bangladeshi leather value chain in a broader perspective, show research needs and conclude.

[6]For reasons of space and own theoretical considerations, this study will not expand on corporate social responsibility (CSR). For a detailed discussion on CSR, see Campbell (2007), Matten and Moon (2008).

References

Bettiol, M., De Marchi, V., Di Maria, E., & Micelli, S. (2011). Economic, social and environmental upgrading in value chains: Social entrepreneurship and the role of emerging economy lead firms. *Working Paper, 4*, School of Environment and Development/University of Manchester, Manchester.

Campbell, J. L. (2007). Why would corporations behave in socially responsible ways? An institutional theory of corporate social responsibility. *Academy of Management Review, 32*(3), 946–967.

Clean Clothes Campaign. (2013). *Frequently asked questions (FAQ) about the Bangladesh safety accord.* Retrieved from: http://www.cleanclothes.org/issues/faq-safety-accord. Accessed December 12, 2013.

Clean Clothes Campaign. (2014). *Presentation: Fatal fashion in Bangladesh.* Retrieved from: http://www.cleanclothes.org/resources/publications/fatal-fashion-in-bangladesh-def.pdf/view. Accessed March 15, 2014.

Dietsche, C. (2011). *Umweltgovernance in globalen Wertschöpfungsketten: Umweltschutz und Qualitätssicherung im Handel mit tropischen Garnelen und Ledererzeugnissen*. Münster: Lit Verlag.

Dusch Silva, S. (2013). Beglaubigung versetzt Berge: Was bringen Siegel und Zertifikate? *iz3w,* 338, Sept./Okt. 2013, 28–29.

Etzold, B., Bohle, H. G., Keck, M., & Zingel, W. P. (2009). Informality as agency—Negotiating food security in Dhaka. *Die Erde, 140*(1), 3–24.

FAO—Food and Agriculture Organization of the United Nations. (2014). *Data.* Retrieved from: http://data.fao.org/dataset-data-filter?entryId=c70af091-56be-41cc-8535-92c2ae460943&tab=data&type=Measure&uuidResource=7b5f0d07-896a-4c2e-9be5-fa0726635fb7. Accessed June 26, 2014.

Gereffi, G. (1994). The organization of buyer-driven global commodity chains: How U.S. retailers shape overseas production networks. In G. Gereffi, & M. Korzeniewicz (Eds.), *Commodity chains and global capitalism* (pp. 95–122). Westport, CT: Praeger.

Gereffi, G. (1999). International trade and industrial up-grading in the apparel commodity chain. *Journal of International Economics, 48*(1), 37–70.

Gereffi, G. (2005). The global economy: Organisation, governance and development. In N. J. Smelser, & R. Swedberg (Eds.), *Handbook of economic sociology* (2nd ed., pp. 160–182). Princeton, NJ: Princeton University Press and Russell Sage Foundation.

GTZ—Gesellschaft für Technische Zusammenarbeit. (2006). *Value chain assessment of the leather sector in Bangladesh,* Dhaka.

Hesselberg, J., & Knutsen, H. M. (2002). Leather tanning: Environmental regulations, competitiveness and locational shifts. In R. Jenkins, J. Barton, A. Bartzokas, J. Hesselberg, & H.M. Knutsen (Eds.), *Environmental regulation in the new global economy: The impact on industry and competitiveness* (pp. 155–219). Northampton: Edward Elgar Publishing.

Hossain, S. (2011). Informal dynamics of a public utility: Rationality of the scene behind a screen. *Habitat International, 35*(2), 275–285.

Human Rights Watch. (2012). *Toxic tanneries—The health repercussions of Bangladesh's hazaribagh leather.* Retrieved from: http://www.hrw.org/sites/default/files/reports/bangladesh1012webwcover.pdf. Accessed January 18, 2013.

Humphrey, J. (2004). *Upgrading in global value chains*. Working Paper No. 28, ILO Policy Integration Department.

Humphrey, J., & Schmitz, H. (2000). Governance and upgrading: Linking industrial cluster and global value chain research. *IDS Working Paper, 120*, University of Sussex, Brighton.

Humphrey, J., & Schmitz, H. (2002). How does insertion in global value chains affect upgrading in industrial clusters? *Regional Studies, 36*(9), 1022–1027.

ITC—International Trade Centre. (2014). *Trade competitiveness map.* Retrieved from: http://legacy.intracen.org/appli1/TradeCom/TPIC.aspx?RP=050&YR=2012. Accessed July 18, 2014.

Islam, N. (2005). Dhaka now: Contemporary urban development. Bangladesh Geographical Society, Dhaka.

Jahangir Alam, M. D. (2014). "The organized encroachment of land developers"—Effects on urban flood management in Greater Dhaka, Bangladesh. *Sustainable Cities and Society, 10*, 49–58.

Jahid Hasan, G. M., & Islam Chowdhury, M. D. A. (2005). Municipal waste management and environmental hazards in Bangladesh. *Pakistan Journal of Biological Sciences, 8*(6), 921–928.

Li, P. P. (2007). Social tie, social capital, and social behaviour: Toward an integrative model of informal exchange. *Asia Pacific Journal of Management, 24*(2), 227–246.

Lund-Thomson, P. (2009). Assessing the impact of public-private partnerships in the global south: The case of the Kasur Tanneries Pollution Control Project. *Journal of Business Ethics, 90*(1), 57–78.

Matten, D., & Moon, J. (2008). "Implicit" and "explicit" CSR: A conceptual framework for a comparative understanding of corporate social responsibility. *Academy of Management Review, 33*(2), 404–424.

Misztal, B. (2000). *Informality: Social theory and contemporary practice*. London: Routledge.

North, D. C. (1990). *Institutions, institutional change and economic performance*. New York: Cambridge University Press.

Ponte, S., & Ewert, J. (2009). Which way is "up" in upgrading? Trajectories of change in the value chain for South African wine. *World Development, 37*(10), 1637–1650.

SEHD—Society for Environment and Human Development. (2002). *Bangladesh environment facing the 21st century* (2nd ed.). Dhaka: SEHD.

Strasser, J., Dannenberg, P., & Kulke, E. (2013). Temporary resource availability and quality constraints in the global leather value chain—The impact of the festival of sacrifice on the leather industry in Bangladesh. *Applied Geography, 45*, 410–419.

Sturgeon, T. J. (2006). Conceptualizing integrative trade: The global value chains framework. *Trade policy research, 6*, 35–72.

Sturgeon, T. J. (2009). From commodity chains to value chains: Interdisciplinary theory building in an age of globalization. In J. Bair (Ed.), *Frontiers of commodity chain research* (pp. 110–135). Stanford: Stanford University Press.

Tewari, M., & Pillai, P. (2005). Global standards and the dynamics of environmental compliance in India's leather industry. *Oxford Development Studies, 33*(2), 245–267.

UN-DESA—United Nations, Department of Economic and Social Affairs. (2014). *World urbanization prospects. The 2014 revision—Highlights.* Retrieved from: http://esa.un.org/unpd/wup/Highlights/WUP2014-Highlights.pdf. Accessed July 17, 2014.

UNDP—United Nations Development Programme. (2014). *UNDP in Bangladesh: Millennium development goals.* Retrieved from: http://www.bd.undp.org/content/bangladesh/en/home/mdgoverview/overview/mdg1/. Accessed March 15, 2014.

Chapter 2
Conceptual Approaches

Abstract The theoretical framework of this study draws on the global value chain (GVC) perspective that is complemented by considerations of informality, subcontracting and middlemen to explore and to uncover the informal dynamics in inter-firm linkages at the lowest end of the leather value chain. Strategies to overcome development constraints are drawn from the debate on economic upgrading in GVCs and embedded in the institutional context to achieve sustained competitiveness. Given its limited practicability, the global production networks (GPN) approach is deemed inappropriate for the extent of this study, although its notion of power, being negotiated in social interaction regardless of the firm's position in the chain, has been integrated. In the end of this section four research questions are outlined to analyse the complexities of inter-firm relationships in Bangladesh's leather industry, their informal dynamics and potential strategies to overcome structural constraints and to reposition themselves within GVC governance.

The theoretical approaches synthesised in Table 2.1 constitute this study's analytical framework to understand the complexity of value chains. Considerations of informality, subcontracting and middlemen are added to the GVC perspective to explore and uncover the informal dynamics in inter-firm linkages at the lowest end of the leather value chain. Strategies to overcome potential constraints are drawn from the debate on upgrading in GVCs and embedded in the institutional context to achieve sustained competitiveness.

2.1 Global Commodity Chains, Global Value Chains and Global Production Networks

Since the 1980s, global division of labour has been facilitating outsourcing of manufacturing and services from the global North to low-cost areas in developing countries. Different theoretical perspectives have emerged to provide a conceptual framework to analyse the governance of globally dispersed but functionally integrated economic activities. The vast body of literature on value chains and

J. Strasser, *Bangladesh's Leather Industry*,
Springer Geography, DOI 10.1007/978-3-319-22548-7_2

Table 2.1 Framework of analysis

Theoretical strand	Analytical category	Dimension	Object of investigation
GVC	Coordination	Complexity of transaction	Middlemen versus producers; producers versus producers; local lead firms versus suppliers; multi-tiered supply relationships
		Codifiability of information	
		Capabilities in the supply base	
GCC, GPN, NIE	Institutions	Formal institutions	Associations; export policy; environmental regulation; international trade regulation (e.g. GSP)
		Informal institutions	Traditions, cultural norms, conventions, practices
GCC, GPN	Power	Resource-based; negotiated in social interaction	Firms, institutions
Upgrading in GVCs	Upgrading	Process, product, functional, inter-sectoral upgrading	Producers, lead firms, development organisations

Source Own composition

production networks originates in the seminal works of Porter's (1985) value chain analysis of the competitiveness of organisations and of Hopkins and Wallerstein (1986) on cross-border commodity chains regulated by the state. Gereffi et al. (1994) revisit the *Global Commodity Chain* (*GCC*) concept from a development perspective, placing emphasis on the strategies and actions of firms. GCC analysis pays attention to spatial inequalities in market access and the distribution of resources. Gereffi (1994) unfolds a binary view of producer- and buyer-driven commodity chains, with the position of the lead firm in the chain based on the distribution of power and the ability to govern all economic activities from the raw material to the final product. Producer-driven value chains are typically found in capital- and technology-intensive industries (e.g. automobile industry, personal computers), where lead firms control up- and down-stream activities, including the production system and retail. Profits are realised by scale, volume and technology (Fernandez-Stark et al. 2011, p. 11). In buyer-driven value chains usually few non-manufacturing firms (e.g. brands, retailers) face a large number of suppliers of labour-intensive, highly standardised consumer goods (e.g. garments, footwear). Here, value and thus profit accrue at stages that are prior to or after assembly (e.g. R&D, design, marketing). Gereffi's framework within which multinational firms act as "conduits for the transfer of capabilities from developed to developing countries" (Sturgeon 2009, p. 115) has been widely received in development studies and development cooperation. Focusing the analysis of upgrading and development on powerful firms instead of on the state allows for a broader set of interventions.

Despite valuable contributions towards analysing the relationship between production and trade, the GCC concept has been criticised for its static view of chain governance, which ignores multi-faceted inter-firm linkages to change over time (Sturgeon 2009). It conceptualises governance as "drivenness" (Bair 2009, p. 26), focusing only on lead firms that use their power to steer production, whereas more complex inter-firm relationships are overlooked.

The *Global Production Networks* (*GPN*) approach develops the dichotomous GCC concept towards a more holistic understanding of the dynamics of globally-organised production activities that are linked to distant markets (e.g. Coe et al. 2004, 2008; Henderson et al. 2002). In a regional development perspective, the GPN approach sees firms embedded within a local and regional institutional environment which is decisive for creating, enhancing, and capturing value (see Coe et al. 2004). They respond to the GCC concept's weakness by adopting an explicitly networked approach, going beyond the quintessential buyer-supplier relation. It examines the inter-linkages and tensions between commercial (firms, agents) and societal actors (workers, civic organisations, consumers) intermingling in networks (Barrientos 2013). Here, power is negotiated in social interaction irrespective of economic resources.

Alongside Global Production Networks, a large body of literature on the *Global Value Chain* (*GVC*) analysis has emerged. The GVC framework portrays the way global firms govern spatially disperse market activities. Gereffi et al. (2005) identified five forms of governance at the interface between lead firms and suppliers (see Fig. 2.1):

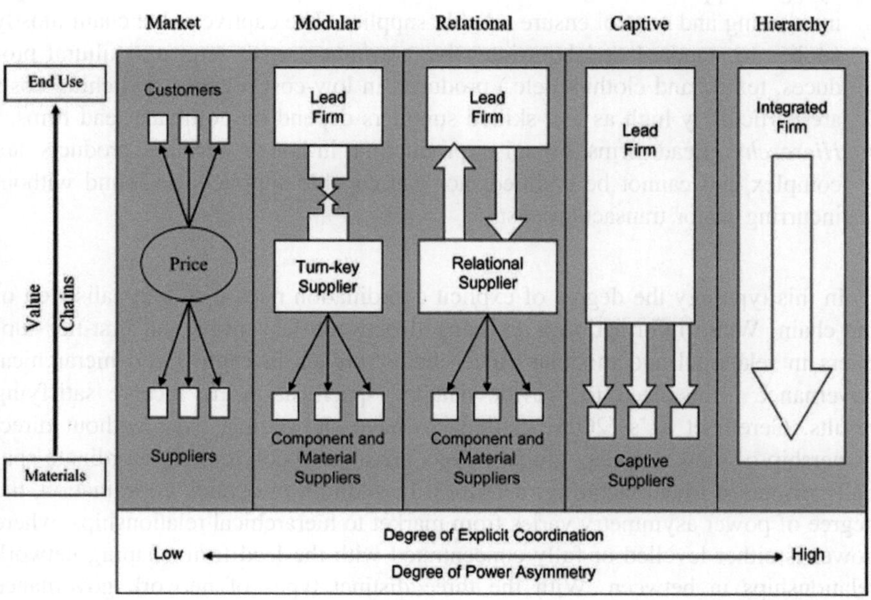

Fig. 2.1 Types of global value chains. *Source* Gereffi et al. (2005, p. 89)

- *Arm's-length or market based relationships*: Competent suppliers make mostly standard products with little explicit coordination by buyers, that is, there is little exchange of information (white block arrows in Fig. 2.1). Product specifications are simple so transactions can be codified easily. Switching costs are accordingly low thanks to the wide range of potential buyers. The linkage is mainly governed by price (black thin arrows in Fig. 2.1).
- *Modular relationships*: Highly competent suppliers are capable of codifying complex transactions (for instance, by technical standards) and of supplying a variety of customers. Conversely, buyers can source from different potential suppliers without needing to invest substantially in the coordination of their supplies. Suppliers in modular value chains often provide turn-key services, covering activities that go beyond mere assembly.
- *Relational relationships*: Product specifications and transactions are complex but cannot be codified adequately. Producers of high technological capabilities and customers in relational value chains need to exchange tacit knowledge to overcome the low codifiability of their products. The mutual dependence created by highly specific assets (Meyer 2011, p. 54) is regulated by trust, reputation, social and spatial proximity, and personal ties. Because relational value chains develop over a long time they require intense inter-actions between buyers and suppliers. Then even spatial distance can be overcome (Sturgeon and Gereffi 2008). Consequently, the costs of finding new business partners are very high.
- *Captive relationships*: A few lead firms control many suppliers with low technological competences competing with each other. Buyers distrust suppliers, perceiving them as unreliable (Humphrey and Schmitz 2000), and minimise risk by tight supplier management. Detailed product specifications as well as tight monitoring and control ensure reliable supplies. The captive value chain mostly applies to standard or labour-intensive consumer goods (e.g. agricultural produces, textile and clothing, etc.) produced in low-cost regions. Switching costs are particularly high as low-skilled suppliers depend on dominant lead firms.
- *Hierarchy*: Lead firms organise production in-house because products are complex and cannot be codified, nor can capable suppliers be found without incurring major transaction costs.

In this typology the degree of explicit coordination rises with verticalisation of the chain. While information is exchanged between lead firms and first-tier suppliers in relational and modular value chains, buyers in captive and hierarchical governance forms need to provide detailed specifications to receive satisfying results. Gereffi et al.'s (2005) merit is to have shown that even without direct ownership of their suppliers global buyers are able to control and coordinate spatially dispersed (manufacturing) activities. In addition to explicit coordination, the degree of power asymmetry varies from market to hierarchical relationships, where power is either levelled or fully concentrated with the lead firm, shaping network relationships in between. With the three distinct types of network governance (modular, relational, captive) Gereffi et al. (2005) added complexity to the GCC approach they had been building on (see Fig. 2.1).

This typology is based on three key factors that are derived from transaction cost economics (Gereffi et al. 2005):

- *The complexity of transactions*: Information and knowledge is exchanged to specify products and processes. The more complex transactions are the more coordination (or interaction) is needed.
- *The codifiability of transactions*: Complex information can be reduced by codification, for instance, through contracts or standards. Suppliers capable of handling codified information provided by their buyers are likely to operate in modular value chains (Sturgeon and Gereffi 2008). Suppliers lacking the competences to act on codification require more coordination (captive).
- *The capabilities in the supply base*: Refers to the producer's ability to deal with complex and codified information. Missing supplier competences (e.g. knowledge, financial, technological, management) lead buyers to monitor and control suppliers tightly (captive) or even organise production activities in-house (hierarchy).

As delineated, the combination of these variables defines the form of governance.[1] The three key determinants take into account that the coordination rises with the increasing asset specificity of a particular transaction, that is, transaction-specific investments are of limited use for actors outside this relationship (Gereffi et al. 2005). This means that transaction costs increase with rising product complexity, so that, for instance, standard products quintessentially used in market relationships are easier to produce and it is easier to find customers for them than for highly specified products. In general, the complexity of transactions determines the transactions costs and thus the coordination of the value chain.

The GVC analysis has been criticised for the simplifying "chain metaphor" (Bair 2009, p. 4) and its highly idealised typology (e.g. Nadvi 2008; Coe et al. 2008) that lacked empirical evidence. It confines inter-firm linkages to global flagship firms governing the entire chain. Multi-tiered and horizontal supply relationships are neglected or assigned to specific forms of governance (e.g. modular, relational). Talbot (2009) and Sturgeon (2009) suggest that complex commodity chains may fork into different strands or threads, entailing multiple forms of governance. Gibbon et al. (2008, p. 323) re-define governance as the coordination of inter-firm relations at specific nodes of the chain. Gereffi and Lee (2012) acknowledge that governance schemes may vary along a value chain. Evidence from this study indicates that there may be more than just one way to coordinate even a specific inter-firm linkage. GPN advocates object to the narrow focus on inter-firm transactions, which ignores other actors (e.g. consumers, state, NGOs) and relationships (Coe et al. 2008). The "Manchester School of global production networks" (Bathelt

[1]Of eight possible combinations three are excluded for being unlikely. See for a detailed discussion Gereffi et al. (2005, p. 87/88).

2006) argues for a multidimensional, multi-scalar, networked approach, stressing global connectivities and interdependencies within production networks (see Coe et al. 2004, 2008; Henderson et al. 2002; Dicken et al. 2001). How this myriad of analytical categories relates to each other remains unanswered. In stressing the relevance of social relations, the GPN approach adds a more dynamic and holistic view of the global economy. But even Coe et al. (2008, p. 290) admit that to understand the organisational complexity of GPNs, their multi-scalarity, and their multi-actor network requires a multinational research team. Notwithstanding the analytical value of the GPN approach, its practicability is highly questioned and thus not appropriate for the extent of this study.

Even though criticism is justified, the GVC approach has sufficient explanatory power to shed light on complex interactions within and beyond the firm-level. The three key variables proved particularly useful in analysing logistically complex value chains shaped by low skilled producers and middlemen in developing countries (see Dannenberg and Nduru 2012). They are also critical to the analysis of this study. Going beyond 'global lead firm-local supplier' linkages, this study incorporates upstream (traders) and downstream (buying houses) actors in the chain analysis as they are assumed to have a profound impact on the coordination. Horizontal relationships (e.g. suppliers of intermediate products, services) support the production network to a large degree, though verticality of material flows and processes is an essential feature of cross-border producer-customer relations. This study therefore uses the terms production network and value chain interchangeably. Taking into account the multi-scalarity of production networks, it is believed that "GVC governance theory operates equally well at any and all of these spatial scales" (Sturgeon 2009, p. 123), which means processes on the local/national level go well with the GVC perspective. Sturgeon (2009), one of the authors of the seminal article on 'The governance of global value chains' (Gereffi et al. 2005), argues that verticality inherent in the chain metaphor should not obstruct the analysis of multi-scalar and organisational complexity as it is rather a "heuristic tool" (p. 127). Instead, he suggests adding power and institutions to the inter-firm linkages in GVC analysis, thereby reviving constitutive elements of the GCC concept.

Power is the essential agency in social relations (Fox 1974) and thus innate to economic transactions. GVC analysis defines power as the availability of resources and capabilities, presuming a concentration of power with large multinational firms. With the degree of power asymmetry rising from market to hierarchical relationships, power determines governance structures. In captive value chains in particular, lead firms command material and immaterial resources. They set prices, place orders and direct the production; in a nutshell, they "wield purchasing power" (Sturgeon 2009, p. 129), whereas suppliers are outclassed in coordination abilities, technological competence, financial resources, and design and marketing skills. In modular chains power among buyers and suppliers is more or less even as both are able to switch partners. Highly skilled suppliers in relational linkages have "competence power" (ibid.) that, if knowledge is tacit, may give them leverage in negotiations with lead firms. This study is amenable to the GPN view that power is negotiated in social interaction regardless of considerable structural differences in resource availability and the firm's position in the value chain (Coe et al. 2008). Qualitative research methods are expected to explore the nature of power in the leather production network and how it materialises in practice.

Institutions defined as a set of rules that regulate social relations and thus economic transactions (North 1990) matter in the analysis of global value chains. The institutional context within which industries have developed is decisive for the way firms adapt to these institutional constraints. As will be set out below, formal and informal institutions may shed light on the intrinsic complexity of business relations at the lower end of the value chain, where the GVC framework remains deficient. For instance, reactions of multinational companies to recent disasters in the garment industry in Bangladesh (Savar/Dhaka, April 2013) and worldwide (e.g. Karachi/Pakistan 2012) indicate that lead firms do not control local suppliers (Silva 2013). Instead, middlemen forward orders to producers with no linkages to their real customers. Multi-tiered supplies disguise competences and responsibilities. Often, producers and middlemen in developing countries resort to informal and even illicit practices to take advantage of dysfunctional institutions or to deal with power asymmetries (e.g. self-organisation, trust, informal employment, tax evasion). Yet GVC analysis lacks conceptual clarity about informality in governance. This study seeks to shed light on where informal practices and strategies are positioned within the value chain, the role they play for market integration and to what extent they modify power relations.

2.2 The Role of Middlemen/Intermediaries in Global Value Chains

Globalisation and trade liberalisation allowed manufacturers in developing countries to become functionally more integrated in global markets, although low capabilities (e.g. product quality, compliance with environmental regulation, logistics, language) in the supply base limit their opportunities for international market entry. The literature has widely acknowledged the importance of middlemen in linking low-skilled producers in developing countries to distant international markets (Dannenberg 2012; Ogouma et al. 2010; Ponte 2009). While product specification and requirements for farmers in agricultural value chains are relatively low, the complexity of transactions rises with the increasing processing degree in manufacturing industries. Asymmetries in knowledge and information keep suppliers dependent on middlemen (Dannenberg 2012; Ogouma et al. 2010; Reeves 2002). In manufacturing industries middlemen or buying agents have been mostly discussed within the framework of multinational corporations organising sourcing on a global level.[2] The key responsibilities of such international purchasing offices

[2]For a detailed discussion on international purchasing offices see Jia et al. (2013), Sartor et al. (2014).

include supplier management, transfer of knowledge, negotiation between buyers and suppliers, marketing support and logistics management (Sartor et al. 2014). Humphrey (2004) observes that global sourcing companies have entered the garment supply chain, assuming competences in logistics, sourcing of materials and translating designs into product specifications. The concentration of capabilities on such strategic intermediary level allows for very flexible sourcing, obstructing upgrading of low-skilled producers. Contrary to the global sourcing strategy, Bangladesh's buying houses have emerged from within the industry, taking on the role of facilitators of buyer-supplier relationships. Interviews with local agents suggest that international traders often encourage them to set up buying offices and establish an exclusive trade relationship. To the author's knowledge, the character of Bangladesh's leather-industry-related buying houses is still that of an intermediary and has not yet evolved to an outsourced office of a global company. Buying houses resolve disputes between producers and customers, manage supplies either locally or by imports and diminish contractual uncertainty (Woodruff 1998, p. 984). They provide assistance in bridging knowledge and cultural gaps between low-skilled manufacturers and powerful multi-national corporations governing the supply chain. Briefly, buying houses mediate an asymmetric relationship (buyer/principal vs. supplier/agent). It is therefore necessary to examine the buying houses' role in terms of power asymmetries towards suppliers and the way the latter adapt to those.

2.3 Subcontracting in Global Value Chains

Subcontracting has increasingly been referred to as a competitive strategy to organise production in vertically disintegrated supply chains (Holl 2008; Van Mieghem 1999; Webster et al. 1997). As it has turned out to be a dominant feature of Bangladesh's leather industry, it is included in this study's conceptual considerations.

The term is often used interchangeably with outsourcing. Either strategy relates to a firm (subcontractor or supplier) providing a service or good for another company, i.e. the contractor, buyer or manufacturer (Van Mieghem 1999, p. 954). This study follows Pratim Sahu (2010) and Webster et al. (1997) in their view of subcontracting, in which the contracting unit (principal or parent firm) hires out the production of parts, components, subassemblies or assemblies of a final product to one or more enterprises (subcontractor or agent) (see Fig. 2.2). Webster et al.'s (1997, p. 830) distinction between industrial and commercial subcontracting in the electronics manufacturing industry is also conducive for this study. Industrial subcontractors feed intermediate products into the parent firm's highly complex manufacturing process. In commercial subcontracting trading companies hire enterprises to produce entire products and market them on their own. The lower the complexity of the product and labour costs the greater the incidence of multi-tiered subcontracting (Pratim Sahu 2010).

Fig. 2.2 Subcontracting production. *Source* Own illustration

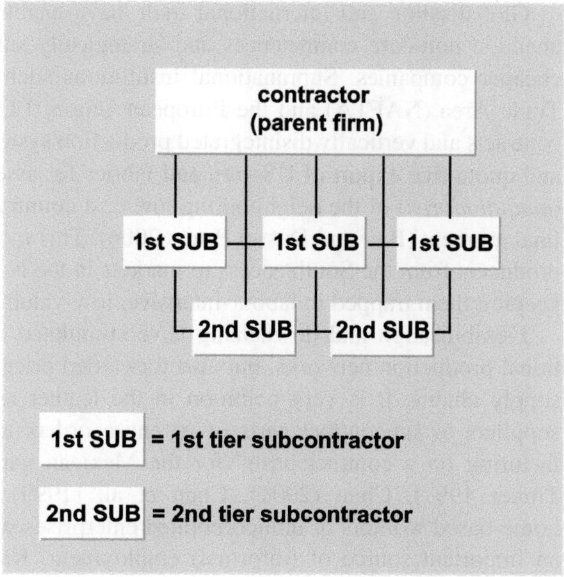

Three reasons for subcontracting relate to production cost factors (Holl 2008; Deavers 1997; Webster et al. 1997):

- Limited capacity and fluctuating production volumes lead to capacity subcontract to meet exceptional surges in demand.
- Getting access to specialised capabilities (e.g. knowledge, economies of scale, labour-intensive activities) which are not available at the contractor's plant.
- Labour-intensive productive activities are subcontracted to low-wage firms.

The advantages for the contracting/parent firm are financial benefits stemming from smaller quantities, specialised production, fewer requirements for legal and environmental controls, and risk of production and quality problems being outsourced (Webster et al. 1997, p. 830). Subcontractors benefit from orders and indirect sales, which confine them, however, to very limited potential for growth, constituting the main disadvantage. Subcontractors have only indirect market access. The risk of being dependent on one single customer is high. Likewise, parent firms may be subject to opportunistic behaviour of the subcontractor (Webster et al. 1997, p. 831). Resources and capabilities between principals and agents are unevenly distributed, reflecting power asymmetries.

Building on Williamson's (1985, 1975) transaction cost approach, Holl (2008) sees the characteristics of the local economy determined by the costs of setting up and governing a bilateral subcontracting relationship. It is important to find a suitable partner who can be trusted and who is capable of realising asset-specific investments (Grossman and Helpman 2005). Costs for specification, monitoring and enforcement of transactions influence the decision to enter subcontracting relationships.

Globalisation and international trade have enabled globally operating firms to abandon non-core competences and strategically subcontract specific activities to cheaper companies. Supranational institutions such as the North American Free Trade Area (NAFTA) and the European Union (EU) facilitated cross-border subcontracts and vertically disintegrated production systems. NAFTA boosted the duty- and quota-free export of US yarn and fabrics for assembly in the production plants (*maquiladoras*) of the neighbouring low-cost country Mexico and re-exports of the final garment (Bair and Dussel Peters 2006). This model of production sharing give producers from the South access to markets in the North, but has been criticised for keeping them trapped in labour-intensive, low-value added activities (ibid.).

Flexibilisation and downsizing have stimulated economic growth and international production networks, but also forwarded price pressure to the weakest in the supply chains. It is very common in the leather and garment industry for local suppliers to subcontract parts of or entire orders to independent workers manufacturing on a contract basis (for the Mexican garment industry, see Prügl and Tinker 1997). Chen (2004), Chen et al. (1999) contextualised self-employed home-based workers or unincorporated enterprises within the informality debate as an important source of (informal) employment. Knorringa (1999) shows for the footwear cluster in Agra/India that producers in times of crisis increased the frequency of subcontracting at specific stages in the production process (e.g. upper). Lacking secure contracts and labour rights are quintessential traits of low-cost subcontracts that are prevalent in labour-intensive manufacturing industries in developing countries. While subcontracting in the leather and garment industry is often a survival strategy (e.g. Prügl and Tinker 1997; Webster et al. 1997), Sudhir Kumar and Bala Subrahmanya (2010) demonstrate for the automobile industry in India that SMEs subcontracted by transnational corporations are assisted in inducing technological innovations which lead to greater economic performance. Technical support and other forms of assistance with regard to learning from lead firms will be examined in Sect. 5.3.5.1.

In Bangladesh's leather industry subcontracting appears to be a common feature. Leather processors supply intermediate products to tanneries of a higher competence level, whereas leather goods and footwear subcontractors transform leather and accessories to leather commodities that are branded and marketed by their lead firm. Each mode of subcontracting (parts assembly, full-package production, self-employment) provides opportunities and displays asymmetries in resources, knowledge and capabilities. How subcontracting relationships are coordinated will be analysed in Sect. 5.3.3.

2.4 Reconceptualising Informality

The GVC approach analyses inter-firm linkages in vertically disintegrated production systems. As power varies with the firm's position in the chain (Gereffi et al. 2005) but is also negotiated in social interaction as GPN studies suggest (Coe et al.

2008), the aid of practices and adaptation strategies outside formal institutions is assumed. This section seeks to define informality, outline its dimensions and contextualise it within the GVC approach.

After pioneering studies in the 1970s (ILO 1972; Hart 1973), informality has been widely received in development studies, but has also been criticised for being a fuzzy concept (e.g. Kanbur 2009; Sindzingre 2006). This study follows the current debate on closing the "formal-informal divide" (Guha-Khasnobis et al. 2006, p. 2) by moving away from dualist (ILO 1972; Hart 1973), structuralist (Castells and Portes 1989) and legalist (De Soto 1989) approaches that are restricted to binary, mutually exclusive, static and juridical conceptualisations of informality.

In the literature on global economic disparities and GVCs, informality has been mostly discussed in case studies on informal employment (e.g. Harris-White 2009; Mehrotra and Biggeri 2005; Barrientos et al. 2003; Maloney 1999), informal economic activity, that is, non-registered enterprises (e.g. Kulke and Staffeld 2009; Murphy 2007), often embedded within a discourse of social inequality (e.g. Sassen 1994), or trust (e.g. Meyer et al. 2012). Kaplinsky and Morris (2001) very instructively illustrate the potential of value chain analysis to reveal inter-linkages between formal and informal activities and their dynamic incorporation into global markets. However, a conceptual integration of informal institutions and practices in GVC analysis is lacking.

New institutional economics (NIE) conceptualise informality from an institutional perspective. According to North (1990), formal and informal institutions constitute a set of rules that delimitate opportunities in society and thus regulate economic transactions. Formal rules are understood as written codifications (e.g. constitutions, laws, market regulations) that, when externally enforced, provide security, but can be quickly modified. Formal institutions may also include (non-) governmental agencies, multi-lateral organisations or trade unions (Sturgeon 2009, p. 130). In contrast, informal institutional constraints comprising traditions, cultural norms and conventions, have evolved over time. They are self-enforced, thus more persistent and less prone to change (North 1990).

Recent studies on informality hinge on North's (p. 46) understanding of a continuum of economic activities ranging from informal to formal (see e.g. Etzold et al. 2009; Kulke and Staffeld 2009; Li 2007; Chen 2004). Li (2007) drawing on research on guanxi, the Chinese way to structure social interactions informally, relates informality to social capital and captures five dimensions of formal-informal extremes (Table 2.2).

According to Li (2007), formal business transactions are written and thus highly codified as opposed to informal arrangements that are made orally and flexibly enforced based on social relations. Formal agreements imposed by abstract laws, regulations or external actors are enforced tightly, i.e. by the authorities, according to the terms and conditions stated. Depersonalised objective processes can be solved by vertical powers within a legal system, whereas peer pressure exerts power in horizontal relationships. Li (2007) further classifies each dimension into sub-groups, determining specific degrees of in-/formal transactions.

Table 2.2 Informal-formal paradigm

Dimensions	Formal ⟷	Informal
Codification	Explicit (written)	Implicit (oral)
Formation	Exogenous	Endogenous
Enforcement of agreements	Tight	Loose
Power relations	Hierarchical	Horizontal
Personalisation	Depersonalised	Personalised

Source Adapted from Li (2007, p. 230). Own illustration

Although Li's approach is useful in overcoming the binary view of informality and was well received in recent studies (e.g. Schiller 2012; Dannenberg 2012; Meyer 2011; Etzold et al. 2009), power has been oversimplified. Etzold et al. (2009) draw on Li (2007), amongst others, to set up a continuum of informal to formal practices and processes that are structured by institutions and dominant players (Table 2.3). Subscribing to Li's perspective, they regard power asymmetries as constituent of vertical relations that are supposed to be prevalent in markets and need to be offset by codification. For instance, written contracts help level asymmetric relationships and ensure trust among unknown business partners. Following this conceptualisation, personal trust is confined to horizontal relationships in predominantly informal interactions. This view ignores the incidence of informal ties in asymmetric power relations as given in global value chains. It also erroneously implies that oral communication and personal trust-based relationships neutralise or are devoid of power asymmetries. Mistzal (2000) adds an instructive view to this study's argumentation as "informality cannot be limited [...] to a local context where there is a relative absence of asymmetries of power" (Misztal 2000, p. 8). With formal and informal interactions coexisting in global trade and production networks, informal practices and processes are inextricably embedded within hierarchical power relations.[3] Empirical evidence of this study is expected to shed light on relations between trust and power in global value chains.

In order to determine the informal nature of transactions in global value chains, four dimensions of informal interactions can be distinguished (Etzold et al. 2009; Alsayyad and Roy 2004; Misztal 2000):

Firstly, *informality is a strategy* to achieve individual goals. Actors make rational choices whether to solve specific situations formally or informally. Misztal (2000) argues from a sociological perspective that a balanced relationship of formal and informal interactions is central to the emergence of trust. In times of global division of labour, informal encounters, trust-based relationships, and tacit understanding are essential to achieving organisational goals (ibid.). Informal ties enable flexible business arrangements to operate within formal structures (e.g. written contracts),

[3]Amendments in Table 2.3 are displayed in italics.

Table 2.3 Continuum of informal to formal practices and processes

Degree of formality	Institutions	Dominant actors	Nature of social ties	Traits of interactions
High: predominantly formal interactions	Generally applicable and legally binding laws; constitutions	State, supranational actors	Law, authority	Discursive knowledge, written communication, legally binding norms, rationality, impersonality, rigidity of rules, vertical relations
Medium-high: mostly formal interactions	Specific articles in directives and contracts	State, corporate enterprises	Market, competition	Discursive knowledge, mainly written communication, codified norms, rationality, impersonality, vertical relations
Medium: both formal and informal interactions	Modes of regulation of an arena	Corporate enterprises, leaders, middlemen	Market, negotiation, contestation	Discursive and practical knowledge, oral communication, socially defined codified norms, horizontal and vertical relations, personalised trust
Medium-low: mostly informal interactions	Unexpressed social norms, taboos, values, customs	Community, peer groups	Social control, identity	Practical knowledge, oral communication, socially defined codified norms, horizontal relations
Low: predominantly informal interactions	Personal agreements	Family, friends	Personal trust	Practical knowledge, face-to-face communi-cation, socially defined codified norms, horizontal relations, personalised trust, strong social ties, intuition

Source Adapted from Etzold et al. (2009)

thus "securing transparency, accountability and partners' rights" (Misztal 2000, p. 4). In other words, informal institutions are deployed to manage transaction risks (Steer and Sen 2010) and to reduce transaction costs incurred by firm-to-firm communication. Flexibility and freedom in making choices provide power.

Secondly, informality can be "*a habit or routine of doing things*" (Etzold et al. 2009, p. 10) understood as an informal institutionalised practice that is deeply rooted in society. Other than Etzold et al. (2009) suggest, routines or institutionalised practices may develop detached from power. For instance, it is more convenient to conclude deals based on faith than on written contracts because transaction costs can be significantly reduced. Practical knowledge is used instead of codification.

Thirdly, actors need to find ways to circumvent dysfunctional formal institutions and therefore *adapt informally* by drawing on tacit knowledge. Adaptation strategies do not necessarily relate to survival activities as recent research on informal economy suggests (Staffeld and Kulke 2009; Etzold et al. 2009); even resourceful players are exposed to formal institutional constraints. Principal-agent relations (e.g. buyer/buying agent vs. supplier) often operate at different scales within dysfunctional formal institutions from which informal institutions emerge to solve arising coordination problems (North 1990).

Fourthly, informal institutions are the *organising logic* (Alsayyad and Roy 2004) of a specific system and structure, for instance, markets and transactions. Such informal regulatory regimes are more dominant and more powerful than formal ones (Etzold et al. 2009, p. 10). Persistency is particularly high and formalisation attempts are likely to fail. These dimensions provide the analytical framework for informal transactions in the leather value chain.

To sum up, informality exists even in the most formal spheres and serves a vital purpose in trust-building processes, innovation and industrial governance. The notion of informality, however, goes beyond mutually exclusive classes. Combining Etzold et al.'s (2009) approach which conceives of informality as an agency, Mistzal's (2000) sociological lens and the NIE's (North 1990) transaction cost approach, this study conceives informality as a process-related, relational and strategic resource that also operates within hierarchical power relations. Within the logic of an informal-formal continuum, informal arrangements spanning informal ties, networks, trust, self-organisation *and* illicit practices may enable entry into highly competitive GVCs. As Wallerstein (2009, p. 86) puts it, "if there are barriers to crossing borders, there are ways to get around them".

2.5 Upgrading in Global Value Chains

It is inherent to the GVC framework that governance may change over time (Gereffi et al. 2005). With reducing complexity of a transaction, increasing codifiability of a product or improving competences, the governance structure and thus power inequalities between buyers and suppliers can be influenced alike.

The activities firms command in a GVC determine the value they are able to capture (Miroudot and De Backer 2012). Most of this value is created at the two ends of the "smile curve" (Li Sun et al. 2010, p. 308) in upstream (e.g. R&D, design) and downstream activities (e.g. marketing, branding), while there is little scope for value creation at the manufacturing and assembly stages (Miroudot and De Backer 2012). With the value resting in non-tangible competences, gains are unevenly distributed in GVCs (see Fig. 2.3).

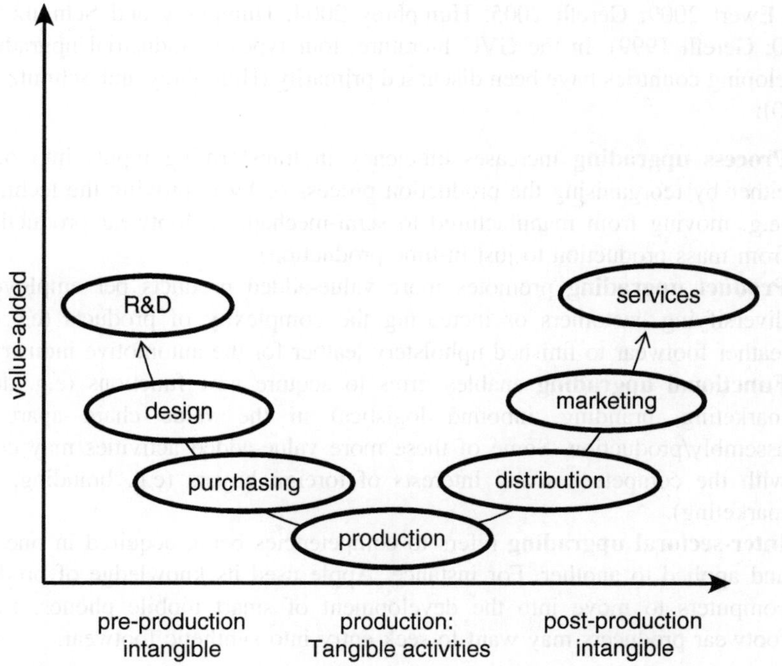

Fig. 2.3 Curve of value-added stages in the apparel chain. *Source* Adapted from Fernandez-Stark et al. (2011). Own illustration

Leaving aside environmental and social aspects,[4] economic upgrading can be defined as "the process by which economic actors—nations, firms and workers—move from low-value to relatively high-value activities in global production networks" (Gereffi 2005, p. 171). Gereffi follows Porter's (1990) economic theory of industrial upgrading that sees nations build up comparative advantages in capital- and skill-intensive industries once the endowment of production factors moves from labour to capital assets and knowledge. The GVC literature is convinced that upgrading is achieved by articulating low-skilled suppliers from the South to resourceful lead firms in developed countries (Gereffi 2005; Humphrey and Schmitz 2000; Gereffi 1999). Several studies provide evidence that upgrading in GVCs may help local producers acquire capabilities and move to new market activities (Ponte

[4]With asymmetric power relationships being an essential feature of global buyer-supplier relationships, issues of social and environmental upgrading have increasingly come to the fore (Barrientos et al. 2010; Jeppesen and Hansen 2004; Tewari and Pillai 2005). As a matter of fact, economic upgrading does not necessarily bring about social and environmental improvements (see Barrientos et al. 2010). It is, however, beyond the scope of this study to expand on the complex relations between economic, social and environmental upgrading. Environmental (e.g. central effluent treatment plant) and social issues (e.g. compliance with firm's or international standards) will only be taken into account in relation to economic upgrading, that is, where the firm's or industry's competitiveness is affected (see Section "Assistance in social compliance").

and Ewert 2009; Gereffi 2005; Humphrey 2004; Humphrey and Schmitz 2002/2000; Gereffi 1999). In the GVC literature, four types of industrial upgrading in developing countries have been discussed primarily (Humphrey and Schmitz 2002/2000):

- **Process upgrading** increases efficiency in transforming inputs into outputs either by reorganising the production process or by improving the technology (e.g. moving from manufactured to semi-mechanised footwear production or from mass production to just-in-time production).
- **Product upgrading** promotes more value-added products per employee by diversifying customers or increasing the complexity of products (e.g. from leather footwear to finished upholstery leather for the automotive industry).
- **Functional upgrading** enables firms to acquire new functions (e.g. design, marketing, branding, inbound logistics) in the value chain apart from assembly/production. Some of these more value-added activities may conflict with the competences and interests of foreign buyers (e.g. branding, direct marketing).
- **Inter-sectoral upgrading** refers to competencies being acquired in one chain and applied to another. For instance, Apple used its knowledge of producing computers to move into the development of smart mobile phones. Leather footwear producers may want to seek entry into synthetic footwear.

Table 2.4 illustrates how the acquisition of capabilities and buyer-supplier relationships determine upgrading trajectories (Humphrey 2004). Drawing on East-Asian countries successfully exporting apparel since the 1970s, Humphrey (2004) and Gereffi (2005) point to the leap from assembly to Original Equipment Manufacturing (OEM) that signifies a major challenge to producers from the global South. Exporters are expected to have capabilities in making samples, procuring raw material and inputs, manufacturing, meeting international standards in terms of price, quality and lead time as well as packaging and shipping the goods (Gereffi 2005, p. 171). Original Design Manufacturing (ODM) and Original Brand Manufacturing (OBM) exports require producers to assume capabilities in designing and marketing. Buyers only provide assistance in increasing capabilities if competition is avoided; that is, producers are expected to develop designs for low-value-added products and to enter marketing channels outside the lead firm's markets. Particularly MSMEs in developing countries, the main object of analysis of this study, have difficulties functionally upgrading at all. They first have to overcome crucial entry barriers such as capacity, quality and lead time to achieve market entry.

The governance structure determines also how and what type of knowledge is transferred. Tight governance schemes such as captive or hierarchical value chains tend to favour product and process upgrading. The buyers secure higher returns from investing in the supplier's capabilities to ensure product quality by transactionally locking them in (Humphrey 2004, p. 15). Large order volumes increase the producer's costs for switching customer. Tacit knowledge which is constituent for relational value chains is very difficult to transfer and requires intense

Table 2.4 Potential upgrading trajectories

Capabilities	Type of upgrading	Description
Assembly	Market entry	Supplier focuses on production according to the buyers' specifications; inputs may be imported or supplied by the buyer
Assembly	Process upgrading	Supplier improves productivity through new capital investment; increases efficiencies in the operation of productive activities
Assembly	Product upgrading	Supplier produces more value-added goods for which better material or higher capabilities are needed
Original Equipment Manufacturing (OEM), "full-package manufacturer"	Functional upgrading	Supplier performs more value-added manufacturing-related activities (e.g. sourcing of inputs; logistics); design and marketing are still the buyer's core competencies
Original Design Manufacturing (ODM)	Functional upgrading	Supplier contributes to design and product development; usually close collaboration with the lead firm's designers; products are sold under the lead firm's brand
Original Brand Manufacturing (OBM)	Functional upgrading	In addition to pre-production and post-production capabilities, the supplier is able to market products under own brand name
		Supplier may closely collaborate with lead firm to market product
		Supplier establishes own distribution channels and operates independently

Source Adapted from Humhprey (2004, p. 8), Fernandez-Stark et al. (2011, p. 16). Own composition

buyer-supplier interactions. Producer competences in both relational and modular value chains are high and require little intervention from buyers. In general, lead firms prevent producers in the South from functional upgrading to avoid competition (Schmitz 2006; Humphrey and Schmitz 2002; Schmitz and Knorringa 1999). This may keep producers trapped in low-wage and low-quality production. Case studies from the Brazilian footwear industry stress the risk of focusing exclusively on production (Humphrey 2004; Humphrey and Schmitz 2000). As buyers are permanently in search of low-cost production sites, other countries might offer similar quality at even lower prices. Without developing anything other than productive functions, low-cost producers take a high risk of losing markets. Hence, upgrading depends on the extent lead firms are willing to share information and knowledge with their suppliers (Bettiol et al. 2011).

It has been widely acknowledged that upgrading is highly conducive to increasing the income of firms in developing countries (Giulani et al. 2005; Dolan and Tewari 2001; Humphrey and Schmitz 2000), even though GVC governance can obstruct local upgrading (Humphrey and Schmitz 2002/2000; Gereffi 1999). Navas-Alemán (2011), drawing on the Brazilian furniture and footwear industry, takes on a quite critical view of exporting and points to the opportunities regional and domestic value chains provide for learning and developing capabilities other than production. Local lead firms were also identified to steer upgrading processes in the Indian automobile (Reps and Braun 2012) and textile industries (Bettiol et al. (2011). Moreover, the pervasiveness of informal practices as a strategy for adapting to complex transactions (e.g. trading in raw hides and skins; international modes of payment) that exceed the supplier's capabilities is often overlooked. Therefore, this study follows Ponte and Ewert (2009) who hold upgrading to be a "better deal" for local producers from developing countries striving to enter global markets, taking into account the informal approaches they have been internalising and the opportunities the domestic market provides. If upgrading is to strengthen the firms' competitiveness, strategies have to be devised for the firms' needs against the backdrop of their socio-cultural context and the degree of their integration into the global value chain. The traditional view of learning from buyers appears to apply more to lead firms directly monitoring large producers in developing countries. Here, spill-over effects such as technology transfer and training of employees are expected to benefit local producers (Li Sun et al. 2010, p. 317). It is often ignored that the competence level of MSMEs in developing countries mostly allows only for mediated buyer-supplier relationships (see Section "Buying Houses—Facilitating or Preventing Market Entry?"). This calls for upgrading strategies that reduce dependencies from downstream actors that prompt unsustainable informal adaptation strategies and harmful illicit practices.

Having outlined the analytical framework, the research questions can be refined as follows.

2.6 Research Questions

Four specific research questions seek to analyse the complexities of inter-firm relationships within Bangladesh's leather industry, their informal dynamics and potential strategies to reposition themselves within GVC governance and to overcome structural constraints.

First, the structure and linkages of the Bangladeshi leather value chain are to be analysed at different spatial scales (local for Dhaka and national), delineating central actors as well as dominant product and information flows along the value chain.

1. How is the Bangladeshi leather value chain organised?
   As Bangladesh's leather industry consists of a highly export-oriented but low-competitive tanning subsector and a more dynamically growing, though from a very low level, manufacturing subsector, both subsectors are expected to

contain specific dynamics. In examining inter-firm interactions with regard to the exchange of knowledge, (intermediate) products and services, governance structures including (inter-)dependencies are expected to be identified.

(a) How is the Bangladeshi leather processing industry organised?

(i) Who are the actors and what are the commodity and information flows in the leather processing industry?
(ii) How is the leather processing chain segment governed?

(b) How is the Bangladeshi leather goods and footwear industry organised?

(i) Who are the actors and what are the commodity and information flows in the leather goods and footwear industry?
(ii) How is the leather goods and footwear chain segment governed?

Having understood the structure of the local production network, it is necessary to analyse power asymmetries and drawbacks that obstruct better market integration. Both formal and informal institutions may explain overt and covert dynamics in the global value chain. The formal institutional framework (policies, regulations, influence of external actors) that firms are embedded within is expected to be crucial to the competitiveness of the leather production network. A major challenge is to explain the importance of informal institutions for value chains.

2. How is the Bangladeshi leather industry integrated into the global market?

(a) What formal institutional framework does Bangladesh's leather industry rely on to join in the global leather value chain?
(b) To what extent are informal arrangements understood as institutions, practices and strategies conducive to global market entry?
(c) What is the impact of informal institutional arrangements on power relations?

In a third step, the practices producers resort to in order to deal with institutional constraints and power asymmetries to uphold competitiveness and manage market entry will be identified.

3. How do export-oriented tanneries and leather goods/footwear producers adapt to power asymmetries in the global leather value chain?
Based on the governance structure and institutional constraints, strategies are to be devised to improve the producers' competitiveness. Upgrading can be achieved by learning from (global) buyers or from external actors (e.g. development organisations). Informal institutions need to be taken into account when looking for a "better deal" for local producers.
4. What upgrading strategies are conducive to improving the competitiveness of Bangladesh's leather industry?

(a) What upgrading strategies does the leather industry require to address weaknesses and seize opportunities in the global leather value chain?
(b) How are upgrading strategies to be devised that cater to the reality of informal dynamics in a GVC in order to improve the local producers' competitiveness?

To examine these research questions, in particular to capture the informal dynamics in economic transactions, it is of vital importance to draw on a suitable methodological approach.

References

Alsayyad, N., & Roy, A. (2004). Urban informality: Crossing borders. In A. Roy & N. Alsayyad (Eds.), *Urban informality: Transnational perspectives from the Middle East, Latin America, and South Asia*. Oxford: Lexington Books.

Bair, J. (2009). Global commodity chains: Genealogy and review. In J. Bair (Ed.), *Frontiers of commodity chain research* (pp. 1–34). Stanford: Stanford University Press.

Bair, J., & Dussel Peters, E. (2006). Global commodity chains and endogenous growth: Export dynamism and development in Mexico and Honduras. *World Development, 34*(2), 203–221.

Barrientos, S. (2013). Corporate purchasing practices in global production networks: A socially contested terrain. *Geoforum, 44*, 44–51.

Barrientos, S., Dolan, C., & Tallontire, A. (2003). A gendered value chain approach to codes of conduct in African horticulture. *World Development, 31*(9), 1511–1526.

Barrientos, S., Gereffi, G., & Rossi, A. (2010). *Economic and social upgrading in global production networks: Developing a framework for analysis.* Retrieved from: http://www.capturingthegains.org/pdf/ctg-wp-2010-03.pdf Accessed August 17, 2014.

Bathelt, H. (2006). Geographies of production: growth regimes in spatial perspective 3—Towards a relational view of economic action and policy. *Progress in Human Geography, 30*(2), 223–236.

Bettiol, M., De Marchi, V., Di Maria, E., & Micelli, S. (2011). Economic, social and environmental upgrading in value chains: Social entrepreneurship and the role of emerging economy lead firms. *School of Environment and Development/University of Manchester, Working Paper 4*, Manchester.

Castells, M., & Portes, A. (1989). World underneath: The origins, dynamics and effects of the informal economy. In A. Portes (Ed.), *The informal economy: Studies in advanced and less developed countries*. Baltimore: John Hopkins University Press.

Chen, M. A. (2004). Rethinking the informal economy: Linkages with the formal economy and the formal regulatory environment. *EGDI and UNU-WIDER Conference*, Helsinki.

Chen, M., Sebstad, J., & O'Connel, L. (1999). Counting the invisible workforce: The case of homebased workers. *World Development, 27*(3), 603–610.

Coe, N., Dicken, P., & Hess, M. (2008). Global production networks: Realizing the potential. *Journal of Economic Geography, 8*(3), 271–295.

Coe, N., Hess, M., Yeung, H. W.-C., Dicken, P., & Henderson, J. (2004). Globalising regional development: A global production networks perspective. *Transactions of the Institute of British Geographers, 29*(4), 468–484.

Dannenberg, P. (2012). *Standards in internationalen Wertschöpfungsketten: Akteure, Ziele und Governance in der Obst- und Gemüse-Wertekette Kenia – EU*. Münster: Lit Verlag.

Dannenberg, P., & Nduru, G. (2012). Practices in international value chains: The case of the Kenyan fruit and vegetable chain beyond the exclusion debate. *Tijdschrift voor Economische en Sociale Geografie, 104*(1), 41–56.

De Soto, H. (1989). *The other path: The economic answer to terrorism*. New York: Harper Collins.

Deavers, K. L. (1997). Outsourcing: A corporate competitiveness strategy, not a search for low wages. *Journal of Labour Research, 18*(4), 503–519.

Dicken, P., Kelly, P. F., Olds, K., & Yeung, H. W.-C. (2001). Chains and networks, territories and scales: towards a relational framework for analysing the global economy. *Global Networks, 1* (2), 89–112.

Dolan, C. S., & Tewari, M. (2001). From what we wear to what we eat: Upgrading in gobal value chains. *IDS Bulletin, 32*(3), 94–104.

Dusch Silva, S. (2013). Beglaubigung versetzt Berge: Was bringen Siegel und Zertifikate? *iz3w*, 338, Sept./Okt. 2013, 28–29.

Etzold, B., Bohle, H.-G., Keck, M., & Zingel, W.-P. (2009). Informality as agency—Negotiating food security in Dhaka. *Die Erde, 140*(1), 3–24.

Fernandez-Stark, K., Frederick, S., & Gereffi, G. (2011). *The apparel global value chain: Economic upgrading and workforce development*. Durham: Center on Globalization, Governance & Competitiveness, Duke University.

Fox, A. (1974). *Beyond contract: Work, Power and Trust Relations*. London: Faber & Faber.

Gereffi, G. (1994). The organization of buyer-driven global commodity chains: How U.S. retailers shape overseas production networks. In G. Gereffi & M. Korzeniewicz (Eds.), *Commodity chains and global capitalism* (pp. 95–122). Praeger: Westport, CT.

Gereffi, G. (1999). International trade and industrial up-grading in the apparel commodity chain. *Journal of International Economics, 48*(1), 37–70.

Gereffi, G. (2005). The global economy: Organisation, governance and development. In R. Swedberg & N. J. Smelser (Eds.), *Handbook of economic sociology* (pp. 160–182). Princeton, NJ: Princeton University Press and Russell Sage Foundation.

Gereffi, G., Humphrey, J., & Sturgeon, T. (2005). The governance of global value chains. *Review of International Political Economy, 12*(1), 78–104.

Gereffi, G., Korzeniewicz, M., & Korzeniewicz, R. P. (1994). Introduction: Global commodity chains. In G. Gereffi & M. Korzeniewicz (Eds.), *Commodity chains and global capitalism* (pp. 1–14). Westport, CT: Praeger.

Gereffi, G., & Lee, S. (2012). Why the world suddenly cares about global supply chains. *Journal of Supply Chain Management, 48*(3), 24–32.

Gibbon, P., Bair, J., & Ponte, S. (2008). Governing global value chains: an introduction. *Economy and Society, 37*(3), 315–338.

Giuliani, E., Pietrobelli, C., & Rabellotti, R. (2005). Upgrading in global value chains: Lessons from Latin American clusters. *World Development, 33*(4), 549–573.

Grossman, G. M., & Helpman, E. (2005). Outsourcing in a global economy. *Review of Economic Studies, 72*(1), 135–159.

Guha-Khasnobis, B., Kanbur, R., & Ostrom, E. (2006). Beyond formality and informality. In B. Guha-Khasnobis, R. Kanbur, & E. Ostrom (Eds.), *Linking the formal and informal economy. Concepts and policies* (pp. 1–20). New York: Oxford University Press.

Harris-White, B. (2009). Work and wellbeing in informal economies: The regulative roles of institutions of identity and the state. *World Development, 38*(2), 170–183.

Hart, K. (1973). Informal income opportunities and urban employment in Ghana. *The Journal of Modern African Studies, 11*, 61–89.

Henderson, J., Dicken, P., Hess, M., Coe, N., & Yeung, H. W.-C. (2002). Global production networks and the analysis of economic development. *Review of International Political Economy, 9*(3), 436–464.

Holl, A. (2008). Production subcontracting and location. *Regional Science and Urban Economics, 38*(3), 299–309.

Hopkins, T. K., & Wallerstein, I. (1986). Commodity chains in the world-economy prior to 1800. *Review, 10*(1), 157–170.

Humphrey, J. (2004). *Upgrading in global value chains*. ILO Policy Integration Department, Working Paper No. 28.

Humphrey, J., & Schmitz, H. (2002). How does insertion in global value chains affect upgrading in industrial clusters? *Regional Studies, 36*(9), 1022–1027.

Humphrey, J., & Schmitz, H. (2000). Governance and upgrading: Linking industrial cluster and global value chain research. *IDS Working Paper, 120*, University of Sussex, Brighton.

ILO—International Labour Office. (1972). *Employment, incomes and equality: A strategy for increasing productive employment in Kenya.* Geneva.

Jeppesen, S., & Hansen, M. W. (2004). Environmental upgrading of Third World enterprises through linkages to transnational corporations. Theoretical perspectives and preliminary evidence. *Business Strategy and the Environment, 13*(4), 261–274.

Jia, F., Lamming, R., Sartor, M., Orzes, G., & Nassimbeni G. (2013). Global purchasing strategy and international purchasing offices: Evidence from case studies. *International Journal of Production Economics*. Available online September 18, 2013. http://dx.doi.org/10.1016/j.ijpe.2013.09.007. Accessed November 25, 2013.

Kanbur, R. (2009). Conceptualizing informality: Regulation and enforcement. *The Indian Journal of Labour Economics, 52*, 33–42.

Kaplinsky, R., & Morris, M. (2001). *A handbook for value chain research*. Retrieved from: http://asiandrivers.open.ac.uk/documents/Value_chain_Handbook_RKMM_Nov_2001.pdf. Accessed March 28, 2013.

Knorringa, P. (1999). Agra: An old cluster facing the new competition. *World Development, 27*(9), 1587–1604.

Kulke, E., & Staffeld, R. (2009). Informal production systems—The role of the informal economy in the plastic recycling and processing industry in Dhaka. *Die Erde, 140*(1), 25–43.

Li, P. P. (2007). Social tie, social capital, and social behaviour: Toward an integrative model of informal exchange. *Asia Pacific Journal of Management, 24*(2), 227–246.

Li Sun, S., Chen, H., & Pleggenkuhle-Miles, E. G. (2010). Moving upward in global value chains: The innovations of mobile phone developers in China. *Chinese Management Studies, 4*(4), 305–321.

Maloney, W. F. (1999). Does informality imply segmentation in urban labor markets? Evidence from sectoral transitions in Mexico. *The World Bank Economic Review, 13*(2), 275–302.

Mehrotra, S., & Biggeri, M. (2005). Can industrial outwork enhance homeworkers' capabilities? Evidence from clusters in South Asia. *World Development, 33*(10), 1735–1757.

Meyer, S. (2011). *Informal modes of governance in customer producer relations. The electronic industry in the Greater Pearl River Delta (China).* Stuttgart: Steiner.

Meyer, S., Schiller, D., & Revilla Diez, J. (2012). The localization of electronics manufacturing in the Greater Pearl River Delta, China: Do global implants put down local roots? *Applied Geography, 32*(1), 119–129.

Miroudot, S., & De Backer, K. (2012). Mapping global value chains. Policy dialogue on aid for trade. *Organisation for Economic Co-operation and Development. Trade and Agriculture Directorate.* OECD Conference Centre, Paris.

Misztal, B. (2000). *Informality: Social theory and contemporary practice*. London: Routledge.

Murphy, J. T. (2007). The challenge of upgrading in African industries: Socio-spatial factors and the urban environment in Mwanza, Tanzania. *World Development, 35*(10), 1754–1778.

Nadvi, K. (2008). Global standards, global governance and the organization of global value chains. *Journal of Economic Geography, 8*(3), 323–343.

Navas-Alemán, L. (2011). The impact of operating in multiple value chains for upgrading: The case of the Brazilian furniture and footwear industries. *World Development, 39*(8), 1386–1397.

North, D. C. (1990). *Institutions, institutional change and economic performance*. New York: Cambridge University Press.

Oguoma, O., Nkwocha, V., & Ibeawuchi, I. (2010). Implications of middlemen in the supply chain of agricultural products. *Journal of Agriculture and Social Research, 10*(2), 77–83.

Ponte, S. (2009). Governing through quality: Conventions and supply relations in the value chain for South African wine. *Sociologia Ruralis, 49*(3), 236–257.

Ponte, S., & Ewert, J. (2009). Which way is "up" in upgrading? Trajectories of change in the value chain for South African wine. *World Development, 37*(10), 1637–1650.

Porter, M. E. (1990). *The competitive advantage of nations*. New York: Free Press.

Pratim Sahu, P. (2010). Subcontracting in India's unorganised manufacturing sector: A mode of adoption or exploitation? *Journal of South Asian Development, 5*(1), 53–83.

Prügl, E., & Tinker, I. (1997). Microentrepreneurs and homeworkers: Convergent categories. *World Development, 25*(9), 1471–1482.

Reeves, P. (2002). Regional diversity in South Asian Inland fisheries: Colonial Bengal and Uttar Pradesh compared. *South Asia: Journal of South Asian Studies, 25*(2), 121–135.

Reps, N., & Braun, B. (2012). Going Green: Ökologische Aufwertungsprozesse und Koordinationsstrukturen in den Wertschöpfungsketten der indischen Kraftfahrzeugsindustrie. *Zeitschrift für Wirtschaftsgeographie, 56*(4), 226–243.

Sartor, M., Orzes, G., Nassimbeni, G., Jia, F., & Lamming, R. (2014). International purchasing offices: Literature review and research directions. *Journal of Purchasing and Supply Management, 20*(1), 1–17.

Sassen, S. (1994). The informal economy: Between new development and old regulations. *The Yale Law Journal, 103*, 2289–2304.

Schiller, D. (2012). Informal dynamics of economic processes. Remarks on the potential of the informality concept. *Zeitschrift für Wirtschaftsgeographie, 56*(1–2), 1–8.

Schmitz, H. (2006). Learning and earning in global garment and footwear chains. *The European Journal of Development Research, 18*(4), 546–571.

Schmitz, H., & Knorringa, p. (1999). Learning from global buyers. *IDS Working Paper, 100*. Institute of Development Studies, Brighton.

Sindzingre, A. (2006). The relevance of the concepts of formality and informality: A theoretical appraisal. In B. Guha-Khasnobis, R. Kanbur, & E. Ostrom (Eds.), *Linking the formal and informal economy: Concepts and policies* (pp. 58–74). New York: Oxford University Press.

Steer, L., & Sen, K. (2010). Formal and informal institutions in a transition economy: The case of Vietnam. *World Development, 38*(11), 1603–1615.

Sturgeon, T. J. (2009). From commodity chains to value chains: Interdisciplinary theory building in an age of globalization. In J. Bair (Ed.), *Frontiers of commodity chain research* (pp. 110–135). Stanford: Stanford University Press.

Sturgeon, T. J., & Gereffi, G. (2008). The challenge of global value chains: Why integrative trade requires new thinking and new data. Retrieved from: http://www.cggc.duke.edu/pdfs/GVCmetrics_Nov202008.pdf. Accessed May 23, 2014.

Sudhir Kumar, R., & Bala Subrahmanya, M. H. (2010). Influence of subcontracting on innovation and economic performance of SMEs in Indian automobile industry. *Technovation, 30*(11–12), 558–569.

Talbot, J. M. (2009). The comparative advantages of tropical commodity chain analysis. In J. Bair (Ed.), *Frontiers of commodity chain research* (pp. 93–109). Stanford: Stanford University Press.

Tewari, M., & Pillai, P. (2005). Global standards and the dynamics of environmental compliance in India's leather industry. *Oxford Development Studies, 33*(2), 245–267.

Van Mieghem, J. A. (1999). Coordinating investment, production, and subcontracting. *Management Science, 45*(7), 954–971.

Wallerstein, I. (2009). Protection networks and commodity chains in the capitalist world-economy. In J. Bair (Ed.), *Frontiers of commodity chain research* (pp. 83–90). Stanford: Stanford University Press.

Webster, M., Alder, C., & Muhlemann, A. P. (1997). Subcontracting within the supply chain for electronics assembly manufacture. *International Journal of Operations and Production Management, 17*(9), 827–841.

Williamson, O. E. (1975). *Markets and hierarchies: Analysis and antitrust implications*. New York: Free Press.

Williamson, O. E. (1985). *The economic institutions of capitalism*. New York: Free Press.

Woodruff, C. (1998). Contract enforcement and trade liberalization in Mexico's footwear industry. *World Development, 26*(6), 979–991.

Chapter 3
Methodology

Abstract Qualitative research complemented by specific quantitative methods has been chosen as an approach to explore and understand specific dimensions of the complexly governed leather value chain. The data source of this study is drawn from empirical field studies in Dhaka, Bangladesh and other sections of the international leather value chain in 2010–2014. Conceptualising the Bangladeshi leather industry within a global value chain served as an analytical framework to define the coordination of inter-firm activities, their business dynamics and power asymmetries at the corresponding nodes in the chain. The complexity of transactions in the chain, the ability to codify these transactions and the capabilities in the supply base were key determinants for an analytical understanding of the value chain. After introducing the research design, which links the development of a conceptual framework, the definition of research questions and data collection coherently, the study site and research methods will be presented. Ultimately, limitations that are inevitably entailed by research in a socio-cultural environment that differs greatly from the author's will be addressed.

Qualitative research complemented by specific quantitative methods has been chosen as an approach to explore and understand specific dimensions of the complexly governed leather value chain. This makes it possible to sketch a multi-faceted picture of the process and activities under study (Creswell 2014). After introducing the research design, which links the development of a conceptual framework, the definition of research questions and data collection coherently (Fig. 3.1), the study site and research methods will be presented. Ultimately, limitations that are inevitably entailed by research in a socio-cultural environment that differs greatly from the author's will be addressed.

Figure 3.1 suggests a linear, hierarchical approach, but many of the stages are interrelated and activities were carried out parallel to each other.

J. Strasser, *Bangladesh's Leather Industry*,
Springer Geography, DOI 10.1007/978-3-319-22548-7_3

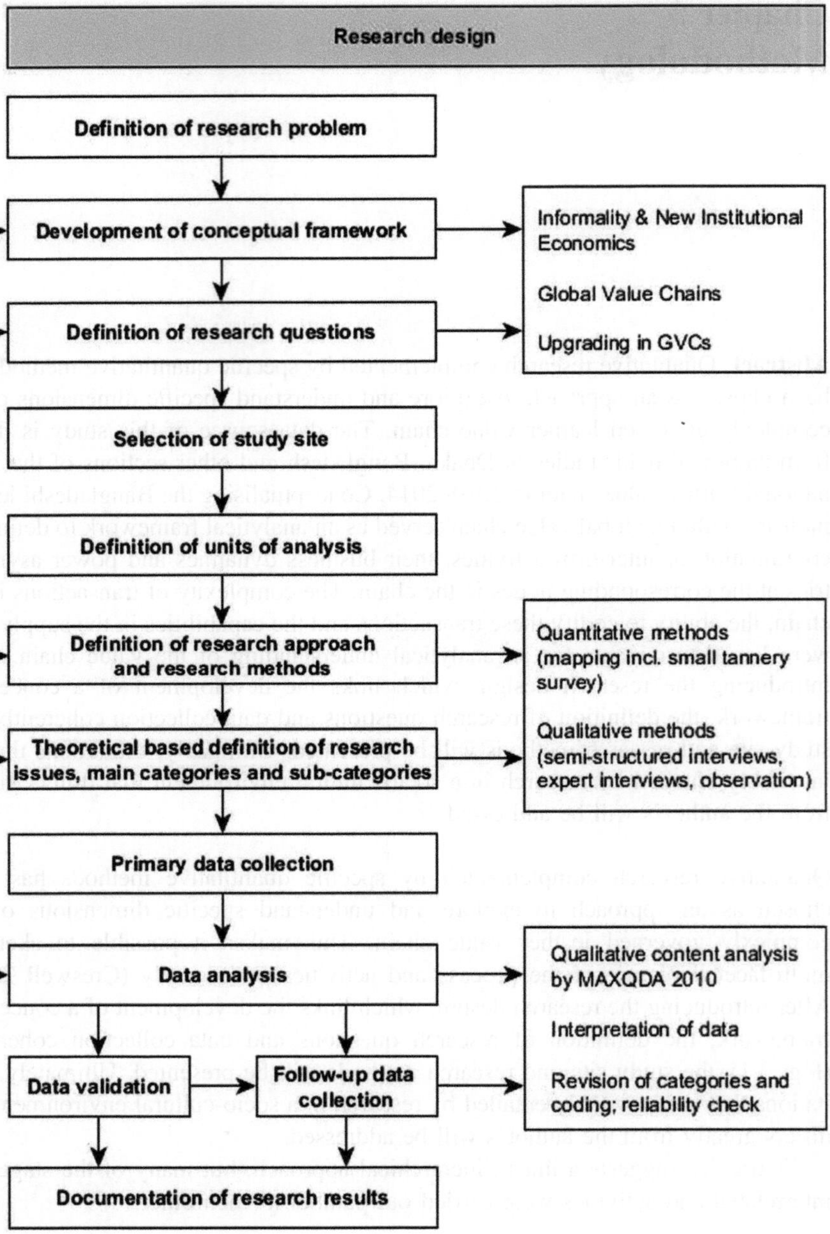

Fig. 3.1 Research design. *Source* Own illustration

3.1 Study Site and Research Methods

This research received funding from the German Research Foundation (DFG) within the priority programme 1233 "Megacities-Megachallenge—Informal Dynamics of Global Change". Dhaka as a monocentric megacity agglomeration represented one of the programme's two focus regions.[1] After prior studies on local value chains in the first research period from 2007 to 2010 this research project was to extend its spatial analysis to the global level. Economic activities that are based in the megacity of Dhaka and embedded in global production networks are scarce. Leather follows woven and knitwear garments, the latter being Bangladesh's largest export earning product being primarily produced in or at the urban fringe of Dhaka. Unlike the clothing sector, the leather industry procures raw material mainly from within the country. This allows for greater possibilities for value addition within the country and makes it possible to devise corresponding upgrading strategies. Moreover, in preparatory visits to leather and garment factories managers of the latter proved to be extremely reluctant to give information on global market integration. Besides a higher level of cooperation in the leather industry, differences in structure (e.g. high concentration of tanneries in Dhaka) and dynamics (e.g. increasing importance of the more value-added leather manufacturing subsectors; own raw material; subcontracting arrangements on different levels) were decisive for analysing the leather industry's integration into the world market and adaptation strategies to the chain's intrinsic power relations.

The data source of this study is drawn from empirical field studies in Dhaka, Bangladesh and other sections of the international leather value chain in 2010–2014. Conceptualising the Bangladeshi leather industry within a global value chain served as an analytical framework to define the coordination of inter-firm activities, their business dynamics and power asymmetries at the corresponding nodes in the chain (Gereffi et al. 2005; Kaplinsky and Morris 2001). The complexity of transactions in the chain, the ability to codify these transactions and the capabilities in the supply base were key determinants for an analytical understanding of the value chain.

The initial assumption of this study was to examine how leather processors and manufacturers, though lacking significant capabilities, still manage to cater to the export market by availing of informal arrangements. The exploratory character of this proposition required a qualitative approach that is capable of unfolding the informal nature of practices, routines and strategies to adapt to power asymmetries or to achieve global market entry. Complementing it with quantitative methods was conducive to gaining an idea of specific magnitudes within the complexly governed leather value chain.

As over 90 % of the country's tanneries are concentrated in the tannery estate in Hazaribagh, a subdistrict in the southwest of Dhaka, the research activities were focused on this region. While mapping all tanneries (n = 168), a small survey

[1]The polycentric Pearl River Delta (China) was the second research site.

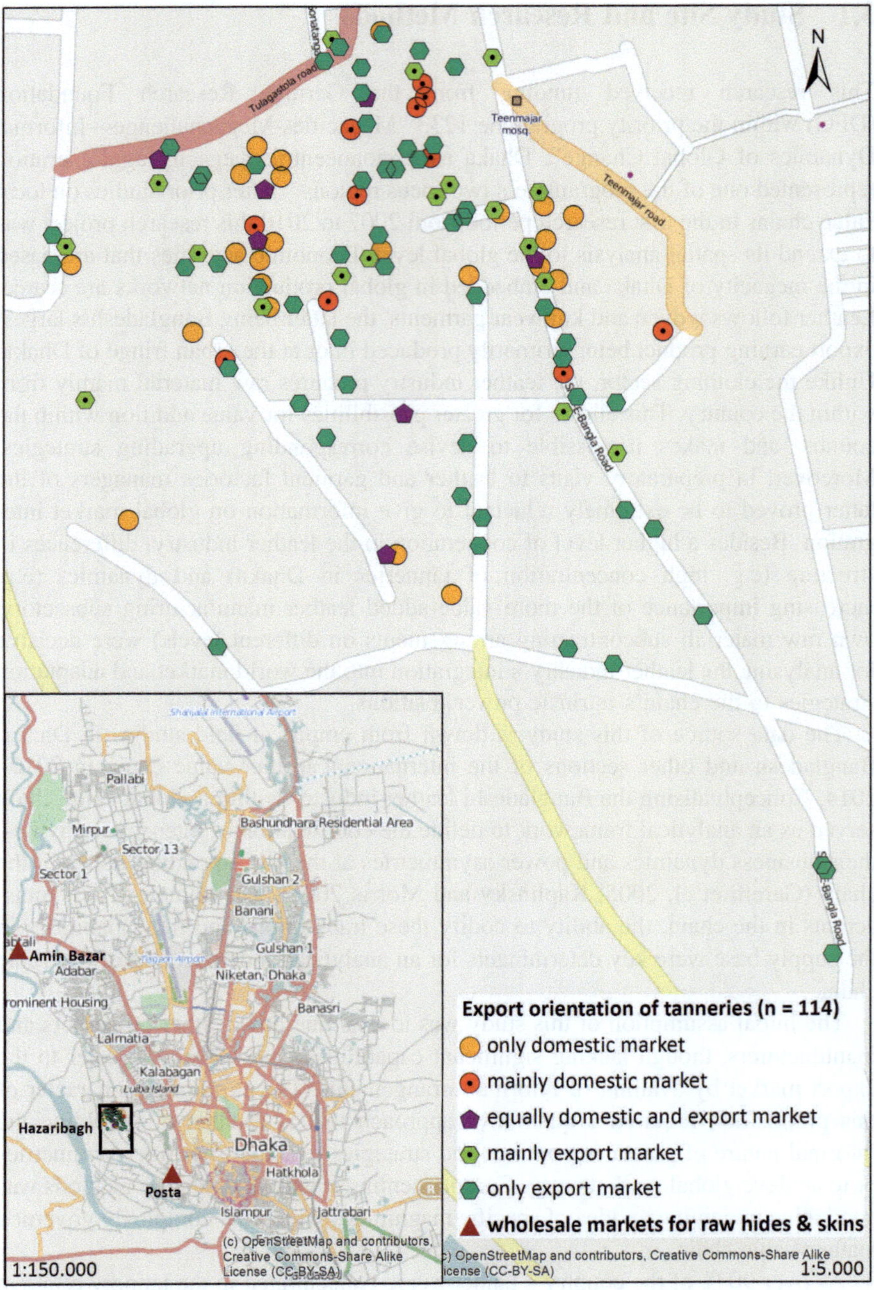

Fig. 3.2 Export orientation of tanneries in Hazaribagh 2011. *Source* Adapted from Strasser et al. (2013)

collected data from operating tanneries (n = 119) on ownership, their production structure (wet blue, crust, finished) and corresponding production volume, their utilisation for own and job work production, their export orientation, and the status of their employees (temporary or permanent). Figure 3.2 highlights the export orientation of Hazaribagh's tanneries in 2011.[2]

Based on the data on operating tanneries, which differs substantially from official figures (e.g. Kumar Bhowmik 2013; interviews with Bangladesh Finished Leather, Leathergoods and Footwear Exporters' Association—BFLLFEA and Bangladesh Tannery Association—BTA), the tanneries to be interviewed were selected according to the theoretical sample approach (Glaser and Strauss 1967). In a few cases, the research team referred to the pyramid scheme (Flick 1998). The potential methodological risks of concentrating information from a similar group were reduced through triangulation. Semi-structured face-to-face interviews (Mayring 2002, p. 67; Flick 1998, p. 105) with selected actors operating at different links along the chain were conducted to provide an "inter-subjective understanding" (Crang and Cook 2007, p. 51) of up- and downstream interactions. In so doing, agencies, dynamics and motivations were portrayed in an in-depth manner that neither statistics nor standardised questionnaires can provide.

The bulk of the interviews with factory owners and managers were carried out in Bengali by student assistants from local partner universities (University of Dhaka, Bangladesh University of Engineering and Technology); these were trained, accompanied and supervised by me, the author of this study. These interviews were transcribed and translated into English. Participants with a command of English or German were interviewed by me. Table 3.1 gives an overview of the actors interviewed along the value chain.

Data collection was stopped when the categories under scrutiny were saturated (Creswell 2014, p. 189). To enhance the validity (or better: credibility) of the data and to expand on specific issues, most of the tanneries and LGF producers were interviewed several times in the course of three years. Transcripts were checked selectively to rule out mistakes during translation and transcription and enhance reliability (Creswell 2014, p. 203).

The principal set of questions during the interviews addressed procurement activities, quality management, challenges in catering to the international market, contract arrangements and payment modes with upstream suppliers and downstream buyers, as well as strategies to improve production processes, to develop products and to increase other activities for value addition (see A.1).

The interview content was analysed and coded by using MAXQDA 2010 qualitative data analysis software. Based on Mayring's (2010) qualitative content analysis, codes were partly developed on the basis of the information collected and

[2]A large number of commercial leather exporters operate on a job work basis, i.e. they rent others' underutilised facilities to produce leather. Thus, Hazaribagh's export activity is assumed to be stronger than pictured in Fig. 3.2.

Table 3.1 Overview of semi-structured and expert interviews, 2010–2012

		No. of actors
Semi-structured interviews		
Producers	Professional butchers	6
	Non-professional butchers	3
	Tanneries	19
	Commercial leather exporters	2
	Leather goods—MSME	6
	Leather footwear—MSME	3
	Leather goods and footwear—local lead firm	2
	Leather goods—foreign lead firm	1
Traders	Regular traders of raw hides and skins	22
	Temporary traders of raw hides and skins	11
	Chemical traders	2
	Buying agents—Bangladesh	4
	Buying agent—Europe	1
Expert interviews		
Experts	Public authorities	5
	Upgrading organisations	4
	Associations	5
	International consultants	3
	Leather technologists	2
	Independent	1
Total interviews		102

Source Own illustration

partly predetermined by the analytical categories provided by the GVC approach (Creswell 2014, p. 199; Gereffi et al. 2005).

Following the interviews with LGF manufacturers, a few questions covered size-specific (employees, turnover, production capacity/volume/area) and socio-economic indicators (education).

A couple of weeks after the interviews with the tanneries, a more extended survey was carried out to collect data on the production process, market conditions, global integration, financial aspects, socio-economic issues and support by business associations. The objective was to enrich qualitative findings with information about quantities.

3.2 Limitations of This Study

The original idea of this research was to examine the entire chain from the raw material to the final product marketed by large overseas retailers, identifying power asymmetries and informal strategies by the producers to deal with those (e.g. Gereffi et al. 2005; Kaplinsky and Morris 2001). With increasing progress in analysing the leather production network in Bangladesh, limitations of time in extending data collection systematically to buyers from selected foreign markets became evident. Particular attention was paid to exploring the nature of economic relations and processes. Given the scope of the illicit practices detected, verification by foreign companies operating at a global scale seemed highly unlikely. Therefore, this study is confined to analysing the local production network and its integration into the global market basically from the view of local producers and buying houses, the latter acting on behalf of foreign buyers. This involves limitations in the inferability of dynamics and processes the author is aware of.

A qualitative approach was considered to be the most appropriate way to research into non-formalised processes in the leather value chain. After exploratory interviews with leather technologists and leather goods and footwear (LGF) manufacturers, illicit practices (e.g. misinvoicing) turned out to determine the leather industry to a much broader extent than assumed. Other studies, mostly in economics, provide empirical evidence on corruption by analysing foreign trade data (for Bangladesh, see Kumar Gupta et al. 2012; for Iran, Reza Farzanegan 2009) or relate restrictive trade policies to illegal capital outflow (e.g. Biswas and Marjit 2007). However, they lack insight into the way such illegal practices are transacted and determine power asymmetries in a specific industry. Qualitative research allowed for an exploration of the producers' meanings, motivations and subjective perceptions in this regard (Creswell 2014). Initial exploratory interviews made the research team realise that semi-structured questions helped the interviewees focus and keep the interview in time. Given my lack of command of Bengali, semi-structured interviews held by local student assistants allowed for more control over the course of the interview (see below). The main challenges were to build up trust and to overcome the language barrier, which often made several meetings necessary. Like Meyer (2011, p. 89) when dealing with the electronics industry in the Pearl River Delta, the term informality was not explicitly mentioned as definitions vary socially and culturally. Furthermore, the interviewees were not to be misled into taking informal to mean the same as illegal. Instead, the questions focused neutrally on the way transactions are carried out to define the nature of interactions and the strategies to deal with power asymmetry within the chain. It required a sensible approach to not affront interview partners. Consequently, the informal institutions and practices that are touched on below are a result of the interviewees' subjective experience and motivation. They have been subject to the principal researcher's interpretation and do not provide a representative picture of the leather industry.

The survey method after the interviews with the tanneries was useful in constructing the classification but proved futile for obtaining reliable data. Most of the very small and small tanneries do not keep accounts or were not used to responding to, for instance, five-point Likert scales. Hence, little of this data considered as supporting information was used in the analysis.

The literature on the leather industry in Bangladesh or on raw material supply is very limited and mostly confined to grey literature published by leather associations or governmental organisations (e.g. GTZ 2006; GTZ-PROGRESS 2006; consultancies hired by UN agencies; European Commission), which, however, represent a rich complementary resource. Those very few academic papers that have been published in English relate exclusively to environmental compliance issues and, thus, can only be made use of in this study to a limited extent. In a few cases information was gathered from newspaper articles (e.g. dynamics on the Festival of Sacrifice; debate on the relocation of the tanneries).

Language constituted a major challenge. The bulk of the interviews were carried out in Bengali by student assistants from local partner universities with me, the principal researcher and author of this study present. These were trained in interview techniques and the research content to ensure reliability by reducing the error margin in both simultaneous and post-interview translations. Due to time constraints and the workload of the student assistants, the interviews could not always be transcribed and translated into English by the same person, thus reducing the overall level of accuracy. Direct quotations in the text are marked in the language the interviews have been taken; they have been slightly edited to enhance clarity and readability. Inaccurate interviews, transcripts and translations required an extremely high level of validation and follow-up questions over three years (2011, 2012, 2014), which unfortunately could not be extended to all producers to the same extent. Cottage and micro leather goods manufacturers producing on subcontract for local lead firms in particular found it challenging to make additional time. Most of these entrepreneurs produce jointly with their workers to the tight schedule of their lead firm.

Likewise, large tanneries were reluctant to provide adequate information. Data inconsistencies were compensated by additional expert interviews with international (UNIDO) consultants giving advice to those tanneries within the framework of the upgrading project Re-Tie Bangladesh. All interviews were carried out in person, except for the last set of follow-up questions with LGF producers in 2014, which were asked by email or over the phone by a student assistant. This method made it possible to check the consistency of responses and provided valuable insights into the producers' development. As a matter of fact, it involves risks in the accuracy of the data (Creswell 2014, p. 202) as subjective perceptions may change over time.

Before proceeding to the empirical part of this study, the historical development of the leather industry and its institutional framework will be portrayed, in order to gain an understanding of the role of specific actors (e.g. business associations).

References

Biswas, A. K., & Marjit, S. (2007). Preferential trade and mis-invoicing: Some analytical implications. *International Review of Economics and Finance, 16*(1), 130–138.

Crang, M., & Cook, I. (2007). *Doing Ethnographies*. London: Sage.

Creswell, J. W. (2014). *Research design. qualitative, quantitative and mixed methods approaches.* Thousand Oaks: Sage.

Flick, U. (1998). *Qualitative Forschung: Theorie, Methoden, Anwendung in Psychologie und Sozialwissenschaften* (3rd ed.). Reinbek bei Hamburg: Rowohlt.

Gereffi, G (2005). The global economy: Organisation, governance and development. In Smelser, N. J. & Swedberg, R. (eds.) *Handbook of economic sociology* (2nd ed.), Princeton, NJ: Princeton University Press and Russell Sage Foundation pp. 160–182.

Glaser, B. G., & Strauss, A. L. (1967). *The discovery of grounded theory: Strategies for qualitative research.* New York: Aldine de Gruyter.

GTZ—Gesellschaft für Technische Zusammenarbeit. (2006). *Value Chain Assessment of the Leather Sector in Bangladesh,* Dhaka.

GTZ-PROGRESS (2006). *A census study on leather sector in Bangladesh & A desk study on status/strategies of the leather sector of the competing countries.* Dhaka.

Kaplinsky, R. & Morris, M. (2001). *A handbook for value chain research.* Retrieved from: http://asiandrivers.open.ac.uk/documents/Value_chain_Handbook_RKMM_Nov_2001.pdf. Accessed March 28, 2013.

Kumar Bhowmik, A. (2013). Industries' location as jeopardy for sustainable urban development in Asia: a review of the Bangladesh leather processing industry relocation plan. *Environment and Urbanization Asia, 4*(1), 93–119.

Kumar Gupta, P., Roy, D., & Ahmad, K. (2012). Close eye or closed eye: The case of export Misinvoicing in Bangladesh. *IFPRI Discussion Paper 0115.*

Mayring, P. (2002). *Einführung in die qualitative Sozialforschung*. Weinheim und Basel: Beltz Verlag.

Mayring, P. (2010). *Qualitative Inhaltsanalyse*. Grundlagen und Techniken: Beltz Verlag, Weinheim und Basel.

Meyer, S. (2011). *Informal modes of governance in customer producer relations. The electronic industry in the Greater Pearl river delta (China).* Stuttgart: Steiner.

Reza Farzanegan, M. (2009). Illegal trade in the Iranian economy: Evidence from a structural model. *European Journal of Political Economy, 25*(4), 489–507.

Strasser, J., Dannenberg, P., & Kulke, E. (2013). Temporary resource availability and quality constraints in the global leather value chain—The impact of the festival of sacrifice on the leather industry in Bangladesh. *Applied Geography, 45*, 410–419.

Chapter 4
The Leather Industry in Bangladesh

Abstract This section gives a brief overview of the historic development of the leather industry in Bangladesh, describes its internal organisation and delineates the institutional framework it is embedded within. Bangladesh's export-oriented leather processing subsector originates from the East Bengal and East Pakistan periods. After Bangladesh's independence in 1971, the tanning industry underwent a restructuring process accompanied by public policies that paved the way for more value addition. Thanks to these policies being inadequately implemented, the tanneries in Hazaribagh, Dhaka keep operating under conditions beyond their capacity and sustainability, while growth of the leather goods and footwear subsectors has been picking up in recent years. Institutions and organisations related to the leather sector were devised to pursue an outward-oriented strategy but failed to boost export earnings. As a result of the deficient institutional framework, both subsectors leather processing and manufacturing suffer from underfunding and require a high level of investment.

4.1 Historical Outline

The tanning industry in the global South has been integrated into global production networks since non-tariff trade barriers such as the environmental regulation in countries of the North were tightened and labour-intensive footwear industry moved to low cost regions (Hesselberg and Knutsen 2002, p. 169). In developing countries leather processing has been a traditional industry that plays a vital role for employment generation and has only recently been integrated in globalised markets.

Bangladesh's leather processing sector came into existence after the country formerly known as East Bengal was partitioned from India in 1947 (Ahmed 2002). During British rule hides and skins were sent for tanning and further processing to regional centres of British India such as Kolkata, Kanpur or Madras, from where also the supply of leather goods and footwear was organised back to East Bengal (ibid.). From 1947 to 1971, East Bengal was declared East Pakistan, a province of

J. Strasser, *Bangladesh's Leather Industry*,
Springer Geography, DOI 10.1007/978-3-319-22548-7_4

Pakistan. During this time, tanneries were established in Hazaribagh (Dhaka) and Kalurghat (Chittagong).[1] West Pakistani tanners controlled the industry, sourcing local raw material, processing it and manufacturing it to leather goods and footwear. Only a few small factories were operated by Bengali entrepreneurs and these produced for the domestic market (BFLLFEA 2014). In the initial stage of the East Pakistan leather processing industry, raw hides and skins were primarily treated with vegetable substances. Once chrome tanning was introduced in 1965, vegetable leather was quickly substituted by the semi-processed tanned wet blue leather that took off as an export good.[2] After Bangladesh attained independence in 1971, the tanning industry underwent a restructuring process, during which the West Pakistani tanners abandoned the country and the government sought to nationalise a substantial part of it (see Ahmed 2002, p. 31). Several attempts to run a number of tanneries publicly failed and ultimately led to privatising the sector. Despite restructuring, the tanning sector experienced significant growth from the 1970s to the 1990s, with export records and the number of tanneries expanding (ibid.). Ahmed (2002) saw a rise from 86 tanneries registered in 1970 to 206 in 1995, a number that leather associations (BFLLFEA, BTA) have kept highlighting in public for many years, while the real number of operating tanneries apparently was decreasing dramatically as this study pointed out (see Sect. 3.1).

Concomitant to Dhaka's rampant population growth, the unplanned expansion of its leather processing industry during the 1970s and 1980s turned Hazaribagh into the centre of Bangladesh's leather industry (Ahmed 2002, p. 5). The Government sought to provide incentives to enhance the value added as, until 1980, only wet blue leather was produced for the export market. Finished leather was of low quality and thus only destined for local consumption. Tax incentives, cash subsidies and duty drawback to semi-finished (crust) and finished leather exports, among other policy measures, were gradually introduced to increase value addition and thus the competitiveness of the leather processing industry. To speed up the latter's development wet blue leather was banned from exports in 1990, inducing an ongoing process of profound restructuring. Many tanneries could not service loans anymore and shut down or were subcontracted by larger tanneries (see Sect. 5.2.1). Interviews with tannery associations and international consultants suggest that this process is likely to be exacerbated once the tanneries relocate to the new site in the outskirts of Dhaka.

With rapid industrial and population growth, the Hazaribagh tanning estate has grown to 70 acres (28 ha) and has been gradually incorporated into Dhaka's urban fabric. The lack of willingness of political and private actors to adjust Hazaribagh to environmental standards to avoid untreated effluents being released into the city's most important river Buriganga has put public health at risk (SEHD 1998, 2002). But it took the government more than 30 years to agree on a site for a new tanning

[1] Chittagong is Bangladesh's second largest city and hosts the primary national sea port.

[2] A detailed description of the production process of leather and the common tanning agents will be provided in Sect. 5.2.1.

estate to be set up outside the city confines. The current site in Hemayetpur in the upazila Savar, a subdistrict of Dhaka District, 25 km northeast of Dhaka City, was eventually selected in 1994 (Ahmed 2002). Since then, governmental bodies and the tannery associations formally agreed to relocate, and a Memorandum of Understanding was signed in 2003; however, there has been a lack of commitment towards quickly devising and implementing plans. A High Court order in 2009 urged the Government to comply with existing laws and regulations. Despite formal pressure, the tanneries keep operating in Hazaribagh under conditions beyond their capacity and sustainability. Section 5.2.4.6 will expand on this issue, contextualising it within locational upgrading.

4.2 The Organisation of the Leather Industry

A familiar argument put forward by North (1990) is that organisations are the agents of institutional change. Firms, a form of organisation, are purposive entities as well as the associations that represent their interests (ibid., p. 73).

The leather industry is dominated by three major leather trade associations, and interviews were carried out with all of them. *Bangladesh Tannery Association* (*BTA*) was already established in 1958 (BLSC 2009) and records the highest number of memberships, covering tanneries (ordinary members, 120) and commercial leather exporters (associated members, 341) at all technology levels (BTA 2014). *Bangladesh Finished Leather, Leathergoods and Footwear Exporters' Association* (*BFLLFEA*) started in 1986 to represent the interests of primarily export-oriented medium-sized and large tanneries that centre on crust and finished leather along with footwear and leather goods production (BFLLFEA 2014). As of 2014, 107 general members[3] and 40 associate members were registered. The *Leather Goods and Footwear Manufacturers and Exporters Association of Bangladesh* (*LFMEAB*), though the youngest (founded in 2003) and smallest association (52 members), appears to be organised best and strives not to be associated with the tanning industry in Hazaribagh (LFMEAB 2014). Most of its members are leather footwear exporters. The leather goods and footwear subsectors have experienced dynamic growth in the last decade, with the latter closing in on the long-time leading leather processors. For reasons of financial constraints mainly large factories are members of LFMEAB. Most of the MSMEs are excluded from the association's benefits and services.

The *Bangladesh Hide and Skin Merchants Association* (*BHSMA*) supports local hides and skins traders in doing business with leather processors. It is noteworthy

[3]If there were in fact "around 200 tanneries" as suggested by BFLLFEA (2014), only roughly half of them would have registered with the association. This would point to a relatively low integration into the tanning industry.

that raw hides and skins (RHS) are only allowed to be traded locally. Prior to the Festival of Sacrifice (Eid-ul-Azha), the peak season for raw material supply, BHSMA deliberates annually with BTA, BFLLFEA and governmental agencies on a fixed price rate per ft^2 of RHS. In 2013, after a three-year break all parties agreed on a price level for RHS of sacrificial animals, publishing it in the media (see Section 5.2.2.3).

Other smaller organisations of manufacturers and traders have a minor impact on the export-oriented leather industry, and thus were excluded from this study.

The leather associations' primary objective is to represent the interests of their members, promoting the leather industry at home and abroad. Their main tasks are to enable businesses to meet and discuss leather-related issues, to inform them about markets, to organise and help them participate in trade fairs, and to negotiate with governmental bodies. Generally, associations play an important role in providing their members with technological know-how, information on fashion trends and quality standards in international markets, and export guidelines. At the time of data collection (2010–2012), BFLLFEA and BTA were engaged in negotiating the terms and conditions for the relocation to the new tannery site.

4.3 The Institutional Framework

Aside from internal organisation, export policy papers from 1997 onwards stipulate that the leather industry is a national thrust sector that requires institutional support (Ahmed 2002, p. 84). By 2011, only few strategies had been implemented or they had proved to be ineffective.

The *Export Promotion Bureau* (*EPB*), an agency under the Ministry of Commerce, is entrusted with promoting the export of leather products. Market research activities such as collecting and disseminating information to the leather (product) exporters, arranging market visits, organising participations in trade fairs in foreign markets and providing the infrastructural facilities are among the EPB's most prominent duties (Ahmed 2002; EPB 2013). Ahmed (2002) and own interviews with EPB officials and LGF producers suggest that the bureau has little knowledge about and capacity to support the leather sector. In line with the export policy's strategic restructuring towards more value addition, the LGF subsectors are given more attention than the tanning industry.

In the same vein, the *Leather Sector's Business Promotion Council* (*LSBPC*) was established in 2004 under the Ministry of Commerce to develop the exportability of leather products from Bangladesh. In addition to EPB's focus on market research, LSBPC is to provide capacity building and facilitate participations in trade fairs to increase the capabilities of leather processors and LGF producers. The interview confirmed that LSBPC's focus is on the more value-added manufacturing subsectors. Under LSBPC's guidance the *Bangladesh Leather Service Centre* (*BLSC*) was created to provide services on product design and development, training, quality testing and certification, market information, international promotion and partnership development as well as financial guidance to SMEs (BLSC 2009). The services these organisations provide can be critical to the industry's competitiveness. The leather production network will be analysed taking into consideration the functionality of the organisational and institutional setting.

Drawing on North's (1990) transaction cost approach, institutions and the technology used determine the firm's resources they need to transform production factors into goods and services. Rules have an influence on *financial and saving institutions*, for instance, in terms of the rates of interest. The tanning industry is highly capital intensive and technically depends on capital from financial institutions. Few development banks provide loans for larger investments such as machinery and equipment (Ahmed 2002); working capital is lent by public and private banks. According to LSBPC, which, together with governmental banks, developed a programme to offer collateral-free loans at 12 %, the market rates approximate 18–19 %. All experts and tannery owners stress that the financial situation of the tanning industry is alarming. High interest rates conflict with the slow processing time for raw material (approximately 20 days) and the huge amount of capital, which is tied to stocked RHS or semi-processed wet blue (Ahmed 2002, p. 84). Ahmed (2002, p. 85) criticises that the lending policy varies from bank to bank, is non-transparent and even changes with new personnel. Moreover, loans are inadequately monitored by banks and thus often used ineffectively. Many tanneries were found shut down or subcontracted as a result of loan default (see Sect. 5.2; Fig. 5.2). As for the LGF subsectors, a BLSC-survey stated serious underfunding of SMEs, which indicates insufficient funding schemes. As a result of inadequate institutional incentives, both leather processing and manufacturing subsectors suffer from poor financial endowment.

Following North (1990, pp. 79–80), institutions structure economic exchange and explain economic performance. Skills and knowledge are driving forces of economic growth. In developing countries the institutional incentives to invest in productive knowledge have often been inadequate. What holds for many sectors in countries of the global South also applies to education in leather technology in Bangladesh.

The *Bangladesh College of Leather Technology* (*BCLT*) founded in 1949 is the country's only educational and training institute for the leather industry. Located in the heart of Hazaribagh, it offers graduate courses in leather technology, footwear technology and leather products, whereas floor-level workers in both leather processing and manufacturing subsectors are trained on the job. Formerly attached to the Ministry of Education, BCLT joined Dhaka University's Faculty of Engineering and Technology as the Institute of Leather Engineering and Technology in 2012. The state owned educational institution is chronically underfunded and cannot stop the exodus of teaching staff and students, says one BCLT professor. Unskilled labour force is a major drawback to the leather industry's competitiveness and reflects North's view of an ineffective use of institutions. He sees the biggest flaw in focusing on higher education instead of increasing the social rate of return by investing in primary education and, in Bangladesh's case, vocational institutes

(1990, p. 80). There is doubt whether BCLT's strategic realignment to Dhaka University is conducive to strengthening the institute's importance in developing the leather sector.

According to Ahmed (2002), several attempts to establish and operate leather *research facilities* have failed since the 1950s. Currently, inadequately equipped and staffed plant facilities on the outskirts of Dhaka (Savar) are not in use.

The availability of *water and electricity* crucially influences the tanneries' production costs and competitiveness. According to Ahmed (2002), small tanneries generally register with Dhaka Water Supply and Sewerage Authority (DWASA). In interviews with experts and tannery owners, large and medium-sized tanneries were confirmed to be using water from their own tube-well for a very low annual fee that is charged per well instead of per water consumption. By the end of 2012, DWASA was reported to have started to install water meters at all tanneries. Electricity supply is highly irregular. Again, medium-sized and large tanneries have invested in generators, while smaller tanneries have little capacity to outweigh failures. Load shedding disturbs production and seriously affects the leather quality. Irregular electricity also alters the LGF manufacturers' productivity, though the mechanisation level in cottage, micro and small industries is low (see Sect. 5.3.1).

With this deficient institutional framework in mind, I proceed to the analysis of the leather value chain, contrasting it with the producers' subjective experiences and motivations.

References

Ahmed, K. A. (2002). *A comprehensive study on leather sector industries of Bangladesh.* Dhaka: Leather Goods & Footwear Exporters' Association, Bangladesh Finished Leather.

BFLLFEA—Bangladesh Finished Leather, Leathergoods & Footwear Exporters' Association. (2014). *About BFLLFEA.* Retrieved from: http://bfllfea.org/index.php/top-blocks/item/43-about-bfllfea. Accessed March 18, 2014.

BLSC—Bangladesh Leather Service Centre. (2009). *The baseline survey on small, micro enterprises & artisans of footwear & leather goods sub-sector in Bangladesh.* Dhaka.

BTA—Bangladesh Tannery Association (2014). *BTA.* Retrieved from: http://bangladeshtannersassociation.org/. Accessed March 18, 2014.

EPB—Export Promotion Bureau Bangladesh. (2013). *Statistics details.* Retrieved from: http://www.epb.gov.bd/detailsexportdata.php. Accessed January 31, 2013.

Hesselberg, J., & Knutsen, H. M. (2002). Leather tanning: Environmental regulations, competitiveness and locational shifts. In R. Jenkins, J. Barton, A. Bartzokas, J. Hesselberg, & H. M. Knutsen (Eds.), *Environmental regulation in the new global economy: The impact on industry and competitiveness* (pp. 155–219). Northampton: Edward Elgar Publishing.

NORTH, D. C. (1990). *Institutions, institutional change and economic performance.* New York: Cambridge University Press.

SEHD—Society For Environment And Human Development. (1998). *Leather industry: Environmental pollution and mitigation measures.* Dhaka: SEHD.

SEHD—Society For Environment And Human Development. (2002). *Bangladesh environment facing the 21st century* (2nd ed.). Dhaka: SEHD.

Chapter 5
The Leather Value Chain in Bangladesh—Results of a Qualitative Analysis

Abstract The main part of this study draws on empirical findings on structures, processes and dynamics of the leather value chain. It looks into the organisation of the industry by analysing interactions of the dominant actors and tracing product flows within both subsectors leather processing and leather goods/footwear. In the leather processing industry emphasis is placed on the procurement of raw material the coordination of which is modified during the Muslim festival Eid-ul-Azha. The access to the international market will be analysed in light of trade and domestic policies and the power asymmetries within the tannery sector. Three areas have been identified as having strategic importance for leather processors to turn to informal practices and strategies to counteract dysfunctional institutions and power asymmetries on the way to global market entry: chemical imports, leather exports, and environmental regulation. Particular importance is attached to subcontracting schemes in the coordination of the leather goods and footwear subsector. The analysis of both subsectors leather processing and manufacturing ends with suggestions to improve their competitiveness. Upgrading strategies in the tanning industry will be assessed against the backdrop of the reality of informal dynamics in the export related areas. As for the leather goods and footwear subsectors, it is explored the extent to which the MSMEs interviewed learn and receive assistance to upgrade from local lead firms. Learning effects by foreign market integration will be examined to the extent that MSMEs have benefited from external development projects.

5.1 The Organisation of the Leather Value Chain—Dominant Actors and Product Flows

The objective of this section is to provide an overview of how the Bangladeshi leather value chain is set up and organised (research question 1). Figure 5.1 depicts the dominant actors and product flows in the leather supply chain.

J. Strasser, *Bangladesh's Leather Industry*,
Springer Geography, DOI 10.1007/978-3-319-22548-7_5

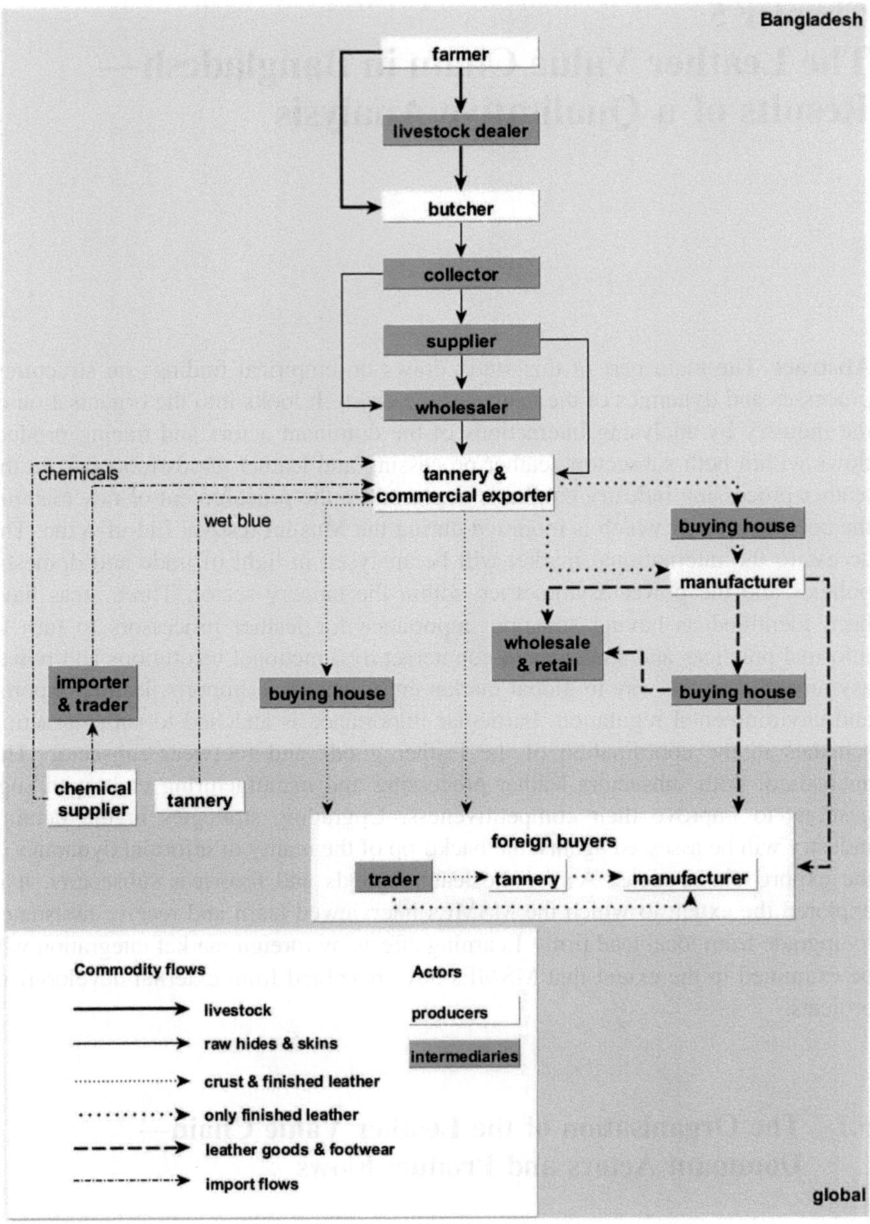

Fig. 5.1 Actors and product flows in the Bangladeshi leather value chain. *Source* Own illustration

Raw hides and skins (RHS)[1] are the raw materials used in the leather industry in Bangladesh. According to BFLLFEA, the country's bovine and ovine livestock population satisfies approximately 75 % of the leather industry's demand for raw material, while the remainder is covered by imports. Land scarcity rules out large-scale cattle farming and thus any related economies of scale. Farmers and merchants trade large (cattle, buffalo) and small ruminants (goat, sheep) on local markets where butchers source for meat production. The collection of RHS is carried out on a very small scale. Based on Ahmed (2002) and on interviews with tanneries and RHS traders, collectors were found to purchase small quantities of RHS from mostly improvised slaughter facilities and distribute them either to suppliers that deliver larger quantities to wholesale markets or directly to wholesalers. Suppliers or wholesalers preserve the hides using salt and store them until they are sold to tanneries and commercial leather exporters. The wholesalers either purchase the hides from their suppliers and sell them to the tanneries independently, or act as brokers between suppliers and tanneries on a commission basis. According to the Bangladesh Hide and Skin Merchants Association (BHSMA), the country's 21 temporary and permanent wholesale markets maintain a powerful position in supplying tanneries and commercial leather exporters with preserved RHS. Aside from the application of salt to prevent the RHS from putrefaction, all middlemen, i.e. collectors, suppliers and wholesalers, add costs without increasing the value and processing degree of the product.

Tanneries carry out the leather production process in three stages (tanning, re-tanning/drying/pre-finishing, finishing), producing three intermediate products (wet blue, crust, and finished leather) that serve as a raw material for further production steps (Heinen Lederfabrik 2014; see Fig. 5.3). Subcontracting arrangements are very common in Hazaribagh. Based on an own survey with 119 operating tanneries, 35 % run only wet blue machinery within their own premises, often carrying out tanning operations on a subcontract basis for leather processors of a higher competence level.

After processing wet blue to higher value-added semi-finished crust and/or finished leather, the supply chain divides into two major strands:

Firstly, both crust and finished leather are exported, either directly or via buying houses to international buyers, who either finish crust leather themselves, or manufacture finished leather to leather goods (e.g. belts, purses, handbags) and footwear (e.g. shoe upper; insoles; ladies' and gents' sandals, shoes and boots).

Secondly, the tanneries sell finished leather to local leather goods and footwear producers, who, after manufacturing, cater the final product to domestic and global markets. Given the low thickness of hides and smaller size of local cattle, leather sourced from Bangladesh does not qualify for either domestic upholstery or automobile upholstery, or for safety shoes, where value addition is highest.

---

[1] Usually, green hides and skins are traded in wholesale markets only in the peak season after the annual festival Eid-ul-Azha, while in the off season wholesalers only deal with salted raw hides and skins (RHS). If not mentioned otherwise, RHS from now on refers to both green and salted hides and skins.

Hazaribagh's leather processors export to three types of buyers, namely traders, tanneries and leather goods and footwear manufacturers. They specify the type of tanning, the degree of processing (crust, finished) or the nature of the finishing (e.g. aniline, semi-aniline, etc.). Asset specificity rises with the increasing degree of processing and complexity of the article (Meyer 2011, p. 55). In particular, finished leather requires a degree of innovativeness and skilled labour force only very few large tanneries possess.

At the manufacturing level, many micro, small, and medium-sized enterprises (MSMEs) produce on subcontract for large local, often export-oriented lead firms primarily to serve the domestic market. While lead firms market their products in own retail shops, the most important marketing channels for MSMEs are large corporate businesses and wholesalers. Direct sales to retail shops are rare. Multi-tiered and horizontal subcontracts within the MSMEs are innate to Bangladesh's leather production network. A more differentiated analysis of the LGF subsectors will be given in Sect. 5.3.

Major importing product flows comprise pre-tanned wet blue leather which serves as a raw material for the exportable semi-finished crust leather, and chemicals which are the principal input component for RHS and leather processing.

A striking feature of Bangladesh's leather supply chain is the intermediaries' dominance in sourcing raw material and final products which leads to incremental costs without adding value. How this dominance plays out in inter-firm relationships with producers will be discussed in the subsectoral analyses on coordination (see Sects. 5.2.2, 5.2.3, 5.3.2, 5.3.3 and 5.3.4.1).

Having given a general overview of the leather value chain, I proceed now to analyse the distinct structure and dynamics of each subsector, unfolding the governance of inter-firm linkages and power asymmetries of these.

5.2 The Leather Processing Subsector

Before analysing inter-firm relations and potential dependencies within the leather processing subsector, it is necessary to unravel the set of actors and product flows (research question 1/a/i).

The tanning industry in Hazaribagh concentrates more than 90 % of the country's tanneries and a wide range of independent leather processors. The results of the mapping of the tanneries (see Fig. 5.2) in Hazaribagh disclose a huge gap to official figures (between 206 and 249 tanneries) that are divulgated by local tannery associations (BFLLFEA, BTA) and cited in studies (Kumar Bhowmik 2013; Ahmed 2002). As of 2011, Hazaribagh hosted a total of 168 tannery buildings, of which 119 were operating tanneries. 17 of these run 19 secondary or tertiary production units. 15 production sites carry out operations other than tanning and 15 factories have already been closed. With the rise of the garment industry, leather has lost importance as a national export earning industry. Tanneries and their associations try to counteract this trend by stressing the industry's role for employment in

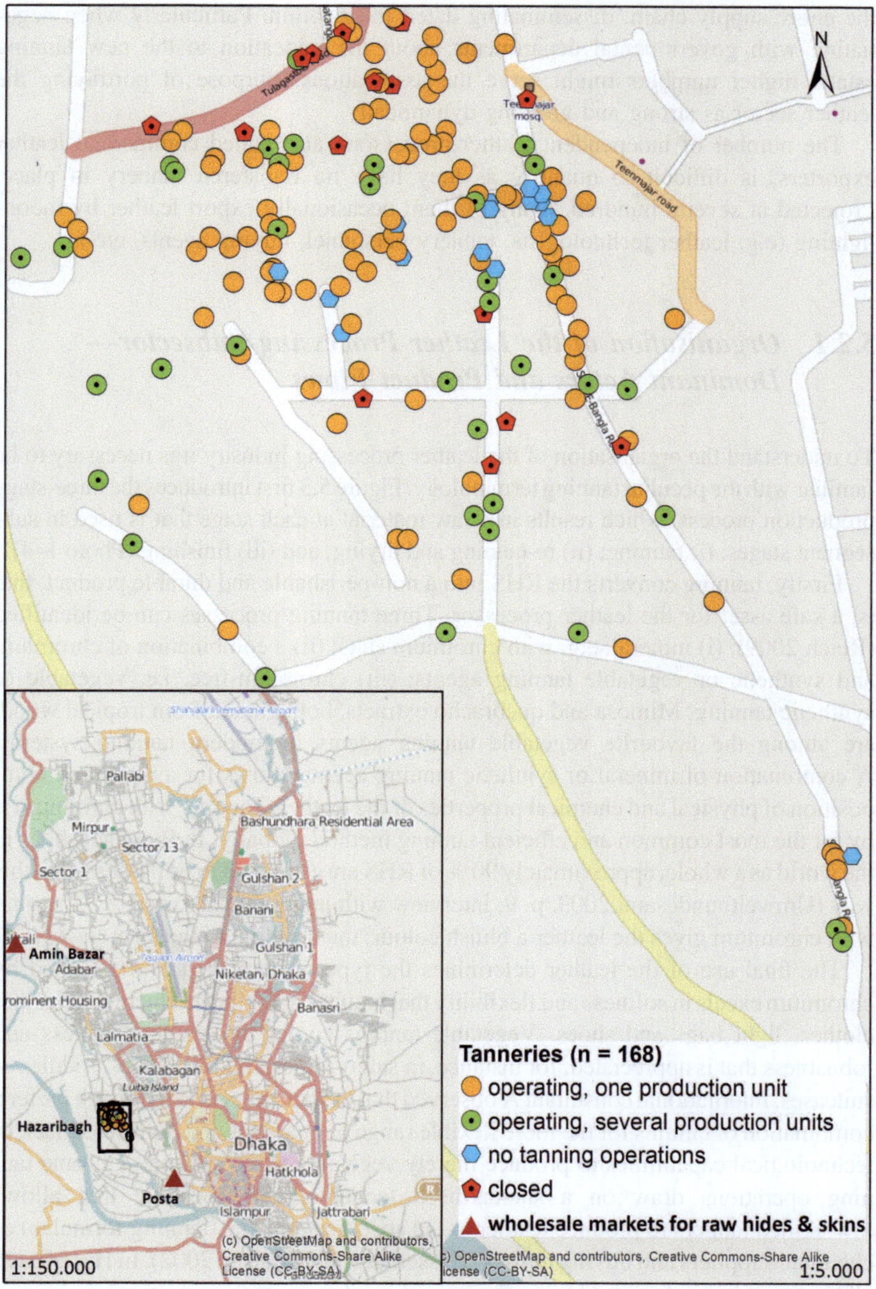

Fig. 5.2 Tanneries in Hazaribagh, 2011. *Source* Data based on own survey conducted in 2011. Own illustration

the entire supply chain, disseminating dated information. Particularly when negotiating with governmental departments about the relocation to the new tanning estate, higher numbers might serve the associations' purpose of portraying the leather sector as strong and growing dynamically.

The number of independent leather processors, also called commercial leather exporters, is difficult to quantify as they have no registered tannery in place. Projected at several hundred, many of them occasionally export leather by moonlighting (e.g. leather technologists, tannery personnel, buying agents, etc.).

5.2.1 Organisation of the Leather Processing Subsector—Dominant Actors and Product Flows

To understand the organisation of the leather processing industry it is necessary to be familiar with the peculiar tanning terminology. Figure 5.3 first introduces the three-stage production process, which results in a raw material at each stage that is used in subsequent stages: (i) tanning; (ii) re-tanning and drying; and (iii) finishing (Photo 1–4).

Firstly, tanning converts the RHS into a non-perishable and durable product, that is, a safe asset for the leather processor. Three tanning processes can be identified (Reich 2009): (i) mineral, e.g. with chromium salts; (ii) a combination of chromium and synthetic or vegetable tanning agents; (iii) chromium-free, i.e. vegetable or synthetic tanning. Mimosa and quebracho extracts, both gained from tropical wood, are among the favourite vegetable tanning agents in modern tanning systems. A combination of mineral or synthetic tanning agents allows for a measured composition of physical and chemical properties of the leather. Tanning with chromium is by far the most common and efficient tanning method globally. In Bangladesh, as in the world as a whole, approximately 90 % of RHS are estimated to be processed in this way (Umweltbundesamt 2003, p. 9; interview with international expert A). Tanning with chromium gives the leather a bluish colour, thus leading to the term '*wet blue*'.

The final use of the leather determines the type of tanning. Leather tanned by chromium excels in softness and flexibility that is suitable for the production of leather clothes, light bags and shoes. Vegetable tannins confer the leather firmness and robustness that is appreciated, for instance, in safety shoes, trekking shoes, saddles or suitcases. International consultant A observed that the tanneries in Hazaribagh prefer a combination of tannins for the more flexible range of final uses and noted their lack of technological capabilities to produce merely vegetable tanned leather. Chrome tanning operations draw on a standardised technological procedure that allows low-skilled tanners to produce leather to the specifications (i.e. tanning formulae) of chemical suppliers and buying houses (Hesselberg and Knutsen 2002). In Hazaribagh all tanneries have chrome tanning facilities (beamhouse) at their disposal.

Secondly, the semi-finished *crust leather* is produced to the customer's requirements. Several processes during retannage give the leather its customer-specific properties. Experience is needed to carry out these production steps (Heinen Lederfabrik 2014).

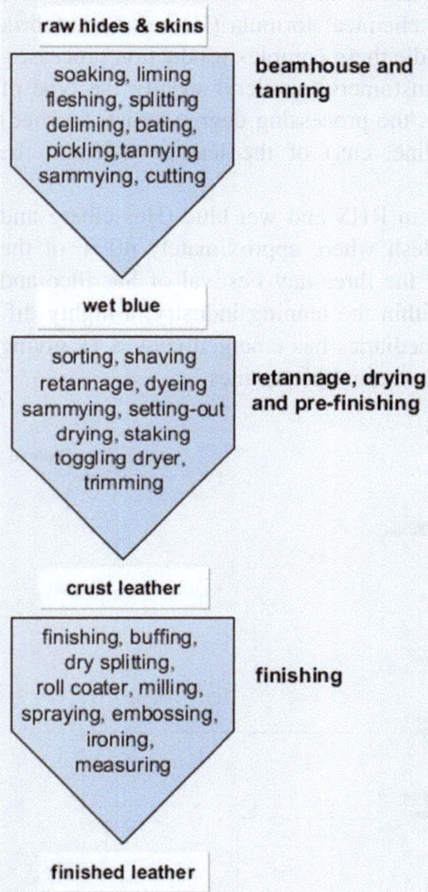

Fig. 5.3 Production stages in the leather processing industry

Photos 1–4 Cattle raw hides, wet blue, crust leather, finished leather. *Source* Heinen Lederfabrik (2014), Verband der Deutschen Lederindustrie (2014). Own illustration and own photos

Thirdly, *finished leather* results from a specific treatment of the leather's surface depending on the type of leather and the requests by the customer. This part involves highly a skilled labour force that knows how to combine machinery and product instructions along with a specific chemical formula (Heinen Lederfabrik 2014). Only experienced personnel can handle these complex production processes. Foreign buyers and their forward-linked customers (retailers) specify the type of tanning (e.g. chromium, vegetable, mixed), the processing degree (crust, finished) and the finishing (e.g. aniline, semi-aniline, etc.) of the leather article to be transacted.

Tanneries tie a huge amount of capital in RHS and wet blue (Hesselberg and Knutsen 2002); even more so in Bangladesh where approximately 40 % of the annual supply of RHS is produced during the three-day Festival of Sacrifice and stocked for months (see Sect. 5.2.2.3). Within the tanning industry, a highly differentiated network of tanneries and intermediaries has emerged (Fig. 5.4), giving account of differing capabilities and strong internal hierarchies.

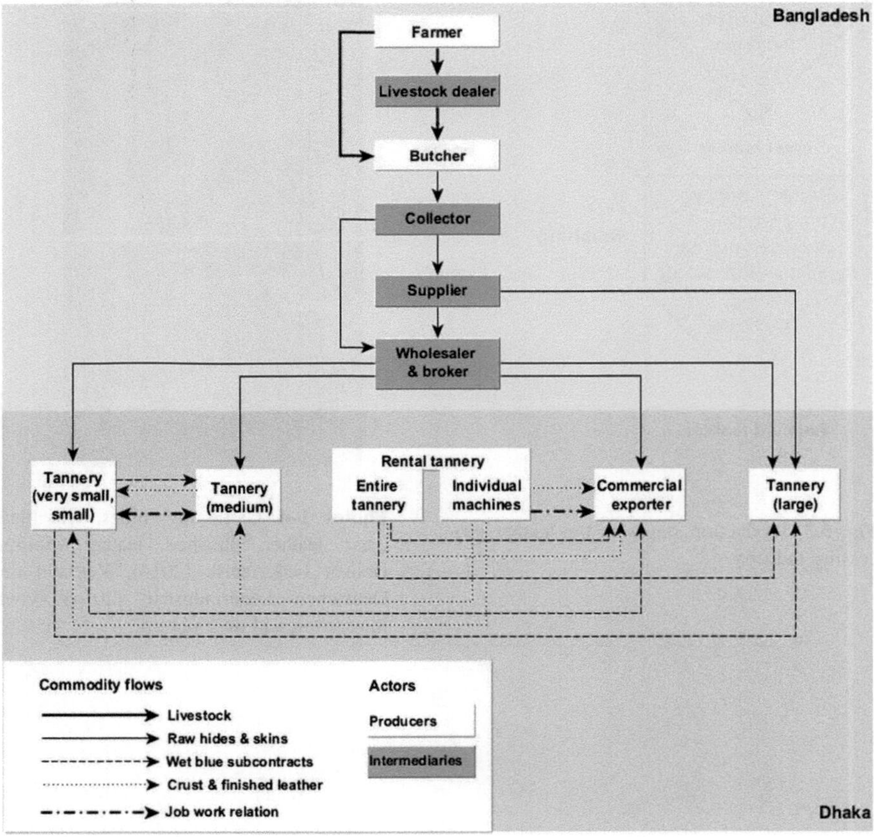

Fig. 5.4 Actors and product flows in the leather processing subsector. *Source* Data based on own interviews conducted in 2011–2012. Own illustration

The leather processing subsector comprises two types of tanneries that are determined by their production activity: firstly, tanneries that mostly run their own production independently; and secondly, tanneries that either rent out the entire of the production facilities or just let individual machines to others for job work production.[2]

The tanneries interviewed were additionally surveyed covering size related indicators (production capacity, turnover, employees, area), among others on the basis of which they have been classified as presented in Table 5.1.

- *Very small tanneries* only have beamhouse and tanning facilities at their disposal. Most of them either have given up their own production, renting out their machinery for producing wet blue on a job work basis, or supply leather processors of a higher competence level with wet blue (subcontracts) or rarely manage to export by producing crust leather on a job work basis in bigger tanneries.
- By contrast, *small tanneries* at times manage to feed into the export market; only one exports on a regular basis. A few of them possess one or two crust machines, but in general carry out crust and, if necessary, finishing operations in job work production either in tanneries exclusively providing this service ('job work tanneries') or in other mostly medium-sized tanneries additionally offering job work production.
- *Medium-sized tanneries* are usually equipped with most of the crust-machines. The operations they cannot satisfy within their own premises, including finishing, they have to demand from job work tanneries. *Job work tanneries* are usually medium-sized tanneries that provide all operations from wet blue to crust and partly finished leather to others. Most of them were forced to give up their own production due to loan default and converted into service providers for others.
- *Large tanneries*, a category under which only five factories in Hazaribagh can be subsumed, have integrated all production steps from tanning to finishing in-house. In peak season, that is, after the Festival of Sacrifice (Eid-ul-Azha), they rent smaller tanneries to enlarge their wet blue capacity.
- *Commercial leather exporters* lack own production plants and rent either entire tanneries or specific machinery on an order to order basis. Thanks to their low overhead costs, they have been able to secure more competitive prices in the international market, vying with medium-sized and large tanneries for market access.

Based on this complex tanning sector, one would assume a high level of specialisation. However, the tanners interviewed pretend to be capable of covering all production steps. Even small tanneries still try to export, though insufficient

[2]Tanneries offering job work rent out individual machines to carry out either single production steps or a full-range production to the desired processing degree (wet blue, crust, finished). Some also provide labour. It is not equal to subcontracts.

Table 5.1 Classification of tanneries in Hazaribagh, 2011

Tannery acronym	Turnover	Employees	Area	Wet blue capacity	Crust capacity	Finished capacity	Sum index	Overall index[a]	Class
A	m.v.	0.00	0.00	0.02	0.00	0.00	0.02	0.00	Very small
B	0.02	0.02	0.01	0.00	0.00	0.00	0.05	0.01	Very small
C	0.00	0.01	0.01	0.04	0.00	0.00	0.06	0.01	Very small
D	0.00	0.00	0.01	0.05	0.00	0.00	0.06	0.01	Very small
E	0.01	0.01	0.01	0.04	0.00	0.00	0.07	0.01	Very small
F	0.01	0.03	0.03	0.02	0.00	0.00	0.09	0.02	Very small
G	0.01	0.01	m.v.	0.07	0.00	0.00	0.09	0.02	Very small
H	0.04	0.02	0.06	0.08	0.00	0.00	0.20	0.03	Small
I	0.07	0.02	0.05	0.08	0.00	0.00	0.22	0.04	Small
J	0.04	0.11	0.02	0.06	0.00	0.00	0.23	0.04	Small
K	m.v.	0.03	0.06	0.05	0.08	0.00	0.22	0.04	Small
L	0.04	0.11	0.00	0.05	0.08	0.06	0.34	0.06	Small
M	0.10	0.06	0.01	0.22	0.00	0.00	0.39	0.07	Small
N	0.58	0.09	0.37	0.07	0.11	0.02	1.24	0.21	Medium
O	0.06	0.32	0.33	0.23	0.40	0.29	1.63	0.27	Medium
P	0.19	0.18	0.46	0.24	0.30	0.29	1.66	0.28	Medium
Q	1.00	1.00	1.00	1.00	1.00	1.00	6.00	1.00	Large

[a]The overall index is calculated by the sum of individual indices divided by the number of indices for which data was provided

Source Data based on own survey conducted in 2011. Own illustration

The validity of the indicator 'employees' is limited as the more modern and automated tanneries are the fewer labourers they employ. However, value-added production steps (crust, finished) carried out by medium and large tanneries are more labour-intensive than the capital-intensive wet blue production and thus might outweigh the effect. For time constraints of the interviewees, three more large tanneries could only be asked a selection of questions and had to be excluded from the analysis production facilities on their own premises in fact compel them to do wet blue production. As classified above, the tanneries interviewed can be characterised by a low technological endowment. Hazaribagh's share of estimated 60–70 % of crust exports also indicates that low technological capabilities prevail in the supply base.

5.2.2 *Coordination Between Leather Processors and Raw Hides and Skins Traders*

As Fig. 5.4 illustrates, tanneries trade leather at different processing degrees among each other and with commercial leather exporters. Qualitative interviews were expected to shed light on the tanning industry's internal power asymmetries as well as on the coordination of inter-firm linkages to upstream traders and downstream buyers.

5.2.2.1 The Procurement of Raw Hides and Skins in Low Season

Hides and skins are a by-product of the meat processing industry.[3] The country's livestock population which ranks eleventh in the world (see Fig. 5.5)[4] provides a significant resource of raw hides and skins (RHS) for value addition.[5]

Bovine hides from zebuine cattle and ovine skins from "black bengal" goats dominate the tanning industry's raw material. Consisting basically of water and protein, RHS need to be collected and preserved to avoid putrefaction and to enter them into valorisation (ITC 2006a). Bangladesh's small-scale farming structure makes it particularly challenging for leather processors and traders to source RHS in an adequate condition and at reasonable costs. A variety of backward-linked traders are central to the procurement of RHS (see Fig. 5.4). What strategies leather processors pursue to procure raw material will be set out in the following.

Bangladesh lacks a functioning RHS market that is determined by supply and demand. Hides and skins are traded at marketplaces and usually sold to the highest bidder, unless firm-to-firm contract relations or personal trust-based relationships are involved. A global selection standard classifies hides and skins under the terms of the following categories: natural defects (e.g. insect bites, scars), man-made defects (e.g. branding, knife cuts), size (area), shape (ir/regular) and weight (ITC 2006a).

---

[3]Apart from some exotic animals or reptiles, only fur animals such as sheep or minks are reared for their fur and meat is just a by-product (ITC 2006a).

[4]It is noteworthy that Bangladesh's goat population estimated by FAO (55 m) differs substantially from BPC (2014) and older sources (GTZ-PROGRESS 2006; Ahmed 2002) that speak of only 34 m.

[5]As only few larger tanneries refer to imports of raw material, these will not be discussed within this study.

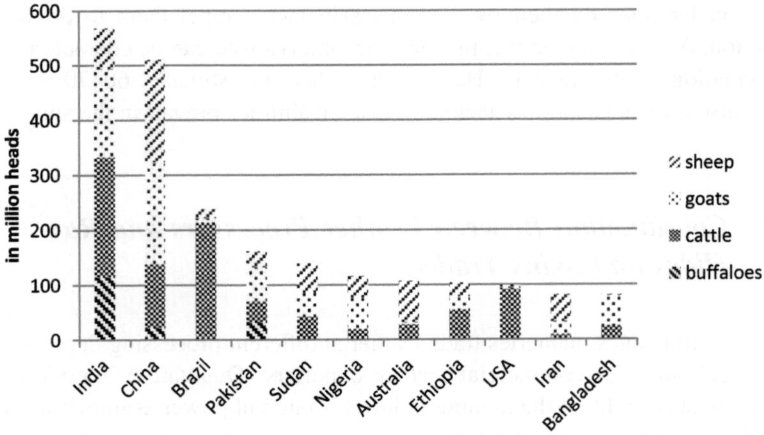

Fig. 5.5 Selected livestock population in top eleven countries, 2012. *Source* Food and Agriculture Organization of the United Nations (2014). Own illustration

Climatic and environmental conditions determine country specific grading systems (ibid.). For instance, brand marks only apply for selection criteria if it is common practice in that country (e.g. USA). Differences in colour matter particularly in Europe as dark coloured hides require more bleaching agents during the tanning process to achieve consistent quality, thereby increasing production costs, says international expert B. He refers to the German market where hides are selected by weight, colour and sex and according to the customers' requirements. Regional studies dealing with constraints in the supply of hides and skins give no account of grading practices (e.g. Wayua and Kagunyu 2012; Jabbar et al. 2002; UNIDO 1997).

In Bangladesh, RHS traders and tanneries lack the financial and technological resources to apply the measurement by weight. Instead, size, thickness and quality are the main price determinants. Ahmed (2002) determines quality of RHS from Bangladesh by the level of dirt (e.g. dung, urine), putrefaction (e.g. red heat, hair slip) and a series of defects (natural, mechanically caused, and flaying).

Selecting and trading RHS rests on tacit knowledge; handbooks or manuals are not available. But hides and skins are a complex commodity. Grain damages can be detected with precision only after the tanning process (crust) and are often missed by both traders and tanneries. The lack of codified information hampers an understandable appraisal of the merchant product. Neither written instructions nor training programs are available to provide information and generate knowledge on how to pick adequate quality. Assessing size, thickness and quality with the naked eye is still the dominant selection method that turns pricing to a matter of experience and tacit knowledge.

> Selection is a matter of experience. We have been in this job for about 26 years; […] I learnt the selection process by experience. (Wholesaler A, Kushtia, Bengali)

Suppliers and wholesalers first classify RHS in high, medium and low quality with corresponding price ranges. After leather processing, a more differentiated quality system ranging from A to H is applied, though without each grade being codified in a documented set of categories. All grades can be processed by the heterogeneous tanning industry. Lower quality RHS are particularly purchased by smaller tanneries and may feed into both export and domestic markets, whereas deficient quality can only be sold to local MSMEs. Tanneries mix different grades of leather per order for three reasons:

First, the highest grade (A, B) of RHS is only sparsely available on the local market and large tanneries only stand a chance of purchasing it during the Festival of Sacrifice.

Second, tanneries seek to sell all grades at an average profit; they mix different grade levels to avoid being left with stocks of unusable (low-graded) material.

Third, customers demand top and lower selection, with the best quality being worked in the more visible parts of leather products (e.g. shoe upper), whereas lower quality leather tends to be used for more hidden parts of the final product, says one leather technologist at a large tannery.

The tanneries interviewed draw on different sourcing strategies depending on their market power and the time of the year. The festival season, when the bulk amount of the annual RHS production is procured, features special dynamics that will be touched on in more detail in Sect. 5.2.2.3. In the low season, the tanneries mostly rely on long-term business ties to local suppliers. A tannery's market position seems to determine the way raw material is procured and what sources are tapped.

Very small and small tanneries buying from suppliers directly tend to refer to trust-based relationships that are very often founded in family relations to home districts. The quantities traded tend to be low so it is more a prioritised than an exclusive supply. When under financial constraints, very small and small tanneries prefer to procure RHS from wholesale markets close to Hazaribagh (Posta, Amin Bazar; see Fig. 5.2), thereby saving transaction costs (e.g. travel and transportation costs).

By contrast, medium-sized tanneries already employ agents to search the most important rural wholesale markets for quality raw material. Those interviewed in this study also consider importing wet blue if prices in the domestic market are constantly beyond their limit. Livestock supply and thus prices of RHS are highly volatile. Diseases such as anthrax in 2010 reduced the availability of local raw material significantly, leading prices to soar and tanners to import (Fattahul Alim 2010). Interviews with tanneries and leather associations also suggest that smuggling activities at the Bangladeshi-Indian border distort market prices. Job work tanneries have technically stopped sourcing RHS for own production.[6]

[6]The interviews conducted give grounds to believe that some job work tanneries continue to produce on their own account covertly, though at a low level.

Large tanneries already started a couple of years ago to procure raw material hierarchically with own agents covering all RHS markets across the country to by-pass costly wholesalers in Dhaka. They run warehouses in all important wholesale markets.

Transportation costs depend on the distance from the wholesale market to Dhaka and the size of the RHS. RHS delivered by the seller are just added to the costs of raw material. If they are excluded from the buying price, leather processors organise transportation on their own, often jointly with others to reduce costs.

It has been shown that off-season sourcing strategies vary depending on the tanneries' size and market power. Neither traders nor tanneries exchange RHS based on codified information. Pricing and quality assessment require experience and tacit knowledge. Before we come to a final conclusion about the governance in the trader-tannery linkage, it is necessary to discuss how power relations between traders and leather processors develop in the low season and how the scenario changes in the peak season when temporary middlemen join in the supply chain.

5.2.2.2 Reverse Power Asymmetries in the Procurement of Raw Material—The Role of Intermediaries

In the GVC framework power conceptualised as the availability of resources and competences varies with the firm's position within the value chain. Bangladesh's leather value chain features an uneven distribution of these characteristics too. When it comes to trading RHS power between traders and downstream tanners is less linear and more negotiated in social interaction than suggested by Gereffi et al. (2005). The tanneries interviewed spend approximately 70–75 % of all production costs on raw material; small tanneries even draw near to 80 %. It is essential for the tanneries' competitiveness to source different grades of RHS at prices that fit their financial capabilities and can be sold at a profit on the international market. Informal dynamics interfere in the governance of the trader-tannery linkage.

Primary wholesale markets excel either in the quality of hides and skins or in their geographic location. The wholesale markets in Natore and Kushtia[7] are well known for the outstanding quality of their RHS, while the markets in Dhaka (particularly Posta, to a lesser extent Amin Bazar) concentrate all grades of raw material from all over the country. The tanneries sourcing from Posta are more exposed to the risk of purchasing RHS of doubtful quality. In particular, very small and small tanneries seem to be affected by some traders' illicit practices. They criticise wholesalers for mixing RHS of different quality, and for withholding information about the region of origin. One must bear in mind that favourable climatic conditions and fertile soils in the northern part of Bangladesh (e.g. Natore, Kushtia) yield hides and skins of better quality than the south where adverse natural conditions (e.g. saline water; low availability of fodder) confine livestock and RHS

[7]Both cities lie about four to six hours by bus in the west and north-west of Dhaka.

to low values. Both the complexity of the natural commodity RHS and the lack of codified knowledge to detect all quality defects make the smaller tanneries vulnerable to illicit practices that affect their price competitiveness. Although both traders and tanners are experienced in assessing the quality of RHS, the former have the advantage of knowing where the hides and skins come from. Besides, the volume of the order determines whether the tanners (or their selectors) can closely scrutinise each hide for faults. The tanneries' informal safeguard against such illicit practices is to rely on personal trust-based relations to upstream traders or source directly from reliable wholesale markets, thereby ensuring RHS quality. Often, however, they are bound to buy from Posta as transaction and transportation costs are significantly lower. This shows that, by withholding information and referring to illicit practices, some traders are able to reverse power asymmetries to specific (weak) downstream actors contrary to their position in the value chain.

Interviews further revealed that payment arrangements seem to have an influence on power asymmetries within the tanneries as well as between traders and leather processors.

Large tanneries order greater quantities of RHS on a regular basis (weekly). They impose prices and payment conditions over wholesalers they usually have a long-term contractual relationship with:

> Q is the largest tannery in Bangladesh; Q is larger than XX [in Jessore; Author's Note]. Q pays 47–48 taka per square foot [for goat skins; A. N.]. But those who are in job work [i.e. commercial leather exporters; A. N.] have lower expenses; they pay 50 taka, 52 taka, 55 taka per [square; A. N.] foot. Their expenses are less; they go from door to door and collect. And Q does not go to the field level directly. (Wholesaler A, Kushtia; Bengali)[8]

Economies of scale allow tannery Q to negotiate prices 10 % below market level if spot payment is agreed upon. Our interviews with traders and tannery Q suggest that large tanneries enforce a down payment in cash at the time of delivery and the remaining amount of the bill after tanning. This payment strategy allows the tanneries to determine quality with precision according to the wet blue selection (A–H) based on which prices are adjusted. Normally, the remaining amount of the bill is met after a period agreed upon beforehand; usually ten to 20 days of supply; but very often it takes up to two to three months of delivery, several traders complained. Although the traders' profit margins are lower than when dealing with other parties, they prefer the regular order inflow commercial leather exporters cannot guarantee.

Wholesalers allow medium-sized tanneries and commercial leather exporters, which place orders only irregularly, to defer payment, but demand a surcharge of 25–50 BDT per cattle hide on average (approximately US$0.35–0.69 or 1.25–2.50 % of the average hides' price[9]). By selling RHS on credit at higher prices wholesalers compensate tight costing imposed by large tanneries, explained one commercial leather exporter. Commercial leather exporters often lack liabilities (e.g. tannery/land

---

[8]Currency converted as of February 24, 2011 (OANDA 2014): 47–48 BDT = US$0.67–0.69; 50 BDT = US$0.72; 52 BDT = US$0.75; 55 BDT = US$0.79.

[9]Currency converted as of February 15, 2011 (OANDA 2014).

to be mortgaged) for bank loans, thwarting their aim to purchase RHS at a large scale. Although deferred payment modes strengthen the wholesalers' position in the supply chain, they also expose them to higher risk. Both suppliers and wholesalers reported that tanners and commercial leather exporters often fail to meet the bill within the agreed time as (foreign) buyers impose their own schedule on them. This may indicate that power asymmetry is passed on from downstream buyers to upstream producers and traders, though wholesalers have developed strategies to reinforce their position in the supply chain.

Spot payment is usually required from very small and small tanneries that are unable to fund with banks. Unfavourable financial conditions constrain their capacity to source an adequate quality and larger quantities of RHS. Tanneries of a low competence level have to buy as is, that is, they are denied the opportunity to renegotiate prices. Potential losses resulting from the wet blue selection have to be borne by them themselves. Very small and small tanneries, however, estimate loss and profit to be balanced as traders face the same constraints. They do not perceive themselves as disadvantaged.

By the time payment is due, the tanners of a higher competence level (medium-sized, large) seem to be able to take advantage of their downstream position in the value chain, reinforcing power asymmetries between them and all kinds of traders. The collectors, suppliers and wholesalers interviewed in both urban (Dhaka) and rural areas emphasised their powerlessness against outstanding payment. It is important to add that traders in rural areas, particularly collectors and suppliers, avoid purchasing green hides and skins on credit due to higher costs. Unlike wholesalers in Posta/Dhaka, who strategically use sales on credit to compensate lower prices by large tanneries, wholesalers in rural areas prefer spot payment in cash as a security for their trading activities. Outside Dhaka, collectors and suppliers prefer to sell RHS via wholesalers who broker between the buying and selling parties on a commission basis if personal ties to tanneries are lacking. However, the longer the supply chain the stronger the upstream traders' exposure to outstanding payment. A supplier accused the medium-sized tannery P, which was also interviewed for this study, of breaking informal agreements:

> They [i.e. tannery P; A. N.] said they would pay in a week. This business is based on faith. The leather business is based on faith. They said they would pay in a week. They said they would pay in cash. But they have gone to Dhaka and haven't paid the money. (Supplier A, Natore, Bengali)

This supplier's deal was set up by a brokering wholesaler who stored the RHS to be sold and charged a regular commission (15–25 BDT = US$0.22–0.36) per piece. As supplier A puts it, trading with RHS depends on trust and is thus to a strong degree informal. The non-personalised trust in a renowned tannery, which is not expected to escape from contractual responsibilities, only works if specific enforcement mechanisms are available. Rural traders usually lack both formal and informal safeguards to enforce payment by larger tanneries. The spatial proximity between traders and tanneries in Dhaka contributes to trust building. Besides, the wholesalers in Posta/Dhaka still play a critical role in the leather supply chain, though their power has been fading since wet blue was banned in 1990 and payment cycles have extended. With the increasing complexity of trade transactions in globally dispersed economic activities (e.g. rising processing degree; complex international payment methods such as letter of credits), payment has been protracted too. The processing time of the exportable crust and finished leather is around 20–25 days provided there is a regular supply of electricity, of which wet blue accounts for ten to 12 days. Consequently, export revenues accrue after one month or (usually) later, which is often passed on to the suppliers of RHS. As a cultural habit, the hide and skin transactions are carried out at a very low formal level. The traded goods change hands only by signing a bill which is ascribed no legal value:

> Solution […] [is; A. N.], that they give the money of their own will. Beside this there is nothing we can do. And we have no document [at hand; A. N.]. There may be a signature, but usually there is nothing on it, ok? We can't do anything with this. This is all done fully on faith. (Supplier B, Natore, Bengali)

Mutual trust between traders of RHS and tanners is vital to compensate for the lack of formal institutional back-up. A weak formal contract is useless when it comes to enforce interests and debts. Collectors and suppliers lack the means to sue buyers. Instead, trust seems to be the dominant mechanism that trade in raw material relies on. Personal trust-based relationships often rest upon kinship ties to home districts and long-term firm-to-firm relationships. Even if payments might not be balanced in time, the personal relationship ensures that money will eventually come in. Interviews with tanneries and traders suggest that transactions with unknown business partners are less likely to engender similar commitment. Formal documents do not have the required judicial strength and thus have no meaning to opposing parties. In the peak season trust is redefined as large concentrations of RHS are available and new middlemen temporarily join in the supply chain (see Sect. 5.2.2.3).

In accordance with the more recent literature on GVC analysis (e.g. Sturgeon 2009; Tran et al. 2013), the coordination of business relations at the lower end of the value chain is more fragmented. Even within the same linkage different ways to exert and receive power exist, contravening the orthodox understanding of linear power asymmetry and explicit coordination. Patterns of relational governance are identified, though both traders and tanners lack the capabilities to define the quality and price of RHS with precision. Even then, there is no such thing as mutual dependence. With wholesalers losing influence since the export of wet blue was banned in 1990, the interaction and negotiation with tanneries has become more contested. Some wholesalers resort to illicit practices to reverse power asymmetries to weak downstream actors (smaller tanneries, commercial leather exporters) contrary to their position in the value chain. Furthermore, they adjust payment arrangements to the market power of downstream buyers, affecting the price competitiveness of smaller tanneries and commercial leather exporters. Here, power asymmetry seems reversed.

Gereffi et al.'s (2005) GVC formulation of global lead firms governing through the chain seems to apply only to tanneries of a higher competence level, which align their payment to the terms and conditions of their (foreign) customers. Here, power asymmetry is passed on from foreign buyers over (large and some medium-sized) tanneries to local RHS traders. In peak season, both trust and power relations are redefined as follows.

5.2.2.3 The Modified Leather Supply Chain on the Festival of Sacrifice (Eid-ul-Azha)

In Bangladesh, internally sourced RHS still dominate the procurement structure, but are subject to cultural-religious traditions. Every year, during the Festival of Sacrifice (also known as Eid-ul-Azha or Qurbani), the second most important Muslim festival, millions of bovine and ovine animals are sacrificed. According to official estimates from BFLLFEA and BHSMA, the three-day Festival of Sacrifice alone accounts for more than 40 % of the annual RHS production in Bangladesh, thus overstretching the capacity of permanent traders and leather processors while also challenging the capabilities of large numbers of temporary hide traders[10] that are only involved during Eid-ul-Azha. Conversely, the religious requirements for sacrificial animals provide trust among business partners and ensure high quality of RHS.

This raises the question of how heavily structural challenges in the production, preservation and procurement of RHS weigh on the growth and competitiveness of the leather sector. Aside from the economic importance of Bangladesh's leather industry (Imamul Huq 2000) and its negative environmental impact (Hasan and Chowdhury 2005; Kumar Bhowmik 2013), little attention has been paid to its natural resource base and the economic implications of its irregular festival-driven supply in a Muslim country. This section aims to discuss the impact of Eid-ul-Azha on the organisation, governance and logistics of the RHS supply in Bangladesh in an ethnically (98 % Bengali, other 2 %) and religiously (Muslim 89.5 %; Hindu 9.6 %) relatively homogeneous society (CIA 2013). It will be explored how the coordination of the local production network adapts in response to the supply of raw material that significantly exceeds the capacity to process it.

On Eid-ul-Azha, the actors and product flows change as depicted in Fig. 5.6. The dashed frame highlights the trade segment and study focus.

During Eid-ul-Azha, the production of RHS reaches volumes that leather and RHS associations consider too large for the regular supply system to cope with. Every Muslim who is able to afford it is expected to sacrifice an animal. The custom is to divide the meat in thirds, one for the family, one for friends and one for the poor. The proceeds from by-products such as hides and skins have to be donated. With the animals being slaughtered on Eid-ul-Azha at the household level, the

[10] Also known as seasonal business men.

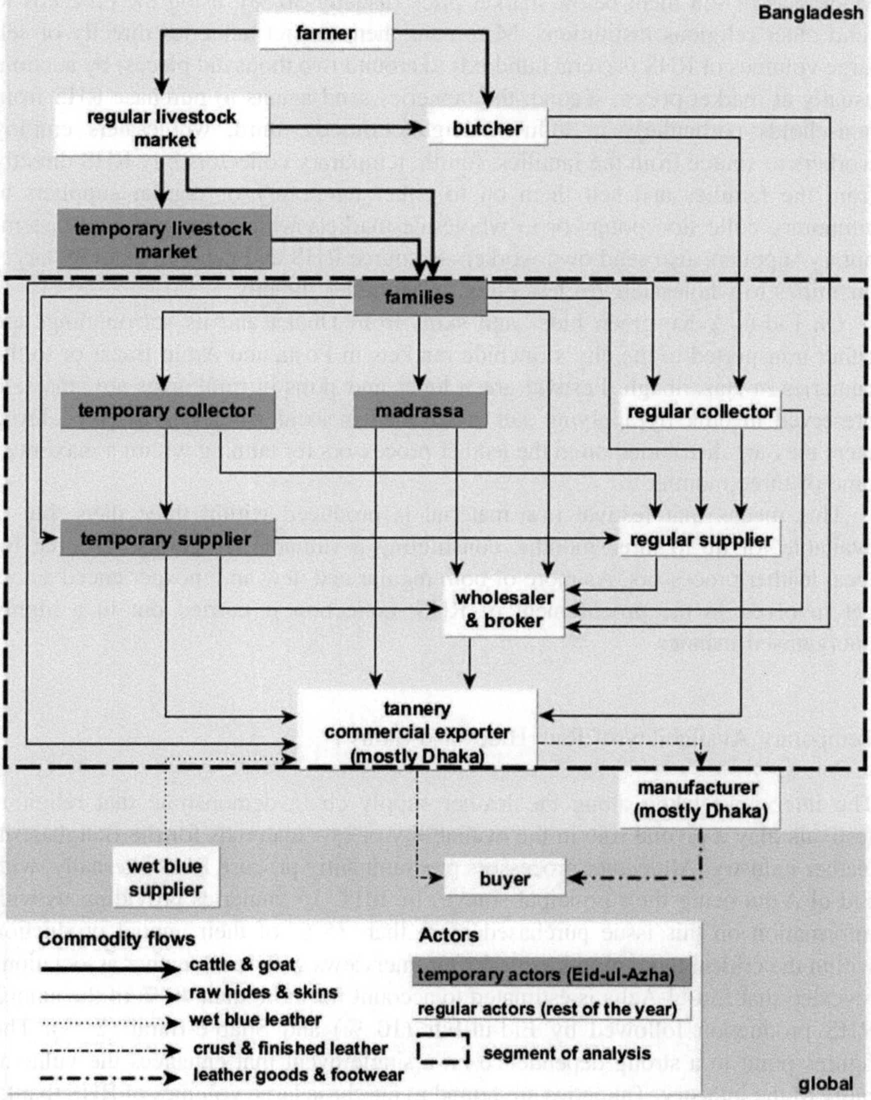

Fig. 5.6 Actors and product flows in the leather value chain around Eid-ul-Azha. *Source* Data based on own interviews taken in 2011–2012. Own illustration

supply segment alters as follows: after purchasing mostly cattle or goat from temporary and permanent livestock markets, the families entrust someone related to a mosque or a Madrassa (Islamic educational institutions) to perform the sacrificial act of cutting the animal's throat. Then, the professional or unprofessional butchers hired by the families proceed to flay the animal and chop it for meat. The resulting RHS reach the tanneries in five ways: first, the families donate the hides to the

Madrassas or sell them below market price (usually 50 %), using the proceeds to fund other religious institutions. Madrassas then contact tanneries directly or sell large volumes of RHS (several hundreds to around two thousand pieces) by auction, usually at market prices; second, the tanneries send agents to purchase RHS from households particularly in affluent neighbourhoods; third, wholesalers employ workers to source from the families; fourth, temporary collectors buy RHS directly from the families and sell them on to either temporary or regular suppliers at temporary collection points or to wholesale markets with warehouses; fifth, temporary suppliers also send own workers to source RHS and generally supply larger quantities to wholesalers or, less often, to tanneries directly.

On Eid-ul-Azha, green hides and skins from Dhaka and its surroundings are either transported to the city's rawhide markets in Posta and Amin Bazar or to the tanneries in Hazaribagh. Festival green hides and skins in rural areas are amassed, preserved in bulk by applying salt and traded in local wholesale markets. From there they are distributed on to the leather processors for tanning within a maximum time of three months.

This means that festival raw material is produced within three days, but is available for up to three months, constituting a valuable temporary resource for local leather processors. As more of both regular and new and inexperienced actors get involved in the procurement of RHS, collection is carried out in a highly unorganised manner.

Temporary Availability of Raw Hides and Skins

The interviews taken along the leather supply chain demonstrate that religious festivals play a pivotal role in the availability of raw materials for the Bangladeshi leather industry. All leather processors predominantly procure RHS internally, with Eid-ul-Azha being their principal source. In 2011, 16 tanneries providing us with information on this issue purchased more than 35 % of their annual production within the critical three-month period. Our interviews with local leather associations revealed that Eid-ul-Azha is estimated to account for more than 40 % of the annual RHS production followed by Eid-ul-Fitr (10 %) and Shab-e-Barat (2 %). The figures point to a strong dependence on a single event that enhances the vulnerability of the industry. Tanneries are bound to purchase large volumes of RHS thanks to the highly concentrated availability and excellent quality ensured by the religious event (see Section "High Quality of Raw Hides and Skins and Systemic Trust on Eid-ul-Azha"). The industry's dependency on sacrificial raw material is briefly summarized by Tanner J's words:

> We buy a lot of raw hides in the time of Qurbani; even more than our capacity. We use these raw hides all year round in our business. (Tanner J, Bengali)

Festival RHS ensure revenues for up to one year. After Eid-ul-Azha, enormous logistic efforts are required to concentrate labour capacities on producing wet blue in order to prevent RHS from bacterial putrefaction. As tanneries cross their capacity limits, job working tanneries such as Tannery O is fully booked just for processing RHS:

> In the Qurbani-season we add some temporary workers and we increase capacity of our machinery by working 24 h a day. In this way, we make the leather wet blue. This lasts up to six months [...]. So these six months are a very crucial period for us because we have to work day and night together. (Tanner O, English)

Unlike medium-sized and large leather processors, very small and small tanneries are unable to produce both wet blue and the more value-added crust and finished leather for the export market at the same time:

> In the time of Qurbani, there are no orders for two months. Then we do only wet blue. (Tanner G, Bengali)

Sales revenues are limited as large volumes of RHS cannot be attended to (i.e. processed) in time. But tanneries are bound to purchase raw material, for quantity and quality abound during that time.

Smaller tanneries with low own production activity are often drawn into job work arrangements by renting out machinery or entire production units to leather processors of a higher competence level. As wet blue is a product of low asset specificity, the tanneries stock and process it further according to the requirements of international buyers. Therefore, export revenues might be ensured for up to one year. Nonetheless, expert B points to the risk of fungal and bacterial infections, which increases with the amount of time that wet blue is kept in stock. In tanning the hides again, grain damages can be reversed in exchange for an augmenting chemical loading.

After the Festival of Sacrifice, tanners have difficulties satisfying their demand for raw material. Structural scarcity of RHS constrains procurement activities in the off season and has been considered by all tanneries interviewed as the most pressing problem. Prices soar and exacerbate the tanners' dependence on festival raw material lying in storage. Very small tanneries that produce little on their own are forced to source RHS locally, whereas some small tanneries have started considering imports of wet blue to serve the demand of their buyers and to remain competitive. Medium-sized and large tanneries are capable of compensating high local prices with imports, though this sourcing strategy bears quality risks in certain markets (e.g. India, Middle East).

Price volatility becomes a burden particularly to very small and small tanneries, but also to medium-sized tanneries that are less flexible in sourcing finances (see Section "Temporary Middlemen—A Limitation to the Development of the Leather Industry?"). This means that a consistent supply, which is critical to organising the leather production process efficiently, is generally not given and is even aggravated by culture-specific, that is, informal institutional constraints (North 1990) deeply rooted in societal practices. Informality as a cultural practice or habit is very persistent to change (Etzold et al. 2009; North 1990).

The extent of unorganised and unregulated (informal) production challenges leather processors to keep up with product quality. Three categories of quality defects in RHS that take on a specific dynamic on Eid-ul-Azha can be identified (Memedovic and Mattila 2008): (i) animal husbandry defects; (ii) slaughterhouse defects; and (iii) post-slaughterhouse defects.

Firstly, deficiencies in husbandry methods are a widespread problem in the global South. Curing faults and parasite infections can often only be detected with precision *after* tanning the RHS. On Eid-ul-Azha, the large quantities of RHS impede rigorous quality inspections. Traders and tanners face restrictions in determining quality but seem less affected as trust is redefined (see Section "High Quality of Raw Hides and Skins and Systemic Trust on Eid-ul-Azha").

Secondly, the major quality defect on Eid-ul-Azha happens when RHS have to be removed from the carcasses with a knife. As authorised (formal) butchers are expensive and scarce, families entrust ordinary people with slaughtering and flaying the animal or, if less affluent, perform the task themselves. The more careful hang flaying method is only applied for goat. BHSMA estimates that damages caused by knife cuts through informal flaying rise from 20 % in the off season to 30 % on Eid-ul-Azha. All tanneries emphasised the substantial declines in quality and prices resulting from insufficient flaying skills. Instead of feeding those hides into the export market, subsequent value-added products such as crust and finished leather may lose up to 50 % in value and have to be sold domestically.[11]

As for the post-slaughterhouse defects, preservation becomes an ever more important issue when Eid-ul-Azha is held during the monsoon season. Salting is a common method to prevent bacterial putrefaction, even in western countries where its use is minimised to optimise the production process and to reduce waste water contamination as well as the corrosion of machinery, explains international consultant B. In Bangladesh, the financial and technical capabilities of leather processors are much lower. Except for one tannery in Jessore, no suppliers, wholesalers or tanneries have cooling systems in place to prevent bacterial invasion and enzymatic activity from beginning six to eight hours after flaying the animal (GME et al. 2006). Once bacterial damage has set in, the opportunity to produce high-quality leather is irreversibly lost, says international expert B. Regular suppliers are usually the first to apply salt. On the first day of Eid-ul-Azha, this duty lies mostly with wholesalers and tanneries. Interviews confirmed that neither is aware of system immanent problems in preserving RHS. High temperatures[12] are barely seen as detrimental to their quality. On the first day of the festival, tanneries start salting the green hides and skins around midnight, whereas the animals had been flayed in the morning. Even after 24 h, one trader was seen with 3,000 pieces of already sold green hides waiting for a tannery to pick them up.

Those quality defects are especially prominent during Eid-ul-Azha and can be understood as a result of institutionalised informal practices reflecting cultural traditions and a strategy to adapt to dysfunctional institutions as professional

[11]Those figures are only estimates. Only large and medium-sized tanneries keep accounts.

[12]Normal maximum and minimum temperatures in November 2011 were 29.7 and 19.2 °C, respectively (Bangladesh Meteorological Department 2014).

butchers are scarce. They affect the competitiveness of the export-oriented leather industry heavily. Aside from quality constraints, the high temporary availability of raw material exceeding the capacity of regular traders encourages temporary middlemen to assume key roles in the supply chain segment.

Adaptation to Seasonal Supply Peaks Through Temporary/Informal Middlemen

As documented in Fig. 5.6, the supply chain during Eid-ul-Azha is temporarily adapted for the large volume of RHS traded on that occasion. This section explores the reasons why temporary intermediaries join in the chain during the festival and the tasks they assume.

Low entry barriers give traders the opportunity to temporarily and informally enter the supply chain. The Ministry of Agriculture of Bangladesh officially obliges RHS traders to obtain licenses and supply certificates to their business partners. According to the Department of Livestock Services (DLS), this practice is not enforced during the festival as the temporary traders' intention is deemed uncommercial. Trading RHS on Eid-ul-Azha is a popular activity, as potential returns are promising:

> There are many businessmen who do business for one day on Eid, such as shopkeepers or fish mongers, who also try to buy hides. (Tanner B, Bengali)

According to BHSMA, enforcing local trade regulation would impinge on the entire leather industry that depends highly on festival-driven raw material and is unable to organise the procurement independently. Thus, formalisation would be counter-productive to the industry.

Seasonal middlemen were regarded by tanneries as a valuable temporary support to ensure the collection and supply of RHS during Eid-ul-Azha. They help feed the hides into the leather value chain, so these are "allocated to […] valorisation" (GME et al. 2006, p. 6) instead of being wasted:

> Actually if there were no seasonal business men, then collecting hides would not be so easy, I think. In seasonal business they collect it [the hides; A. N.] from various areas, from house to house. In this way the collection of hides goes fast. (Tanner C, Bengali).

During Eid-ul-Azha, regular intermediaries cannot cope with quantity and dispersion of the RHS, BHSMA assures. This allows new actors to join in and transact with business partners at arm's length. Thanks to their piecemeal procurement, temporary middlemen significantly reduce transaction costs for downstream actors. Unlike their bigger rivals, smaller tanneries also maintain direct linkages to temporary intermediaries who supply them small quantities.

After Eid-ul-Azha, only a few large temporary suppliers with storing and salting capabilities stay in the market. Festival RHS from all over Bangladesh are traded at local wholesale markets for up to three months and are eventually distributed to Dhaka's tanneries.

As laid out above, seasonal middlemen are accepted as a temporary and informal support to compensate for the failure of the regular supply chain. Nevertheless, their interference has substantial negative consequences for regular actors within the chain.

Temporary Middlemen—A Limitation to the Development of the Leather Industry?

Trade transactions are more complex than temporary middlemen interpret them. RHS are subject to fluctuating market prices and, as a by-product of the meat industry, are inelastic. Price constituting factors at Bangladesh's RHS markets are size, thickness and quality. Four reasons for increasing prices on Eid-ul-Azha in 2011 have been identified in interviews with tanneries and associations: Firstly, an apparent slump in the supply of festival-livestock was ascribed to serious transportation problems on the arterial roads to Dhaka. Secondly, temporary middlemen are involved in organised illegal activities, such as smuggling RHS across the Indian border, causing prices of animals and RHS to soar. Thirdly, temporary intermediaries are accused of stock-piling RHS for the longest possible time after Eid-ul-Azha, pressuring tannery owners to purchase before the raw material begins to putrefy, so they attain higher prices. Apart from allegations concerning price-rigging in accord with tanneries, here, power relations reverse, as temporary suppliers realising that tanneries need to stay in the market control the supply; fourth, the mark-up on RHS traded by temporary intermediaries can be related to their lacking capabilities in determining product quality and prices. This point will be elaborated on in more detail.

Financing raw material on Eid-ul-Azha is a costly and risky undertaking. Temporary collectors—who are normally shopkeepers, caretakers or leather workers—have no way of receiving a bank loan to finance this seasonal business. They usually invest in a single- or low double-digit amount of RHS. Only a few temporary suppliers manage to procure larger quantities. Interviews suggest that downstream regular intermediaries and smaller tanneries generally lack the collaterals to render them credit-worthy. Their funds for raw material come from their operating business, family or friends. Lacking both the ability to obtain information about regional price differences and the market power to exert pressure on suppliers, small tanneries are confined to purchasing hides in smaller quantities, often of lower quality.

Medium-sized and large tanneries, while acknowledging the temporary intermediaries' small-scale collection at the household level, blame them for pushing prices unseemly:

> Suppose the leather costs 2,000 Taka: then what he does is buy that at 1,000 or 1,200 Taka and then sell them to us at 2,000 Taka. So if we could buy […] it at 1,800 Taka, the supplier or the person who sells it could have some profit. We could also have 200 Taka profit. So […] that person pulls off a huge profit. (Tanner P, Bengali)[13]

[13]Currency converted as of February 5, 2011 (OANDA 2014): 2,000 BDT = US$28.62; 1,000 BDT = US$14.31; 1,200 BDT = US$17.17; 1,800 BDT = US$25.75; 200 BDT = US$2.86.

In November 2011, margins plus costs of temporary collectors interviewed range from 20 % to almost 60 % (200–1,000 Taka/piece).[14] They usually work independently or jointly with partners and incur low transportation costs using rickshaw, motorcycle-taxis or cargo bicycles. Downstream temporary suppliers are better organised and employ workers for collecting larger volumes, though profit tends to be less (100–150 Taka/piece).[15] This and more differences between regular and temporary traders are laid out in Table 5.2 which shows the extent of the constraints facing temporary middlemen when they collect hides and skins. Note that Table 5.2 is an abstraction. Some traits may also apply to the rival middleman (e.g. systemic trust) as will be stressed in the next section.

Temporary traders present an economic risk to regular intermediaries and bigger tanneries aiming for economies of scale. A regular collector explains the dynamics in pricing on Eid-ul-Azha:

> They don't know about the market. Suppose the hide is sold at 80 Taka per feet, they give 90 Taka here. They don't understand good or bad; they buy everything. This is why we face problems. […] We also have to purchase at higher prices. (Regular collector A, Kushtia, Bengali)[16]

Instead, interviews suggest that regular intermediaries tend to avoid maximising individual benefits and maintain personal trust-based relationships to both upstream suppliers and downstream customers. They have limited capabilities to pass on prices to wholesalers and tanneries that refer to either market power or trust to pressure them. It is convenient, though, for both tanners and suppliers to agree on lower margins for regular orders in return.

Table 5.2 The traits of regular and temporary traders of raw hides and skins

Regular middlemen	Temporary middlemen
Small- and large-scale collection	Small-scale collection (door-to-door; max. 500 pc)
Often advance payment	Own capital
Mostly known buyer	Often unknown buyer; sometimes prior agreement
Long-term personal trust-based relationships	Systemic trust
No instrumental methods and codified knowledge for assessing quality/price of RHS → tacit knowledge	No instrumental methods and codified knowledge for assessing quality/price of RHS → learning by doing

Source Data based on own interviews conducted in 2010–2012. Own illustration

[14]Currency converted as of November 7, 2011 (OANDA 2014): 200 BDT = US$2.66; 1,000 BDT = US$13.30.

[15]Currency converted as of November 7, 2011 (OANDA 2014): 100 BDT = US$1.33; 150 BDT = US$1.99.

[16]Currency converted as of February 24, 2011 (OANDA 2014): 80 BDT = US$1.15; 90 BDT = US$1.29.

By contrast, seasonal traders are not able to resort to tacit knowledge from a lack of training and experience. Remarkably enough, medium and large tanneries rather than smaller tanneries view them as price boosters and as an incalculable risk to their business. Higher overhead expenses and financial dependency on banks seem to make them more concerned about costs. Thanks to their market position and export orientation, they enjoy access to a preferential loan system that allows them to purchase raw material during and after the festival. Servicing loans might make them invest more cautiously. As the lending policy often lacks transparency (Ahmed 2002, p. 85) and the financial situation of some tanneries is critical (e.g. Tanneries N/O/P), it is challenging to obtain loans for working capital. On Eid-ul-Azha 2012, two medium-sized tanneries (N/P) had difficulties with achieving funding for their raw material from governmental banks.

Since tanneries procure the bulk amount of their annual collection within three months, they are sensitive to price surges. They tend to wait until they understand the actual supply base:

> […] But I buy very small quantities because if I lose money, why would I buy? The price is crazy at the moment. I will maybe wait a month until I buy. (Tannery M, English)

As a matter of financial constraints and disparate international market prices, this tanner waits until prices are decreasing. After a period of seven to ten days, during which salt has to penetrate the RHS to prevent putrefaction, tanners start inspecting the quality at wholesale markets. The big tanneries aiming for better quality tend to buy good and large quantities of Qurbani raw material within 15–25 days when prices normally have reduced in relation to the first Eid-day, despite an all-time peak thereafter.

This involves the risk of being put under pressure by temporary suppliers keeping back raw material, although quality diminishes after one month, too. RHS prices are volatile: during Eid-ul-Azha 2011, the average rate at the temporary collection points (see Photo 5) was around 80–85 Taka (US$1.06–1.13) per ft^2, two weeks later, the wholesale price rose to 100 Taka (US$1.33).[17]

In festival season not all temporary middlemen make a profit, tanners and traders maintain. By definition, they lack the know-how to adequately assess the quality of RHS and run the risk of underestimating market developments. Most of them have no capacity to preserve the raw material and feel urged to dispose of their goods fast. Others do have facilities

> to store the hides and thus the price rises. Then we [i.e. the tanneries; A. N.] have to buy them for 200 taka [per cattle hide; A. N.] more […]. (Tanner C, Bengali)[18]

[17]Currency converted as of November 7, 2011 (OANDA 2014).

[18]Currency converted as of February 7, 2011 (OANDA 2014): 200 BDT = US$2.85.

Photo 5 Temporary collection point in Dhaka, Eid-ul-Azha 2011. *Source* Own photo

Temporary middlemen know about the large volumes of RHS coming in on Eid-ul-Azha and they know about the tanneries' need to buy at any cost as the festival is the prime season for raw material supply. If raw material cannot be bought at adequate prices, the operative business suffers dramatically in the following months:

[…] out of desperation to collect leather the price becomes high. (Tanner E, Bengali)

To limit the negative effect of price surges on the tanning industry, the tannery associations, BFLLFEA and BTA, previously agreed with the government to offset the low capabilities in the temporary supply base by recommending a price rate. Most of the tanneries doubted that this approach would keep prices at a constant rate, providing security and trust in raw hides markets. Some smaller tanneries complained about counterproductive fixed price rates, suggesting that buyers take advantage of and impose them as sales prices. The lack of a guiding price rate for Qurbani 2011 and 2012 proved confusing for temporary traders when assessing the value of the hides, particularly in the early stages of collection. Nevertheless, it was re-established in 2013. The lack of a price information system is typical for hide and skin markets in the global South (for Balochistan/Pakistan, see Rodríguez et al. 1993, p. 267).

It has become apparent that the price volatility of RHS is intensified by the low capabilities in the temporary supply base on Eid-ul-Azha and has serious negative impacts on the financial capacities and competitiveness of downstream actors, in particular the tanneries.

High Quality of Raw Hides and Skins and Systemic Trust on Eid-ul-Azha

Despite the temporary intermediaries' low competence in determining quality and prices, Eid-ul-Azha is well known for excellent quality RHS. As set out before, the quality of RHS is determined by the level of dirt, putrefaction and a series of defects (natural, mechanically caused, and flaying). As a result of lacking instrumental methods and available codified knowledge, regular intermediaries and tanners largely select the size, thickness and quality of RHS with the naked eye. They are able to resort to tacit knowledge acquired by experience and constant interaction with upstream and downstream actors, constituting personal trust-based relationships:

> It is our habit. I can identify good or bad hides by looking at them. We learn it practically. The majority of the people working with hides learn it practically. They do not learn it theoretically. (Wholesaler A, Dhaka, Bengali)

By contrast, temporary intermediaries lack capabilities to build up knowledge, experience and personal trust to business partners. Instead of "learning by interacting" (Bathelt and Glückler 2012, p. 241), they have to learn by doing it in a very short business period. Occasionally, to ensure quality on Eid-ul-Azha and in exchange for raw material, regular intermediaries transfer knowledge to their temporary fellows, BHSMA reports.

Despite their lack of tacit knowledge in determining quality and prices, temporary intermediaries can rely on a higher quality standard than usual. Apart from the quality defects already discussed, special quality criteria the Qu'ran imposes on sacrificial animals turn out to be beneficial for RHS on Eid-ul-Azha. Hence, animal husbandry defects can be ruled out by those requirements. Animals that are "free from blemish" (Masri 1989, p. 123) also ensure hides and skins that are devoid of diseases, parasite infections or corrosion damages, among others. Another positive effect is that the size of sacrificial animals is larger than in the off season and produces larger RHS, too. This effect, however, may well be outweighed as cattle hides exceeding 25 ft^2 need to be cut into halves to fit the machinery, thereby losing area and, thus, markets of more value-added leather products (e.g. automotive, upholstery). Tanneries say that foreign buyers are also aware of the large quantities and good quality of RHS coming in on Eid-ul-Azha, adjusting to these dynamics. They tend to ignore stocked low quality wet blue until festival leather has been processed.

Eid-ul-Azha as a cultural-religious institution provides codified information on the quality of sacrificial animals and thereby also on RHS. Thus temporary intermediaries succeed in offsetting structural deficiencies. Trust is created and ensured among unknown business partners. Unlike regular intermediaries who usually maintain "thick linkages" (Sturgeon 2002, p. 41) with downstream players, temporary collectors are only weakly tied to forward-linked actors without incurring major transaction costs. Temporary suppliers take a higher risk in trading with larger volumes of RHS and therefore often contact potential customers before Eid-ul-Azha. They tend to have a certain level of experience by trading annually with festival RHS or by being professionally tied to the leather industry (e.g. leather technologists, chemical traders, buying agents), which provides them with contacts and reduces risk.

This means temporary intermediaries are able to count on "systemic trust" (Bathelt and Glückler 2012, p. 190) guaranteed by the high quality of RHS that are produced consistent with religious requirements. Though product specification for RHS in theory is complex, religious requirements engender trust that allows for a simplifying interpretation of the transaction. On Eid-ul-Azha, both buyers and suppliers assume high-grade raw material, which apparently makes them ignore the complexity of the transactions. The large quantities of RHS traded during the three-day festival cannot be scrutinised at length; neither tanneries nor regular traders have time for it. Any asymmetry in information and power to temporary middlemen is offset, too. (Regular) middlemen often rely on personal trust-based relationships that—being forged in constant interaction with their business partners—reduce uncertainties (e.g. lead time, quality) between them. Following Shapiro's conceptualisation of "impersonal trust" (1987), Bathelt and Glückler (2012, p. 190) argue that dealing with unknown business partners requires another type of trust that is founded in institutions or systems providing security (e.g. contracts, transactions with banks). Cultural-religious institutions like Eid-ul-Azha encourage unprofessional middlemen to join the supply chain, though they are unlikely to rely on personal trust-based relationships because of their temporary business activity. The lack of formal and informal self-organisation in the leather (processing) industry as well as the high concentration of raw material during a limited timeframe enables temporary middlemen to participate in trade transactions. The religious festival provides security concerning quantities and quality of RHS, thereby establishing systemic trust. Moreover, the overall discourse of good quality festival-hides seems to prevail over negligent practices at different levels in the supply segment. Asked about the advantages and disadvantages of Eid-ul-Azha, the general secretary of the tannery association BTA confirms its importance for the tanning industry but shies away from mentioning possible drawbacks:

> Actually we are Muslim; Eid-ul-Azha is our yearly festival. We always consider the religious side. […] Everybody who has money gives [on; A. N.] the Qurbani Eid-ul-Azha in the name of God. So if you say, it is an advantage, this is ok. If you say this is a disadvantage, it is also ok. But we will do it because these are religious activities of the personal appearance [i.e. festival/event; A. N.] of the people. The advantage we have is that we get maximum leather at this time. Moreover, quality is good because everybody wants to slaughter good cattle in the name of God. […] Secondly, a huge quantity of raw hides becomes available, and the price is also suitable at this time. I cannot tell you of any disadvantages because this is a religious appearance [i.e. festival/event; A. N.]. So I cannot say. (General Secretary BTA, English)

The tannery association seems aware of the constraints Eid-ul-Azha involves but eschews a critical debate for religious reasons. Interviews with tanners also suggest that the industry does not differentiate yet between the religious event which naturally is beyond question and the logistical bottlenecks that do have a negative impact.

A culture-specific religious event like Eid-ul-Azha can have a decisive effect on the production and processing of renewable resources of an export-oriented industry. Eid-ul-Azha poses key challenges to traders and tanners, resulting in temporary solutions for the logistics of the RHS supply and in the subsequent leather production process. This, however, impinges on the production of RHS (slaughtering), further leather processing activities and the final product quality, even though the religious requirements for sacrificial animals positively affect the quality of RHS. Regular middlemen refer to tacit knowledge to define quality and deal with lacking codified specifications. The main weakness of the modified supply segment during the festival is the large number of temporary intermediaries lacking the experience and competences to adequately assess quality and price. Thanks to "systemic trust" during the festival, traders are able to enter the supply chain, maintaining market relationships. Structural deficiencies, however, cannot be completely balanced. Tanneries suffer from preventable quality constraints and face serious problems in sourcing RHS at adequate prices, which restricts their competitiveness in international markets. Potential interventions in how to increase efficiencies and improve the competitiveness of leather processors while keeping the character of the religious festival will be presented in Section "Increasing the Capabilities in the Supply of Raw Material".

5.2.2.4 Concluding Remarks on the Coordination of the Tannery-Trader Linkage

Trust is the dominant mechanism that trade in raw material relies on. Personal trust-based and long-term firm-to-firm relationships constitute the tanneries' sourcing strategies in the off season. In response to the lack of codified information, traders in RHS and tanners refer to tacit knowledge to define price and quality. In accordance with the GVC formulation defined by Gereffi et al. (2005), only large tanneries appear to pass on power asymmetry from foreign customers to upstream traders of RHS. The rising complexity of international transactions has weakened the power of RHS-wholesalers, which is now more contested in interaction with upstream traders and downstream smaller leather processors. The position in the value chain appears to matter less; wholesalers vary the terms of payment with the market power of the downstream leather processor, which enables them to exert power selectively.

In peak season the scenario changes. Temporary middlemen join in the supply chain during Eid-ul-Azha to benefit from the large availability of RHS which renders personal trust-based relationships and tacit knowledge less important. They are able to rely on systemic trust thanks to the codified information Eid-ul-Azha as a cultural-religious institution provides on the quality of sacrificial animals and thus on RHS. Trust among unskilled and unknown business partners is ensured, though codification (e.g. contract) is lacking. Due to the large concentration of RHS business partners who do not know one another in particular agree on spot payment in cash, thereby reducing risks and offsetting power asymmetries. Thanks to systemic trust in festival RHS the rather relational governance in the off season is superimposed by more market-based governance in the peak season. Trust, an informal institution, redefines power relations. However, informal interventions at different stages (production, collection, processing) increase the vulnerability of downstream leather processors who have difficulties sourcing faultless quality at internationally competitive prices.

5.2.3 Coordination Between Leather Processors and (Foreign) Buyers

After learning about the structure of the local leather production network, it is necessary to analyse how the tanning industry is integrated into the global market and the way supplier-foreign buyer relationships are coordinated. Before research question 2 and its corresponding sub-questions are addressed, the tanning industry's linkage to the domestic market needs to be briefly characterised.

5.2.3.1 Domestic Market Activities

Hazaribagh's tanning industry has been described as highly export-oriented (BFLLFEA, BTA, Ahmed 2002). To explore the structural constraints in access to foreign markets and their strategies for dealing with this, the tanneries interviewed were preselected for their export orientation. Hence, domestic market activities play either a minor or no role whatsoever in their portfolio.

The interviewees mentioned four reasons why they consider the domestic market unsuitable for supply:

- First, the internal purchase power is too low to fuel a sustained demand for leather products, the production costs of which are too high to earn decent profit margins.
- Second, banks are reluctant to provide loans to tanneries that only engage in the domestic market; export orientation is a necessary, though not sufficient, condition for funding with banks.
- Third, until 2012 tanneries benefitted from fiscal incentives on the exported value which were not granted for sales in the domestic market (see Section "Institutional Framework").
- Fourth, defaulting customers and unreliable commitment to agreements and contractual terms are major concerns for tanneries when catering to the domestic market. Tanneries with little market power (very small, small) in particular do not consider local companies as trustworthy business partners.

Interviews showed that export-oriented tanneries only supply the local market under the following premises:

Firstly, large export-oriented leather goods and footwear manufacturers source semi-finished leather (wet blue, crust) in Hazaribagh to cut costs. Enquiries revealed that even a multinational leather footwear manufacturer who runs a fully integrated and environmentally compliant tannery outside of Dhaka procures wet blue from very small tanneries in Hazaribagh on a regular basis. Some companies based in the Export Processing Zones (EPZ) of Dhaka and Chittagong purchase leather at prices similar to the export market where the final product is destined for. Others have the facilities to finish the leather in-house. The only disadvantage for the tanneries is that sales to companies in EPZs do not qualify them to apply for financial incentives ("rebate") that are only granted for cross-border trade.

Secondly, foreign buyers reject the product quality submitted and the specificity of the leather makes it impossible to find another international buyer. In this case, the inferior quality is to be sold to wholesalers or small manufacturers in local leather clusters such as Bangshal/Old Dhaka. Prices for lower grade leather to non-export-oriented local manufacturers tend to be approximately \$1 per ft^2 below export prices (\$1.80–2.20 for crust; \$2.80–3.40 and more for finished leather).

Third, tanneries that run their own leather goods or footwear factories sell leather on to their sister concerns that may partly be involved in export activities. This increases both efficiencies and value added captured within the firm.

The tanneries interviewed put little faith in the development of the domestic market. Low reputation and low margins prevent them from diversifying their sales strategy, even though regular order inflow from foreign buyers is lacking. The primary goal is to attain highest possible revenues through foreign market integration.

5.2.3.2 Access to the International Market

The objective of this chapter is to analyse the way Bangladesh's leather processing industry connects to the global market (research questions 2 and 2a). The magnitude of exports will be discussed against the background of domestic and foreign policies the industry relies on. In Section "Buying Houses—Facilitating or Preventing Market Entry?" entry barriers and the role of buying houses in linking tanneries and foreign customers will be analysed.

The leather industry accounts for only 2 % of the country's export earnings (ITC 2014). Leather exports, though prone to economic fluctuations (GTZ-PROGRESS 2006, p. 5) such as the financial crisis in 2008, are still ahead of the more value-added leather goods and footwear subsectors (Fig. 5.7).

Data based on an own survey conducted in 2011 say that almost 80 % of Hazaribagh's tanneries show export activity, underscoring the sector's strong

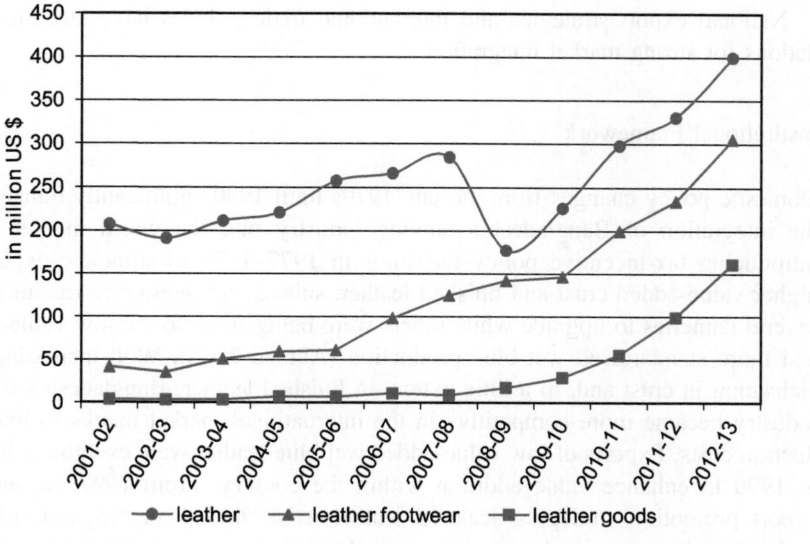

Fig. 5.7 Subsectoral export performance, 2001–2013. *Source* Export Promotion Bureau (2014). Own illustration

outward orientation (see Fig. 5.8).[19] What matters, however, is the nature of exports, which is not recorded statistically. The tannery associations estimate that Hazaribagh's leather processing industry exports 60–70 % of the lower value-added crust leather. Only few large tanneries have finishing technology and capabilities, which impinges on the export record.

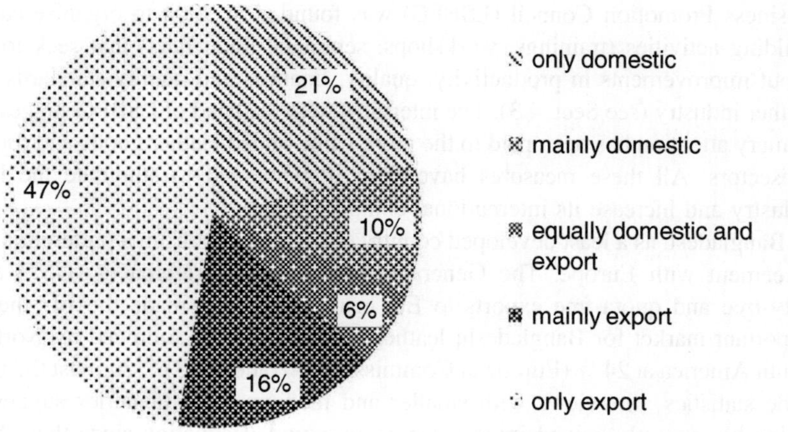

Fig. 5.8 Export orientation of tanneries (n = 114), 2011. *Source* Data based on own survey conducted in 2011. Own illustration

[19]An unregistered number of commercial leather exporters operating on a job work basis have not been included in this survey.

National export strategies and international trade policies have laid the foundations for strong market integration.

Institutional Framework

Domestic policy changes from the late 1970s until 1990 significantly transformed the integration of Bangladesh's tanning industry into the world market. After introducing tax-incentive policy measures in 1977–1978 to stimulate exports of higher value-added crust and finished leather, subsequent internal restructuring led several tanneries to upgrade while others were being stuck to the low value-added and more standardised wet blue production (Ahmed 2002). With increasing specialisation in crust and, to a little extent, in finished leather, Bangladesh's tanning industry became more competitive in the international market thanks to low production costs. Exports of low value-added wet blue leather were eventually banned in 1990 to enhance value addition within the country. From 1997 on, national export promotion strategies declared leather as a "thrust" or "highest priority" sector to achieve a significant increase in foreign currency earnings (Ministry of Commerce of the Government of the People's Republic of Bangladesh 2007; interview with EPB). Financial and fiscal incentives were introduced to encourage exports of higher value-added crust and finished leather (Ahmed 2002). Interviews with EPB officials revealed that export subsidies were lowered successively to 3 % for crust and 4 % for finished leather in 2011–2012, and eventually cut in 2012. Meanwhile, funds have been diverted to the more value-added leather goods and footwear subsectors, currently amounting to 15 % of the FOB-value (Board of Investment 2011). In addition to incentives and subsidies, the Leather Sector Business Promotion Council (LSBPC) was founded in 2004 to organise capacity building activities (trainings, workshops, seminars, trade fairs) that seek to bring about improvements in productivity, quality, finances and quality standards in the leather industry (see Sect. 4.3). The interview with the head of LSBPC suggests that primary attention has been paid to the more value-added leather goods and footwear subsectors. All these measures have been implemented to stimulate the leather industry and increase its international competitiveness.

Bangladesh as a least developed country (LDC) benefits from a preferential trade agreement with Europe. The Generalised Scheme of Preferences (GSP) allows duty-free and quota-free exports to EU markets and has made the EU the most important market for Bangladeshi leather products (45 %) followed by North and South America at 24 % (European Commission—Trade 2013).[20] Against the official trade statistics, interviews with smaller and medium-sized tanneries suggest that China has recently gained importance as an export destination since these buyers grant higher margins and impose fewer requirements for social and environmental compliance than EU customers. Most of the interviewees maintain both export ties to

[20]The GSP facilities for the second most important market "American region" do not include leather products.

buyers in Asia (particularly China/Hong Kong, Taiwan, Korea and Japan) and Europe where they focus on Italy. A few also mentioned to export to Spain. Only two very small tanneries have not had any linkages to countries outside of Asia (China, Hong Kong, Taiwan). Two medium-sized and large tanneries have diversified their business relations to companies all over the globe, even in North and South America. As most of the transactions are made with international trade offices in, for instance, Hong Kong or Italy, very little can be said about final consumer markets.

Buying Houses—Facilitating or Preventing Market Entry?

But even though trade and domestic policies have encouraged the exports of Bangladeshi leather products, the low capabilities in the supply base have been a persistent constraint to direct market access. Although almost two-thirds of the tanneries cater mainly or exclusively to the export market, they rarely maintain direct business relations to foreign customers:

> […] the buyers do not come here directly; they do not place an order here. We produce but they [i.e. American buyers] place an order in Hong Kong. The Korean party purchases from us. American buyers purchase from the Korean party and do not purchase from us directly. (Tanner A, Bengali)

According to interviews with tanneries and buying agents, only large tanneries seem capable of acquiring international customers directly, whereas small and medium-sized tanneries generally depend on the assistance of local buying houses linking them to international buyers. Only one small tannery interviewed managed to export directly on a regular basis thanks to a long-term, trust-based relationship to one foreign trader.

Policy changes in the 1990s significantly transformed the integration of Bangladesh's tanning industry in the world market. After the export ban on low value-added wet blue leather in 1990, buying houses gained in importance by linking poorly-skilled producers to powerful foreign customers. The government's aim of boosting the industry clashed with many tanneries' financial inability to upgrade to the more complex and more value-added crust and finished production. Though concomitant financial and fiscal incentives successfully increased the industry's export earnings, conditions for investing in machinery were insufficient (Ahmed 2002). Poor capabilities in management, as well as in the appraisal and monitoring of bank loans have continued to aggravate the competitiveness of Hazaribagh's tanneries (ibid., p. 85). As a consequence of constraints in funding with banks, many tanneries were either forced to close down their productions, or have been driven to rent out their production facilities to commercial leather exporters, or have ended up supplying low value-added wet blue to leather processors of a higher competence level.

Constraints in achieving direct sales to international buyers relate to the low capabilities of Hazaribagh's leather processors, and to the complexity of the product and trade transactions. Local tanneries produce to the detailed specifications (size, thickness, grade, chemical formula, type of finishing, etc.) of foreign buyers and, moreover, need to have an understanding of international payment methods. Among the leather processors interviewed, Letter of Credit (L/C) and Telegraphic Transfer (T/T) are the most common payment methods. The buyer's (issuing) bank issues an L/C, a written document, to the seller's (accepting) bank to guarantee timely payment for goods or services. In theory, both parties are provided with a high level of security, though the L/C does expire after a certain time period (Business Dictionary 2013). Leather processors in this study classified the L/C by the time payment is due:

- At-sight-L/C: after examining the documents (bill of lading), the buyer's bank immediately pays the consignment.
- L/C of 30/60/90/120 days: the seller receives payment at the time stipulated in the L/C upon presentation of documents, complying with the terms and conditions of the L/C.

L/Cs are issued either as revocable or irrevocable. An irrevocable L/C cannot be amended or cancelled unilaterally unless both parties agree to change terms and conditions. It provides the highest payment security to the selling party. In practice, buyers can impose conditions on their suppliers who are in need of selling (asset-specific) products.

By contrast, T/T is a payment method that in former times transferred money via telegraph or telex, meanwhile through banks (Business Dictionary 2014). Thanks to the quick bank transfer, it is still a common practice in developing countries. Usually an advance payment is agreed between both parties. The exporter sends documents along with the shipment of the goods. After clearing customs and picking up the goods with the documents, the importer pays the remaining amount to the exporter. In practice, T/T payment signifies a risk to both parties: the buyer advances a percentage of the final payment without having received the order and the seller delivers the goods without having received full payment. L/C and T/T transactions differ in their complexity and formality (e.g. complete payment after a specified time period versus negotiable advance) including a degree of trust (e.g. neither party can amend changes without the consent of the other versus advance payment before party receives the order).

Most of the small and medium-sized tanneries lack the judicial and language knowledge to record those terms and conditions according to the agreed payment method accurately. Hence, their ability to codify those transactions is low. Local buying houses fill in this gap by acting as brokers between producers and customers. They explore markets, arrange business contacts, and issue contract and shipping documents (e.g. bill of lading, commercial invoice, air waybill, packing list). According to interviews, buying houses have three options for dealing with an order:

- First, they attend to the order themselves in a non-transferable L/C, subcontracting smaller tanneries for production. Buyers would not trust the smaller tanneries' capabilities if they inspected their production site.

- Second, production is outsourced to medium-sized rental tanneries. Very often it is a mix of subcontracting smaller tanneries for the more standardised beam-house process (wet blue) and outsourcing the higher value-added crust and finishing production steps to tanneries of a higher competence level.
- Third, buying houses ask to forward a transferable L/C to known tanneries.

Depending on the technological and financial competences of the supplying tannery, buying agents are often in charge of monitoring the production process:

> It depends on the people, but it is not possible to continuously stay beside the drum just like a doctor and like a prescription [of; A. N.] how to make leather. The procedure is […] this can do this person, and the drum man who runs the drum and measures the chemicals part by part [has to give this chemical] after one hour, after two hours, after half an hour. 'This chemical runs one hour. If you put it in the drum, after one hour this chemical will go. […] Then after half an hour this chemical will go.' (Buying agent A, English)

The complexity in producing crust and finished leather lies in applying chemicals according to the formula provided by the buyer. Technicians from buying houses give assistance in making sure these requirements are met. They instruct supervisors and workers on specific production steps, but give little explanation on how chemicals react under specific conditions. In this way, knowledge and capabilities are unlikely to be built up. Buying houses maintain their powerful function.

In theory, buying houses are expected to represent both the buyer's and supplier's interests, with the latter (seller) being responsible for their commission. In practice, they are more loyal to their order placing customers, thereby contributing to keeping the tanneries trapped in captive relationships:

> Actually European buyers, they don't directly trust the Bangladeshi tannery owners. That's why they put some middlemen to see to both parties' interests, mainly the buyers' interests. So we work just to balance for the party, so that the buyer gets the ordered goods correctly. For this reason we take 3–5 % commission and mainly this commission is provided by the shipper, not the buyer. (Buying agent B, English)

Buyers distrust suppliers in low-cost countries (see Humphrey and Schmitz 2000). Distrust of Bangladesh's tanneries is often founded upon infrastructural limitations such as an irregular power supply and insufficient production capacity, both of which compromise lead times. Particularly smaller tanneries lack (adequate) electric generators resulting in delays, quality defects (e.g. spots on the leather), and an increase in production costs:

> For this [power cut; A. N.] I have to pay extra wages and I also have to pay extra electricity costs. We have to give them a tiffin expense as well. So the costing has gone high. (Tanner L, Bengali)

Buying houses ensure buyers do not reconsider their order, while keeping up pressure on the tanneries. In addition to infrastructural problems, Hazaribagh lacks a central effluent treatment plant (CETP), which causes serious environmental problems (see Section "Informal Institutionalised Practices in Environmental Regulation") and weighs on the reputation of the tannery estate. Interviews with tanneries and a European trader suggest that international buyers prefer not to be directly related to Hazaribagh firms. Mediated relationships may be a reason for the low buyer pressure on local producers. Except for the regulation on the import of restricted substances in the EU and US market (see Section "Compliance with Regulations on Restricted Substances"), China and Europe as the main producer and consumer markets have not demanded international standards on product quality or production processes yet. Mediated relationships, however, are prone to asymmetries of power (see Dannenberg 2012; Ogouma et al. 2010; Reeves 2002). Smaller tanneries are denied personal contact with their customers, so that a trusted (long-term) relationship with foreign buyers can neither be developed nor expensive intermediaries bypassed.

The inadequately implemented export policy has enabled buying houses to assume a strategic position in the leather value chain, though power asymmetries both within the tanneries and in customer-producer relations have emerged. Buying houses compensate the tanneries' lack of ability to produce to the buyers' detailed specifications and to handle complex (payment) transactions, but keep low-skilled leather processors highly dependent. In response to power asymmetries and dysfunctional institutions, tanneries seek informal ways to remain competitive in the export market.

5.2.3.3 Informal Practices and Strategies in Global Market Entry—Analysis of Three Areas of Global Impact

This study's qualitative approach enabled the researcher to identify practices that seem to have had the most significant impact on the grounded realities and perceptions of the actors participating in the chain. Three areas have been identified as having strategic importance for leather processors to turn to informal practices and strategies to counteract dysfunctional institutions and power asymmetries on the way to global market entry (research question 2b/3): chemical imports, environmental regulation, and leather exports.

Informal Practices and Strategies in the Chemical Market

Chemicals are an indispensable input component for all stages of the production process (wet blue, crust, finished) and constitute a regular element of expenditure for all tanneries and commercial leather exporters.[21] Bangladesh's government has neglected to foster an indigenous chemical industry, so forward-linked export earners (garments, leather) hinge on costly imports. The tanneries interviewed indicate that chemicals burden their cost structure by approximately 15–20 %. Raw

[21] Despite a low (1 %) import duty on capital machinery and spare parts, financial constraints prevent tanneries from sourcing capital-intensive machinery, even reconditioned, on a frequent basis, which gave us reason to exclude it from our analysis on informal arrangements.

material amounts to 70–75 %, whereas labor costs account for maximum 5 %. According to the buyer's requirements of the final product, high-quality chemicals are imported from Europe, whereas lower quality chemicals are brought in from regional markets such as India and China. Depending on the chemical, a customs duty is charged at rates between 30 and 75 %.

Export-oriented companies have the option of applying for a bonded warehouse license that allows for a duty-free import of raw material and chemicals, provided the items are used and fully re-exported by the companies. An interview with the National Board of Revenue (NBR) in December 2011 revealed that 31 tanneries had held such a license. All tanneries that are not eligible for the bonded system are requested to apply for the duty drawback scheme[22] that allows a part of the customs duty paid at the time of import to be abated once the imported goods are further processed and re-exported. NBR expects applicants for bonded warehouse licenses to meet requirements on legality (e.g. registration with Board of Investment and other departments), infrastructural conditions (e.g. road access to tannery), production (e.g. fully own production; 80 % export orientation) and financial solvency, amongst others. This regulatory framework provides the export-oriented bonded tanneries a strong competitive edge over tanneries refunding within the duty drawback scheme. The latter turn to or end up being drawn into informal (and often illicit) practices and strategies at different spatial scales.

Firstly, tanneries infringe formal regulations to become license holders or remain covered within the bonded license scheme. According to leather technologist A, export records are 'modified' to meet the requirements. Interviews with tanneries and NBR also suggest inconsistencies in the allocation of bonded licenses. If NBR required bonded license holders to export at least 80 % of their production, the financially buffeted tannery N would not be eligible for duty-free chemical imports:

> They provide only 50–60 % bonded chemical. But our use depends on export, but […] in this moment our export is low. So we cannot use 100 % bonded chemical. (Tanner N, English)

The remaining 40 % are covered by local chemical traders, boosting tannery N's chemical costs by 20–25 %. The medium-sized and large tanneries' purpose is to source chemicals at the lowest possible cost to export leather at competitive prices. Illicit arrangements with governmental agencies are strategies to uphold competitiveness.

Secondly, license holders misuse the bonded warehouse facility by importing chemicals beyond their capacity and leaking the excess amount to non-bonded chemical traders or smaller leather processors. This informal strategy to pursue particularistic goals has been institutionalised for two reasons: first, NBR is said to authorise higher import quantities against bribes; second, bonded license tanneries are said to give money to customs officials to turn a blind eye to conspicuous invoices. Although, obviously, none of the license holders reported or confirmed

[22] Non-bonded tanneries can apply for a duty drawback of 4 % of the exported value.

this practice, several chemical traders, buying agents and small tannery owners termed it an open secret:

> Now they charge 15 % duty to import a chemical. If it is imported by [the; A. N.] tannery [of bonded license; A. N.], the duty is less. Everyone now imports by tannery. The shopkeepers buy the products from the tanneries; then we buy from the shops. (Tanner G, Bengali)

The common sourcing practice for small tanneries such as tannery G is to purchase chemicals at local trade shops. The latter either source from chemical traders who also import at a charge (e.g. 15 %) far below official rates or from bonded license tanneries who distort the chemical market by entering it. Traders importing at legal customs duty would not be able to survive. Smaller leather processors such as tannery G consume low quantities of chemicals and have few opportunities to procure chemicals from large bonded-license tanneries:

> It costs me less if I can collect it from other bonded license tanneries. (Tanner G, Bengali)

Even if import duty is low or nil, adding retailers as another intermediary to the supply chain translates into higher costs. The legal arrangement to refund imported chemicals within the duty drawback scheme is not sufficient to maintain price competitiveness, considering this practice to be institutionalised and widespread. Instead, bonded license holders increase their revenues and reinforce their competitiveness by informal local chemical sales on both scales locally with the competitive edge over non-bonded leather processors being ensured and globally as international competitors may be underbid (research question 2c).

Thirdly, some chemical importers and commercial leather exporters adapt informally to respond to unfair competition by bonded-license tanneries. As revealed in interviews with tannery E and leather technologist A, license holding tanneries are approached to import chemicals on their license against an illegal commission that usually falls below the duty value. This informal adaptation strategy enables non-license holders to source at competitive costs and reinforces the powerful position of bonded-license tanneries in the chemical market.

Fourthly, chemical importers resort to misinvoicing[23] practices to maintain their competitiveness in the local market. According to prior agreement with international chemical companies, they import chemicals below invoice, which means only a certain percentage (usually around 50–70 %) of the imported goods are declared for invoice and thus subject to tax. The remaining amount reaches the exporting company tax-free (often via front men). It goes without saying that both foreign chemical companies and Bangladeshi leather processors benefit from such illegal practices that have been confirmed as widespread in Hazaribagh. One chemical trader complained about the dominance of bonded-license tanneries leaving him with no option but to do the same:

[23]Misinvoicing means that a country's reported imports differ from its trading partner's reported exports, which Kumar Gupta et al. (2012) explain by undervalued imports at the border in order to evade taxes.

If we want to survive, there is no other way. (Chemical trader A)

Chemical traders adapt to the misuse of bonded licenses in the chemical market through under-invoicing, a clearly illicit practice. Such arrangements originate in dysfunctional local (formal) institutions but can only be overcome at the global level. This indicates a strong degree of trust that has to be established between international chemical companies and leather processors in Hazaribagh to agree on and carry out such risky arrangements.

From the analysis of the chemical market two types of informal arrangements are derived: first, tanneries make strategic use of their bonded-license to control the national chemical market and strengthen their price competitiveness in international markets; second, non-bonded leather processors have developed adaptive strategies in response to unfair competition, including illicit agreements (under-invoicing) with global partners.

An amalgamation of interests between large tanneries and powerful buying houses involved in chemical trade seems to prevent inquiries from state departments with integrity. It also eliminates any attempt to establish an indigenous chemical industry that would allow for creating and capturing value within Bangladesh. The informal and illicit practices that have become institutionalised within the chemical market have created an informal regulatory regime (organising logic) as conceived of by Alsayyad and Roy (2004). The informal institutions developed are persistent and systemic; that is, the formalisation of harmful illegal practices is likely to fail unless the entire chemical market (e.g. rates of import duty; allocation of bonded licenses) is overhauled.

Informal Institutionalised Practices in Environmental Regulation

Leather processing is based on a wide range of chemicals (organic, inorganic, tanning/dying agents, finishing chemicals, etc.) that, if released unregulated, impact heavily on the environment, contaminating soil, water, and air (Umweltbundesamt 2003). Along the production process tanneries produce a significant amount of effluents, solid waste and air emissions that require appropriate treatment. Although enforcement is poor, other south Asian countries (Pakistan, India) have managed to establish a Pollution Control Board to monitor and regulate the environmental contamination caused by tanneries (e.g. Dietsche 2011; Lund-Thomson 2009; Reps 2008; Schjolden 2000), while Hazaribagh lacks such facilities. Several studies point to the implications for the environment and public health without analysing the governance failure (e.g. Kumar Bhowmik 2013; Azom et al. 2012; Hossain et al. 2007; Hasan and Chowdhury 2005).

The current environmental regulation in Dhaka stipulates that tanneries have an effluent treatment plant to be eligible for an Environmental Clearance certificate, according to information by the Department of Environment (DE). Although Hazaribagh's leather processors do not meet these conditions, the law is not enforced; they keep operating, polluting waterways and topsoil. The overt infringement of environmental regulation in Hazaribagh has always been a bone of contention. A Memorandum of Understanding (MoU) signed by the leather associations BFLLFEA and BTA and the Bangladesh Small and Cottage Industries Corporation (BSCIC) in 2003 offset the existing environmental regulation. Under the MoU the Government of Bangladesh provided the tanneries with financial and technical support to relocate their production plants within three years, preventing DE from imposing penalties. A decade later, DE-officials are frustrated:

> Actually there is a law, but we are not doing anything. (DE, English)

The final relocation has been postponed several times and construction activity had not even started by November 2012. Unlike other countries of the global South (for Pakistan, see Ortolano et al. 2014; for India, Dietsche 2011; for Brazil, Hesselberg and Knutsen 2002) where in recent years more effort has been devoted to environmental concerns and cleaner production, although monitoring and enforcement are still weak, in Bangladesh pressure from environmental regulation and civil society has failed to address pollution caused by the tanning industry (Hoque and Clarke 2013; Azom et al. 2012). As the share of Bangladesh's leather industry in the world market is minuscule (0.4 %; ITC 2014) in contrast to India or Brazil, the demand from Europe and the US is accordingly low. Consequently, pressure from global buyers sourcing low-cost quality on local stakeholders to environmentally upgrade has been little.

Such state-tolerated informality responds to the organising logic Etzold et al. (2009) adopted from Alsayyad and Roy (2004). An existing formal regulation has been formally informalised to protect the industry's interests at the expense of the environment and public health. Despite its comparatively low export performance, leather is an economic sector of national importance for employment, which appears to make the government cautious about enforcing costly environmental regulation. But changing consumer awareness of environmental conditions and product quality (e.g. Kulke 2009, p. 135; Baksi and Bose 2007) may downsize competitive edges through non-enforcement. Interviews with tanneries and upgrading organisations revealed that a Human Rights Watch Report (2012) on the labour conditions in and health effects of Hazaribagh's tanning industry led international customers and tradeshows to cancel orders and invitations to large tanneries. This might have been just a knee-jerk public outcry as real changes need time. The effect on Hazaribagh's tanning industry appears to have been low: prior to and after the report leather processors showed little awareness about the low standards in environment, health and labour conditions.

Informal Strategies in Leather Exports to Connect to the Global Market

Like the informal dynamics on the chemical market, misinvoicing practices have been identified in leather exports. According to Buehn and Eichler, misinvoicing means "the true value of exports or imports deviates from the amount of exports or imports businesses report to the authorities" (2011, p. 1263). While over-invoicing of exports is to maximise the benefit from export subsidies, under-invoicing is meant to evade taxes (Kumar Gupta et al. 2012). Interestingly, Kumar Gupta et al. (2012) conclude from export data from the garments and leather industries in Bangladesh that domestic policies (export subsidies, import duty) seem to provide incentives for misinvoicing practices in international trade. Non-fiscal incentives such as export subsidies on the Freight on Board (FOB) value have been gradually lowered to 3 % for crust leather and 4 % for finished leather; they were eventually cut in 2012.

Our interviews suggest that it was rather power asymmetries at both local (commercial leather exporters vs. tannery associations) and international/global levels (buyers vs. tanneries) that encouraged under-invoicing while over-invoicing did not seem to be an issue.

According to buying agent C, commercial leather exporters are considered as "trespassers" by large tanneries and are fined by the export certificate providing tannery associations[24] (BFLLFEA, BTA) on direct leather exports. As a result of these coercive measures, they seek to compensate for the additional costs for buying houses through misinvoicing. It has naturally been difficult to explore whether such illegal practices have become institutionalised among the tanneries. Only tanner E reports under-invoiced leather exports, for he was a victim of insufficient payment:

> He [i.e. the buyer; A. N.] agreed to full payment and he would give the remaining 50 % after receiving the product. After receiving the product he gave us 15 cent [per ft^2; A. N.] less. […] He picked the right moment because I mentioned before that I do under-invoicing. Under-invoicing is illegal. As I did under-invoice, he could cancel the whole 50 % payment because he is legal: 'this is my L/C [i.e. Letter of Credit; A. N.], I gave full payment'. He is right. (Tanner E, Bengali)

In the wake of the global economic downturn in 2008 when Hazaribagh faced a severe decline in orders[25] (see Fig. 5.7), Tanner E agreed to a Chinese buyer's proposal to export leather by 50 % under-invoice. At the time of delivery, the foreign buyer paid the agreed 50 % of the real exported value. Once the remaining 50 % became due, the foreign buyer claimed quality defects and reduced the rate by 15 US cent per ft^2. Irrespective of the real grounds for the price reduction, the tanner and his buying agent were unable to sue the buyer, as a legal basis for the second payment was lacking. Unlike dynamics in the chemical market, the risk in exporting leather under-invoice undoubtedly lies with the exporting company.

Another example confirms the risk low-skilled suppliers are exposed to when resorting to illicit practices. The critical part of under-invoicing lies in the final payment. Buying agent C, who executes 80 % of his exports under-invoice, emphasises that "I must trust my customer 100 %" to receive a payment from

[24]Despite biennial elections of its chair, one association is dominated by one tanner who is an influential land owner in Hazaribagh and a powerful buying agent with many associated small tanneries as his clients. Commercial leather exporters compete with tanneries for market share; they are not entitled to become full association members.

[25]The slump in leather exports in 2008–2009 (see Fig. 5.7) can be explained by a decline in orders after the global economic recession. It might also be plausible that exporting leather under-invoice as a strategy to adapt to low global demand has distorted official statistics.

under-invoice transactions. This can be effected either at the time the customer comes for the final selection, by front men declaring the money as remittances (!), or by importing enterprises arranging fake deals, among others. Such trust, however, can only be built up in constant and direct business relations, from which small tanneries like tannery E with low and irregular export activity are excluded. Buying houses negotiate directly with buyers and are central to securing informal transactions, while risk is mainly outsourced to the suppliers.[26] Trust appears to be fundamental for illicit practices to be secured in asymmetric buyer-supplier relationships; otherwise the selling party ends up with lower export revenues, less capacity to reinvest and overall poorer competitiveness.

Exporting leather under-invoice is an instructive example of how local actors adapt either to unfavourable power relations at the local level or to critical conditions in the international market, thereby exposing themselves to high levels of risk. In both cases close cooperation and trust with international partners are indispensable for risk control. These results suggest that informal practices and those trespassing legal boundaries may succeed even in asymmetric power relations, as long as they pay off for both parties (see North 1990). More research is necessary to analyse who are the driving forces behind such arrangements and to find out under what conditions global buyers accept that transactions be carried out this way.

Aside from the abovementioned clearly illicit practices, several informal strategies have evolved to adapt to power asymmetries and structural constraints in connecting to the global market.

Firm-to-firm transactions at international level are complex and require adequate codification (e.g. contracts, shipping documents; see Section "Buying Houses—Facilitating or Preventing Market Entry?"). Buying houses reduce complexity for their clients. They handle orders in two ways:

- First, they transfer the L/C to tanneries with sufficient production capacity. Often they additionally subcontract standardised production steps (tanning) to smaller tanneries without the buyer's knowledge, thereby saving costs.
- Second, they sell leather on their own account and place the order with smaller tanneries. This is a widespread but highly risky practice as tanneries are not stated in L/C or T/T and have no judicial means to sue the buyer in the event of a breach of contract. Lacking market knowledge, they are easily drawn into captive relationships:

> All of the dealing is done through the buying agent. The buying agent may say that 'your goods are not up to the mark; you will have to charge five [US; A. N.] cents less. […] They [the buyer; A. N.] will not give the payment, they will tell the bank and will give instructions to them and the payment will be stopped'. So we do it under compulsion. But sometimes we have seen that it is not done by the buyer but by the buying agent. (Tanner B, Bengali)

[26]Buying houses are affected by losses as the commission is paid by the supplier.

The high asset specificity of crust and finished leather both tailored to the customer's individual needs allows buying houses to put pressure on prices. The tannery's power to re-negotiate is significantly deteriorated after production. Small tanneries in particular complained about buying houses bringing forward supposed quality defects. Even formal bank-to-bank LCs cannot guarantee enforcement. Small and medium-sized tanneries lack the financial and judicial capabilities to sue foreign buyers. They trust their buying agent to settle payment conflicts, often without satisfactory results (see tannery E).

To overcome structural constraints in market entry and power asymmetries (e.g. in information regarding buyers) to downstream actors, tanneries have discovered informal strategies. Tanner G who is running a low-capacity wet blue tannery tells how powerful buying houses can be successfully bypassed in market entry:

> XX forwarded it only to me and I subcontracted it to other tanneries. It was a huge order and I had to do it. Like: If any large tannery gives me an order of 100,000 ft^2, then I subcontract 20,000 to 30,000 [ft^2; A. N.] of it to others. (Tanner G, Bengali)

Joint production, often on a subcontracting basis, allows smaller tanneries to cater to the export market, keeping transaction costs, for instance, for shipping documents to a minimum. Such horizontal informal networks are critical to market entry at affordable costs. To bypass powerful buying houses such as B (see Section "Buying Houses—Facilitating or Preventing Market Entry?") smaller tanneries produce on a subcontract basis for the contracting tannery. The case above shows that the medium-sized job work tannery XX acts formally as the contracting tannery but transfers the order to a third party (first-tier subcontractor = tannery G) due to temporary capacity constraints. A written contract has been set up to specify the product (e.g. type of tanning, colour) and other terms and conditions. It clarifies, for instance, whether the production is based on per piece or per ft^2 and sets the prices per machine for crust leather production which small leather processors usually have to rent from tanneries of a higher competence level. Then tannery G splits the order informally (oral agreement) to other small tanneries (second-tier subcontractors) to secure production within the lead time.

All subcontracted small tanneries produce to the specifications provided (via the buying house) by the contracting tannery. The latter is aware of the multi-tiered subcontract, but monitors only the production process of the first-tier subcontractor. According to tannery G, the buying house B found out about tannery XX's subcontracts during production, accepted the deal, and monitored the production of tannery G from which it now sources directly. Such 'direct' relationships to the buying house involve a high degree of monitoring and control, but also increase margins as well. The risk, however, remains with the tannery (see tanner B; above).

Tannery G's benefits from subcontracts are profit margins from export revenues that amount to 2–4 %. There are also a number of disadvantages. The contracting tannery retains the export subsidies of 3 % of the FOB-value which were granted until 2012, depriving the subcontracted tannery of substantial earnings. The first-tier subcontractor tannery G cannot take advantage of a sustained and trusted business relationship with a foreign buyer. Buying houses and contracting tanneries give instructions but do not impart knowledge. The buying house's major concern is to ensure quality and lead time. If the tannery (subcontracted or not) is unable to deliver as per agreement for any reason, the buying house withdraws from the contract.

In multi-tiered subcontracts power relations are more complex at the lower end of the supply chain. Other than assumed, control does not continuously decrease from one end to the other. Buyers give buying houses explicit information on the product and payment arrangements but often leave the supplier management to the intermediary, thus exerting little control over production. The brokers have faith in the production capabilities of leather processors of a higher competence level (medium-sized, large tanneries). They know the contracting tannery can handle the complexity of the production. This is different with low-skilled small tanneries, often acting as first-tier subcontractors: buying houses give clear instructions on the production process in order to keep the lead time and exert high control over these (Fig. 5.9). For instance, leather technologists from buying house B pay regular visits to tannery G (first-tier subcontractor) with whom the contract was concluded. Tannery G is responsible for checking the quality of its fellow tanneries to which it maintains a personal trust-based relationship:

> The buying house only thinks about the supply and the quality of the goods. They do not care how you manage it. (Tanner G, Bengali)

This involves risk for all actors, which increases, however, towards the lowest end of the supply chain (see Fig. 5.9):

Firstly, with second-tier subcontractors being excluded from monitoring and control by buying houses, the risk of supplier failure increases. Three low-skilled suppliers have to produce using exactly the same chemical formula. Significant quality differences, for instance, in terms of colour or fastness, may give foreign buyers or buying houses grounds to demand price reductions (see tanner E) or even reject parts of an order, which would affect both first- and second-tier subcontractors.

Secondly, bypassing the buying houses informally may impair the reliability of the contracting tannery in the domestic market. Buying houses may avoid placing orders to tanneries that further subcontract without their knowledge. In Hazaribagh subcontracts are widespread and risk is generally accepted, provided that quality and price are ensured:

> The buying house accepted; it did not become angry as it needed the goods as early as possible and it could not change the delivery time. […] The buying house realised that XX was not able to do the whole production on its own. (Tanner G, Bengali)

The risk for tannery XX, however, has materialised. Since that transaction, tanner G has been dealing directly with this buying house, which allows him to gain higher profit margins (4 %) plus export subsidies he did not have before.

Third, buying houses may have to delay the lead time or entrust other tanneries with the production if quality is deficient, generating unexpected reputational and financial costs. As tanner B illustrates (see quote from above), the pressure is just forwarded to the suppliers being beaten down.

Figure 5.9 portrays the coordination and risk involved in subcontracted leather processing for the export market.

These findings seem to show that adaptation to power asymmetries within the tanning industry through subcontracts ensures market entry but involves substantial risks that increase upstream. Multi-tiered subcontracts and in particular informal transactions at the lowest end are prone to quality inconsistencies that affect both the producers' and the subsector's competitiveness, though power imbalance favours downstream customers in price setting. Subcontracts exclude any knowledge exchange with buyers or buying houses who along with the contracting tannery give instructions instead of imparting knowledge. Learning and sustained competitiveness appears unlikely to be achieved, just for the sake of (informal) market entry. More research is necessary to define whether and how tanneries manage transaction risks (for Viet Nam, see Steer and Sen 2010)

Central to understanding the importance of informal practices and strategies in the leather production network is their value for dealing with uneven power

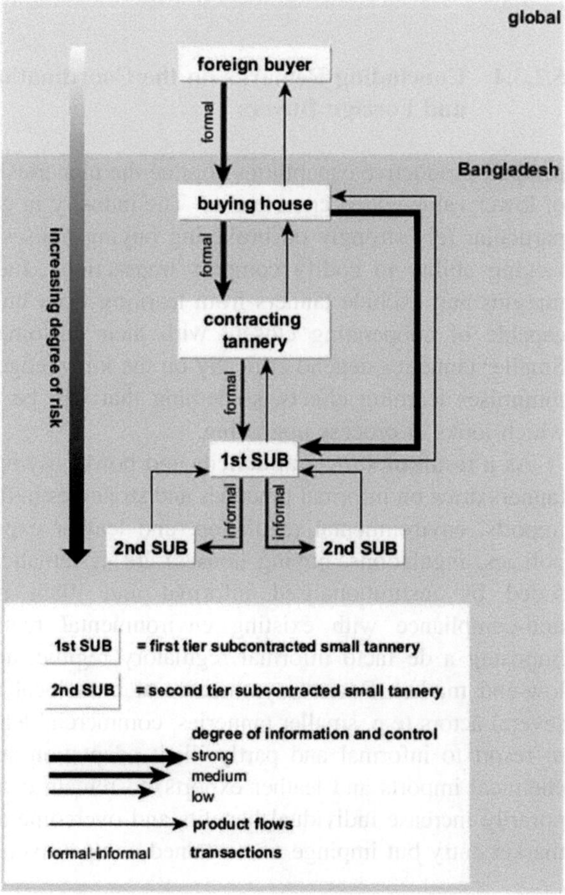

Fig. 5.9 Subcontracted relations in leather exports. *Source* Own illustration

relations. This chapter presented how low-skilled producers draw on informal institutions to adapt to power asymmetry on the way to the export market, thereby attenuating it. Multi-tiered subcontracts allow tanneries of a low competence level to cater to foreign markets. Trusted alliances with more powerful partners (first-tier subcontract) and informal horizontal networks with peers (second-tier subcontract) prove useful for overcoming decisive gatekeepers (e.g. buying agents). But the individual benefit is confined to export revenues. Tanneries are excluded from learning from buyers and constant interaction as long as business relationships are mediated. Buying houses carry out the transactions and are interested in keeping their linking function between producers and customers, thereby controlling information. Turning to illicit practices such as misinvoicing can expose firms and the entire sector to high risks, undermining corporate integrity and reliability in the market. Being pervasive, these practices would seriously impair the sector's competitiveness under formal conditions, that is, if regular import duty for chemicals were paid. The results also signalise that more research is needed into the extent to which informal practices and strategies influence risk and how this can be managed.

5.2.3.4 Concluding Remarks on the Coordination Between Tanners and Foreign Buyers

Limited productive capabilities confine the tanneries interviewed largely to exports of lower value-added crust leather. The industry in general and the interviewees in particular rely strongly on brokering buying houses that compensate the tanners' lacking ability to codify complex transactions. Indirect export relations reduce margins and exclude tanners from learning from buyers. Only large tanneries are capable of cooperating closely with their customers to achieve better quality. Smaller tanneries depend critically on the knowledge of chemical suppliers, which minimises learning effects, something that will be expanded on in Sect. 5.2.4.2 which looks at process upgrading.

As a result of structural deficits and power asymmetries along the value chain, tanners draw on informal practices and strategies in three relevant sectors: chemical imports, environmental regulation, and leather exports. Formal institutions (e.g. policies, regulations, buying houses) are systematically being evaded and superseded by institutionalised informal and illicit practices. The state-tolerated non-compliance with existing environmental regulation has been formalised, imposing a de facto informal regulatory regime, and keeps the tanneries in the low-end market. Power asymmetries at both local and global level have caused several actors (e.g. smaller tanneries, commercial leather exporters, buying agents) to resort to informal and partly illicit adaptation strategies (e.g. under-invoicing chemical imports and leather exports) to remain competitive. Such practices temporarily increase individual benefits and overcome asymmetric power relations in market entry but impinge on sustained competitiveness.

The findings from Sects. 5.1, 5.2.1–5.2.3 call for holistic upgrading strategies that encompass a reformulation of the institutional framework. Improvements to processes during and prior to production may help contain the negative effects of informal and illegal practices.

5.2.4 Strategies to Improve the Competitiveness of Bangladesh's Leather Processing Sector

The complexity of the governance structure and institutional constraints substantiates that strategies must be devised to the specific needs of each set of actors along the value chain. This chapter's objective is to point to weaknesses within the production network and find solutions to improve the producers' competitiveness (research question 4a). It will also consider the value of non-harmful informal institutions that may serve the purpose of achieving a "better deal" (Ponte and Ewert 2009) for local producers (research question 4b).

5.2.4.1 Public Local Governance: Macroeconomic Development Strategies and Policies

The initiatives and needs of economic upgrading at the firm level will be contextualised within macroeconomic development strategies and policies to understand institutional constraints.

Bangladesh prides itself on offering the most liberal investment climate in South Asia (Board of Investment—BOI 2011, p. 6). Constant economic growth rates over the last two decades, a huge low-cost workforce, low energy costs as well as export and economic zones provide prima facie good conditions for local and foreign investors (BOI 2010, p. 5).

Contrasting those parameters with results from interviews with tannery owners reveals that, for instance, energy costs (gas), though available at a low cost, eventually may add up to incalculable expenses. The leather processors complain about countless power failures generating additional costs for emergency power generators and hampering the production process, which often affects the final product quality. In addition to this, frequent nationwide strike actions (*hartals*) particularly before elections point to political instability and seem to have discouraged foreign companies from investing on a larger scale as displayed in Fig. 5.10. These might be reasons why despite a, by and large, increasing trend towards investment, with the exception of a steep drop after the economic crisis in 2008, Bangladesh still lags far behind regional competitors such as India, the undisputed leader, and Pakistan.[27]

[27]India ranks first with US$34,613 m followed by Pakistan with US$2,387 m (Board of Investment 2010, p. 47).

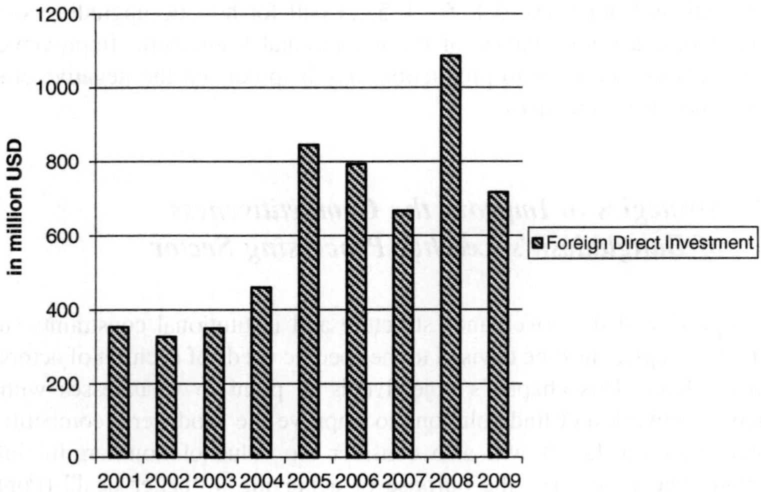

Fig. 5.10 Investment trend in Bangladesh. *Source* Board of Investment (2010). Own illustration

Within the FDI policy framework a myriad of fiscal and financial incentives such as tax and duty exemptions, export subsidies, 100 % ownership, no restrictions on issuing work permits to foreign nationals, amongst others, are granted. Differentiating FDI inflows in 100 % FDI and joint venture investment, the bulk per unit was directed to foreign investors having full ownership (BOI 2010, p. 15).

Bangladesh's investment policy is generic and abstains from focusing on a certain sector, explains the deputy director of BOI. In 2010, services—at 65 % (US$ 4,575,901)—captured the bulk amount of full ownership FDI (BOI 2010, p. 17). In the manufacturing sector FDI were largely directed to the chemical (US$1,985,938 m; 28 %) and textile industry (US$221,259 m; 3 %), with the latter also providing the highest employment opportunities. Agriculture-based industries have benefited from US$154,291 m. Only four "tannery and rubber product" units received a minor investment of US$4,013 m despite export promotion strategies declaring leather a thrust sector. In 2010, United Arab Emirates (US$2,229,898 m), Kingdom of Saudi Arabia (KSA; US$1,850,406 m) and United Kingdom (US$952,035 m) were among the top investing countries, whereas China ranked only 10th.

In joint venture investment services account for 66 % (US$6,693,352 m) followed quite a way behind by chemical (US$1,413,025 m; 14 %) and textile industries (US$1,093,168 m; 11 %). Investment in leather only amounts to US$85,754 m (1 %), in spite of a higher number of units (42) benefiting from foreign investors. KSA (US$2,275,663 m), Norway (US$1,651,704 m) and the United States (US$1,045,679 m) invest most (see Fig. 5.11).

The figures illustrate that there is little interest from foreign investors in the leather industry, a trend which is assured by the Board of Investment:

> We are intending to simply abandon the raw material [i.e. crust and finished leather; A. N.] of the leather sector. (Deputy Director Board of Investment, English)

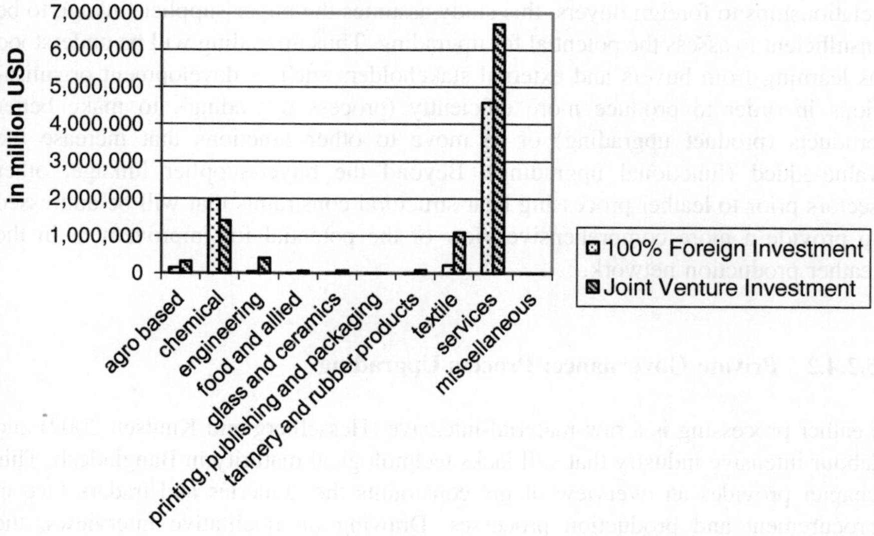

Fig. 5.11 Sector wise investment in Bangladesh, 1991–2010. *Source* Board of Investment (2010). Own illustration

Low value addition and extensive environmental pollution in Hazaribagh make the leather (processing) industry unattractive to foreign investors. Industrial policy has apparently contributed little to improving the image of the tanning subsector in particular. With the relocation to the new tannery site pending, potential investors have little certainty about future infrastructural conditions, functionality of facilities and costs. In accordance with Humphrey (2004, p. 12), they will abstain from giving assistance as long as the benefits are unclear. At present, investments in manufactures are mostly directed to Export Processing Zones (EPZ) around the major urban centres, Dhaka and Chittagong, which ensure adequate infrastructure (e.g. access roads, industrial electricity, telecommunications) for industrial use. Interviews have provided information pointing towards a considerable FDI-inflow in leather to economic zones outside EPZs in the reference time (1991–2010),[28] whereas Hazaribagh was not able to benefit accordingly. The new tannery site in Hemayetpur/Savar is expected to play a critical role in developing an environmentally compliant and technologically modern tanning industry.

Research on upgrading has shown that "power relations may inhibit upgrading and limit knowledge flows" (Humphrey and Schmitz 2002, p. 1020) within a global value chain. It has been suggested in the literature on upgrading in GVCs that learning from global buyers is crucial to overcoming entry barriers (e.g. Gereffi 2005; Humphrey 2004; Humphrey and Schmitz 2002). In view of very few direct

[28]In 1997, a German leather goods company set up a factory outside of Dhaka (100 % FDI). Another major leather footwear manufacturer (LFM D; see Sect. 5.3) incurred a strategic partnership with an Italian company in 1996, which developed into a strategic alliance in 2006.

relationships to foreign buyers, this study assumes the buyer-supplier linkage to be insufficient to assess the potential for upgrading. Thus upgrading will be understood as learning from buyers and external stakeholders such as development organisations in order to produce more efficiently (process upgrading), to make better products (product upgrading) or to move to other functions that increase the value-added (functional upgrading). Beyond the buyer-supplier linkage, other sectors prior to leather processing bear structural constraints that will be addressed to provide a more comprehensive view of the potential for improvement in the leather production network.

5.2.4.2 Private Governance: Process Upgrading

Leather processing is a raw-material-intensive (Hesselberg and Knutsen 2002) and labour intensive industry that still lacks technological maturity in Bangladesh. This chapter provides an overview of the constraints the tanneries and traders face in procurement and production processes. Drawing on qualitative interviews, the objective was not to give an exhaustive list of limitations, but to reflect the tanners' subjective needs in order to maintain or regain a competitive position in the market. Results from the interviews with tanners and traders were triangulated with the opinions of leather technologists, buying agents and experts from upgrading projects.

Insufficiently developed backward linkages cause chronic shortages of raw hides and skins (see Strasser et al. 2013), or make leather processors reliant on importing machinery and inputs such as chemicals. When it comes to exporting leather products, mark-ups due to higher prices for raw material and, if legally imported, chemicals weigh on the tanneries' price competitiveness. At the moment, the industry pins its hopes on minimum labour costs, where Bangladesh ranks lowest compared with international benchmarks.[29] Although one leather footwear OEM emphasises that "cheap China is over" (see Sect. 5.3) and Bangladesh stands a good chance of soon becoming the world's factory for labour-intensive consumer goods, whether this approach is sustainable is being publicly questioned more than ever (see Burke 2013; ZDF 2013; Human Rights Watch 2012).

A closer look at the production costs of the tanneries interviewed compared with a European tannery apprises of a stronger financial burden arising from raw material (70–75 %) and chemicals (20–25 %) due to little-developed backward linkages (Table 5.3). Labour costs are minuscule; expenses for environmental compliance (e.g. pollution abatement costs) do not even exist yet. The striking dependence on raw material and chemical supply requires place-specific strategies to reduce the industry's vulnerability and improve its competitiveness.

[29]The hourly wages (including social security) in the Bangladeshi factory of a German leather goods manufacturer are lowest compared to subsidiaries in other countries: Tunis: €1.90; Ukraine: €2.20; China: 1.10; Bangladesh: €0.50.

Table 5.3 Production costs in European and Bangladeshi tanneries

	European tannery (%)	Tanneries interviewed in Hazaribagh/Dhaka (%)
Raw material	55	70–75
Chemicals	10	20–25
Labour	12	1–6
Energy (gas, electricity, water)	3	Not specified
Other costs (e.g. environmental compliance)	20	Not specified

Source Hesselberg and Knutsen (2002, p. 168). The data based on own interviews conducted in 2011 are estimates. Own composition

Increasing the Capabilities in the Supply of Raw Material

Section 5.2.2 introduced the supply segment of the value chain and the tanneries' sourcing strategies for internal raw material. Being a renewable resource, RHS can generally provide a competitive advantage and an opportunity to move up the value chain (Gereffi 1999; Hassler 2004). However, efficiency in inbound logistics is required. With more than 40 % of the annual RHS being produced in only three days, the dependency on a single cultural-religious event is striking. Shortcomings, however, are not confined to culture-specific institutional constraints; they exist throughout the year at various stages of the supply chain (animal care and husbandry; production, collection, preservation, and processing of RHS) where they have not been adequately addressed by governmental and non-governmental organisations. Figure 5.12 displays where these need to intervene to achieve better results as regards raw material. This section draws on interviews with tanners and traders, contrasting their subjective perceptions of deficiencies with expert opinions and experiences from other case studies in order to define potential points of intervention. It shows that constraints in the supply of raw material are not an isolated issue but require an exchange of knowledge, technical assistance and institutional support to be overcome.

Traits of Indigenous Raw Material

The large livestock population provides a significant resource of RHS for value addition. Apart from breed-, sex- and age-related defects that are not considered in this analysis, the natural features of the local raw material will be very briefly touched on in order to understand its upgrading potential.

The quality of bovine and ovine hides from Bangladesh has been lauded both by national leather associations and international experts. Bos indicus cattle, as the zebu are scientifically known, originate in Asia and have proved highly adaptable to severe climatic, nutritional and sanitary conditions (Leather International 2004). The tropical climate produces zebuine hides that are lighter and thinner than in Europe (ibid.). Thanks to the fine grain pattern and low difference in thickness

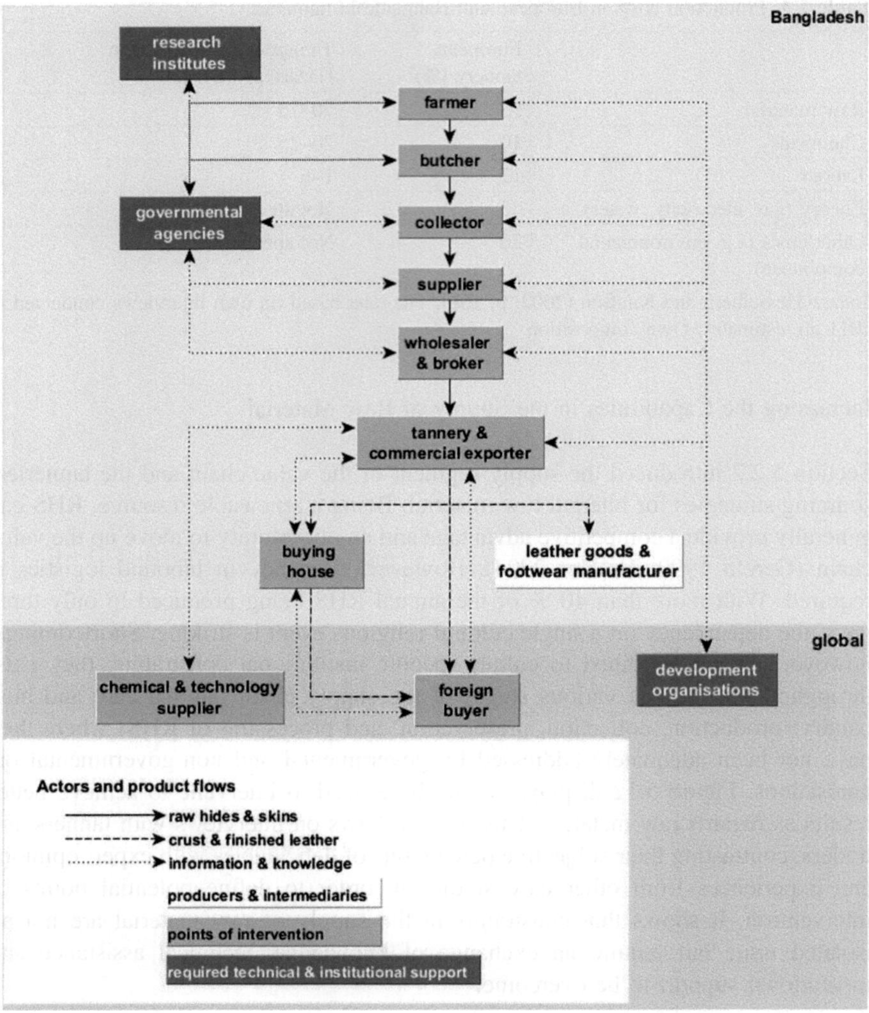

Fig. 5.12 Suggested points of intervention in the production, collection, and preservation of raw material. *Source* Own illustration

between back and belly, zebuine hides are in high demand on the international market (Leather International 2002). Various natural conditions (e.g. sweat glands, sebaceous glands, fat blisters) make them less suitable for leather footwear, but an excellent choice for upholstery and garment leather, provided size suffices (ibid.; international consultant B).

International expert B ascribes "black bengal", the dominant goat breed in Bangladesh, a very good ratio between the core area and the belly and neck area. The fine grain and pore structure are equally deemed of high quality. However, size limits its use to small garments, leather goods and footwear.

Livestock Production and Animal Husbandry

According to the Department of Livestock Services (DLS), 97 % of livestock in Bangladesh is reared on a small scale. Smallholders face several limitations in terms of land size, resources, productivity or market access, which restrain them mostly to subsistence farming (Todaro and Smith 2011). In Bangladesh 90.6 % of farms operate on an area of 5 ha or below; the average operational farm size amounts to only 1.6 ha (Todaro and Smith 2011, p. 421). With each farm rearing only small numbers of ovine and bovine animals, Bangladesh's livestock is highly scattered throughout the country. Hence, contrary to what most of the smaller tanneries fear, it is the current farming structure that proves challenging for a reliable collection and supply of RHS. The lower surface area[30] of Bangladeshi zebuine hides and goat skins is partly also a result of the prevailing structure of poor smallholders lacking sufficient animal feed. Technological limitations aside, the tanners see the small and inconsistent size of indigenous bovine hides as a barrier to product upgrading (e.g. automotive upholstery).

With animal husbandry being operated at a very small scale, there is little control of the conditions of livestock production and the quality of hides and skins. According to international consultant B, smallholder farmers in Bangladesh lack knowledge about the consequences inadequate animal care has for the value of hides and skins and thus for the entire leather industry. Poor parasite management exposes the tanneries' low skills in finishing as it requires a number of chemical and physical processes to correct scars on the surface (Triple Line Consulting Ltd 2002). Full-grain (aniline) leather that commands the highest price on the international market is unlikely to be achieved, says expert B. Governmental departments barely act preventively; DLS, for instance, only attends to epidemic diseases that endanger animal and public health.[31] Services on how to avoid pre-slaughter human-made raw material defects (e.g. urine and faeces irritations; scars from fences; calluses from harnesses) are lacking. Experiences from Sub-Sahara African countries (Jabbar et al. 2002) advert that a holistic approach is indispensable for tackling such interrelated problems. Tanners, traders and farmers need to exchange knowledge and jointly address deficiencies, supported by governmental and non-governmental agencies (see Fig. 5.12).

Mostly medium-sized and large leather processors criticise the sluggish development of large-scale cattle and dairy farming that is expected to be better capable of meeting the industry's demand for a constant supply of RHS in terms of volume, size and quality. Both dairy and cattle farming allow for a better organisation of fodder and husbandry conditions, which is expected to increase the predictability of output and minimise hide defects. Industrialising livestock farming could also

[30]A 12 % dewlap in zebu numerically compensates the surface area lost by the hump (Leather International 2004), though the latter produces discontinuous leather. To a certain extent, professional cutting would allow for product upgrading, for instance, to upholstery leather.

[31]After the outbreak of the anthrax disease in 2010, DLS has vaccinated several million animals.

provide the tanning industry with incentives for technological upgrading to enhance mechanisation and automation.

However, the dominant smallholder farming system with limited land availability and small farm size is a bar to those prospects. Local inheritance laws are likely to further subdivide land parcels among family members (LANDac 2012; Your Commonwealth 2011). DLS-officials see no scope for large-scale cattle farms in Bangladesh, which currently operate with between 50 and 300 animals, a size that is insufficient to achieve economies of scale. Moreover, dairy farms do not necessarily produce better RHS quality. Dairy cows are reared for late slaughter in order to maximise the milk yield, making the quality of the hides deteriorate over the years. This indicates that smallholder farming is likely to continue to be the dominant agricultural system in Bangladesh, securing livelihoods and a consistent food supply. It explains why tanneries do not care about backward linkages (e.g. joint ventures) to farmers or cattle-dealers to verticalise the supply of RHS:

> We have no connection with the farmers. We just buy the leather. (Tanner Q, English)

Smallholder livestock production and non-commercial animal husbandry tend to foment a more deficient quality of raw material. It will be necessary to reach out to the rural communities via associations and, as the degree of organisation of smallholders is expected to be low, through local leaders and awareness-raising television programmes to impart knowledge on proper husbandry, the value of intact hides and skins for the leather industry, potential quality defects and how to avoid these. Programmes operated by governmental agencies need to address such flaws. Any failures that occur at this stage, tanneries have to be remedied by tanneries during the tanning process. Natural irregularities (e.g. growth marks) are to a certain extent inevitable and give the leather its uniqueness. Human-made defects require more costly chemical and physical treatment, reducing value and productivity (Triple Line Consulting Ltd 2002, p. 13). But good livestock management and animal husbandry pays off: full grain leathers accrue the fewest pre-slaughter defects and are corrected the least, which is why they obtain the highest price.

Production of Raw Hides and Skins

The actual implications of Eid-ul-Azha on prices and the availability of raw material unfold during the off season. All interviewees consider the scarcity of RHS without question to be the most taxing problem in their operational business. None of them explicitly related the religious festival to an economically unsustainable sourcing pattern that restricts the all-year supply of indigenous raw material. As a cultural-religious institution, Eid-ul-Azha is deeply rooted in the Muslim society. Instead of citing it, tanneries refer to inadequate livestock production and management (see above) as well as other reasons, which are set out below, to explain the structural shortage of RHS. These deserve a critical review in order to derive policy implications:

Price volatility of raw material is a prominent feature in the leather industry, which is exacerbated by a seasonal festival of such massive extent. This applies even more to Bangladesh where RHS are sold to the highest bidder, unless transactions are carried out in trust-based or long-term firm-to-firm relationships. Export duty on RHS has decoupled the domestic market from international developments. Experts consulted within this study regard prices for local raw material as surprisingly high, i.e. above world market level. This implies that dynamics on the local RHS-market vary from global tendencies.

Secondly, tanners complain about the extensive illegal cross-border smuggling of both cattle and RHS. This practice is particularly prevalent during the festival season but has severe implications for the all-year round availability of RHS. Though widely covered by the media (e.g. Fattahul Alim 2010; Ullah Mirdha and Saha 2012), governmental departments and the state remain inactive in stopping these practices favouring a powerful competitor. India ranks among the top ten leather exporting nations and is subject to its own cultural-religious constraints.[32]

Thirdly, contrary to some tanners' assumption that nutritional patterns have changed over the past years, meat consumption in Bangladesh has expanded, though at a very low level (FAO 2009). It remains to be seen whether the high share of both urban and rural population currently living in poverty will be able to increase their incomes significantly to shift towards a more meat-based diet in future, which, moreover, can be met by local supplies. Implications for livestock farming would be expected.

In addition to quantitative limitations, the quality of RHS is constrained by low capabilities in the supply base. When it comes to slaughtering and flaying the animals, the poor infrastructure affects the quality of the raw material. The Department of Livestock Services counts a minimum of one governmental abattoir in each of the 64 districts in Bangladesh; Dhaka as the most populated district has five. Only two slaughterhouses in the entire country are privately operated. In 2011, more than 12 m ovine and bovine animals were registered to be professionally killed in both governmental and private facilities.[33] While quantities are already held to be insufficient, DLS-officials consider the technological and hygienic conditions in governmental slaughterhouses as "not so good". The semi-automatic hang-flaying method is only practiced in private slaughterhouses; in governmental facilities bovine animals are still slaughtered and flayed on the floor, soaking the hides in faeces and blood, thereby accelerating bacterial invasion. Veterinary control in governmental slaughterhouses is also held to be "not so good" (DLS). Modernising the technical infrastructure in slaughterhouses is necessary but not sufficient. A significant though not quantifiable percentage of bovine and ovine animals is slaughtered at open markets by both professional and non-professional

[32]Cattle are considered sacred in the Hindu religion and it is forbidden to kill them for consumption or further production. The Indian leather industry dominates in regions with a mainly Muslim population and uses buffalo or imported hides.

[33]This number is disaggregated as follows: cattle: 6.05 m; buffalo: 0.3 m; goat: 5.73 m; sheep: 0.242 m. Data on the production of hides and skins provided by the Food and Agriculture Organization of the United Nations (FAO) are estimates based on local trader associations and methodologically not unambiguous so we have refrained from referring to them.

butchers. Informal slaughtering at open markets is not subject either to veterinary surveillance or quality control. Adequate technological facilities are also lacking; bovine animals are killed and flayed on the floor. As long as governmental slaughterhouses do not vary significantly in their hygienic and technical conditions to slaughtering and flaying animals from informal markets, there is little reason for advocating abolishing informal structures. Moreover, remote rural areas rely on informal markets; this means it will require more efforts to work with the community, raising awareness about adequate husbandry conditions, slaughtering facilities and flaying capabilities.

Several adjustments to *peak season dynamics* seem necessary to minimise quality defects due to insufficient slaughtering facilities and flaying capabilities.

Holding the sacrifice in joint premises (for Saudi Arabia, see Brooke 1987) may ensure organised and professional flaying with positive implications for the collection rate of RHS and the final leather quality. Sheltered facilities may reduce the climatic vulnerability (e.g. monsoon rainfalls) RHS are exposed to. The dimension of 5–6 m bovine and ovine animals, as estimated by leather associations in 2011, to be killed within a maximum of three days, challenges the capacities for providing joint premises for an organised mass sacrifice. In general, affluent urban areas have the highest sacrificial activity and are the most suitable for finding joint facilities, whereas rural areas are more difficult to be covered adequately.

Manual flaying particularly by non-professional butchers is prone to knife cuts and other slaughtering defects. Some of these can be detected only after tanning and are thus very costly for the tanning industry. At present, weeks before the festival training programmes (oral presentations) are run for professional butchers in Dhaka to minimise quality defects caused by inadequate flaying. One suggestion is to organise these programmes on a sufficiently small scale (i.e. upazila and ward level)[34] all year round to ensure countrywide all-season quality leather. The automatised hang flaying method as practiced in Western abattoirs removes the hides and skins accurately from the cattle carcasses, but is too costly to be implemented countrywide and, moreover, technically and logistically unsuitable for temporary use during the festival. Instead, semi-automatic constructions that enable the butchers to flay hanging carcasses manually may have economic and logistical advantages for a proper set up in joint premises. But still, the large concentration of sacrificial animals during a period of a few days makes it very difficult for the limited number of professional butchers to carry out flaying with reasonable care. As butchers on Eid-ul-Azha unlike in the off season do not trade with RHS, they have little interest in producing flawless hides and skins.

Consequently, it is necessary to disseminate information on proper flaying and the value of intact hides and skins for the leather industry countrywide at all administrative levels to all potential actors. TV spots currently broadcasted prior to

[34]Bangladesh is structured into 7 divisions and 64 districts, each of which is divided into subdistricts (Upazila). Cities and towns are subdivided into wards for administrative purposes (Wikipedia 2014).

Eid-ul-Azha explaining the appropriate treatment of RHS to achieve maximum valorisation for the export earning leather industry should be aired all year round to achieve the sustained impact of such information among the target groups (farmers, non-professional butchers).

Collection of RHS

Collecting RHS is particularly challenging during Eid-ul-Azha. If the production of festival hides and skins is properly organised (e.g. joint premises), the collection rate from currently 75 % (est.) could increase significantly.

Although seasonal middlemen contribute significantly to collection, medium-sized and large tannery owners want the government to be more active in prosecuting them. The Department of Livestock Services, however, argues that seasonal middlemen trade only temporarily and not commercially in RHS; they are thus exempted from acquiring a trade license. Newspaper articles (e.g. Fattahul Alim 2010; Hossain 2012) and interviews with tanners and RHS-merchants clearly point out that temporary intermediaries are involved in commercial activities. Some of these remain longer in the supply chain and retain large quantities of RHS in order to achieve higher prices. Stricter law enforcement (e.g. control of trade licenses) at least during the three-day festival may discourage temporary traders to take the risk of joining in the supply chain. This approach, however, will only be successful if the tanneries organise themselves to procure raw material.

Informal self-organisation might be more conducive to increasing efficiencies in governing the supply chain on Eid-ul-Azha. Tannery associations would have to take the lead in managing and systematising procurement activities during religious festivals. The current collection rate[35] of only 75 % (est.) on Eid-ul-Azha implies that collectors still miss certain areas. Tannery associations would have to assess in which areas collection has to be improved to cope with the large concentration of raw material. This might conflict with the economic interest of organisations and groups related to political parties, which are very often in control of the hide and skin supply in certain neighbourhoods on Eid-ul-Azha as several temporary intermediaries report. Smaller tanneries, for instance, might jointly organise sourcing activities in order to enhance their collective negotiation power versus upstream suppliers. A network of agents collectively organised by a group of tanneries could more systematically cover a larger catchment area, thereby increasing the collection rate. A stronger internal organisation may be a prerequisite for governmental departments to provide an adequate infrastructure for sacrificing and flaying activities.

[35]Reliable data on the slaughter and collection rate are not available in Bangladesh, for the slaughter activity is not fully covered by private and governmental abattoirs (see above). The collection rate is an approximation made by tanners' and traders' associations.

Preservation of RHS

Preservation matters throughout the year, but the large availability of raw material on Eid-ul-Azha exceeds the tanneries' capacity to immediately process green hides and skins to wet blue. Various methods are discussed against the socio-cultural and geographic backdrop.

First, preservation through ground and wind drying is unreliable in climates with high humidity (Triple Line Consulting Ltd 2002, p. 74).

Second, cold storage could entail economic benefits for the tanneries if financed and used along with other leather processors and upstream wholesalers. International consultant B appreciates the advantage of green hides and skins being processed without contaminating waste water or corroding the machinery by sodium chloride (salt) that is alternatively used for preserving hides and skins (see below). The unstable and costly supply of electricity makes cold storages an idea that is difficult to implement in Bangladesh. Tannery owners, however, may be encouraged to provide their new factories in Hemayetpur/Savar with appropriate preservation facilities, drawing on lessons from the most modern and only tannery in Bangladesh with a cold storage.[36] There, hides and skins are wrapped to prevent them from getting pressure marks and palletised to let them cool down. According to international consultant B, this method requires less capital input than storing cattle hides hung up as European hide merchants often do.[37] He adds that cold storage facilities are not an indispensable asset but provide traders and tanneries with the necessary flexibility to react to price fluctuations.

Third, salting is still considered to be the economically and practically most suitable preservation method in developing countries (Triple Line Consulting Ltd 2002, p. 74). Putrefaction can be avoided if salt is promptly and properly applied and supplementary bactericides are incorporated. The widespread lack of knowledge and awareness in Bangladesh is probably the most daunting challenge. During Eid-ul-Azha 2012 many professional RHS traders were seen stockpiling unsalted hides totally unaware of appropriate storage, preservation time and the risk of bacterial putrefaction. It is therefore of paramount importance to impart knowledge about the negative effects of putrefactive damage on the leather quality as well as the price competitiveness of downstream tanners. Madrassas, as another temporary trader, should be encouraged to auction smaller batches of green hides and skins after a maximum of three hours after sacrificing to enable the tanneries timely preservation. Furthermore, it will be necessary for traders' (e.g. BHSMA) and tannery associations (BTA, BFLLFEA) to reach out to small-scale hide and skin collectors to impart knowledge about timely collection and adequate preservation by using salt.

[36]In Noapara, Jessore; approximately 235 km or about 7 h by bus from Dhaka.

[37]A German trader puts the hides in boxes, covers each layer with flake ice to cool them down and stores them in dedicated facilities.

If efficiencies in the supply of raw material are to be increased, trainings and awareness-raising campaigns cannot be limited to peak season events or professionals only. A large population (i.e. farmers, non-professional butchers, collectors) needs to be addressed throughout the year by both disseminating codified information and public service media, translating complex information in simple ways for ordinary people to understand.

To conclude, more attention has to be given to developing the performance in economic sectors prior to leather processing, namely animal husbandry, animal health, slaughtering methods and slaughtering facilities. Table 5.4 summarises constraints in the supply of RHS and refers to actions required to overcome these.

Table 5.4 Constraints and required actions to improve the domestic trade and quality of hides and skins

Sector	Constraints	Potential interventions	Target groups	Institutions
Animal husbandry, animal health	Human-made raw material quality defects (e.g. diseases, physical and mechanical damages)	Improved animal husbandry and disease control (e.g. use of correct harness and proper medicine)	(Smallholder) farmers; cattle dealers	Farmers' associations; traders' associations; veterinary organisations; government departments
Production of RHS: off-season	Insufficient number of and low technological level in abattoirs	Construction and modernisation of governmental slaughterhouses; improving slaughtering facilities in informal markets in rural areas	Butchers	Government departments (e.g. Department of Livestock Services, Department of Agricultural Marketing); butchers' associations
	Abrasion of RHS during transportation; heating of RHS as a result of inadequate storage	Proper handling of animals and of RHS; proper storage of RHS	Cattle dealers; traders of RHS; leather processors	Traders' associations; tanners' associations

(continued)

Table 5.4 (continued)

Sector	Constraints	Potential interventions	Target groups	Institutions
Production of RHS: Eid-ul-Azha	Unorganised slaughtering	Holding sacrifice in joint facilities	Imams and students related to religious educational institutions; ordinary people	Governmental agencies; religious institutions; public service media (newspapers, radio, TV, etc.)
	Quality defects due to inadequate flaying	Manual hand flaying in joint facilities by professional personnel; use of proper tools and techniques; awareness raising programmes on adequate flaying	Butchers; ordinary people	Butchers' associations; public service media (newspapers, radio, TV, etc.)
Preservation	Putrefaction of RHS due to delays in the application of salt	All-year awareness-raising programmes (e.g. TV, radio), teaching and trainings on timely preservation; (joint) cold storages in new tannery site	Farmers; collectors; suppliers; wholesalers of RHS; leather processors; ordinary people	Hide and skin merchants' association; tanners' associations; trade/export promotion councils; public service media (newspapers, radio, TV, etc.); national standards associations; financial institutions
Collection	Unskilled temporary traders boosting prices	Monitoring trade license holders; law enforcement; organised collection by regular traders and tanners	Temporary traders; regular traders; tanners	City corporation; municipality councils; hide and skin merchants' association; tanners' associations

Source Adapted from Triple Line Consulting Ltd (2002) and Ministry of Agriculture of the Government of the People's Republic of Bangladesh (2013). Own composition

Codification to Increase Efficiencies in Trading RHS

The structural scarcity of raw material and the low capabilities in the supply base weigh on the leather industry's competitiveness. Instrumental methods to adequately determine the price based on size, thickness and quality of RHS are lacking and increase inefficiencies in procurement. Assessing the size of RHS manually or with the naked eye is a strategy for adapting to both the deficient technological capacity for applying the measurement by weight and the large volumes of RHS on Eid-ul-Azha. Trading RHS on an inaccurate calculation basis is prone to human errors, putting both trading parties at a disadvantage. It also favours wheeling and dealing to evade taxes, adds international consultant B. Interestingly, both traders and (smaller) tanners trust that profit and losses from calculation inaccuracies are eventually balanced out in long-term relationships.

Codification in the supply of RHS faces a variety of challenges. A weight-based pricing system requires reorganisation, that is, centralising the widely scattered collection and distribution network to introduce instruments for weighing countrywide in slaughterhouses, at wholesale markets and in tanneries. This is expensive even if investments of that scale are centralised in, for instance, common facility centres in the tannery estate and in each of the 21 wholesale markets. Above all, it is likely to reduce labour-intensity and thus employment for large population groups. Instead of introducing a costly weight-based pricing system, it appears to be more practical to improve the existing one by reducing its proneness to informal practices that are detrimental to the tanning industry's competitiveness.

Tacit knowledge is needed to define the quality and price of RHS, increasing the complexity of the transaction. This knowledge cannot be acquired within a few days of the year. Temporary intermediaries are able to ignore that complexity because of the religious requirements for sacrificial animals and the lacking codified information on the trade of RHS. Introducing codification through a set of intersubjectively comprehensible criteria on how to select, grade and price raw material may prevent temporary intermediaries from joining in the supply chain. Tanners and (regular) traders would first have to agree on terms and conditions about the way hides and skins are removed (e.g. cutting lines; an exact definition of the constituent parts of RHS, i.e. legs, head, tail). Drawing on practices in developed countries, such agreements could be arranged by the corresponding associations and communicated to all members and associates, suggests international expert B.[38] Written instructions and practical trainings may help both experienced traders and tanners to better understand the size and quality of the merchant goods. More control over negative effects (e.g. price mark-ups) and more precision in dealing with RHS may encourage investments in technology to assess the size more accurately. Such an increase in complexity could discourage non-professional middlemen from joining in the supply chain for fast and high margins. Cutting out

[38]The guideline this expert refers to has been developed for the German market and is dated. Codification does not necessarily determine the application of rules.

inexperienced middlemen, however, is only an option if the supply chain can be reorganised more effectively (see above).

The codification of merchant goods under current festival dynamics is practically impossible. Mass sacrifices and professional flaying in joint premises might stimulate it. The way transactions (payment) are handled involves power asymmetries that seem more difficult to resolve.

Formalisation

In low season trust is the dominant mechanism in trading raw material between tanneries and traders. Personal and long-term firm-to-firm relationships compensate for the lack of a formal contract; terms and conditions are negotiated based on mutual understanding. Problems arise when firstly, tanneries delay the payment, making use of their power; and secondly, the payment arrangements exclude smaller tanneries from renegotiating potential quality defects. Likewise, spot payment in quasi-market relations during Eid-ul-Azha prevents tanners from resorting to sanctions in case quality turns out worse than expected. Their business risk increases during the festival season and is only partly offset by systemic trust (see Section "High Quality of Raw Hides and Skins and Systemic Trust on Eid-ul-Azha").

Formalising transactions between collectors/suppliers/wholesalers and tanners is only useful if all parties accept those contracts to be binding and payment is adjusted after tanning. This could secure transactions and level out power asymmetries. However, as long as formal documents are weak because, for instance, they lack amendments on conflict resolution (see Meyer 2011) or cannot be enforced, raising awareness of the benefits of formalisation is likely to prove futile. The large number of regular intermediaries engaged in the trade of RHS makes formulating legally enforceable contracts a daunting task. Under current conditions any attempt to formalise transactions is likely to fail. A more organised production and collection of festival hides and skins is more likely to reduce potential risks.

The measures and suggestions set out above and displayed in Table 5.4 relate to structural constraints at all stages from husbandry over production to collection and preservation of RHS. They do not claim to deliver a complete account of all problems in the supply segment but are devised to address crucial actors.

If foreign buyers are to gain confidence in the Bangladeshi tanning industry, the dependence on a single event for the procurement of raw material and on inexperienced temporary intermediaries needs to be governed more effectively. Codification and formalisation of transactions between traders and tanners might partly be conducive to drive out unwanted middlemen, but do not serve as a blueprint for all transactions. For instance, the reliance on personal trust-based and long-term firm-to-firm relationships with professional merchants increases the reliability of a constant supply with RHS.

In the long run, the relocation to Hemayetpur/Savar is expected to entail a concentration of both leather processors and wholesalers with the objective of verticalising the supply of hides and skins. With larger quantities of RHS being traded, higher levels of formalisation and codification may be required. This may lead to emerging market relationships and more even power relations. Smaller wholesalers will possibly be downgraded to suppliers or collectors or even cut out of the supply chain. It remains to be seen how such reorganisation will influence upgrading paths.

Increasing the Capabilities in the Use of Chemicals

Chemicals constitute the major input component for processing hides and skins to leather. With only a few substances locally available (e.g. ammonium sulfate, sodium chloride, sodium carbonate), approximately 90 % of all chemicals needed for tanning and finishing operations have to be imported by trading companies. This weighs significantly on the tanneries' production cost structure in which chemicals amount to more than twice the percentage of a European tannery (see Table 5.3). Considering the dominant illicit import practices (under-invoicing; see Sect. 5.2.3.3), the real costs are assumed to be even higher. Such dependence on external actors and knowledge limits the tanning industry's innovative capacity for experimenting with chemicals in the production process. In addition to sourcing chemicals at convenient prices, the tanneries need to increase their capabilities to use chemicals efficiently. Figure 5.13 shows what stages governmental agencies and development organisations need to intervene at in order to build up and strengthen a local chemical industry. This section will discuss the interlinkages between local and global actors in providing knowledge for the adequate use of chemicals.

Hesselberg and Knutsen see the capacities of European tanneries' resting on "craftsmanship and tacit knowledge" (2002, p. 169) rather than on cutting-edge technology. Interviews with experts and tanners suggest that leather processors in Hazaribagh lack both. Indirect and short-term buyer-supplier relationships exclude the tanneries from "learning by interacting" (Bathelt and Glückler 2012, p. 242; see Section "Buying Houses—Facilitating or Preventing Market Entry?") with foreign customers. Knowledge can hardly be transferred under these circumstances. In general, buyers indicate the product specifications of an article in international contracts (e.g. L/C, T/T) and entrust buying houses with communicating and enforcing these terms with their suppliers. One of the country's largest tanneries admits its limited innovative capacity and dependence on foreign, particularly European buyers, in terms of fashion trends:

> We gain knowledge at a very late stage [...]. Fashions come to Asian countries one year later. Then we follow, we copy. (Tanner Q, English)

Ahmed (2002, p. 42) ascribes the lack of technological know-how in applying chemicals in tanning and finishing operations to the incomprehensive theoretical and practical education graduates receive from the Bangladesh College of Leather

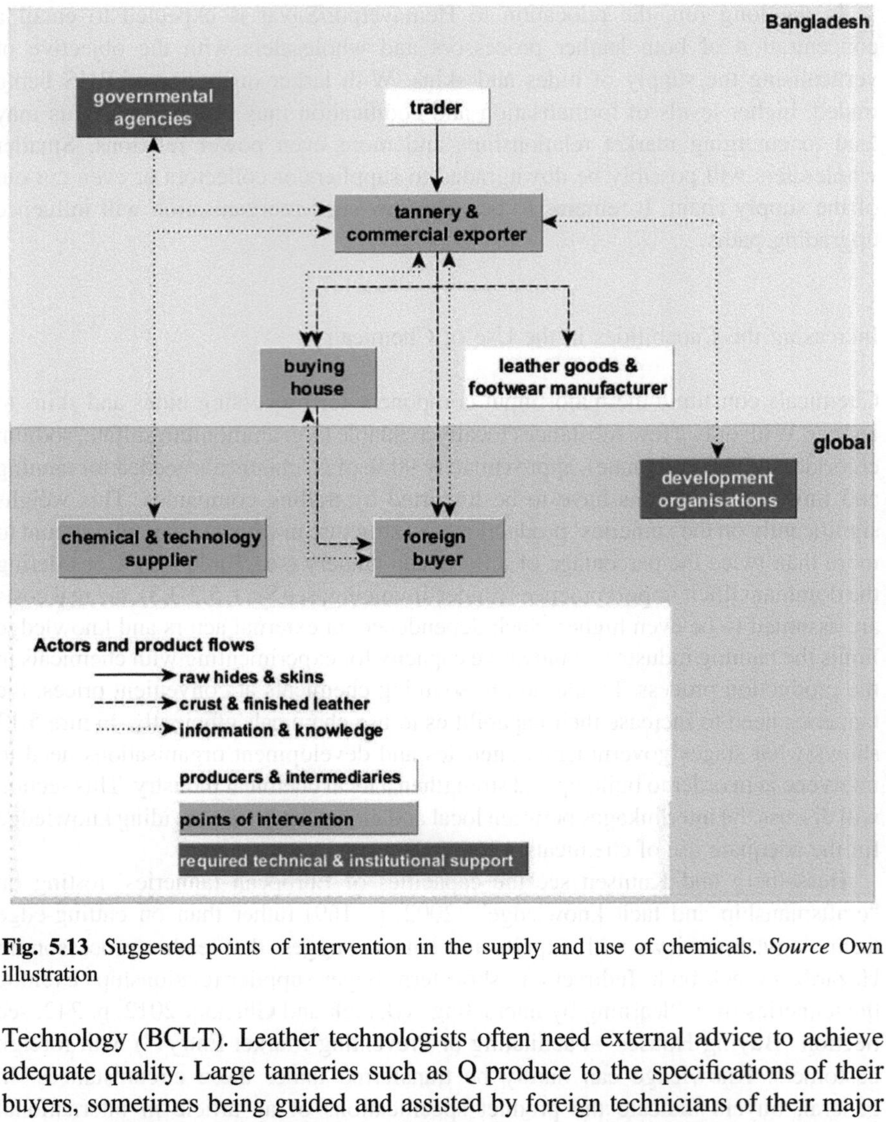

Fig. 5.13 Suggested points of intervention in the supply and use of chemicals. *Source* Own illustration

Technology (BCLT). Leather technologists often need external advice to achieve adequate quality. Large tanneries such as Q produce to the specifications of their buyers, sometimes being guided and assisted by foreign technicians of their major customers. Smaller and medium-sized tanneries do not qualify for this approach; as a result of the lack of direct relationships to buyers, inadequate technology, low production capacity and unskilled labour, they follow the formulae provided by chemical suppliers. Their dependence on the knowledge of service providers makes them incapable of researching and developing specific leather articles, constraining value addition within Bangladesh.

Apart from local power asymmetries in organising the chemical market, the complexity of the chemistry and the lacking knowledge seem to have suppressed any impetus to invest in a domestic chemical industry. Tanning relies on a simple standardised process that can easily be carried out to the instructions of chemical suppliers or buying houses[39] (Hesselberg and Knutsen 2002). After washing and soaking the hides and skins, the beamhouse process follows a standardised procedure. Here, codification can be both explicit in the form of written indications (i.e. tanning formulae) from customers or chemical suppliers and implicit in the form of instructions on location from buying agents. This is different for finishing leather, the complexity of which is based on craftsmanship and tacit knowledge rather than on standardised chemical processes. Resources (time, money, knowledge) are necessary to experiment with costly raw material in order to develop new leather articles. Smaller and even medium-sized tanneries have little capacity to afford this. The gap to tanneries in the North seems huge:

> Actually, the Italian artists make rubbish leather beautiful; because they research, […]. They are researching every day and the chemical companies [are; A. N.] mostly now in Italy. (Tanner Q, English)

Calling Italian tanneries ‘artists’ shows Q’s admiration for and distance to the craftsmanship and knowledge his overseas counterparts have acquired in collaboration with leading European chemical companies. Resources are invested in finished leather where value addition is highest.[40] Italian companies are market leaders in finishing technology and have little interest in sharing knowledge with low-skilled suppliers. They place orders for crust leather in Bangladesh and finish them at home, thereby maintaining their comparative advantage.

A proper application of chemicals is inextricably related to an efficient use of water. The low automation level in Hazaribagh’s tanneries makes it very difficult to optimise the use of chemicals. Quantities of both chemicals and water are calculated and applied manually and are thus prone to imprecision. Process control can direct important factors such as savings, effluent and quality (Leather International 2006). According to buying agent B and international expert B, a simple water and chemical management system (e.g. Aquamix) feeds the exact quantity of water/chemicals into the drum that is supported by a temperature control unit. It helps to achieve a more rationalised use of chemicals (e.g. in colour matching), keeps the discharge of liquid effluents to a minimum and ensures consistent quality. Hazaribagh’s tanneries are still not ready for such technological upgrades, buying agent B criticises. Only one footwear OEM that also operates a tannery outside of Dhaka has adopted a water management system; tanneries in Hazaribagh have been wary of investing in technology that is costly to implement, to operate, to maintain and repair, and eventually to relocate to the new tannery site. The industry pins its hope of a technological upgrade to the still undated relocation, meanwhile missing out on enormous potential for value addition.

[39] Buying houses in Hazaribagh very often run chemical import businesses.

[40] Value addition from crust to finished stage is estimated to account for 9 % (GTZ 2006, p. 66).

Increasing the Capabilities in the Use of Machinery

Tanning and finishing are more capital-intensive production activities compared to the higher value-added but more labour-intensive leather goods and footwear manufactures. Sourcing and using machinery properly impacts heavily on the tanneries' competitiveness. Apart from technical assistance by buyers, machinery suppliers and development organisations to use modern technology closely interrelated with the proper application of chemicals and water, it is also necessary to consider trade policies (e.g. tax on imported machinery) and funding schemes (Fig. 5.14).

The tanneries cannot source sophisticated technology from a domestic engineering industry. Only drums for soaking and liming RHS, i.e. the initial step of processing RHS to wet blue, are available on the local market. Other machinery needed for subsequent production steps is procured either locally from tanneries

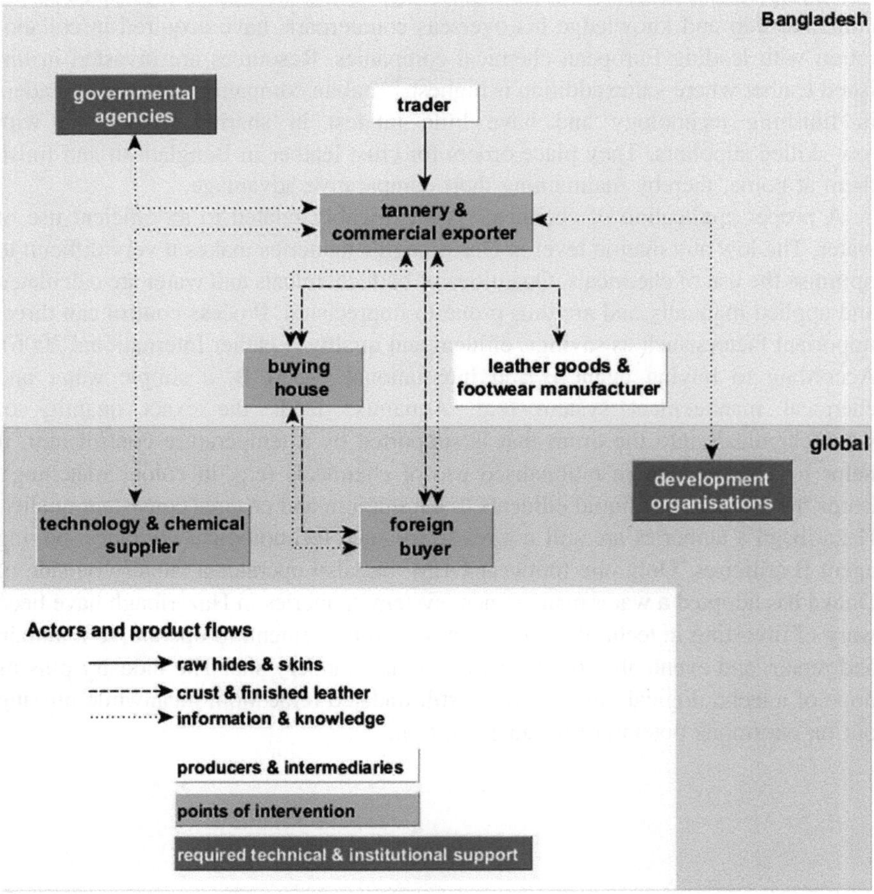

Fig. 5.14 Suggested points of intervention in the supply and use of machinery. *Source* Own illustration

that have shut down and sold on their remaining means of production, or it has to be imported via brokers. Up to now, if tanneries sought to renew their stock, most of them fell back on reconditioned or second-hand quality to cut costs.

Specific machinery that increases precision in trading wet blue is lacking, so that inaccurate measurement practices that already set in at the RHS-stage continue:

> In a tannery you can't measure accurately. Wet blue sometimes needs trimming, and so the area then sometimes shrinks; sometimes [it turns out; A. N.] bigger, [...]; we have no machines to measure the wet blue. So we measure the crust, and wet blue is measured by hand. (Buying agent A, English)

No tannery in Hazaribagh is able to determine with precision the size/area of stocked wet blue, which would, however, be useful when grouping batches to the specifications of incoming orders. Most of the smaller tanneries produce wet blue on a job work basis or supply tanneries of a higher competence level. Since 1990, an export embargo on wet blue has made investments in area-measurement machinery unattractive. Moreover, frequent power cuts outweigh potential financial and logistical advantages and induce high costs for repair and maintenance instead, explains one international consultant.

In Hazaribagh only a few large and medium-sized tanneries operate a digital measuring machine that is used for calculating the area of crust and finished leather. Leather processors of a lower competence level are forced to rent these machines from their more powerful rivals on their way to the export market, thereby reinforcing power asymmetries immanent to the chain. The tanneries widely agree with buying agent A who believes that inaccuracies from measuring the leather surface at the raw and wet blue stage can be balanced out in trade relations. He assures that foreign buyers are aware of the limited technological capabilities of their suppliers and agree to an error margin of 10 % in terms of size (and colour) at the crust stage. Inaccuracies that eventually can be adjusted are idiosyncratic for processes prior and during production. The introduction of technology in area-measurement can reduce the complexity in the transactions between wet blue buyers (medium-sized/large tanneries; commercial leather exporters) and sellers (very small and small tanneries), making calculation less reliant on non-tangible assets such as experience. While awareness would have to be raised to promote the effectiveness of such technology, it can be assumed that tanneries prefer to carry on with this practice thanks to the low error margin. Other machinery is considered more valuable and thus prioritised. Within the tanning industry the use and availability of machinery varies strongly.

Very small and small tanneries either capitalise from factory closures or source low quality machinery mostly from India (e.g. fleshing machine, split machine). However, they are unable to renew their technological equipment on a regular basis. Like other tanneries of his size, tanner K suffers from the deplorable state of his machinery:

> [...] the problem is that spare parts are not available. There are some two or four sellers who sell the parts. These parts are not always available. The machines I have are too old; that is why I face problems almost every day. (Tanner K, Bengali)

Tanner K's machinery—most of it purchased more than 20 years ago—is now outdated and in a bad state. Like him, other tanners complain about the low operationality and high costs for repair and maintenance, compromising leather quality and lead time:

> […] there are wrinkles; it [i.e. the hides; A. N.] gets stuck […]. If we had new machinery, this would not happen. There is always a huge spot in the middle because of the split machine. If it were new, it wouldn't be like that. (Tanner G, Bengali)

Small and very small tanneries such as G's with interrupted export activity and difficulties with funding from banks suffer most from machine-related quality problems. As they are very often subcontracted by tanneries of a higher competence level or mediated by buying houses, they have few means to oppose buyers downgrading their leather. Wrinkles, for instance, are very often a result of malfunctioning machinery the causes of which and how to repair these most tanneries are unaware of, says international consultant A. This case shows that the impact on quality can be substantial, particularly for tanneries producing only wet blue.

The medium-sized tanneries interviewed set up operations in the 1980s with what was then new machinery. Investment in machinery stock since then has been low; hardly any equipment has been added to and almost nothing renewed. Hence, the financial burden for repair and maintenance is high, as spare material has to be imported or tanneries need to use the technical services of either in-house or external mechanics:

> We have no spare or excess materials, accessories. That's why we have to do repair and maintenance work, which costs us more than any other expenses. (Tannery N, English)

Financially solvent medium-sized competitors (e.g. tannery O) seek to maintain their technological level by investing in reconditioned machinery. In recent years, these tanneries have preferred the low-cost reconditioned and second-hand devices from China and Taiwan to the more expensive European quality.

Large tanneries are reportedly more capable of investing in (new and better quality) productive gear, though I was not provided with specifics on that issue. The international expert A assures that their working environment is generally better organised than that of their smaller rivals, though all lack a separate and well-established workshop where spare parts and tools are stored and classified according to their use.[41]

> YZ stands out to me as a more dedicated company than the rest. They have a workshop, not badly equipped, but with problems of inaccuracy, [and; A. N.] not given enough resources […]. (International consultant A, English)

YZ is considered to be technologically ahead its large rivals and determined to improve its own standards. A proper workshop and machinery setup is essential for effective repair and maintenance, particularly in peak season when production

[41] This could not be verified for tannery Q since we were not allowed to visit the entire of the tannery.

capacity is overstretched and machines run around the clock for months. Despite decent organisation of their workplace, YZ still lacks equipment and, more importantly, a certain level of knowledge that is necessary for an accurate handling of machinery. It is still struggling to make effective use of its technological advantage. So it is the only tannery in Hazaribagh that is able, though with difficulties, to split the hides after liming into two (or more) layers to maximise their valorisation (GME et al. 2006). As all other tanneries irrespective of the firm size split their hides after tanning, the tanning formulae are adjusted to thick hides that are more time consuming to process and therefore produce inconsistent quality. YZ's biggest disadvantage is, as he is completely alone with this technological knowledge, he cannot engage in any exchange with competitors, says consultant B.

Both experts describe the technical and mechanical skills of Hazaribagh's tanneries as poor. Improper use, which was confirmed in interviews with tanneries of all sizes, eventually impinges on operability and reduces the machine's lifetime:

> A spraying machine obviously should filter the exhaust air. From what I saw here, the exhaust air filtration system was turned off first because maintenance and repair is very costly and the employees are not capable of carrying it out. So they turned it off and still blow the overspray into the filtration. (International consultant B, German)

The spraying machine is part of the equipment for finishing and therefore only available at large tanneries or at some medium-sized tanneries providing their plants for job work. Having such technology at their disposal does not qualify them for proper use of it. New machinery, which is already a challenge in itself, is also not sufficient to generate knowledge. Awareness and trainings are needed to gain practical knowledge about how to correctly use and maintain machines. In peak season the lack of knowledge about repair and maintenance hits the tanneries most, which struggle with constant breakdowns. Being used to follow instructions, operators and technicians have difficulties building up practical knowledge:

> Because as a leather technologist you first tell someone to tell the operator what you want from him and then the operator does it. But a feeling for the material cannot be communicated like this. And knowledge cannot be translated into practice; this means they know what they have to do, but they don't know why and they don't know how everything is related to each other and therefore cannot take innovative steps […]. (International consultant B, German)

Rigid social hierarchies in a paternalistic society accompanied by a lack of vocational institutes (see Sect. 4.3) for leather workers translate into an ineffectively operated production process, discouraging innovations, and poor skills development. Knowledge transfer seems to be difficult even in in-house operations and contributes to worsening the tanneries' competence level, minimising their opportunities to reposition within the global leather value chain. Insufficient equipment and an inadequate use of technology impinge on product quality and thus value addition. Leather technologists criticise that the tannery owner's or manager's negligence very often leads to inefficiencies in the use of machinery.

Results from workshops on preventive machine maintenance operated by the two UNIDO consultants (A + B) within the larger development project Re-Tie Bangladesh (see Section "Upgrading Initiatives to Improve Production Processes") show that awareness has to be raised among managers in order to increase efficiencies and put new ideas into practice. Participation in those workshops was nil among managers and turned out to be lower than expected among leather technologists. Keeping the results apart from technical issues and organisational dysfunctions within a larger perspective, the workshops confirmed two things:

First, the language barrier still hampers an adequate knowledge transfer. Upgrading projects would have to direct more resources into effective training methods provided in both languages, Bengali and English. Codified information (e.g. manuals) on the right use of modern machinery is useless if it is in English or if the workers are illiterate. Both consultants advocate more practical trainings. Technicians could be multipliers for workers if persistent socio-cultural idiosyncrasies did not bar an effective knowledge transfer to 'subordinate workers' (see above).

Second, the tannery owners and managers are extremely conservative in adopting knowledge and suggestions from actors outside the industry. In interviews they mostly expressed their concern to find buyers, while they were barely aware of the prerequisites for attracting those. A major setback for the UNIDO consultancy was that it proved very difficult to convince managers of the economic benefits of improving working procedures and of upgrading measures that touch base with both productive and management activities.

In addition to the widespread lack of awareness and skills, investment behaviour may have contributed to the low technology level. In the light of the relocation debate that has been ongoing for decades planning activities for the new tannery site in Hemayetpur/Savar seem to have made the tanneries reluctant to invest in their means of production in Hazaribagh. They are worried that investments will fail to amortise while production is in Hazaribagh or that they might be damaged during transportation to the new site 25 km away. Irrespective of size, all tanners interviewed maintained that they were committed to modernising their technological assets for their new factories. National and international experts, however, consider very small and small tanneries with outdated machinery financially unable to relocate.

It has been shown that the chronic undersupply of technology and the improper use, maintenance and repair of existing machinery are costly and affect product quality. Financial constraints are a major barrier to investment and can only be overcome in collaboration with the banking sector. For sustained competitiveness, it is vital to raise awareness and teach practical know-how.

Constraints to and Opportunities for Increasing Capabilities in the Production Process

Despite defects resulting from different stages of the supply chain, Hazaribagh's tanneries are considered to produce "decent quality" (international consultant B). There is, however, enormous scope for increasing efficiencies in the production process and improving the quality of the final product as presented in Fig. 5.15. The following chapter presents constraints to and opportunities for improving tanning operations that are essential for all classes of leather processors. Interventions should include buying houses that on behalf of foreign buyers often monitor and thus interfere in the production process. Ideally, the industry exchanges knowledge with educational facilities (e.g. BCLT), research institutes and development organisations committed to increasing the performance in tanning. Finishing capabilities that are pivotal for more value addition will be discussed within product upgrading (see Section "Constraints to and Opportunities for Increasing Finishing Capabilities").

The tanneries interviewed have difficulties identifying and resolving problems during the production process. Internal quality management is far from meeting

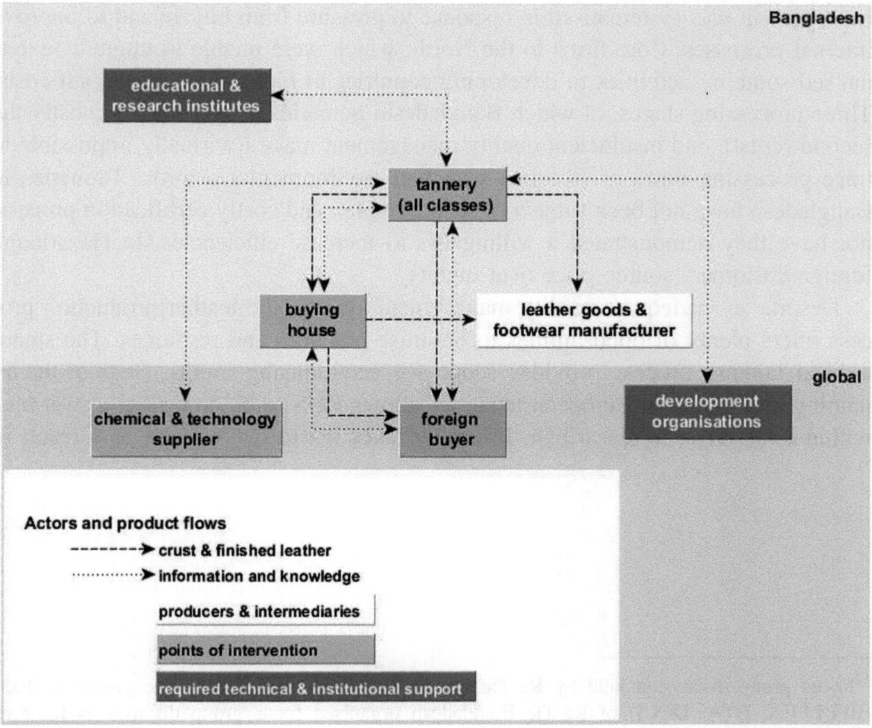

Fig. 5.15 Suggested points of intervention in leather processing. *Source* Own illustration

international standards, consultant B explained. Leather technologists criticise insufficient automation and the fact that tannery owners stipulate few requirements for monitoring the production process adequately.[42] To ensure quality the leather is usually inspected after the major production steps (wet blue, crust, finished). Physical tests are conducted only for the final product, that is, crust or finished leather. This leads to hides and skins being further processed, although quality problems resulting from, for instance, machine failure or wrong application of chemical formulae could have been detected much earlier. Effective process control that relies on technology to oversee critical operations is not in place in any of the interviewed tanneries. Only large and to a lesser extent medium-sized tanneries would be financially capable of realising investments but defer these, for instance, to input (chemicals) and resource-saving (water, energy) technology due to the unpredictable costs they expect from the relocation to the new tannery site (see Sect. 5.2.4.6). In mediated buyer-supplier relationships, buying houses monitor the production process and ensure quality by giving technical instructions (e.g. chemical formula, dying operation).

By contrast, European tanneries gradually implemented the ISO 9001 quality management system to meet statutory, regulatory and the customers' standards (e.g. production batches numbered consecutively; use of chemicals; variations in production; change of suppliers). Hesselberg and Knutsen (2002) argue that quality management was systematised in response to pressure from buyers and to improve internal processes. Core firms in the North, which were unable to upgrade, externalised sourcing activities to developing countries to hide pollution and cut costs. Three processing stages, of which Bangladeshi tanneries tend to supply mostly the second (crust), and insufficient quality management make it virtually impossible to trace processing flaws or factories with bad environmental records. Tanneries in Bangladesh have not been subject to such complex and costly certification process, nor have they demonstrated a willingness to increase efficiencies. In Hazaribagh foreign customers source price over quality.

Despite an inadequate quality management system, the leather production process offers plenty of opportunities to optimise practices and resources. The standardised tanning process provides scope for economising inputs. State-of-the-art tanning knowledge in European tanneries allows RHS to be processed to wet blue within three days; in Hazaribgh, it usually takes ten to twelve days as a result of

[42]Focus group discussion held by Re-Tie Bangladesh on April 6, 2011: The project partners (BFLLFEA, BTA, DCCI) of Re-Tie Bangladesh organised focus group discussions for their members, to which leather technologists were invited to participate in on a regular basis (monthly). The objective was to identify the main challenges in supply chain activities (marketing, finances, production process, human resources) and to compile potential solutions to overcome those.

frequent power cuts, cumbersome chemical formulae, low automation and an insufficiently organised production process as reported by tanners and international consultant B.[43] According to the latter, three major drawbacks curb the tanneries' performance:

Firstly, flat belt drives in soaking, liming and dying drums are outdated and need more time (and more water) to make tanning agents diffuse and penetrate proteins. Efficient drive technology with speed control, heating system and automation, among others, could save time, money and resources and could increase quality.

Secondly, with the exception of one tannery, all leather processors in Hazaribagh are unable to split the hides after liming into two (or more) layers. Besides maximising valorisation, splitting serves to tan thinner hides. This favours short floats and a maximum fixation of tanning agents, i.e. if the hides are split at the right moment, chemicals and water can be used more efficiently.

Thirdly, chemical processes such as penetrating the proteins with tanning agents require precise temperature control (e.g. through a water management system such as Aquamix) which Hazaribagh's tanneries cannot provide. Instead, this process relies on experience and implicit knowledge.

Tied up with the lack of temperature control is the lack of incentives to economise the use of water, which is a central resource in tanning operations. In Hazaribagh water resource management was barely organised until 2012 when UNIDO consultants helped install water meters in some tanneries, which quickly became defective. In general, medium-sized and large tanneries have their own well to pump water at their convenience, whereas almost every very small and some small tanneries interviewed were registered with the local water supplier (DWASA) and had relatively higher expenses than their competitors'. This shows that competitive conditions among the tanneries are highly unequal and reinforce power asymmetries and price competitiveness. As water for industrial use in general is cheap and liquid effluents remain untreated, tanneries add water by eye, caring little about an efficient use. International consultant B compares the water consumption of a large tannery in Hazaribagh (80–100 m^3) per ton of raw material with that of a medium-sized German tannery *before* water saving modes of operation lowered water consumption to 15–20 m^3. This shows that there is huge potential to reduce quantities through process optimisation

Water quality also varies considerably. Consultant A blames the hard and pollutant groundwater quality, which in principle is not suitable for tanning, to the lack of a water treatment plant in Hazaribagh. The new tannery site is designed to provide treatment facilities for the water to become soft enough to clean the hides and absorb the tanning chemicals effectively. Aside from rational dosage and maximum fixation of tanning agents, all tanneries lack a water management system that ensures consistent quality in different production batches (see Section

[43]According to consultant B, a regular European tannery needs two days to process wet blue to crust and another three days to finish the leather. In Hazaribagh the entire production process can take between 20 and 25 days.

"Increasing the Capabilities in the Use of Chemicals"). The less consistent quality is, the more leverage customers have to renegotiate in their favour, forcing tanneries to accept losses.

The current disproportionate use of both water and chemicals is related to lacking financial incentives as well as a profound lack of technical and practical knowledge among technical personnel. To achieve a more effective penetration of hides and skins by chromium tanning agents, it was common sense in all tanneries to add 8 % chromium, says leather technologist A. However, if temperature, pH-value and osmotic pressure were adjusted, 6 % input would suffice, assures consultant B. Then costs could be minimised, while the physical quality could be maintained.

The inefficient use of chromium has resulted in an informal practice among leather processors: the effluents are so rich in chromium that the load is reused for tanning low-graded leather. Smaller tanneries regularly source effluents from bigger tanneries to process low-quality hides or split leather, which are said to cater to the domestic market (see Photos 6 and 7).

One tanner (G) was seen to reuse chromium effluents to tan split leather destined for the Chinese market. As the precise (chemical) content is unclear, reusing chemicals is obstructive to producing consistent quality batches. Although two tanneries in Hazaribagh were granted chromium recovery plants from prior upgrading projects, neither of them is capable of operating it, criticises consultant B. The tannery owners are alleged to have shut them down on profitability grounds, which may even hold true if such machines are neither used nor maintained adequately; moreover, spare material is often costly to import. Consultant B also points to the few incentives for tanners to operate and maintain such machines as neither sewage fees nor surcharges have to be paid, while chromium is available at a low cost. Additionally, at least one—usually influential—member of staff earns a great deal of money from selling on chromium-rich wastewater and therefore is interested in keeping things as they are.

To put it briefly, the informal practice of reusing tanning effluents is detrimental to the environment and the quality of products that are mostly destined for the less demanding domestic market. As benefits accrue for both buying smaller tanneries

Photos 6/7 Workers collecting effluents from large tannery for reuse. *Source* Own photos

and selling larger tanneries, the latter see little need to adopt and invest in clean technologies.

Results of waste-water load tests in a large tannery carried out by international consultant B showed an average load of 5 g chromium per litre of water as compared to 2 g chromium per litre of water from a German tannery, with the difference being that the latter treats its effluents. The high chromium load is down to an inefficient use of chemicals and favours informal practices (see above).

Chromium, a naturally occurring mineral, exists "in several chemical forms and valence states in the environment" (EPA 1998, p. 26). According to the international experts interviewed (A, B) and literature referring to epidemiological studies (e.g. EPA 1998; Umweltbundesamt 2003, p. 9), trivalent chromium has not yet been proven to harm human health and can be used for tanning; only hexavalent chromium is classified as a human carcinogen (Zuther and Marschner n.d., p. 5). If discharged untreated into rivers trivalent chromium is toxic to aquatic life, adds consultant B. With 80–90 % of all leathers being tanned by chromium, it is still the most common and most efficient tanning agent available (e.g. GME et al. 2006; Reich 2009; international consultants A/B).[44] Waste management is critical to process upgrading and sustained competitiveness.

After tanning, the intermediate wet blue leather is kept in stock. Time constraints and the large concentration of RHS in the peak season (Eid-ul-Azha) force tanneries to process large quantities of wet blue for subsequent stockpiling. This involves logistical challenges particularly for very small and small tanneries that lack storage space. The tanneries can only proceed with crust and finished leather production once the customers place orders and define product specifications (e.g. grade, thickness, surface area, colour, type of finishing). Lower graded wet blue remains stocked for months and sometimes even for years, thereby deteriorating the quality significantly, explains consultant B. Bigger tanneries often have more permanent customers and are able to process some wet blue batches to crust leather. At this stage they are able to examine the leather for natural features and damages (e.g. insect bites, scars) to 100 %, says consultant B.

This section has pointed to technological and logistical challenges Hazaribagh's tanneries are exposed to. The constraints outlined here do not claim to be exhaustive but point to potential points of intervention along the production process.

---

[44]It is not entirely resolved which tanning method results in a better life cycle assessment. Only 5.5–6 % of (trivalent) chromium suffices to produce leather as opposed to the high input (25 %) of vegetable tanning agents, which are gained from tropical wood and are more complex to treat (Silvateam 2013).

Upgrading Initiatives to Improve Production Processes

The tanneries interviewed have not been found to pursue a strategy to improve their competitiveness. Being largely unaware of individual and structural shortcomings, they stick to business as usual.

By the time of this study, only Re-Tie Bangladesh ("Reduction of Environmental Threats and Increase of Exportability of Bangladeshi Leather Products"), an international development project, was in place to improve production processes and impart knowledge about the competent use of machinery. In the past, national (e.g. SEHD 1998) and international organisations (e.g. GTZ 2006; UNIDO in the 1990s) highlighted the need for environmental improvements, but never engaged over a longer period as tanners were held "very traditional" and "inconvincible" (interviews with SEHD and GTZ).

The primary objective of Re-Tie Bangladesh was to increase the exportability of leather products by making production processes cleaner and more efficient. The project operated by Sequa gGmbH and its partner organisations[45] received funding from the European Commission during 2009 and 2013.

As depicted above, the initial situation was miserable: Old and disused machines, a lack of spare parts, disorganised workshops, and sometimes even good machines that fail to survive only a few repair processes (UNIDO 2012). Re-Tie's upgrading activities aimed to raise awareness about environmental sustainability and eliminate drawbacks from inadequate machinery handling. Workshops to demonstrate the relation between machinery and quality were carried out by UNIDO consultants and were well received among the technicians. Tannery owners and managers known to be cautious to introduce innovations allowed their technical personnel to attend these events without getting personally involved. Communication and dissemination of information at this level proved challenging, says the head of Re-Tie Bangladesh. Equipment (e.g. solar heating system, protective gear) was provided along with technical assistance to empower technicians and operators to help themselves. The project consultants pursued a self-help approach, encouraging the technologists to learn from failure. Several steps were initiated to achieve improvements in introducing cleaner technologies and using energy more efficiently in tanneries of all sizes. Technologically more challenging measures were confined to tanneries that were held capable of implementing and continuing them; this procedure made it difficult for smaller tanneries to participate in upgrading activities.[46]

First, the tanneries received technical assistance in managing resources (water, chemicals) efficiently. Particular emphasis was placed on pollution prevention and

[45]Partners were United Nations Industrial Development Organization (UNIDO), bfz gGmbH, Dhaka Chamber of Commerce and Industry (DCCI) and Bangladesh Finished Leather, Leathergoods and Footwear Exporters' Association (BFLLFEA). Bangladesh Tanners Association (BTA) was an associate partner.

[46]Very small and small tanneries benefited mostly from improvements in Occupational Health and Safety (OHS).

pollution load, adjusting the industry's liquid waste management to the conditions of the new tannery site (e.g. CETP). UNIDO's (2012) technical report identified various achievements in the adoption of new techniques:

- Manuals and interactive tools on the treatment of tannery effluents were provided to prepare tanners for liquid waste management at the new tannery site.
- Ten national experts and at least 120 technicians received guides, demonstration videos, solid waste management preparations and practical demonstrations, through which reductions were achieved in water consumption (30 %), in chromium load in wastewater (15 %) and in chemical oxygen demand (COD) in wastewater (15 %; UNIDO 2012).
- Water meters were provided by UNIDO but stopped functioning soon after installation due to impurities (e.g. sand, dust).
- The tanneries improved process parameters such as volume of the float, control of pH, duration of drumming, temperature of float, among others, to increase the uptake of chromium from 50–60 % to over 85 % (UNIDO 2012). With decreasing batch-to-batch variation in chromium content, a more consistent and higher quality of wet blue leather was produced. This gives huge scope for future process improvements by modern technology at the new tannery site. High chromium exhaustion which, according to UNIDO, is practiced by 30–35 tanneries in Hazaribagh has reduced chromium consumption by 71 % and chromium content in wastewater by 38 %.
- UNIDO (2012) assures that the entire tanning industry in Hazaribagh has benefited from water-saving modes of operation. Although less than 50 % of the tanneries participated, water consumption was reduced by 21 %.[47]
- One large tannery was granted a hair-saving machine, decreasing its COD by 40–60 %. This technology is expected to become a valuable asset in the modernisation of the tanning industry in Hemayetpur/Savar.
- 30 tanneries have adopted a modified liming process that needs less sodium sulphide (25 %) and improves the quality of the limed pelt. For unknown reasons, no progress has been made in reducing water consumption in de-liming.

In a second step, national experts and technicians were trained in energy consumption management, achieving significant reductions (30 %) in selected factories (e.g. gas, CO_2).

- Solar water heating systems were introduced in a few tanneries to make use of sustainable solar energy for tanning. After initial technical problems, other tanneries came forward to set up a similar technology.
- Energy audits conducted by national and international experts resulted in guidelines for improving the power factor, protecting electrical motors from overheating and overloads, and providing training on corresponding issues.

[47]Some tanneries did not have adequate infrastructure at their disposal to implement water-saving technologies (see Footnote 46).

National experts managed to convince 18 tanneries to invest in the necessary infrastructure. Despite significant improvement, UNIDO points to the limited effect technical assistance has on the dilapidated infrastructure (e.g. haphazard electricity lines; inadequate electrical equipment) in Hazaribagh.

In sum, UNIDO's consultancy within the development project Re-Tie Bangladesh has had a positive impact on technicians, national experts and the participating tanneries in increasing efficiencies in tanning operations. The commoditisation of water, better know-how and modern technology proved to be useful instruments in reducing the consumption of water, chemicals (e.g. chromium) and COD in wastewater. Although according to UNIDO, "all numerical targets were achieved" (2012, p. 8), the scale and scope are still insufficient to induce a thrust towards internal development of the tanning industry. Development projects are highly recommended to regularly inspect production sites and verify the effectiveness of the upgrading measures implemented, otherwise sustained improvement is unlikely to occur.

Upgrading by Introducing Process Standards and Compliance Initiatives

The myriad of challenges Hazaribagh's tanning industry faces in environmental and economic terms calls for comprehensive upgrading strategies. Re-Tie Bangladesh's main objective was to improve the economic and ecologic performance of tanneries producing leather for the world market. Specifically, the project aimed to reduce waste and pollution, improve Occupational Health and Safety, Corporate Social Responsibility (CSR) and ensure compliance with other international standards (see Switch-Asia 2013).

Very early on, the project partners learned about the limitations in the tanning industry in terms of compliance with international social and environmental standards. UNIDO's technical report (2012) has criticised the lack of "adequate pollution control measures, wastewater treatment and rather poor working conditions" (UNIDO 2012), which put the competitiveness of the entire tanning industry at risk. The time period the project operated within (2009–2013) proved way too short to solve environmental and social concerns on that scale.

In addition to financial and technical assistance in implementing sustainable cleaner production, Re-Tie Bangladesh focused on skills development. Trainings and practical workshops were organised for managers, leather technologists and workers to raise awareness about environmental sustainability. Only tanneries with adequate financial and management capabilities were considered eligible to adopt clean technology, so that the project's target group (SMEs) could not fully benefit. The original primary objective of providing employment and income opportunities to environmentally sustainable SMEs failed:

> It is going to be difficult for small and medium-sized tanneries which cannot keep pace with the bigger ones and do not have the capacity to adapt to this change. (Head of Re-Tie Bangladesh, German)

Small and, to some extent, partly also medium-sized tanneries lack opportunities to obtain funding from banks for investing in technology and trained personnel. Development projects such as Re-Tie Bangladesh need quick and positive results that only large factories are generally able to provide. It has to be questioned to what extent project objectives are geared towards the reality of local SMEs.

By the end of the project period, the introduction of environmental standards was still an unresolved issue. The CETP, a prerequisite for any international environmental certification scheme, had not been constructed yet. The national government and the tannery associations have not yet agreed on a roadmap for the relocation. Meanwhile, the tanneries in Hazaribagh keep operating, ignoring half-hearted public and buyer pressure:

> [...] we are getting many, many warnings from buyers that 'you should immediately [...] follow the rich [countries; A. N.]', you know the German law, on the website they provide a book like this, 'this is the regulation of leather [products; A. N.], you must follow the rich [countries; A. N.].' We are trying, but it is the road we cannot follow. [...] many German customers push us to follow the rich [countries; A. N.] immediately. We follow the rich [countries; A. N.] in terms of chemicals; we cannot follow in terms of the environment of the area. (Tanner Q, English)

Large tanneries such as Q with customers in different markets are admonished to improve their environment. The entire tanning industry has ignored its responsibility for this environmental disaster, though problems are largely institutional. The MoU between the tannery associations and the government offsets the enforcement of environmental regulations (see Sect. 5.2.4.6). At the present time, Hazaribagh is environmentally too degraded to go for compliance and set up effluent treatment plants. Moreover, many tanneries have never built up financial reserves to support individual or joint solutions. Only outside Dhaka do a few leather footwear manufacturers operate an individual effluent treatment plant, demonstrating that environmental compliance within certain limits is possible.[48] According to experts (A, B) and own observations, large tanneries barely invest in their production facilities; they are already planning for the new site. Consultant B has observed that wages are being squeezed to keep returns on sales between 10 and 20 %, while European (and smaller Bangladeshi) tanneries get by with 3–5 %. It pays off to be cheap.

Small and medium-sized tanneries seem to be exposed to less pressure from their customers. Tanner H who maintains two long-term business relationships to traders in China and Korea describes his buyers' interests in Hazaribagh:

---

[48] Outside the export processing zones (EPZ) only one global and one large local leather footwear manufacturer have established their own effluent treatment plant, though the latter does not have a beamhouse section. Both factories take pride in their efforts to achieve environmental compliance—and remain silent about the fact that they keep sourcing wet blue from rented tanneries in Hazaribagh.

> Actually, when they come there, they always count their profit, most of the buyers count their profit; how can they make profit in their country. They buy leather from us, they make goods, they make materials, [and; A. N.] they make shoes, bags. So how can they make profit? Actually […] very few buyers ask us about the environment. (Tanner H, English)

Low production costs attract buyers from low-end markets. Smaller customers in markets with lower consumer awareness (e.g. China) seem less concerned about labour conditions and environmental compliance than those from more regulated markets (e.g. U.S., EU). Hence, low pressure from foreign customers and financial constraints seem to have contributed towards smothering the tanneries' willingness to change. Very few have been as straightforward as this chief leather technologist at a large renowned tannery:

> We are screwing the environment! (Leather technologist B, English)

As long as current business practices harm both the environment and public (and the workers') health, social standards such as the Business Social Compliance Initiative (BSCI) or SA 8,000 cannot be implemented either (Social Accountability International 2013; BSCI 2014). Acknowledging this limitation, Re-Tie Bangladesh focused on explaining certification schemes and benefits. However, the head of the project is aware that only very few large tanneries will qualify to join international standards in the distant future. He argues that compliance improves the corporate reputation and image of the location, which ultimately affects the industry's competitiveness in a positive way. Negative publicity in turn can seriously impact on business. The Human Rights Watch Report (2012) about the devastating environmental and labour conditions in Hazaribagh was published shortly before an important leather fair in Bologna and thereby managed to exert high pressure on the tanning industry. Trade fair participations and orders from foreign customers were cancelled, as tanners and consultants confirmed. Hazaribagh's negative image was communicated to a large audience. Some large tanneries (at least officially) pretend to have understood that Hazaribagh is detrimental to their business and that relocation is pivotal to the industry's future. Smaller and medium-sized tanneries do not yet seem to realise the link between non-compliance and order inflow. As their business transactions are usually mediated by buying houses, they are more detached from their customers' needs and expectations.

Awareness of social compliance among both tannery owners and workers was found to be extremely low (UNIDO 2012). Re-Tie Bangladesh trained national experts as multipliers in OHS and CSR for the tanneries. Workshops and presentations on housekeeping and hazardous production conditions were organised; information on safety measures was disseminated. Re-Tie installed lighting systems to enhance illumination, secured electricity connections and machinery (e.g. drums), and provided protective gear to the workers (e.g. gloves, aprons, boots). The tanners interviewed appreciated such measures, though visits to production sites confirmed that, for instance, protective gear was very often not regularly replaced by the employers, nor was it frequently used by the workers as a force of habit. Better practices that have no immediate financial benefit and are not reflected in the final product have not become routinized yet. In informal talks, tannery owners often ignore and belittle the impact of such measures on the environment and their workers' health.

With the aim of raising awareness of environmental and social compliance in other industries and other countries, Re-Tie Bangladesh organised study tours for a selected group of tanners within Dhaka and abroad. The Leather Working Group was visited in Brussels to show tanners how to bring together both environmental and social compliance in one international standard (see Leather Working Group 2013). However, even the largest and technologically more advanced tanneries are far away from being certified, says the head of Re-Tie Bangladesh.

Visits to tanning industries of neighbouring countries such as Kanpur in India may be useful to draw on good practices of public-private partnerships (PPP). It is, however, important to heed their failures.[49] At BSCI's office in Dhaka the tanners learned more about the activities this initiative is carrying out in other export-oriented industries (e.g. garment) and the opportunities that social compliance brings about for producers. In 2010, leather technologists were invited to participate in a workshop on clean production processes in Germany. Some of the participants were keen to introduce those ideas into their production processes, but ultimately they very often ended up frustrated by their superior's reluctance to revisit established practices. The fear of change and innovation is widespread in Hazaribagh.

Re-Tie Bangladesh initiated several steps towards more compliance, but ultimately the tanning industry is far away from adhering to international standards. Awareness that is critical to change remains low. Environmental compliance requires regulatory enforcement and corporate commitment. Only large tanneries are capable of investing in cleaner technologies and more compliant practices, but they lack the determination to do so, until the relocation becomes more concrete. A four-year, small-scale project that is limited in scope is not sufficient to initiate change.

Compliance with Regulations on Restricted Substances

While environmental and social compliance are widely ignored in Dhaka's tanning industry, international pressure has led to an initial regulation of the use of chemicals. Compliance does not increase the value-added but ensures access to regulated markets.

The legislations in two major consumer markets are the main drivers for an increasing control of restricted substances (e.g. azo dyes, formaldehyde, pentachlorophenol, chromium VI, lead, cadmium) in leather products:

- The EU's General Product Safety Directive 2001/95/EC seeks to guarantee that products are safe for consumption (European Commission—Enterprise And

[49] For India, see Dietsche (2011), and for Pakistan, Lund-Thomson (2009) in implementing pollution control in the tanning industry.

Industry 2013); in this regard, the REACH regulation (Regulation on Registration, Evaluation, Authorisation and Restriction of Chemicals) enacted in 2007 protects human health and the environment from unforeseeable risks from restricted substances (European Commission—Health and Consumers 2013).
- The United States Consumer Product Safety Commission aims to ensure safe consumer products (US CPSC 2013).

Based on several international laws, a list of restricted substances encompasses over 150 hazardous chemicals (SGS Bangladesh Limited 2011). In general, overseas customers specify clearly what chemicals are to be used:

> So they have this [internal; A. N.] standard and they used to say: Don't use this type of dyes and other indicators [i.e. substances] like this. […] We use this leather for hospitals and […] some orthopaedic purposes, so don't use this type of chemical here. (Tanner O, English)

The tanneries produce to the prescribed chemical formula and send a sample for testing, the results of which are to be submitted to the buyer before going into production. Product standards and regulations such as REACH are to guarantee that products are devoid of restricted substances and thus safe to be consumed in northern markets. Consumer confidence in the North goes hand in hand with the imposition of new production methods in the South. This complexity and additional costs raise the bar for some producers to join the value chain (e.g. Ponte and Gibbon 2005). The literature and experts view standards as a means of regulating access to northern consumer markets (e.g. Dannenberg 2012; Kaplinsky 2010; Nadvi 2008). Third-party controls make sure that importers have low transaction costs (Dietsche 2011, p. 37). The tanneries are expected to prove that their product is devoid of restricted substances. Independent testing, inspection and certification agencies such as SGS and Bureau Veritas run chemical and physical tests that are mostly demanded by medium-sized and large tanneries. The Bangladesh Standards and Testing Institution (BSTI) and a laboratory at BCLT provide the industry with public testing services at lower costs, which have been demanded by some of the small and very small tanneries interviewed. Some international buyers distrust testing institutions based in Bangladesh and order their suppliers to go abroad to ensure reliable results:

> But the foreign people do not accept our test because we [are said to; A. N.] give a good report instead of a bad report and a bad report instead of a good report. That might be the case. That's why I do it in India. (Tanner J, Bengali)

It has been reported that bigger tanneries send their samples to Singapore for testing. Standards and certificates codify transactions to the extent that "institutionalised trust" (Fox 1974; see also Shapiro 1987 on impersonal trust) among unknown business partners is ensured. Local testing facilities and even renowned international certification agencies based in Dhaka have yet to gain the buyers' trust. Some smaller tanneries report having used restricted substances imported from India (e.g. formaldehyde) until only a few years ago. Costs for testing samples are either shared or borne by the suppliers only. For small tanneries such as L's, this signifies that more effort has been given to clean production. Italian buyers ask him "to write that we do not use it [i.e. azo dyes; A. N.] and we have to submit a certificate too" (Tanner L, English), while his Chinese buyers never ask for any certification.[50] Requirements for the use of chemicals and restricted substances vary with the consumer market. On the domestic (Bangladesh) market no regulation or enforcement of the use of chemicals is in place that would demand tests or a scrupulous quality control. To cut costs, cheaper but harmful substances are supplied, which are still available on the market. As long as restricted substances are produced and marketed, tanneries will process these where appropriate. Tanner L points to the EU's hypocrisy in the trade and use of restricted substances:

> For example we do not use azo dye chemicals. Who makes these chemicals? They are made by the Europeans. Asia does not make these chemicals. But they [i.e. the Europeans] produce them and also restrict them. (Tanner L, Bengali)

Indian companies have also engaged in producing substances that are restricted to be processed and re-imported as intermediate or final products. This means that tanneries producing for both Asian and European markets need to comply with different requirements if they want to produce as cost-effectively as possible.

Despite REACH, the EU remains the most important market for Bangladeshi leather products. Asian buyers such as L's Chinese customer, that do not push for compliance, are likely to market their products locally. The chief technologist of tannery XX speaks openly about the discrepancy of product requirements and production costs:

> If you sell a shoe for US$5, how can you expect me to put US$20 of chemicals into it? (Leather technologist B, English)

Customers get what they are willing to pay for. High-quality, non-harmful chemicals are only supplied if demanded and they are suitably reflected in the production costs. Only one tanner commented on the assumed benefit of using non-restricted substances:

> If my products are disease free, my grade will be higher and then I will be more confident about my product. And if my product is disease-free I can bargain with buyers about the price and can upgrade my prices. (Tanner E, Bengali)

While others tend to see testing as a burden or vital for the export business, this tanner, despite only irregularly exporting (or because of it) understands the certificate as to adding value to his product, thus enabling him to tap new buyers. Compliance with REACH is a prerequisite for the EU market. Tanner E is unlikely to attain higher prices; by acquiring knowledge and processing skills he just makes sure he has access to a highly regulated market.

Interviews have shown that international regulatory pressure can be a driver to implement standards within the leather value chain. State-imposed standards for health and safety (see Kaplinsky 2010) such as REACH safeguard consumer interests; they also seem to be an effective instrument for introducing cleaner

[50]It remains unclear to what consumer market tanner L's customer sells his leather.

processes to producers, though market-specific unsustainable practices persist. Violations are registered by randomly checking samples, though negative lists do not exist yet.[51] By contrast, environmental and social standards address production conditions and require local governance which faces challenges in implementation. Transgressions cannot be traced in the final product, and are thus more easily ignored by final consumers. Global buyers welcome state-imposed improvements to procedures that rule out risks for consumers and do not infringe their core competences. Rising costs can be justified by mandatory regulation.

The chapter on process upgrading revealed a large number of structural weaknesses along the leather value chain and discussed a variety of interventions. In a more holistic approach, the complexity of systemic constraints was addressed by including procedures upstream from leather processing. Results have shown that processes prior, during and after the production of raw material have decisive effects on the leather quality. As for the tanning industry, process upgrading cannot rely on a set of globally regulated standard-intensive procedures. Many shortcomings have to be resolved within the local production network. It requires local governance to ensure animal health, to improve livestock management, to guarantee a consistent supply and quality of raw material, and to use more efficient technologies. Regulatory pressure from foreign markets has proved effective in introducing cleaner inputs; in the long run more attention has to be given to more comprehensive standards in terms of the environment and production conditions. By now, lacking awareness and the lack of debate of, for instance, culture-specific constraints stands in the way of better performance by the local production network. Short-term development projects give useful but insufficient impetus to initiate change; long-term commitment of public, private and civil society stakeholders is necessary to achieve sustained improvement.

5.2.4.3 Private Governance: Product Upgrading

By improving procedures it is not just efficiencies that are increased; there is more scope for developing higher value-added products if better skills and superior technology are used. To produce more complex leather articles, it is vital to improve productive and in particular finishing capabilities. Different actors (educational and research institutes; development organisations) would be required to impart finishing knowledge to the tanneries and stimulate innovation as the following chapter discusses (Fig. 5.16).

[51]The EU's Rapid Alert Warning System (RAPEX) lists dangerous non-food products found in test samples.

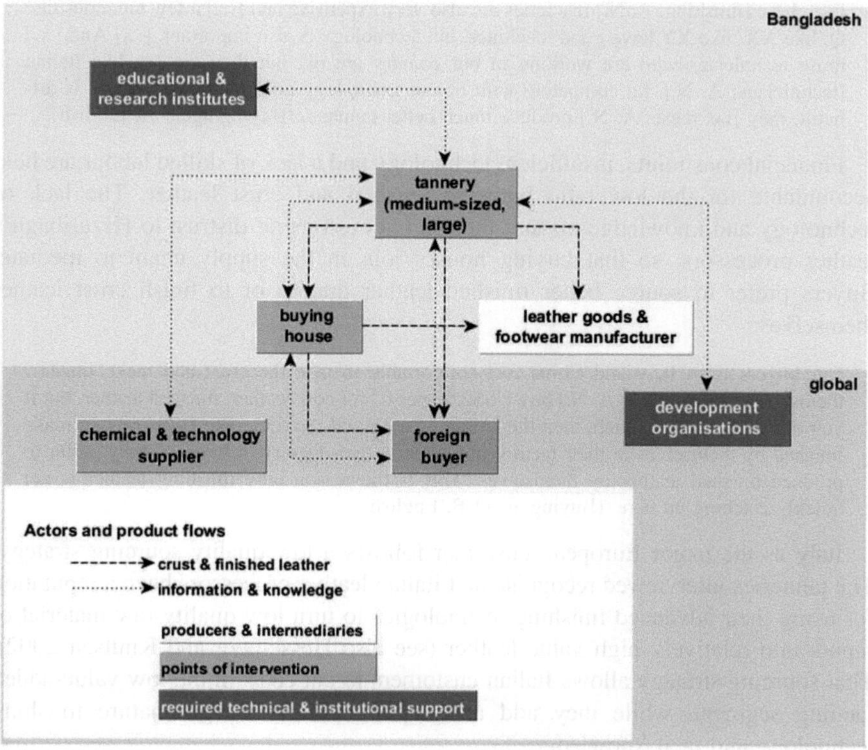

Fig. 5.16 Suggested points of intervention in increasing productive and finishing capabilities. *Source* Own illustration

Constraints to and Opportunities for Increasing Finishing Capabilities

Hazaribagh's tanning industry predominantly exports crust leather (70–80 %), although value addition is highest in finished leather. The majority of exported leathers forego a value addition of 9 % (GTZ 2006, p. 66).

With reference to this study's mapping data, 20 large and medium-sized tanneries indicated that they use in-house finishing technology.[52] Smaller tanneries and commercial leather exporters need to rent finishing machinery or outsource finishing operations to tanneries of a higher competence level.[53] Buying agent B refers to the lack of finishing capabilities in Bangladesh:

[52]The mapping survey excluded the number of finishing operations carried out in-house. Some tanneries only have a few finishing machines.

[53]Consultant B and buying agent B assure that only two tanneries that were not included in the qualitative part of this study manage to export more than 50 % finished leather.

> […] these [finishing; A. N.] machines are also very expensive and […] a few tanneries like Q, like XX, like XY have good machines, but technology is also important. […] And […] those technicians who are working in our country are ok, but they are not like Italian [technicians; A. N.]. So competing with Italian technology and Italian technicians is difficult; they [i.e. these; A. N.] produce much better tannage. (Buying agent A, English)

Financial constraints, insufficient technology and a lack of skilled labour are held accountable for the low ratio between finished and crust leather. The lack of technology and knowledge nurture the foreign customers' distrust to Hazaribagh's leather processors, so that buying houses join in the supply chain to mediate. Buyers prefer to source better finished leather quality or to finish crust leather themselves:

> Our buyers from Italy and China feel comfortable to take the crust and make finished themselves. So you [can; A. N.] buy US$2.50 per ft^2 for cow leather, finished leather, but if you don't like it very much, then the feeling is not good. So they take US$1.60 and make finished by themselves in their factory in China, in their factory in Italy. So they prefer to produce finished leather by themselves. This is the reason why finishing leather is not quickly catching up here. (Buying agent B, English)

Italy as the major European customer follows a low quality sourcing strategy. The tanneries interviewed recognise that Italian leather processors have a reputation for using their advanced finishing technologies to turn low quality raw material or inputs into relatively high value leather (see also Hesselberg and Knutsen 2002). That sourcing strategy allows Italian customers to cut costs in the low value-added tanning segment, while they add and capture value through mature finishing technology and tacit knowledge.

International consultants (A, B) see strong variations in the quality of finished leather, though they ascribe Hazaribagh's tanneries the potential to live up to international standards. Variations in quality have to do with the fact that there are few standardised procedures and with the manual production techniques, explains consultant B. Large tanneries have good finishing technology available that has allowed them to introduce a certain degree of standardisation. Medium-sized tanneries are struggling with producing consistent finishing quality as a result of poor and insufficient equipment, untrained operators and competitive market conditions that demand them to respond flexibly to market requirements. Smaller tanneries lack human resources, skilled labour and finances to experiment with costly raw material and chemicals to attain satisfactory results. If need be, finishing operations are subcontracted to tanneries of a higher competence level, limiting entrepreneurial innovation and creativity as tanner M indirectly confirms:

> We depend on XX, we use XX technicians, who also work on a commission basis; [they do; A. N.] job work on a per ft^2 basis and we pay them. They make the test, we tell them the recipe [i.e. the chemical formula; A. N.], the customer plant gave them [actually: us; A. N.] their recipe, 'you use this chemical, then you get good quality leather'. (Tanner M, English)

Tanner M runs a chemical import business, a buying house and from 2005 to 2013 also a small tannery for wet blue production to reduce his dependence from other tanneries.[54] Because of the dearth of technology and skilled personnel he outsources re-tanning, dyeing and finishing operations to medium-sized tanneries that provide machinery, chemicals and qualified technicians. There, leather is produced according to the foreign customer's specifications. Knowledge and information tanner M depends on remain concentrated within tanneries of a higher competence level such as XX, which are specialised in providing more value-added services and operations. Hence, power asymmetries are reinforced as smaller tanneries refuse to or cannot build up skills. The following provides a review of the reasons for the limited finishing quality in order to define potential points of intervention by drawing on expert opinions (A, B):

First, the lower the quality of raw material the more complex the finishing and the more skills are needed. Despite fine grain pattern, RHS from Bangladesh very often contain surface defects (e.g. growth marks, ticks) due to negligence in animal care (see Section "Increasing the Capabilities in the Supply of Raw Material"). Tanneries need to know how to process RHS to achieve consistent quality of crust leather. The structural lack of finishing knowledge and technology has to do with insufficiently developed institutional structures (e.g. education). In 1987, Bangladesh College of Leather Technology (BCLT) established a finishing department that was to provide training facilities mainly to smaller tanneries seeking to export crust and finished leather (Ahmed 2002, p. 32). The embargo on wet blue exports three years later was to boost value addition from crust and finished leather production. But concomitant measures for upgrading were lacking so many small and medium-sized tanneries ended up in subcontracting arrangements. The result is that innovation has been obstructed and dependence on tanneries of a higher competence level increased. By the time these interviews were taken, no tannery was using any of these facilities for product development:

> When I visited the Bangladesh Leather College I was stricken by the excellent technological and machinery equipment they have, which, however, appears to be unused. […] So it isn't used; it is maintained for the sake of showing only, but not to do research, […]. (Inter-national consultant B, German)

This expert ascribes the lack of research culture in Dhaka's leather industry to the sharp stratification of Bangladesh's society which prevents graduate personnel such as leather technologists from 'getting their hands dirty'. Bangladesh's hierarchical and rather impermeable society may contribute towards obstructing knowledge transfer and innovation. More importantly, BCLT provides the industry with graduates in leather technology, footwear technology and leather products, but has no cooperative ties with the tanneries at all. The industry seems totally detached from the educational institution in Hazaribagh. In turn, the tanners are accused of being utterly traditional and reluctant to change. Although graduate leather technologists enter the tanning industry (or in chemical companies) annually, there

[54] M's relatively high turnover (see Table 5.1) is very likely to be related to his activities as buying agent, which unfortunately could not be separated from each other. In 2013, financial problems forced M to give up his tannery and return to his core business as a commission agent.

seems to be little exchange of knowledge and needs between both institutions. Being chronically underfunded, it remains to be seen whether BCLT gains importance by joining Dhaka University's Faculty of Engineering and Technology in 2012. Following North (1990, pp. 79–80), it requires institutional incentives to invest in productive knowledge that have often been inadequate, for instance, by establishing vocational institutes for tannery operators.

Second, scope and application of finishing technology rests on a fruitful alliance of adequate machinery and the technical know-how about operation and preventive maintenance. Some large tanneries, for instance, are reported to use modern roller coating and spraying machines (with spray gun control, partly funded by Re-Tie Bangladesh), but are weak in maintaining these adequately. He considers it a major drawback that operators are trained on the job and if literate, usually lack English language skills to use instructions of machines originating from Europe. Instead, knowledge is highly concentrated with a few leather technologists who instruct operators on the correct use. Quality assurance rests upon tacit knowledge borne by selected employees (technicians). Education of operators and adequate codification in Bengali may reduce the tanneries' vulnerability to powerful employees tacit knowledge is tied to.

Third, the quality of finishing chemicals determines the final leather quality. The tanneries interviewed reported that they use finishing chemicals (e.g. binders, pigments, lubricants) of standard quality (mostly from Europe) along with the corresponding formulae provided by customers and chemical suppliers to warrant adequate leather quality. They follow the instructions of their chemical suppliers without learning a more critical and experimental use of chemicals. Techniques to apply those chemicals are partly dated (manual production techniques), putting consistent quality at stake. Consultant B, for instance gives account of large tanneries releasing finishing chemicals in easily inflammable organic solvents that are more time consuming and harmful to health. Some refer to high-boiling solvents of low volatility, which can be traced long after production. European tanneries in turn use almost exclusively aqueous systems that have a better solubility, are chemically cross-linked and thus more resistant. Table 5.5 summarises constraints, suggested interventions and the objectives for pursuing an improvement in finishing competences.

The challenges outlined above require technicians to be trained on the adequate use of machinery and chemicals. The overall goal is to increase the share of finished leather exports. It will be paramount for the tanneries' competitiveness to catch up on finishing capabilities and technology if dependency on expensive intermediaries is to be reduced and internal value addition increased.

Other Constraints to Product Upgrading

The final use of the leather (e.g. lining, shoe upper, leather bags, suitcases, upholstery, automotive leather) is determined by the type of raw material (cattle

Table 5.5 Constraints and potential interventions in the increase of finishing capabilities

	Constraints	Interventions	Objective
Finishing technology	Only few tanneries with finishing machinery	Define tanneries with ability to invest in finishing technology	Disseminate and extend finishing technology in Hazaribagh
		Devise loan programmes with financial institutions and development organisations	Make finishing technology accessible
	Outdated technology	Supplant and renew finishing machinery by means of loan programmes	Modernise finishing technology
	Lack of spare parts	Reduce tax on machinery and spare parts	Make spare parts available and repair processes less costly
Finishing capabilities	Lack of skilled labour	Improve education in BCLT; offer trainings for leather technologists and machine operators	Reduce the dependence on subcontracts and buying houses
		Provide instructions in Bengali	Reduce the dependence on chemical suppliers
		Provide trainings on use and maintenance of finishing machines	Reduce machine failure

Source Data from interviews conducted in 2011–2013. Own composition

hides, goat skins), quality parameters such as size and thickness, the type of tanning and finishing as well as the leather processor's capabilities.

Low levels of technology and know-how affect product upgrading. According to experts, the capabilities even among the few large tanneries differ widely. Tannery Q, for instance, produces approximately 80 % of leather for bags compared to other large rivals who mainly supply their customers with shoe upper leather. In the latter, leather consumption is less and value addition more, so that

> sometimes while you are selling two bags, you sell 20 pairs of shoes (Tanner Q, English).

Obviously, the grade of the leather determines value addition, too. But the development of new articles requires willingness and sufficient investment in R&D, both of which are lacking at tannery Q, says consultant B. As a public limited company Q, is bound to attain high sales on a regular basis and is thus less interested in taking a risk of diversifying the range of products and customers. Medium-sized tanneries export mostly crust leather, though of lower quality, for both leather goods and footwear manufacturers. Smaller tanneries usually process lower-grade raw material and export—in line with their tanning capabilities—low value-added leather for leather goods as well as upper and lining leather.[55]

At the moment, Hazaribagh's tanneries lack the skills to produce fully vegetable tanned leather, thereby missing value addition in product lines such as safety/trekking shoes, saddlery or suitcases. Those tanneries engaged in vegetable tanning combine mineral and vegetable agents. Vegetable tanning is more expensive, more complex in treatment and more time consuming than chrome tanning:

> So you can't make shoes in the same way. You have to use a much slower and less profitable process if you are making a vegetable shoe. (International consultant A, English)

Considering market requirements, the high costs for developing vegetable tanning skills, and sustainability[56] criteria, chrome tanning seems the most suitable choice for Hazaribagh's tanneries, though environmental issues need resolution.

Quality parameters such as size and thickness also determine the potential for product upgrading. Indigenous cattle hides are unsuitable for the more value-added automotive upholstery leather. Zebuine hides are thinner and smaller (20 ft^2 or approx. 1.9 m^2 on an average) than, for instance, European ones (40–50 ft^2 or approx. 3.72–4.65 m^2). Large imported hides[57] or hides from sacrificial animals that exceed 25 ft^2 are very often not suitable to the existing machines and have to be processed in halves, thereby losing area and potential for more value addition. However, more critical to value addition are technology and know-how; size can be made fit by better cutting skills and technologies, says expert B. Satisfactory finishing capabilities are essential to outweigh limitations in the availability of adequate raw material. But neither personnel nor technology, both indispensable for developing new articles and growing in new markets, are up to the international standard. Although the automotive leather market is highly lucrative—the demand is soaring and returns on sales are high—Hazaribagh's large tanneries do not qualify for entering such markets. They would be unable to fulfill the automobile industry's requirements of synchronising all supplies with the production given the high proneness for failure during leather processing, assures consultant B. And even if they were capable of ensuring quality, the automotive leather market is averse to take such risk, he adds. Before accepted as new suppliers, tanneries would have to invest in the market, offering substantial discounts to automobile producers; a challenge Hazaribagh's tanneries are not up for yet. Consequently, it requires not

---

[55]Unfortunately, precise indications about the final use were lacking in most of the interviews.

[56]Unsustainable cultivation practices—the mimosa tannin is gained from the bark of an acacia species that is cultivated in monocultures in tropical countries, whereas the heartwood of the quebracho tree provides tannins for extraction only after 80 years—impinge on the ecological performance of vegetable tannage (Silvateam 2013). The high demand for leather articles collides with a sustainable use of vegetable tanning agents. Consultant A emphasises that the combination of tanning methods makes effluent treatment very complex and costly.

[57]Normally, hides are imported in the form of the tanned intermediate wet blue leather. The Middle East is one of the most important sources for imported hides, though tanners assess the quality to be low.

just technology and skills to treat hides and skins to their final use and determine value addition, but also financial solidity as well as infrastructural and political stability to ensure just-in-time quality.

It has become obvious that Hazaribagh's tanneries face a variety of structural constraints to product upgrading. To follow the path of developing more sophisticated products and entering new markets, technology has to be acquired and skills have to be systematically learned. Constraints in the availability of raw material are breed-related and thus difficult to overcome. Tanneries are well advised to invest in R&D to build up knowledge and firm-specific competences that may provide a competitive advantage in the leather value chain (see, for instance, Humphrey and Schmitz 2002, p. 1017). The current logic of maximising benefits by squeezing labour costs and disregarding environmental compliance has induced a "race to the bottom" (for India, see Tewari and Pillai 2005), which still attracts buyers, but is detrimental to moving up the value chain. Long-term strategies need to be designed for those tanneries that are able and willing to invest in capacity building and technology to catch up with international competitors (see Cattaneo et al. 2013).

5.2.4.4 Private Governance: Functional Upgrading

Humphrey and Schmitz (2002) point to the inequality between global buyers and local producers shaping upgrading trajectories. Buyers coordinate their leather suppliers in Hazaribagh through buying houses and competitive pricing. Such captive relationships confine the tanneries to production, while up- and downstream services are made available by buyers (e.g. R&D, design) and other parties (e.g. buying houses). The fabrication of labour-intensive low-cost products constrains the producers' margins substantially. Moving into higher value-added activities can be achieved by extending the range of functions that are performed within a GVC (Cattaneo et al. 2013; Fernandez-Stark et al. 2011; Humphrey 2004). However, developing capabilities in "pre- and post-production stages" (Cattaneo et al. 2013, p. 33) often interferes with the core competences of foreign buyers or their intermediaries. This section discusses the potential for functional upgrading of the tanneries interviewed.

Developing Marketing Functions—Cutting Out the Buying House?

Hesselberg and Knutsen (2002) assume power relations in the global leather value chain to be buyer-driven. These study's interviews confirm that leather processors are subject to price pressure from buyers, which is channelled through intermediary commission agents (see Section "Buying Houses—Facilitating or Preventing Market Entry?"). Trade linkages to foreign buyers are largely lacking, so that knowledge and information cannot be exchanged. It requires external help to empower tanneries to transact without intermediaries (Fig. 5.17). How buying

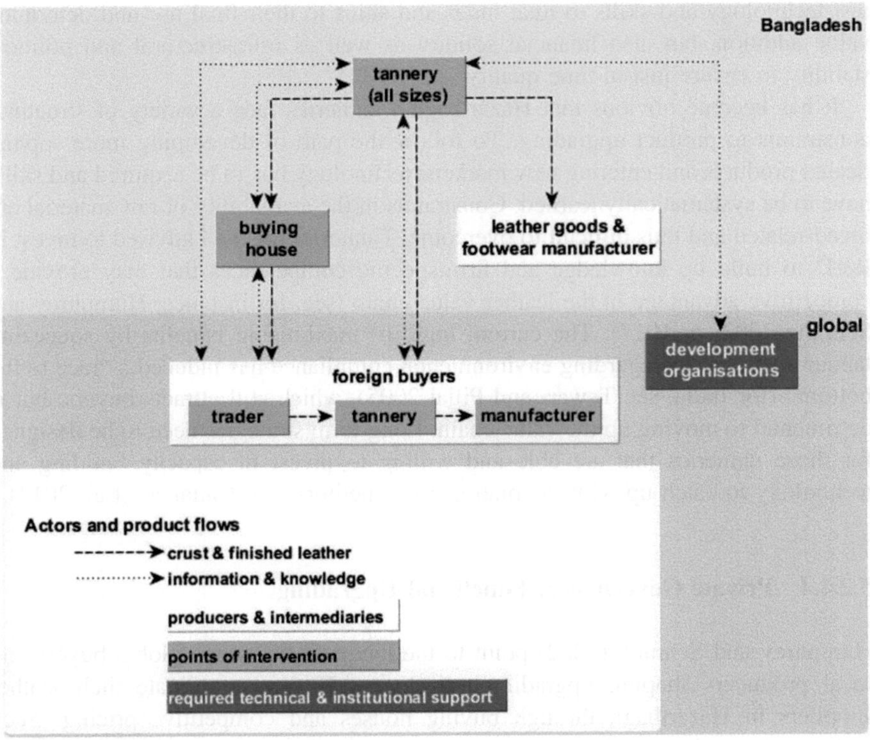

Fig. 5.17 Suggested points of intervention in developing marketing functions. *Source* Own illustration

houses affect the tanneries' competitiveness and what the latter can do to reduce dependence will be set out in the following.

Researching and connecting to international markets has been in the hands of buying houses since wet blue exports were prohibited in 1990. In brokering at the interface between buyers and suppliers buying agents have developed a competitive edge over tanneries in market knowledge. Tanneries, however, are not always satisfied with their agents' capabilities in finding and handling buyers:

> […] they have to gather more knowledge in this sector; because some agents are very weak. They cannot negotiate all the problems with the foreign buyers. So we need strong agencies, strong agents, […] [so; A. N.] they can handle all these problems. And they [have to; A. N.] know the marketing system, they [have to; A. N.] know the channel of setting the leather, and also they have to gather a lot of knowledge in the international market. So we need very good agencies to sell the leather from Bangladesh. (Tanner O, English)

A certain lack of negotiation power is justified on the grounds of captive chain governance (see Gereffi et al. 2005). The buyers' favourable position in the value chain allows them to select from among a multitude of suppliers and to impose on them their terms and conditions. Buying houses provide services to the tanneries, so that these can focus on leather processing. In case of quality claims or delays in lead time, buying houses are entrusted with re-negotiating terms and conditions, trying to balance the interests of both buyers and sellers.

Though apparently specialised in brokering between buyer and supplier, tanner O criticises buying houses for failing to support and advocate their clients' interests. After the export of (standardised) wet blue was banned, most of the leather processors were not prepared to market complex transactions of value-added crust and finished leather to foreign markets. Buying houses[58] that already had traded in wet blue before saw a promising niche to fill in. Many others followed suit, so that meanwhile the tanneries have been outnumbered.[59]

Lacking capabilities in trading leather may relate to low formal entry barriers. Except for a number of licenses (e.g. trade license, export/import license), there are no requirements for joining this business. Knowledge is gained on the job. As the labour market in tanneries is highly competitive, many graduate leather technologists from BCLT end up in chemical import companies or buying houses or start up their own buying agency. But market knowledge develops over time. Many buying agents are inexperienced in setting up trade relations to customers and negotiating favourable terms and conditions for their clients. Particularly small tanneries that achieve exports only on an irregular basis are more likely to agree to risky conditions negotiated by their buying houses. To get into the business, newcomers often accept any order without securing the transaction properly. The son of tanner P tells how he tried to succeed in the broker's business and how informal agreements ultimately turned back on him and the tannery:

> I was actually very much younger and inexperienced. So one of the buyers came to Bangladesh and ordered some leather […] He said 'I will come and I will inspect and I will take the leather'. So afterwards what happened? He didn't come; I am calling his mobile phone, he is not receiving. I am sending mails [for; A. N.] many, many months but he is not responding. (Buying agent D, English)

After eventually localising the foreign buyer in Dhaka and threatening to take legal action

> […] he told 'OK, I agree to buy your leather, but I have to inspect that before'. So he inspected [it; A. N.], 'OK, everything is fine, […] 'So I will go back to Brazil and I will send you T/T money'. But when our car dropped him at the airport and he took so many samples from many, many tanneries and we found out that […] he had taken already 50 to 60 pieces, big pieces of leather, so this is fraud […]. But later on he didn't pay us the T/T [after; A. N.] he went back to his country. […] We called him many, many times, but he didn't [pay; A. N.]. Now what can I do? (Buying agent D, English)

---

[58]Already in the 1980s buying houses were engaged in trading wet blue leather, though at a lower scale.

[59]The number of leather trading buying agents draws on estimates from tannery associations, tannery owners and buying agents. With the increasing number of commercial leather exporters, the demand for the services of buying agents has risen, too.

Several small tanneries complained about foreign buyers comparing offers, obtaining samples and placing orders without issuing a secure (irrevocable) L/C. Their low export activity makes them highly vulnerable to informal practices eventually turning on them. With unknown buyers, the transaction risk increases significantly. The buying house's job is to assess the buyer's credibility and secure the transaction. As reported above, the inexperienced buying agent D was duped by his buyer; moreover, he lacked the financial and judicial means to sue him. He was unable to protect his father's tannery for which he brokered, though thanks to these family connections claims could be settled and losses adjusted elsewhere. Almost all tanneries reported having been affected at least once by trusting buyers and buying houses without opening a secure L/C. As a result of lacking knowledge and an unstable order situation, transactions are informalised, though reference to formal agreements might have helped provide security between unknown business partners.

Specialisation in handling buyer-supplier relations implies knowledge. This is all the more important as mostly smaller tanneries might want to stick to production and resist to capacity building:

> Do we produce leather or search for buyers!? (Tanner J, Bengali)

Tanneries of a low competence level benefit from the assistance provided by buying agencies. Due to a lack of knowledge, awareness of the opportunities and resources to invest in human capital, they see little need for developing competences other than production. Rather than developing marketing skills it is more important for these tanneries that buying houses offer better services.

Mediated relationships may expose tanneries to power asymmetry and harmful illicit practices. These are often played out when it comes to negotiating the agent's commission. The official rate must not exceed 5 % of the exported value and is usually subdivided into the foreign trader (2–3 %) and the local buying house (2 %). The quality of the leather and the buying agent-supplier relation determine the commission. If the price has been fixed to the detriment of the tannery, the agent may concede to a lower commission rate in order not to lose the buyer. If the transaction turns out higher than expected thanks to the agent's negotiating skills or if the buying house insists on a higher commission rate than agreed, tanneries have no choice but to give into their demands:

> It is like he didn't give me any L/C; I made a contract with him for US$1.25, but he has brought in US$1.30. Then he said that 'I brought in US$1.30, you have to give my percentage.' If I have good relation with him then I give it, or I don't give. If I don't give, in future he will never give me any orders. (Tanner G, Bengali)

This case shows the vulnerability smaller tanneries are exposed to in exporting. They have difficulties achieving exports on a regular basis and producing on a subcontract basis without being issued an L/C; tanner G struck the deal only with the buying house. Trust between agent and supplier is essential for keeping the tannery in the market. This may involve underhand dealings contrary to the terms and conditions set:

Yes, we say them to take [an additional; A. N.] 2 %. And this 2 % is unofficial and in the L/C it will be mentioned that the local agent gets 5 %. (Tanner L, Bengali)

Such informal dealings were confirmed by other tanners and are done under-invoice, that is, in the same way chemicals are imported to save taxes or leather is exported to attract orders during economic crises. Tanner L is bound to pay the additional commission if he wants to keep supplying buyer and buying agent.

The analysis has shown that buying houses refer to illicit practices to keep the tanneries in the market but also to impose higher commission rates. This eventually impinges on the tanneries' competitiveness. Buying houses offer crucial services particularly to tanneries that want to focus on production. Development projects such as Re-Tie Bangladesh should consider extending consultancy to buying houses, for instance, in legal terms, to enable them to offer better services, thereby benefitting upstream producers. To capitalise on exports and to overcome their structural dependence on buying houses tanners need to build up capabilities in market knowledge, language skills, and, as the latter cases confirmed, in payment methods, which will be set out in the following chapter.

Enhancing the Security of Payment Methods and Reducing the Tanneries' Vulnerability to Informal Arrangements in Trade Transactions

In mediated buyer-supplier relations buying houses also negotiate payment terms. Interviews revealed that the complexity of financial transactions varies with the stability of buyer-supplier relations (one-off/new buyer, long-term/regular buyer) that in turn determine power relations and the use of informal arrangements.

One-off business relations give buying houses little leverage to advocate to the benefit of the tanneries. Here, trust has not been established yet. To ensure quality and payment business transactions require a higher codification level and are thus more formalised. Results from interviews suggest that most of the tanneries prefer to deal with new buyers only if the latter agree to open a secure L/C. For liquidity reasons, tanneries favour short payment periods (at-sight L/C, L/C 30 days). By contrast, buyers prioritise L/Cs to be paid within 60 days and more, which weighs on the tanneries' financial capacity. Only a few small tanneries were ready to accept T/T payment if the customer advances a substantial percentage (30–50 %) of the final export value before production starts. In doing so, tanners are able to finance part of their production and to increase the customer's commitment to take the product.

Generally, small volume orders and a history of transactions with that buyer encourage (all kinds of) tanneries to accept T/T, which is a very simple and fast payment method, but which also requests buyers and suppliers to trust each other. Depending on the down payment and honesty of both parties, power asymmetries can be either levelled out or are reinforced. A risk of the other party betraying one's trust remains. Hence, one-off transactions would involve a more complex payment method (L/C) as a safeguard, which in principle leaves little room for informal arrangements. An irrevocable L/C cannot be amended or cancelled unless both parties agree (see Section "Buying Houses—Facilitating or Preventing Market Entry?"). Any deviation from the contractual agreements gives foreign buyers a natural advantage over suppliers (and intermediaries) to re-negotiate terms and conditions thanks to their position in the value chain. Interviews with tanners suggest that in the event of delays or insufficient quality, new buyers are more likely to compel the supplier to strictly adhere to the terms and conditions stipulated in the irrevocable L/C instead of re-negotiating an acceptable deal for both (e.g. extension of lead time; discount; payment/quality could be settled with the next order). The risk for the supplying tannery increases if the buyers propose T/T payment to accelerate the delivery and the final payment is informally agreed:

> The 30 % [advance; A. N.] they give us, they sometimes request 'OK, you send us the goods and we arrange another T/T. I need these goods very badly.' We believe [them; A. N.] and send [the goods; A. N.]. And these people never opened the L/C [for the final payment; A. N.]. (Tanner Q, English)

Even Q, the largest tannery in Hazaribagh, is not immune from giving into insecure payment methods. Trusting a little known business partner exposes the supplier to high risk. Almost all tanneries interviewed have experienced losses through payment defaults, though they have been affected to different degrees. Large tanneries such as Q's have the capacity to compensate losses or find other buyers to take their goods. However, depending on the volume and the leather quality, outstanding payment can severely affect exporters. Smaller tanneries and commercial leather exporters trading smaller quantities are more prone to payment defaults due to the higher risk they are taking to achieve exports.

Tanner C, who runs a very small tannery with wet blue facilities that are usually rented by leather processors of a higher competence level arranged a small order of 25,000 ft^2 (approx. US$58,000) for a customer in Hong Kong. The transaction was arranged on documents against acceptance (D/A), a payment method that was only mentioned by a few smaller tanneries. After signing an agreement that the importer's bank is allowed to transfer the payment to the exporter's bank after a period stipulated in the D/A (usually 30/45 days), the importer is delivered with the documents and thus the goods (Wirtschaftslexikon 2013). The bank is neither liable for accuracy and correctness nor for cashing the documents. Unlike an L/C, a D/A does not provide any guarantee to the seller that the buyer is willing and able to pay for the goods (ibid.). Consequently, D/A is a very insecure payment method if trust among the business partners has not been established yet. For more than four years tanner C has been claiming and calling in local leather-related authorities (tannery associations, Export Promotion Bureau) to locate the importer or to get in touch with his bank or his chamber. By the date of our interview, Tanner C had received only US$5,000. To claim the outstanding US$53,500 he would have to resort to legal proceedings:

> There are several problems in this case, like I have to go Hong Kong. There I have to find a lawyer to help me. For this I have to spend US$5,000 to US$10,000. And if I don't get the money, my investment to get US$53,000 will go to the dogs. Then how will I survive? (Tanner C, Bengali)

Family disputes hinder tanner C from investing in his one-storey factory which lacks space and consists of very basic and outdated machinery (soaking drum; pit; fleshing machine). To make use of his tannery and to achieve exports, he started a commercial leather export business which allows him to produce wet blue in his tannery and crust leather in rental tanneries. While this legal construction prevents him from servicing banks, tannery C's competitiveness is obviously impaired by a lack of capital and deferred investment. This critical situation forces him to accept almost any buyer without him or her sufficiently proving their creditworthiness.

Suppliers have to give careful thought to the way they deal with buyers. Sustainable business relationships require trust that cannot be built up in one-off transactions. Even several low volume orders processed on an L/C basis can be just preparatory steps to gain the supplier's confidence and ultimately cheat on him. Buying agent A relates the risk buying houses (and tanneries) are exposed to:

> You and me it is the first time that we are doing business, OK? First time I give 5,000 ft^2 and you'll open the L/C. Against your L/C I'll give you 5,000 ft^2, OK? Then after two months you give me [an order of; A. N.] 10,000 ft^2; I give you 10,000 ft^2, you give me the L/C. But after three months, everything is OK. After three or four months, the fourth order comes; but that order [is; A. N.] 20,000 ft^2. [Buyer says; A. N.] 'you open 10,000 ft^2 L/C. OK, give me the due, I will send you the money against next L/C', but you don't [the buyer doesn't; A. N.] give me the money. (Buying agent A, English)

Customers make their suppliers commit to a deal by gradually increasing the order volume, testing their reliability (quality, lead time). As a matter of fact, payment defaults and cheating are the exception rather than the rule, but they particularly affect the most vulnerable suppliers, i.e. very small and small tanneries and commercial leather exporters. Just like buying agent A explains, tanner C was given a number of orders consecutively until the payment suddenly stopped, either deliberately or because of the buyer's insolvency. Even though this buyer was still relatively new to tanner C, the latter did not insist on a secure transaction by issuing an L/C. As a result, his competitiveness has been significantly harmed.

Trust in the other's commitment is the major reason why tanneries prefer to trade with known buyers. A common understanding on quality issues and lead times developed over time makes buyer-supplier relations more sustainable. Apart from the buyer's requirements that suppliers may be unable to meet, volatile market prices often make it compulsory for buyers to re-negotiate, adjusting prices irrespective of prior agreements:

> Yes, the market comes down and he doesn't allow us to open the L/C […]. 'I need to re-negotiate. Say, we sell in 1.75 Dollar [per ft^2; A. N.].' Then the market comes down and then he says 'I cannot sell for 1.75 [Dollar; A. N.], you must agree to 1.60 [Dollar; A. N.]. Ok, 1.60 [Dollar; A. N.] and we'll make some bargaining and agree to 1.70 [Dollar; A. N.]. (Tanner Q, English)

Though bargaining is a natural part of the leather business, 5 US Cent make a significant difference. Tanner Q is bound to re-negotiate if the market price decreases and he wants to sell a product of high asset specificity. There is "nothing to do; no choice", he says, confirming the power asymmetry in captive value chains.

Even though an irrevocable L/C in theory levels power between exporters and importers, market volatility and the buyer's position in the value chain justify the latter in pressuring sellers to agree to amendments. Thus even formalised structures cannot grant security to Hazaribagh's tanneries held in captive relationships.

Other than stated by Li (2007) or Etzold et al. (2009), formality does not imply or ensure equal power relations. Apart from asset specificity and the buyer's desire to want that product, the regularity of business relationships to buyers seems to determine the suppliers' negotiation power. This means that intangible assets or informal institutions such as trust matter more than formalised contracts.

Long-term relations to buyers may help reduce the power asymmetry between buyers and suppliers but are difficult to establish. Buying houses control the link and refuse to pass on contact details to the tanneries. Buyers need to have an interest in bypassing brokering agencies so they can source directly from the tanneries. With the tanneries giving the commission rate, there is little reason for foreign buyers to take that risk. Usually a regular business relationship draws on a certain leather article (e.g. shoe upper, lining) a customer demands on a regular basis from a local agent. Catering to a foreign buyer frequently reduces the complexity of the transaction substantially as tanner N sets out:

> But when […] we're doing business for a long time, ten to 12 years […] sometimes you deliver the goods as a verbal order. But it's a small quantity […]. (Tanner N, English)

For this tanner verbal orders with his customers include product specifications and price via email communication. Unlike an L/C that implies a highly codified bank-to-bank transfer, an email communicates along low formal ties and is hardly judicial binding. After a business relationship of more than ten years, trust in the producer's quality and lead time and the customer's payment behaviour is strong enough so small orders can be managed at such a low level of formality. Here, buyers and suppliers have a more balanced business relationship without having to play power games. Small tanneries have more difficulties managing to set up permanent business relations to foreign buyers, most of which demand that their suppliers offer in-house production from wet blue to finished leather.

Enduring relationships create trust and allow for a more flexible interpretation of business transactions. Interviews also suggest that some buyers prefer T/T over L/C as it is less expensive in issuance and favours a quick delivery (e.g. sample, low quantities). This is why tannery Q receives 100 % down payment from its German buyer, whereas its Chinese customers only advance 30 %. In permanent relationships buyers and suppliers transact rather relationally. They leave room for informal arrangements and a flexible interpretation of the market situation:

> If we have good relationship with the buyer, then we can complete L/C documentation even though we cannot supply 100 % of the goods in one process. Under these circumstances, the C&F [i.e. cost and freight; A. N.] agent agrees to accept one part of the goods which we adjust to full amount in the subsequent consignment. As the banks are involved in this process, accountability is assured. (Commercial leather exporter A, Bengali)

Mutual understanding among the parties gives this commercial leather exporter time to organise finances for his production. This applies very much to the arrangements an Italian trader agrees with his Bangladeshi buying agent from whom he has been sourcing leather since 1996. He anticipates the unpredictability of the lead time and is ready to adjust if needs be, recognising the unstable production conditions (e.g. irregular electricity supply, nationwide strike actions) in Bangladesh:

> What can I do? We need the leather and we already program the delay. […] If you work a lot with Asian countries you must adapt to this type of delay, to this type of mentality. You must be realistic. (International trader, English)

It is only thanks to a trustworthy long-term relationship that such adjustments can be handled verbally. As long as quality can be ensured, minor delays are accepted for the sake of staying in the market he has built up with his Bangladeshi counterpart.

In any case, to strengthen the capabilities in the supply base, proper knowledge about the nature and risks of the most important payment methods (L/C, T/T, D/A, Documents against Payment D/P) seems necessary. One of the tannery associations in collaboration with Re-Tie Bangladesh addressed this deficit by organising a two-hour seminar on the functionality and advantages of L/C payment. More trainings and workshops for both tanners and buying houses are necessary to raise awareness of insecure payment methods.

In sum, the nature of buyer-supplier relations seems to determine the complexity of the payment method and the use of informal practices. As a result of structural limitations, few tanneries have been able to benefit from long-term business relationships. Those who have transact with their buyers rather relationally; power does not play a role. Transactions such as T/T that include a degree of informality increase the supplier's risk of payment default in one-off or short-term buyer-supplier relationships. More formalisation (e.g. L/C) cannot resolve power asymmetries but may prevent weaker parties from being taken advantage of in informal practices. More capacity building in payment methods is needed to reduce the tanneries' vulnerability in international transactions.

The main argument of this section has been that downstream competences in, for instance, negotiating contracts or finding own distribution channels could remove the dependency on costly buyers and intermediaries. However, only a few (mostly large) tanneries in Hazaribagh qualify for expanding towards higher value-added activities. Prospects for smaller tanneries lacking financial means and knowledge to invest substantially in technology, labour and marketing are rather gloomy. The next section will elaborate on the dilemma of functional upgrading of smaller enterprises (MSMEs) in GVCs.

Limitations of Functional Upgrading in Captive Value Chains

Interviews with tanners and experts suggest that entire Hazaribagh is struggling to live up to international standards for leather quality. The industry's upgrading imperative furthered by projects such as Re-Tie Bangladesh is to increase productivity and efficiencies in the production process by introducing modern technology and developing a skilled labour force. Lacking knowledge of strategic services in pre- and postproduction stages is currently being provided by foreign buyers (e.g. R&D, design) or compensated by external service providers (e.g. buying houses, chemical companies). Almost none of the tanneries interviewed are able to encroach in economic activities prior to and after production; the few large ones with potential to succeed are expected to face enormous challenges (international consultant B).

Naturally, externalised complementary services restrain the producer's capacity for innovation as interaction that is pivotal for upgrading (Humphrey and Schmitz 2002, p. 1018) is lacking. It may well be more cost-efficient to produce leather articles according to the customer's or the chemical company's specifications than to develop own products. It hinders, however, a critical examination of quality and a creative exchange of ideas with up- and downstream business partners. Certainly some particularly large tanneries are working on extending their product range, but as noted by tanner Q, they are late in following international trends and copy articles from leather fairs.

In general, only large tanneries are asked to develop products based on a sample provided by the customer. Given the limitations in knowledge, technology and infrastructure (e.g. constant power supply) such product development is costly, time-consuming and not always successful, says leather technologist A. Moreover, tanneries are not allowed to supply an article specifically developed for one buyer to other customers (asset specificity). In this case, functional upgrading does not apply; external parties (buyers) take the decision to further the development of specific products (see, for instance, Fleury and Fleury 2001, p. 118). As R&D has not been strategically incorporated into the leather processor's range of activities, learning is limited.

In two cases it was seen that buying agents had increased their functional competences by moving into leather processing. Building on extensive market knowledge, they sought to add productive capabilities to their core competence of brokering transactions by taking over wet blue tanneries. Neither invested in machinery to carry out crust and finished production in-house; instead, they rented facilities from tanneries of a higher competence level. In both cases the acquisitions were used to improve the agents' positions on the local market instead of modifying the governance to buyers as will be briefly set out in the following.

Tanner M had been brokering leather for two decades before he ventured into production by taking over a wet blue tannery in 2005. His aim was to increase his tanning capacity to satisfy the rising needs of his buyers. It is important to add that exporting by the tannery's license is more lucrative than as a buying agent, for:

- only tanners/producers are entitled to duty drawback for re-exported chemicals;
- buying houses were not eligible for subsidies for crust and finished exports (3; 4 %).

However, financial distress forced M to give up his tannery in 2013 and to return to his core business to meet outstanding liabilities.

Buying agent D is a large landowner in Hazaribagh who owns three wet blue tanneries. Two of these were inherited and rented out to tannery Q and other job working leather processors. He uses the third's license to export crust and finished leather he purchases from other parties. Instead of developing productive activities and turning into a real tanner, agent D uses his tannery license to save money and gain influence. A powerful advisory role in one of the tannery associations enables him to hold sway over a large number of small tanneries[60] (buying agent A[61]) to which he transfers orders regularly and on a subcontract basis. With middlemen like buying agent D controlling market access and business associations, small and medium-sized producers are more vulnerable to unfavourable business deals (e.g. commission rates, subcontracts) or illicit practices (see Sect. 5.2.3.3). This case substantiates that emerging domestic actors seek to strengthen their position in the local production network rather than looking outwards. As a consequence, new power imbalances to weaker actors within the network arise, while old ones are reinforced.

Under current conditions the tanneries interviewed are not able to meet the challenge of functional upgrading. Captive relationships with buyers tie the tanneries to low-cost production and low-price competition. A prerequisite for functional upgrading is substantial "intra-firm investment in equipment, organisational arrangements and people" (Humphrey and Schmitz 2002, p. 1024), which most of the tanneries are unable or reluctant to perform due to future uncertainties (relocation). The strategy of organising production processes more efficiently supports product quality and increases the returns to labour and capital for the producers. It is applicable to all sizes of firms and seems to be the more sustainable way of improving performance and competitiveness in a labour-intensive industry. However, if large tanneries happen to invest and manage to functionally upgrade, particularly after the relocation, the technological and financial divide among the tanneries is expected to rise. This may bring opportunities to large competitive tanneries, whereas smaller leather processors are likely to be shaken out the market.

5.2.4.5 Prospects of Inter-sectoral Upgrading—Combining Leather Processing and Manufacturing

Adding downstream strategic functions to production may be one solution to set themselves apart from other low-cost regions. Another is to use knowledge and inputs from leather processing in order to move into new (side) chains such as leather goods or leather footwear. Provided that certain competences can be

[60]To the author's knowledge, at least three of the tanneries interviewed (E, G, and I) are managed by this buying agent. Many others are said to be handled by him.

[61]Buying agent A is an employee of buying agent D.

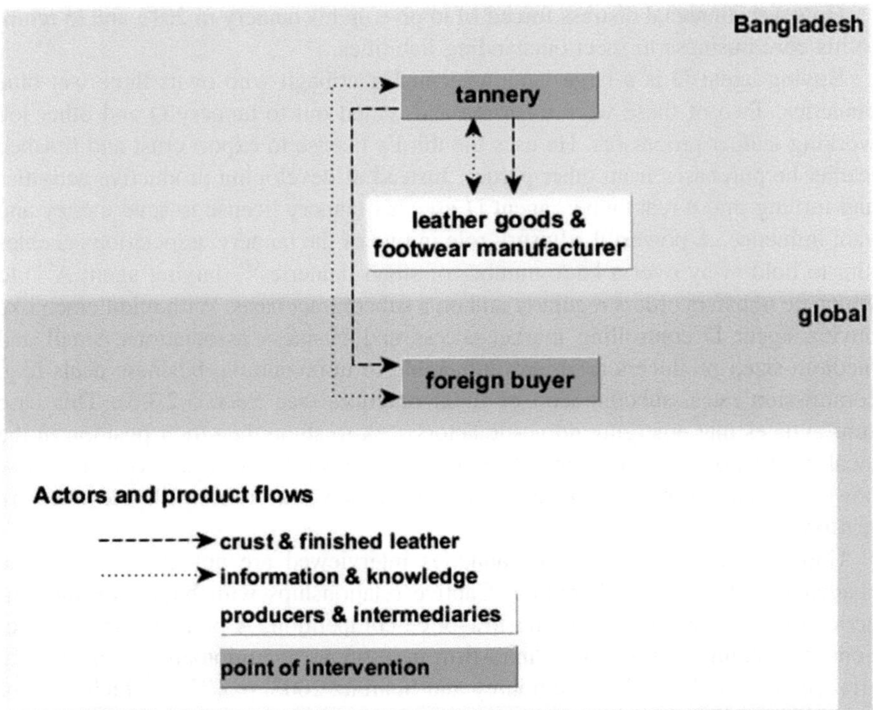

Fig. 5.18 Suggested points of intervention in inter-sectoral upgrading. *Source* Own illustration

acquired, often from local or foreign manufacturers (e.g. joint venture), inter-sectoral or chain upgrading may offer higher value addition[62] (see Fig. 5.18).

All of the leather processors interviewed are aware of the current dynamic development in the leather goods and footwear subsectors, which is about to change the dominance of the tanning industry. Relocation for which investment has been deferred is expected to boost both leather processing and manufacturing. Many tanners express their intention to invest in leather manufacturing, but keep a low profile because of the financial implications. The medium-sized tannery O, officially highly indebted because of a loan default, aims to link tanning with footwear production at the new site because:

> […] you cannot survive only on leather export. […] you have to do footwear also. (Tanner O, English)

---

[62]Strictly speaking, inter-sectoral upgrading refers to the competence acquired in one activity of a chain that is applied to a new sector (Humphrey and Schmitz 2000, p. 4). For instance, a contract manufacturer in electronics uses his/her knowledge to move into developing own designs and brands (e.g. Samsung). This study assumes leather processing to be different from manufacturing, constituting two single chains.

Plans have not been communicated yet—or are yet to be designed as the relocation date is still uncertain.

The other two medium-sized tanneries interviewed already combine tanning and manufacturing, supplying leather goods and footwear to the low-end export market. Tannery N exports small leather goods (purses, belts) and leather footwear (gents' shoes) to Chinese and Italian buyers. Despite external assistance in terms of design (Italy) and machinery (China) to live up to international quality standards, the major problems for price competitiveness are the availability of accessories, the high prices of raw material and adequate finishing quality, says tanner N. Finances, foreign assistance and sourcing capabilities seem to define upgrading trajectories. It remains to be seen how N's currently underperforming tannery[63] determines the strategic planning and direction of its leather footwear subsidiary. Large tanneries already use their domestic market power to direct more value-added leather products to new markets.[64] Here, more research is needed to analyse specific inter-(sub-) sectoral upgrading trajectories.

Small tanneries usually do not count on the financial resources or on knowledge to set up an export-oriented factory. Very few have tried to succeed in manufacturing activities, manufacturing low-complex leather goods such as purses (Tanner I) or shoe upper (Tanner H). Tanner K failed due to a variety of flaws and errors:

> We started a footwear business 15 years ago. At that time we lacked technical support and we didn't have sufficient instruments. We didn't build it for the local market, exclusively for export. We had no idea about the costs. [...] After we spent our money in land development, chemicals and machineries, we didn't have enough working capital [any more; A. N.]. For that reason we couldn't run our factory. We bought machines worth five crore [i.e. 50 m; A. N.] taka. (Tanner K, Bengali)

Unprofessional planning made tanner K's leather footwear venture go awry. Limitations in design capabilities, technology and skilled labour aggravated financial miscalculations. The lack of marketing channels and high overhead costs eventually led the factory to close after only one year, binding a huge amount of capital in machinery and chemicals, which have remained unused since. Tanner K's primary objective now is to seek a strategic partnership with a local investor in order to rebuild business, using still available production utilities and inputs. This case illustrates the lack of sustainable business strategies. An export-oriented strategy without experience either in manufacturing or in the domestic market and without partners providing technical and financial assistance is likely to fail. As most of the tanneries are used to processing leather for the export market, working on the domestic market seems cumbersome and not very profitable. A local development strategy, however, could pave the way for further export ambitions as

[63]As a result of high prices for raw hides and skins, tannery N struggles with financial difficulties that led to a substantial decline in leather exports from 250,000 to 50,000 ft^2 per month in 2012.

[64]Family members of tannery Q have been engaged in leather footwear production since 1990 (see Section "Enhancing the Security of Payment Methods and Reducing the Tanneries' Vulnerability to Informal Arrangements in Trade Transactions").

the cases of medium-sized tanneries N and P illustrate. Both started using low-grade and rejected leather to manufacture simple leather goods (e.g. belts, purses, bags) and later on footwear for the local market. Once established in the domestic market, they sought opportunities abroad offered by their buying houses and leather purchasing customers. While N has been gradually augmenting sales, tannery P's export activity appears to be discontinuous.[65]

As a result of a complete lack of FDI in the tanning industry in Hazaribagh and positive prospects for leather goods and footwear in the global market, local authorities (Board of Investment, Export Promotion Bureau) advocate realigning export promotion strategies and investment policies. The rising demand for leather goods and footwear in the world market encouraged several tanneries to venture into new chains and markets with varying degrees of success. More consultancy and advice seem essential to avoid tanneries taking incalculable risks.

This section has shown that chain upgrading, here understood as moving from leather processing to the manufacturing subsectors, is at quite an early stage. Size, financial constraints, lacking strategic partnerships and lacking know-how appear to compromise ventures in leather goods and footwear production. More research is needed to understand what factors matter. The political discourse may be decisive for shaping future upgrading strategies in the leather goods and footwear subsectors without weakening the tanning industry.

5.2.4.6 Public–Private Governance: Site Upgrading—Relocation to the New Tannery Estate

Despite all shortcomings in organising production processes and developing up- and downstream strategic functions, growth rates in the leather processing industry picked up after an overall economic downturn in 2008. In the fiscal year of 2012–2013, leather poured almost $1 billion of export revenues into the nation's coffers. At the same time, international NGOs (Human Rights Watch 2012) and media (e.g. ZDF 2013; Renton 2012) have brought unacceptable labour and environmental conditions in Hazaribagh to the attention of a wider public in consumer markets. Bangladesh's national government and the tannery associations have not paid sufficient heed to those critical voices. Ongoing negotiations about land development and financial compensation have delayed the relocation process. In addition to the government adjusting the site to the industry's needs, development organisations can provide more technical assistance for an operational setup (Fig. 5.19). Global standards on the requirements of environmentally compliant leather can accelerate the process. Tewari and Pillai (2005) demonstrate for the Indian leather industry that both effective domestic regulation and pressure from foreign markets (e.g. ban on leather exports from Bangladesh) is needed to induce change.

[65]Unfortunately, no details were given about the dynamics in footwear exports.

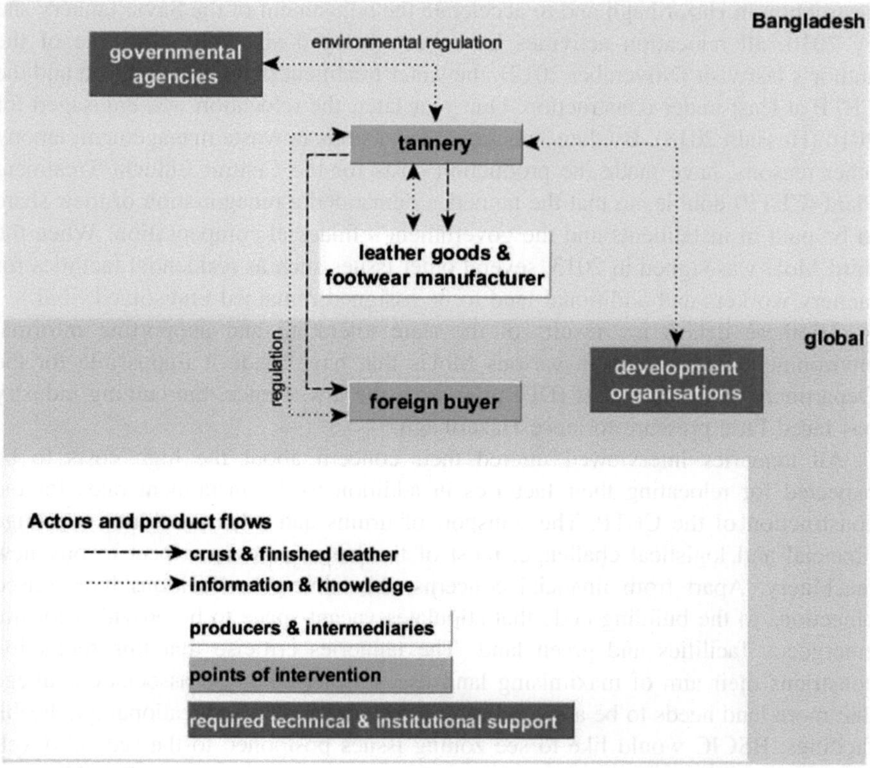

Fig. 5.19 Suggested points of intervention in site upgrading. *Source* Own illustration

After Bangladesh gained independence in 1971, the tanning industry in Hazaribagh had seen continuous growth without any adjustments to infrastructural facilities. Instead of investing in production technology, productivity and waste management to keep up with international competitors, the tanneries have opted for a regulatory race to the bottom by relying on cheap labour, pollution and hazardous working conditions. In 2013, Green Cross Switzerland (2013), an NGO, ranked Hazaribagh among the world's ten most polluted places.

Since 1962 already, many political and judicial attempts have been made to relocate the tannery cluster to the outskirts of Dhaka.[66] In 2003, after a series of court rulings the tannery associations (BTA, BFLLFEA) and a governmental agency (Bangladesh Small and Cottage Industries Corporation—BSCIC) agreed upon a Memorandum of Understanding (MoU) to shift the tanning industry by 2005 to the new site in Hemayetpur/Savar. In 2007 a new MoU was signed to define responsibilities in the construction of infrastructural facilities and the costs to be borne. Despite a High Court order from 2009 to end the environmental

[66]See for more details on the relocation process, Ahmed (2002, pp. 34–35).

destruction in Hazaribagh and to accelerate the adjustment of the Savar tannery site by 2010, all relocation activities have been delayed since. By the time of the author's last visit (November 2012), the water treatment plant was finalised and the CETP at least under construction. One year later, the relocation was envisaged for 2016 (Hossain 2013). By then, functional extensions in waste management, among other reasons, have made the production costs for the Central Effluent Treatment Plant (CETP) double, so that the tanneries demanded a renegotiation of their share to be paid in instalments and the government's financial compensation. When the third MoU was signed in 2013, several other issues such as residential facilities for tannery workers and additional land to be assigned remained unresolved (ibid.).

All these delays are results of the state tolerating and supporting informal environmental regulation in various MoUs that have made it impossible for the Department of Environment (DE) to enforce the law. Hence, the tanning industry has faced little pressure to leave Hazaribagh.

All tanneries interviewed uttered their concern about the high costs to be expected for relocating their factories in addition to the instalment rates for the construction of the CETP. The transport of drums and other machines is a huge financial and logistical challenge; most of the tanneries even expect to buy new machinery. Apart from financial concerns, the tannery associations have raised objections to the building code that stipulates vacant space to be provided for fire emergency facilities and green land. The tanneries criticise that this regulation constrains their aim of maximising land use. Furthermore, the associations allege that more land needs to be assigned to housing for workers, educational and health facilities. BSCIC would like to see zoning issues postponed to the second development phase. The tanneries interviewed, however, take the view that BSCIC has to provide infrastructure and services including the full operation of the CETP first, before they start constructing factories. In this conflict the tannery associations, one of it advised by the powerful tanner, landowner and buying agent D, have demonstrated political weight and negotiation skills to extend the process for the industry's interests.[67]

Based on the principles set down in the MoU, the tannery site in Savar covers 200 acres of industrial use that are to be developed with adequate facilities (e.g. CETP, water treatment plant, solid waste management) for the tanning industry. BSCIC provides other infrastructural services such as electricity, internal roads, telecommunications, post office and bank, among others. According to BSCIC, 155 (!) tanneries had acquired land by November 2012, with plot sizes ranging from 10,000 ft^2 to more than 100,000 ft^2. No layout plans had yet been submitted by any tannery.[68]

Expert opinions drastically differ from the current design of BSCIC. Consultant A holds that the number of operating tanneries will be critical for the

[67]It is beyond the scope of this study to answer the extent to which real estate and property speculation of tannery owners expecting Hazaribagh to be converted into "West-Dhanmondi" has had an influence on the delay of the relocation. Dhanmondi is a middle class housing area that borders in the east on Hazaribagh.

[68]According to this study's mapping data, only 119 tanneries were found operating in Hazaribagh.

functionality of the new site. In his view, the area is not suitable for more than five to ten tanneries; additionally, one or two tanneries can emerge from a joint venture by several smaller tanneries. The rest of the existing tanneries he considers as not competitive enough and thinks they should be closed. In consideration of the implications for the entire tanning sector, it is unclear to what extent this expertise will be incorporated in the final design. By January 2014, Re-Tie Bangladesh and UNIDO had not applied for a follow-up project yet.

While waste-water treatment appears to be resolved, questions remain over how solid waste management amended in the MoU of 2013 and essential for an environmentally compliant industry will be treated in Savar. In late 2012, neither BSCIC nor consultant A was aware of any official projects. The current situation in Hazaribagh is disastrous. The tanneries informally dispose the entire solid waste generated during the production process by selling it on to scrap leather processors that operate without a license in the west of the tannery area. Off-cuts of RHS[69] and wet blue leather are further processed as inputs to fish and poultry feed (see Hossain et al. 2007), animal glue or cloth hardener, among others, instead of being chemically neutralised and properly disposed of (see Photos 3 and 4). The remainder of crust leather is used as a combustion agent for the vats the RHS and wet blue off-cuts are boiling in. The resulting intermediate products constitute completely new side chains that to the author's knowledge feed into the domestic market[70] (Photos 8/9).

Scrap leather processors operate without a license, that is, fully informally. They have been tolerated by the DE, the police and other governmental bodies—very often against bribes as several scrap leather processors assure. The tanneries have established truly informal rules of environmental regulation that structure solid

Photos 8/9 Leather off-cuts boiling and sun-drying for further processing to input for fish and poultry feed. *Source* Own photos

[69]Tanners estimate approximately 10 % of RHS to be wastage.

[70]One chemical company located in this area produces matches, the tip of which is made of animal glue. While some scrap leather processors admitted to supply this company with raw material for animal glue in production peaks, a manager denied using contaminated wet blue off-cuts from this area and assured that he sourced only trimmed RHS directly from the tanneries.

waste management. Here, informality is the organising logic of urban space, as Alsayyad and Roy (2004) observed. The following incident illustrates how informality is constantly negotiated by public and private actors:

In February 2011, a few weeks ahead of the Cricket World Cup in Bangladesh, three leather off-cut processing factories were closed by the DE. The scrap leather processors interviewed classified these shutdowns to be a government move for two reasons:

First, air pollution from boiling (RHS, wet blue) and burning[71] (crust) leather off-cuts was to be reduced during the games to avoid negative public relations. The government was keen to present a "clean city" to the world.

Second, the authorities demonstrated action when solid waste consumption peaked three months after Eid-ul-Azha. This gave them leverage on re-negotiating informal terms and conditions (i.e. bribes) with the scrap leather processors, says one of them. After negotiations between the DE, influential tanners and scrap leather processors along with their corresponding business associations, and the Police, the factory owners were fined. A couple of days later, however, they were allowed to resume their operations. All parties had stakes involved and agreed on continuing the informal practice of hazardous solid waste management. The tanneries pursue the (informal) strategy to save costs and keep externalities to a minimum, whereas scrap leather processors make a living from processing leather waste. DE and the police are bribed to turn a blind eye to these practices.

The commoditisation of solid waste seems to vary with the size of the tanneries. Interviews with leather technologist A and several scrap leather processors suggest that managers of medium-sized and large tanneries make contracts about solid waste. The large availability of off-cuts recently even led to auctions that are held on an annual basis. Scrap leather processors offering the highest bid are awarded the contract to collect all leather wastage during a certain time period (usually one year). Smaller tanneries produce only low volumes of leather wastage, so that supervisors are reported to monetise waste for their own benefit.

Small scrap leather processors tend to source from several tanneries depending on the latter's production activity. Some interviewees mentioned that the processing of leather off-cuts to an (8 %) input of fish and poultry feed has experienced a boom since import duty on proteins significantly increased in the beginning of the 2000s. Since then, RHS and leather off-cuts have been ascribed commercial value:

> Before, this was a business of poor people, now everybody wants to get in. (Scrap leather processor A, Bengali)

Competition has become fierce and made scrap leather processors more vulnerable:

[71]Plastic material is also used as a combustion agent and considered more harmful by the authorities, according to several scrap leather processors.

> Because I can't bid with other parties. The other parties hiked prices more than me. The rate has increased from 2 lakh [i.e. 200,000; A. N.] taka to 4 lakh [i.e. 400,000; A. N.] taka. As the competition increased, prices did too. (Scrap leather processor B, Bengali)[72]

By 2011, approximately 80 scrap leather processing facilities were estimated to operate in Hazaribagh, most of them on a very small scale with only one to three workers. Air pollution as well as respiratory and skin diseases as deleterious side effects of this booming informal industry have been reported by scrap leather processors and Human Rights Watch (2012). Scrap leather processor A died at a young age in February 2014 after suffering for two years from inexplicable paralysis and kidney insufficiency. The consequences of this extremely dangerous organising logic for public health cannot be estimated. The tanning industry is not willing to take responsibility for the damage it has caused.

The dynamics in environmental regulation of the tanning industry are highly informal and even illicit. Instead of implementing a formal system of solid waste management, the tanneries have used tripartite MoUs to keep externalities low and exculpate from responsibility. The way public and private actors closely interact to manage waste informally corresponds to a truly organising urban logic. The relocation debate has blocked for decades any initiative to find on-site solutions. Now DE classifies Hazaribagh as totally toxic; air, soil and water limit values are exceeded by far. It has been recommended that the entire area be put under quarantine for a minimum of 25 years. Questions remain about how environmental compliance can be achieved in the new tanning estate without compromising the livelihoods of many scrap leather processors and slum dwellers. It requires an inclusive strategy to not just regulate industrial waste but also to deal with the social costs.

5.2.4.7 Upgrading and Informal Dynamics in the Tanning Industry

This section briefly wraps up core results of the discussion of how upgrading strategies can be devised to fit in with the reality of informal dynamics in three important export related areas (environmental regulation, chemical imports, leather exports) of the global leather value chain in order to improve the producers' competitiveness (research question 4b).

Tewari and Pillai (2005) demonstrated for the Indian leather industry that it is critical to compliance to get the state involved. Bangladesh's government lacks this commitment. The tripartite MoU de facto formalises a state-tolerated informality. The enforcement of environmental regulation has been offset, while the relocation process is stuck in negotiations over financial compensation for the tanneries. Process (or in this case locational) upgrading can be conducive to preventing institutionalised informal practices from staying in place or invading in

[72]Currency converted as of February 19, 2011 (OANDA 2014): 200,000 BDT = US$2,766; 400,000 BDT = US$5,533.

non-negotiable public realms after relocation. The new tannery site in Savar can put an end to informality as an organising urban logic (Etzold et al. 2009; Alsayyad and Roy 2004). It could re-introduce regulation and enforcement, thereby establishing trust with new buyers. Provided that internal restructuring (e.g. suitability of the site for 155 tanneries) and technological upgrading take place, the relocation offers an excellent opportunity to boost an environmentally compliant industry (e.g. CETP, solid waste management).

Upgrading strategies need to take account of formal and informal institutions that interfere in the industry's competitiveness and exacerbate power asymmetries. Formal institutional constraints such as payment methods or import duty on chemicals may reinforce power asymmetries at both global and local scales within the leather production network. Interviewees adapt by turning to risky low-formal arrangements (e.g. with new buyers) or even illicit practices (e.g. under-invoicing). Institutionalised illicit practices, for instance, with global chemical companies obstruct any impetus to establish a domestic chemical industry. In particular, the bonded license scheme reinforces power asymmetries within the tanning industry and needs to be revamped. Better control mechanisms for the import and consumption of chemicals may prevent misuse and sales in the black market. Turning a blind eye to these illicit practices harms individual firms, the industry's competitiveness and society at large. However, a trade-off between formalisation and price competitiveness can be assumed. While formalising practices and processes may reduce the smaller leather processors' dependencies on large tanneries, fully taxed imported chemicals make re-exported products more expensive. Therefore, it is suggested that the duty drawback scheme be continued for crust and finished leather to avoid smaller tanneries being driven out of the market. This scenario gives an idea of how complex solutions may turn out to be.

National agencies (EPB, BOI) propose banning the exports of crust leather for the sake of a higher value-added through finishing and manufacturing. This strategy, however, requires concomitant measures such as the assessment of the technological potential of the supply base to prevent factories from closing or ending up subcontracted, as happened in the 1990s (Ahmed 2002). The current share of crust leather exports (60–70 % est.) conflicts with a rash and indiscriminate policy change. Instead of pushing towards inter-sectoral upgrading, fiscal incentives could be provided to introduce cleaner and more modern technologies to optimise production processes. Lessons can be learned from export policies that were inadequately implemented in the past. The embargo on wet blue exports has borne out asymmetric power lines within the tanning industry, as a response to which smaller tanneries developed informal adaptive strategies (e.g. informal subcontracts) with often only temporary benefits. They may be useful in achieving direct transactions with buying houses, but their scope in sustainably modifying innate power asymmetries remains narrow. Learning is limited. Collective action could be more effectively used if small firms grouped cooperatively to increase their capacity and improve their facilities jointly.

An institutional overhaul seems inevitable to address dysfunctions systemically. Where the formal is not just enabling the informal but even the illegal (e.g.

chemical imports, environmental regulation), it seems appropriate to argue for formalisation and stricter law enforcement accompanied by supportive measures to enable the industry to find its own (informal) solutions (e.g. collective factory organisation instead of higher single rates). Table 5.6 summarises the informal dynamics of each outlined sector, the stakeholders, risks and power asymmetries involved, and the impact these entail. It points to strategies that deal with informal dynamics intrinsic to the Bangladeshi leather value chain and perhaps enhance the industry's competitiveness.

5.2.4.8 Concluding Remarks on Scope and Focus of Upgrading Strategies for Hazaribagh's Tanning Industry

The results from expert and semi-structured interviews with selected stakeholders along the value chain suggest that Bangladesh's tanning industry is strongly dependent on foreign buyers. Hazaribagh's integration in the global market follows the paradigm of a race to the bottom (for India, see Tewari and Pillai 2005). Price as the major sourcing parameter translates into low-quality production and devastating environmental conditions. Pressure from global buyers for upgrading is low and only addresses improvements in production processes (e.g. technology, chemicals, productivity) that positively impact product quality, too. Coordination through private standards (Ponte and Gibbon 2005) such as the Leather Working Group or BSCI is unrealistic under the current conditions of environment and labour in Hazaribagh. Mandatory standards such as REACH have proven effective in restricting the use of harmful chemicals in products entering the EU market. Bangladeshi tanneries were forced to shift to safer substances. Following Tewari and Pillai (2005), nation states and supranational regions such as the EU are able to exert pressure, shaping upgrading paths of producers in the global South. Apart from REACH, little has happened yet.

The literature on upgrading emphasises that captive value chains create barriers to functional upgrading, while they are supportive of process and product upgrading (Giuliani et al. 2005; Humphrey and Schmitz 2000, 2002). Most of the leather processors interviewed lack capital and human resources to move into higher value-added strategic functions. Missing buyer-supplier interaction in mediated export relations deprives tanners of learning by exporting (see for example Navas-Alemán 2011). The tanneries' primary competence is production which increases dependence on powerful middlemen controlling market access and concentrating knowledge (buying houses, chemical companies). Thereby, particularly smaller but also medium-sized producers are systematically held captive.

The heterogeneous tanning industry requires strategies that are devised to the group-specific needs of the tanneries. An export-oriented strategy seems to be appropriate for particularly large tanneries, the capabilities of which are closest to the export market's requirements. Expert interviews suggest that the major challenge will be to encourage these tanneries to invest in technology and the training of employees. A skilled labour force is a basic prerequisite for optimising production

Table 5.6 Informal dynamics in relevant areas of the leather processing industry and strategies to deal with them

	Chemical imports			Leather exports		Environmental regulation
Dominant informal practices and strategies in the leather processing sector	Bonded license tanneries leak duty-free chemicals to local market	Third parties import chemicals by using the tanneries' bonded license in return for payment	Traders import chemicals under-invoice	Tanners export leather under-invoice	Multi-tiered/joint subcontracted production	Suspended law enforcement of environmental regulation in tannery estate, Hazaribagh
Type of informality	Informal strategy to achieve particularistic goals; pervasive institutionalised illicit practice	Adaptive strategy; pervasive institutionalised illicit practice	Adaptive strategy; pervasive institutionalised illicit practice	Adaptive strategy; illicit practice	Strategic resource	Informality as an organising urban logic; state-tolerated informality
Actors	Medium-sized and large tanneries with bonded license	Selected chemical traders, small commercial leather exporters	Chemical traders/importers	Individual tanneries, commercial leather exporters, buying houses	Several tanneries	All tanneries in Hazaribagh; scrap leather processors
Scale	Local	Local/Global	Global	International	Local	Local
Frequency	On a regular basis	On a regular basis	On a regular basis	Irregularly	Irregularly	On a regular basis
Aim	To export leather at competitive prices; to obtain additional	To stay in the chemical/leather market	To stay in the chemical market	Market entry; to overcome temporary (order) crises	Market entry; to overcome structural constraints (e.g. production capacity); to reduce costs for	To export leather at competitive prices

(continued)

Table 5.6 (continued)

	Chemical imports			Leather exports		Environmental regulation
	revenues from sales on the local market				shipping documentation	
International competitiveness	Competitive prices in international market	Competitive prices in international market	Competitive prices in international market	Competitive prices; higher returns for buyer and supplier	Market entry, but possibly quality differences	Competitive prices, but environmentally non-compliant products
Impact	Missing incentives for establishing own chemical industry			Lack of price competitiveness under formal conditions		
	Lack of price competitiveness under formal conditions					
Power relations	Asymmetry to non-bonded leather processors reinforced	Asymmetry to non-bonded leather processors reinforced	Asymmetry between bonded tanneries and chemical importers established	Asymmetry between buyer and tanneries reinforced	Asymmetry to powerful gatekeepers (e.g. buying houses; contracting tanneries) temporarily overcome	No effect on power relations
Risk	Low; institutionalised practice with informal (e.g. trust) and illegal (e.g. bribe) safeguards	Low; institutionalised practice with informal (e.g. trust) and illegal (e.g. bribe) safeguards	Low; institutionalised practice with informal (e.g. trust) and illegal (e.g. bribe) safeguards	Very high, informal safeguards (e.g. trust) not always ensured	Medium (e.g. supplier failure, quality differences)	Low (MoU between government and industry as formal safeguard)

(continued)

Table 5.6 (continued)

	Chemical imports	Leather exports		Environmental regulation
Strategies to deal with informality	Monitoring of bonded licenses and law enforcement; modernisation of application process (computerisation, less direct personal contact to officials)	Improvement of management, marketing and distribution capabilities of supply base to minimise proneness to such arrangements	Better harmonisation with other leather processors to improve efficiency in collective production; can increase individual competitiveness	Implementation of existing environmental regulation; annulment of MoU; relocation to new compliant tannery site
	R&D in own chemical industry			

Source Data based on own interviews conducted from 2010–2012. Own composition processes. Large tanneries are hesitant to invest in technology until the terms and conditions of the relocation to the new tannery site are defined. The longer they wait the less they will be able to catch up with more compliant regional competitors (e.g. India, Vietnam). Raising awareness among tanners and managers of the benefits of process upgrading for costs and product quality will be crucial to the industry's success.

Medium-sized tanneries are struggling to keep up the leather quality. Loans are usually prioritised for the purchase of raw material during peak season (Eid-ul-Azha), while investment in high-value machinery and, more importantly, in repair and maintenance, tends to be forgone. Insufficient access to finance and a lack of direct marketing are major constraints to the development of this tannery group. Both medium-sized and large tanneries will have to develop marketing channels to increase margins and to reduce dependency on powerful buying houses.

Small and very small tanneries are given few chances to survive. Experts believe the relocation to entail a shake-out. The tanneries of this group are not held to be creditworthy of funding with banks. Their technological assets are mostly confined to wet blue equipment; few also operate single crust machines. A technological upgrade to produce crust leather within their own premises is not financially feasible, so that dependencies on tanneries of a higher competence level are expected to remain high. Very small tanneries already stopped their production and rent out machinery to commercial leather exporters or tanneries of a higher competence level.

Building a robust supply base by enhancing its capabilities may be a "better deal" (Ponte and Ewert 2009, p. 1637) for the tanning industry. This does not necessarily translate into increased export values, but in the long run may help build up trust to (hitherto reluctant) buyers. Unskilled labour force has been identified unanimously by all tanners as a major constraint to high leather quality and ought to be adequately addressed in trainings and practical seminars. Managers recognise the limited knowledge of labour in using, maintaining and repairing machinery, but do not question the prevalent system of learning on the job. Upgrading projects are suggested to place more emphasis on education and skills development on the operator and technician level. The tanning industry may increase competitiveness by establishing vocational institutes that complement the graduate courses in leather technology provided by the Bangladesh College of Leather Technology (BCLT).

Though the strategy of organising the production process more efficiently is insufficient to reposition a firm in a GVC, it is a *conditio sine qua non* to develop its competitiveness. More sophisticated production methods and improved quality may help establish trust and pursue long-term relationships to foreign buyers; the latter are particularly important when it comes to safeguarding international contracts of varying degrees of formality (e.g. L/C, T/T). Process upgrading can also change Dhaka's tanning industry's negative reputation and strengthen ties to more regulated markets. This, however, has to be rewarded in higher returns if an exodus to less regulated markets (e.g. China) is to be avoided.

In the long run, private standards may provide an opportunity for few large tanneries to produce compliant high-quality leather. It is by all means necessary to strengthen small and medium-sized tanneries that are unable to fulfil those requirements and run the risk of ending up excluded from the global market (for the horticulture industry, see Dannenberg 2012). Re-Tie Bangladesh confirmed that distrust of a traditional industry towards learning and introducing new production methods has to be dismantled first in order to achieve sustained upgrading.

It will be challenging to reduce the divergence of export and domestic market requirements which are currently unable to offer either adequate prices or quality. With the attraction of foreign leather goods and footwear (LGF) manufacturers in local EPZs, domestic sales meeting export requirements can be raised, but still local LGF producers need to be strengthened to build up a solid domestic market (see Sect. 5.3).

In light of the above, industrial upgrading is an evolutionary process, the success of which will rely on close collaboration between the public sphere and private stakeholders. Both parties have evolved institutionalised informal and illicit practices, many of which only provide individual benefits, while society at large is harmed. A major revision of the institutional framework seems indispensable to start a fundamental change towards more compliance and to ensure the tanning industry's competitiveness in the global market without compromising domestic values.

5.3 The Leather Goods and Leather Footwear Subsector

After discussing development constraints, adaptation strategies and the potential for upgrading for the leather processing industry, I proceed to explore the dynamics of the higher value-added leather goods and footwear (LGF) subsectors. First, I will look into the structure and organisation of the LGF manufacturers (see Sect. 5.3.1). Before discussing global market integration of the producers interviewed (see Sect. 5.3.4), I will delve into the coordination of the local production network (see Sects. 5.3.2 and 5.3.3), which is expected to shed light on research question 1/b/ii. In Sect. 5.3.5, it is investigated what upgrading trajectories have been taken to improve the manufacturers' competitiveness.

5.3.1 Organisation of the Leather Goods and Footwear Subsector—Dominant Actors and Product Flows

This section provides an overview of the organisation of the leather goods and footwear (LGF) subsector (research question 1bi). Figure 5.20 depicts the dominant actors and product flows.

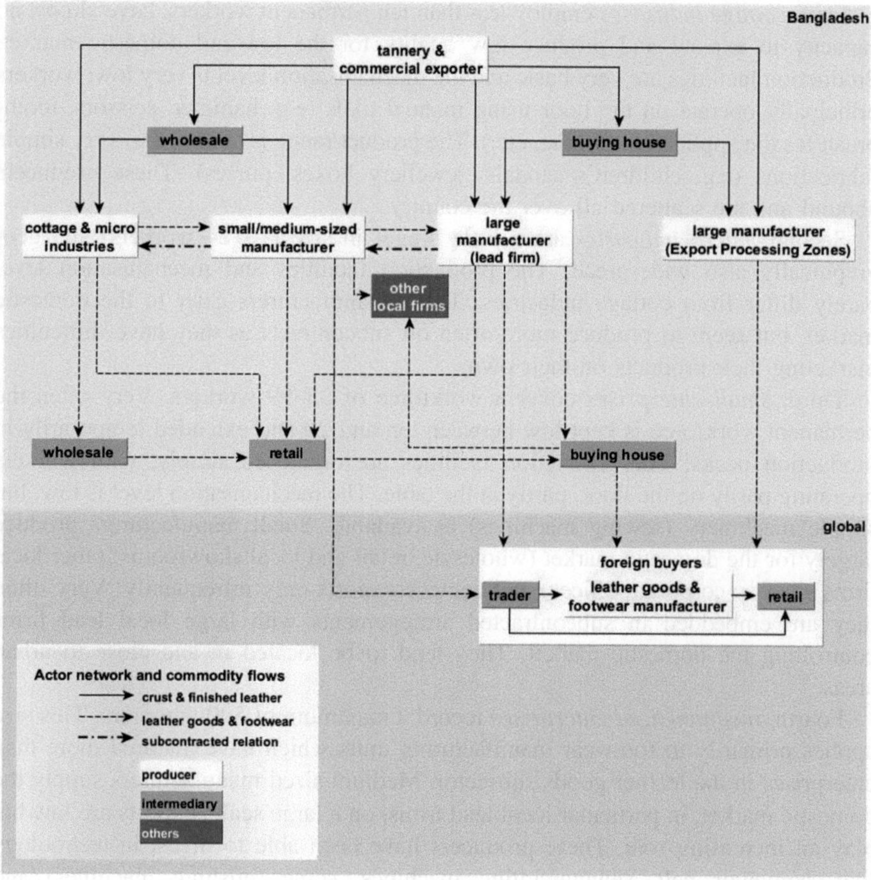

Fig. 5.20 Actors and product flows in the leather goods and footwear subsector. *Source* Data based on interviews conducted in 2010–2012. Own illustration

The LGF industry is forward linked to the leather processing subsector from which it procures a variety of raw materials (crust/finished leather, lining leather, insole-leather, outsole-leather) for subsequent manufacturing.

Adapted from the Bangladeshi SME Foundation's classification of firm sizes (interview SME Foundation) and enriched by findings from own interviews with manufacturers, the LGF industry can be categorised as follows[73]:

[73]The SME Foundation provides also reference values on the annual turnover of each manufacturer's class. Due to data inconsistency these could not be verified for all of this study's interviewees. The indicator 'employees' is only to a limited extent applicable to the reality of Dhaka's LGF manufacturers. Very often micro and small industries employ only few workers on a permanent basis but hire temporary workers during production peaks.

First, *cottage industries* employ less than ten permanent workers, have almost no capacity to expand and produce low quality for the low-end domestic market. Production facilities are very basic and the mechanisation level is very low; workers principally operate on the floor using manual tools (e.g. hammer, scissors, toothbrush for the application of glue, etc.). The product range is confined to very simple fabrications (e.g. children's sandals, jewellery boxes, purses). These producers abound and are scattered all over the country.

Second, *micro industries* are a little bigger in size (10–24 workers) and geographically also widespread. The production facilities and mechanisation level barely differ from cottage industries. These manufacturers cater to the domestic market, but seem to produce more often on subcontracts as they have difficulties marketing their products on their own.

Third, *small enterprises* cover a workforce of 25–99 workers. Very often the permanent workforce is kept low between ten and 20 and extended temporarily in production peaks. The production facilities are organised simply, with workers operating partly on the floor, partly at the table. The mechanisation level is low, but simple machinery (sewing machines) is available. Small manufacturers produce largely for the domestic market (wholesale, retail and local showrooms; other local firms such as corporate offices) and achieve exports only infrequently. Very often they are embedded in subcontracted arrangements with large local lead firms controlling the domestic market. They tend to be located in and close to urban areas.

Fourth, *medium-sized enterprises* record a maximum of 500 labourers. This size applies primarily to footwear manufacturing units which have matured more than enterprises in the leather goods subsector. Medium-sized manufacturers supply the domestic market, in particular local lead firms, on a large scale; exports are low but play an increasing role. These producers have been able to invest in technology (e.g. conveyor belt, sewing/cutting machines, some finishing machines) and industrialise production processes. They are primarily found in large cities and due to space constraints at the urban fringe.

Fifth, *large manufacturers* exceed 500 employees. They play a critical role on the domestic market by drawing on micro, small and medium-sized manufacturers (MSMEs) for subcontract. Exports are achieved on a regular basis, though the domestic market remains the core business. Despite a high level of mechanisation (e.g. conveyor belts, cutting machines, modern sewing machines, last machines, finishing machines), labour productivity is still one of the lowest in the world.[74] Manufacturing facilities are outside the urban centres.

Sixth, *large manufacturers* are also found *in export processing zones* (*EPZ*) around Dhaka and Chittagong. These firms are exempted from certain taxes to cater exclusively to the export market (BOI 2011). They have been excluded from this

[74]After 15 years of operation the labour productivity in the Bangladeshi plant of a German leather goods company amounts to only 44 % of the German factory. A Tunisian subsidiary set up in the late 1970s has reached 90 %.

study because the conditions under which they have access to the global market (e.g. tax holidays, bonded licenses, FDI) differ significantly from companies operating outside EPZ.

This study focuses on MSMEs which make up the vast majority of Bangladesh's LGF industry (BLSC 2009; GTZ 2006; GTZ-PROGRESS 2006; Ahmed 2002). The participants selected and interviewed were firstly classified according to structural data such as number of employees, production capacity, capacity utilisation, size of the production site, and turnover (see Table 5.7). Data inconsistency of cottage and micro producers in particular (e.g. LGM A, LGM B) makes it difficult to inter-subjectively comprehend the way participants have been grouped, but insights from semi-structured interviews support the outcome.

Figure 5.21 gives an overview of the spatial location of the different types of factories. Most of the small producers interviewed are based in Hazaribagh; only one (LGM F) is located outside Dhaka City Corporation (DCC). Ganaktuli, another leather cluster which lies south of the tannery estate on the way to Old Dhaka, hosts several cottage and micro producers three of which were interviewed because of their relation to the large retailer and leather goods manufacturer LGM G (see Sect. 5.3.3.3). One medium-sized (LFM C) and one large footwear producer (LFM D), both closely cooperating—as we will see in Sects. 5.3.3.3 and "Subcontracting for the Export Market—Developing Capabilities or Becoming Invisible Exporters?"—have their factories in the district of Gazipur, which is adjacent to Dhaka. Another medium-sized footwear manufacturer expanded his factory within Hazaribagh.

The original objective of this study was to shed light on the challenges and constraints local LGF manufacturers face in catering to the export market and how they try to overcome those. The first interviews (February–April 2011) disclosed intense interrelations between MSMEs and local large manufacturers as a striking feature of the local production network, whereas the importance of exports was rather downsized. Follow-up questions in early 2014 revealed that this picture apparently had changed towards a stronger export-orientation among the MSMEs interviewed, the reasons and dynamics of which unfortunately could not be fully revealed anymore. Hence, the coordination in the manufacturing segment through subcontracting activities seemed critical to the MSMEs' competitiveness and thus was highlighted in this study's analysis.

Section (5.3.2) relates the manufacturers' strategies to source raw material to their class and examines their value for competitiveness. New actors displayed in Fig. 5.20 will be introduced.

Table 5.7 Classification of leather goods (LGM) and leather footwear manufacturers (LFM), April 2011

Manufacturer acronym: Leather goods	Manufacturer acronym: Leather footwear	Number of employees (in 2011)	Production capacity (in pieces/pairs per month)	Capacity utilisation / production volume (in pieces/pairs per month)	Area (in ft^2)	Turnover/sales (in BDT)	Class
LGM A		m.v.		2011: 100 pc (bags); 500 pc (jewellery boxes)		m.v	Cottage
LGM B		12	m.v	m.v	m.v.	m.v.	Micro
LGM C[a]		20	2010: 1,500 pc (wallets, bags, jewellery boxes)	2010: 73 %	2011: 400	m.v.	Micro
			2013: 3,500 pc (wallets, bags, jewellery boxes)	2013: 70 %	2013: 1,420		
LGM D[a]		8	2010: 400 pc (bags), 20,000 pc (small garments)	2010: 60 %	2011: 1,000	2011: 8 m	Small
			2013: 800 pc (bags), 32,000 pc (small garments)	2013: 60 %	2013: 1,800	2013: 12 m	
LGM E[a]		12	2010: 1,000 pc (bags)	2010: 55 %	2011: 850	2010: 6–7 m	Small
			2013: 2500 pc (bags)	2011: 60 %	2013: 3,500		
				2013: 60 %		2013: 10–15 m	
	LFM A[a]	46	2010: 3,000 pairs	2010: 75 %	2011: 1,000	2010: 20 m	Small
			2013: 4,000 pairs	2011: 80 %	2012: 2,500	2013: 35 m	
				2013: 70 %			
LGM F		35	2010: 10,000 pc (bags)	2011: 25–30 %	2011: 5,000	m.v.	Small
			2013: 10,000 pc (bags)	2013: 40 %	2013: 5,000		

(continued)

Table 5.7 (continued)

Manufacturer acronym		Number of employees (in 2011)	Production capacity (in pieces/pairs per month)	Capacity utilisation / production volume (in pieces/pairs per month)	Area (in ft^2)	Turnover/sales (in BDT)	Class
Leather goods	Leather footwear						
	LFM B	250	2011: 30,000 pairs; 1,000 pc (bags); 500 pc (garments);	2010: 100 % (footwear)	2011: 6,000	2010: 130–140 m	Medium
			2013: 30,000 pairs; 20 pc/day (jackets)	2011: 100 % (footwear)	2013: 6,000	2013: 30 m	
				2013: 20 % (footwear)			
	LFM C	350	2011: 1,400 pairs/day	2011: 70–85 %	2011: 25,000	m.v.	Medium
			2013: m.v.	2013: m.v.	2013: 38,000		
LGM G[b]		28	2010: 3,500 pc/month	2010: 65 %	2011: 4,350	2010: 16 m	Large
			2013: m.v. (closed in 2014)	2013: m.v.	2013: 2,900	2013: 11 m	
	LFM D[b]	>5000	2012: 15,000 pairs/day (export); 4,500 pairs/day (local)	2011: 100 % (export);	m.v.	m.v.	Large
				40 % (local)			

Source Data based on interviews conducted in 2010–2014. Own illustration

[a]LFM A, LGM D and LGM E moved in late 2011 from a residential area to a larger production site; LGM C moved to a larger production site in 2013

[b]Data applies only to own factory. The subcontracting intensity approximates 90 % of LGM G's and 40 % of LFM D's overall production

The manufacturers were classified by the type of product they predominantly offer. All manufacturers interviewed were related either directly (first-tier subcontractor) or indirectly (second-tier subcontractor) to at least one of the two large (lead) firms (see also Table A.1)

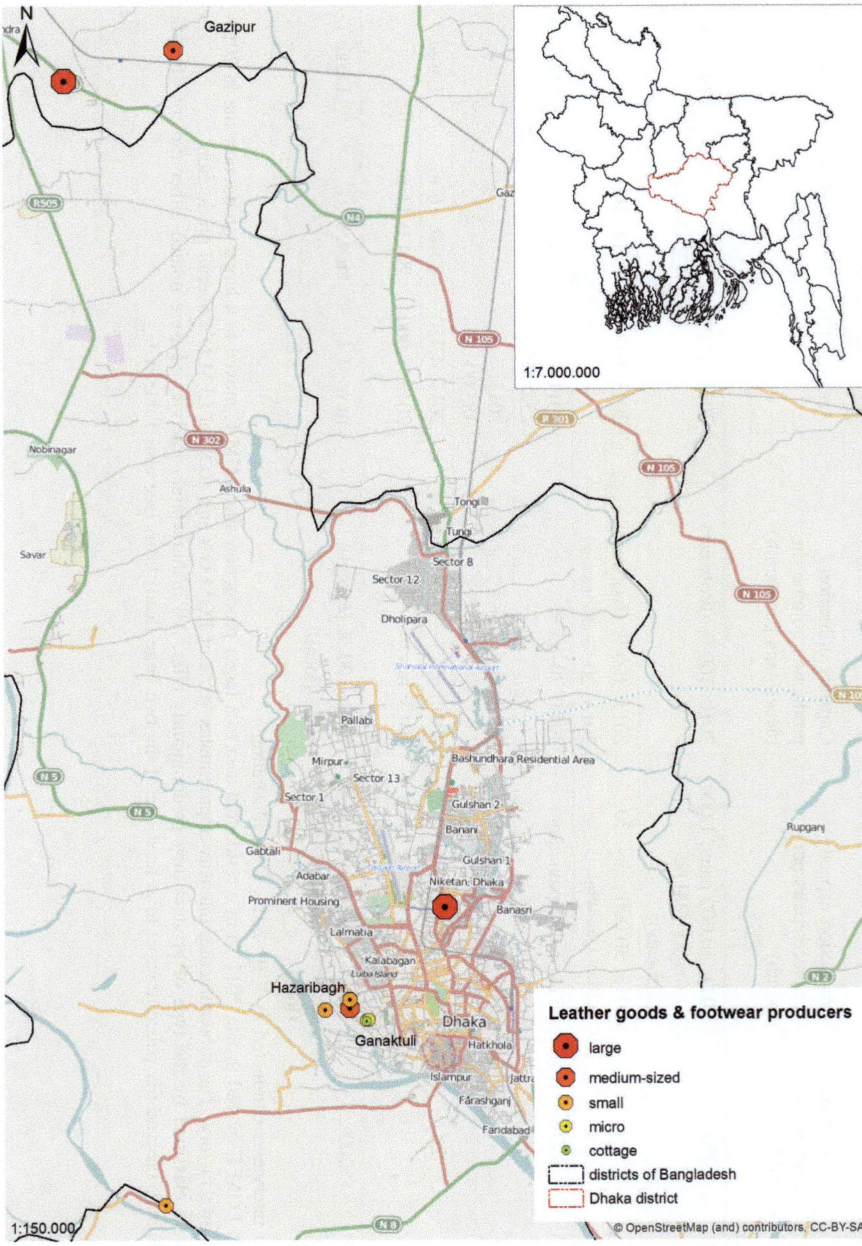

Fig. 5.21 Leather goods and footwear producers interviewed, 2012. *Source* Own illustration

5.3.2 Coordination Between Leather Goods/Footwear Manufacturers and Leather Suppliers

Interviews with LGF manufacturers on their strategies to source raw material from tanneries aimed to explain how this chain segment is coordinated and controlled (research question 1bii).

Cottage industries usually buy inferior leather quality from leather wholesalers in Old Dhaka where cottage, micro and small LGF producers are concentrated (e.g. Bangshal, Agamasi Lane).[75] Occasionally, they purchase low-quality finished leather (e.g. dyeing by manual spraying) and sometimes also crust leather directly from small tanneries, using RHS of inferior quality (e.g. cattle heads). Some manufacturers apply a rudimentary finishing on their own (e.g. manual application by brushes) or are provided the service from within the leather clusters in Old Dhaka. Targeting the low-end domestic market, cottage industries are not subject to tight product specifications by their buyers which are usually wholesalers, retailers or local showrooms (GTZ 2006). Some appear to be integrated into multi-tiered subcontracting schemes on the domestic market, that is, leather is supplied by the contracting (first-tier) manufacturer (see Sect. 5.3.3.4). In general, competition is high; cottage industries operate on a very price-sensitive level, where the quality of the leather and the finishing, amongst others, are a matter of secondary importance. Given their lack of export relations and apparently few linkages to local lead firms, cottage industries were of minor importance to this study and thus excluded from the analysis.

Thanks to a larger production volume, *micro, small and medium-sized manufacturers* tend to buy crust and finished leather directly from leather processors in Hazaribagh. Sometimes micro and small factories source small volumes from wholesalers in Old Dhaka. Specific finished leather articles unavailable in Hazaribagh are purchased outside Dhaka, usually from a tannery in Chittagong.[76] MSMEs operate to their customers' detailed product specifications on raw material and the type of finishing. If subcontracted by large local firms such as LGM G or LFM D (see Table 5.7), the requirements placed on product quality and thus of raw material increase. One medium-sized footwear producer (LFM C) occasionally buys crust leather and finishes it in medium-sized rental tanneries on his own account. This, however, seems to be a rare practice as knowledge and skilled personnel need to be hired.

As indicated already in Sect. 5.2.2.3, the supply of raw material is determined by the Festival of Sacrifice:

---

[75]Information on cottage and micro industries were gained mostly in informal conversations while looking for potential interviewees.

[76]According to the tannery associations and expert interviews, there are two tanneries in Chittagong.

> […] before Eid-ul-Azha most of the tanneries want to clear their stock. So if you have money, you can buy the leather at a cheap price now. For the long term it is very helpful for the business, but you need money. […] To some extent I'm trying. I already bought some leather for the jacket [production; A. N.] because in our country winter is coming. So I just stock in some leather for the jacket. (LGM E, English)

The tanneries are keen to clear their stock of low-quality RHS that has accumulated over the year to make room for high-quality raw material coming in on Eid-ul-Azha. This is the opportunity for small factories such as LGM E's to stock up on raw material at a relatively low cost, provided that funds are available. The main challenge is to finance raw material ahead. Micro and small producers usually do not qualify for bank loans nor are they able to repay funds raised from relatives and friends for only a very short term (usually 10–20 days) in time as orders are not in place yet (see Section "Insufficient Access to Finances"). Own capital is also limited. In order to economise they purchase rather small quantities of low-quality raw material at a low cost. The period before Eid-ul-Azha opens a window of opportunity only solvent manufacturers can use. After the festival, prices increase:

> After Eid-ul-Azha, after the Qurbanir Eid, we pay extra 15–20 taka per ft^2. But the buyers, they don't give us extra money. (LGM E, English)[77]

Large amounts of RHS are accessible after the Festival of Sacrifice (see Sect. 5.2.2.3). With varying availability and quality of RHS, prices fluctuate, too. Contracts set up before and up to three months after the festival involve risks as (foreign) customers deny re-negotiating terms and conditions.

The quality of raw material and therefore also the type of tannery from which leather is sourced seems to vary with the customer. Local buyers and particularly large business corporations placing orders for customer gifts (e.g. folders, bags) apply different standards to the quality of the leather:

> […] because our main customer is a local customer and they don't want to provide much money. They need better things [i.e. products; A. N.] but at a cheap price. That's why we go to medium or small tanneries and collect this type of leather; not graded leather because the price is a factor. […] But for the foreign buyers we collect the leather from large tanneries. (LGM E, English)

Price matters in the local market. Small manufacturers such as LGM E source low-quality leather from small and medium-sized tanneries to produce cost-effectively. Mechanical/physical and chemical tests to certify product quality are not required from domestic buyers. This scenario changes for the export market. Here, MSMEs usually need to comply with regulations on restricted substances and submit clearance certificates (see Sect. 5.3.4). According to LGM E, only a few tanneries can ensure safe quality.

Payment arrangements with leather processors often vary with the terms and conditions agreed on with the downstream customers. In general, micro and small

[77]Currency converted as of February 9, 2011 (OANDA 2014): 15 BDT = US$0.20; 20 BDT = US$0.27.

manufacturers have to advance between 20 and 50 % of the final payment. This may rise to 70 % for large tanneries if a special leather article is needed. The remainder is to be paid upon delivery. This generally works as long as other payments come in.

The transactions between tanneries and manufacturers are little codified. Contracts tend to be concluded on a low-formal level, with basic specifications being stated on pads and bills. Samples are requested from all leather processors. Low order quantities and low codification of contracts give micro and small manufacturers little leverage for (re-)negotiating with large tanneries. In general, all LGF manufacturers tend to source raw material from a few trusted tanneries. Small producers such as LGM D were particularly exposed to tanners making use of their power in the first years of their business:

> Yes, I faced a lot of problems. […] maybe they [i.e. the tanneries; A. N.] give a sample, […] and they say that this was 100 Taka per ft^2. But when I get the order -and buyers never want to give more time- then they [i.e. the tanneries] say that 'oh, that was an old deal, it is now 130 Taka. And no other tannery […] has that leather [article; A. N.]. So I don't have enough time to buy or to create new leather or to go to another tannery, so I have to give [the new price; A. N.]. That was a big problem. (LGM D, English)[78]

As an inexperienced manufacturer, LGM D faced sudden price increases several times contrary to the terms and conditions agreed upon with the tannery. Trust had not been built up yet. Tanners used their power to impose changes in prices, taking advantage of the manufacturer's lead time.[79] Very often also infrastructural limitations such as power cuts cause delays and quality failures. Micro and small manufacturers that supply low value-added products to the domestic market source leather from low-cost tanneries which have difficulties rising to international requirements concerning, for instance, leather softness and colour matching, says expert B. Rejected leather can hardly be substituted or even re-exported within the lead time. New production would entail a minimum of seven to ten days. Later on, LGM D had gained more experience in the market and had forged enduring relationships to trusted suppliers. Irrespective of the power asymmetries in manufacturer-tannery relations, raw material prices fluctuate; particularly in Bangladesh where slaughter activities and RHS are scarce in the off season. Increases of 10–20 BDT (US$0.14–0.29)[80] are difficult for small manufacturers such as LGM D to compensate:

> That is a big problem because in a passport holder we need four to five ft^2; then […] for a big order it is very difficult to profit. It fluctuates [within; A. N.] one day, even [within; A. N.] half a day. Sometimes the tannery owners are not supporting us. When they see that my order is urgent and I need it, then they don't negotiate. (LGM D, English)

[78]Currency converted as of February 8, 2011 (OANDA 2014): 100 BDT = US$1.43; 130 BDT = US$1.86.

[79]In Hazaribagh, processing RHS to finished leather takes minimum 20 days (see Sect. 5.2.1).

[80]Currency converted as of February 8, 2011 (OANDA 2014).

Wedged in between powerful leather suppliers and forward-linked customers, small manufacturers either accept losses as buyers do not renegotiate or the buyer withdraws from the contract because the tannery refuses to accept lower rates. Both ways illustrate the micro and small manufacturers' vulnerability to the fluctuation of raw material prices.

According to the two *medium-sized manufacturers* interviewed, the payment varies with the supply volume and the relationships to upstream and downstream customers. Advances tend to be rare and low (10 %); the final payment is given after delivery and quality control. Medium-sized factories with rather low but regular export activity (e.g. LFM C) are able to use back-to-back letter of credits (L/C), where one (international) L/C serves as a collateral for another (e.g. at the national level). Occasionally the bill is settled upon payment by the foreign customer's, which indicates a slight power imbalance in favour of the manufacturer. In general, however, power asymmetries seem to materialise less within this group.

The *large manufacturers* (LGM G, LFM D) interviewed produce a part of the final goods in-house, while others are outsourced to smaller manufacturers (see Section "Magnitude, Characteristics and Importance of Subcontracting for Lead Firms"). In-house production, though substantially varying between both lead firms, draws on raw material from mostly large leather processors. Market power exempts these lead firms from down payment; the bill is cleared upon receiving the materials. Instead, their producers are entrusted with the procurement of raw material based on a (product) sample. If the countersample passes inspection, subcontractors place the order with the tannery. As subcontractors take care of their raw material individually, quality differences can be assumed. Lacking competences in leather processing make the lead firm LGM G reluctant to assume the liability for externally produced leather.[81] Lead firms provide only very specific accessories (e.g. outsoles).

The procurement of raw material is a matter of finance that particularly affects micro and small manufacturers. Local lead firms outsource the risk of fluctuating raw material prices to their suppliers. Lower quantities exclude these from economies of scale and make them more vulnerable to leather processors (mis-)using their power in setting prices. Medium and large firms are able to source from medium-sized and large tanneries at arm's length and often on a trusted basis. In general, leather quality varies with the consumer market. MSMEs source from low-cost tanneries for the domestic market and refer to large tanneries to meet international requirements.

[81]Only fabric and garment producers, LGM G's core business, can count on the provision of raw material that is being imported or produced in-house.

5.3.3 *Coordination Between Leather Goods and Footwear Producers and Customers on the Domestic Market*

Leather goods and footwear manufacturers differ in structure, size and market orientation from the tanning industry. The bulk of the leather goods and footwear production is based on cottage, micro and small industries which primarily cater to small local buyers such as wholesalers, retailers or showrooms (GTZ 2006). Small and medium-sized manufacturers often supply larger domestic buyers and achieve exports, though not always on a regular basis.

Interviews with MSMEs and two local lead firms in leather goods and footwear manufacturing and retailing, each the largest of its kind, confirmed subcontracting to be the dominant coordination scheme for productive activities in the domestic market. Before the dynamics in local subcontracts are elaborated on (see Sects. 5.3.3.3 and 5.3.3.4), other possible coordination schemes on the domestic market will be briefly touched on (see Sects. 5.3.3.1 and 5.3.3.2).

5.3.3.1 Coordination Between MSMEs and Wholesalers

The local wholesale-retail distribution network is mostly fuelled by cottage and micro industries and small manufacturers. Though margins from wholesalers are quite attractive (approximately 10–20 %), all small manufacturers complained about the institutionalised payment system of local buyers, which considerably affects their competitiveness:

> But the main problem is […] their payment system is very bad and that's why I am just stopping with these two buyers [who pay in time; A. N.] because I don't have enough money to get the order and deliver the product on time because the majority of the local buyers pay for their product after getting the product; it may be five or six months later. (LGM E, English)

LGM E is unable to supply more than his two regular domestic buyers as the local terms of payment leave him in an unfavourable position. Down payment for production and delayed payment by his customers would expose him to huge risk. The local payment system predominantly practiced by wholesalers and retailers is an informal institution that has been persistent to change.

The supplier is given a percentage of the final sum up to one month of the delivery of the product. Another smaller percentage may be arranged within the next month. The remainder, usually between 30 and 50 %, will be settled before Eid-ul-Fitr which closes Ramadan. This means the manufacturers deposit 30–50 % of each order to wholesalers; capital that is excluded from being valorised. With their finances being blocked for up to one year, better skilled MSMEs have few incentives to cater to domestic buyers of this type.

Delays in payment are the reason why LGM D tries to avoid supplying middlemen in the domestic market. When she started her business after graduating from

BCLT, she tried to enter the domestic market via intermediaries. Soon she learned that formal contracts provide no guarantee about timely payment:

> We might do something about the contract but our local laws are not so strong. So maybe we have to go to the court and nothing results. […] And the people who gave the order, they are mainly big companies. We are small, smaller than those. (LGM D, English)

Formal institutions such as contracts are useless if enforcement is poor. Weak political and judicial institutions have proved futile in solving cases in time. Small manufacturers such as LGM D tend to avoid these costs and await their payment. After initial problems as a female newcomer in a male dominated industry (and society), LGM D has adapted to the systemic constraint of pre-financing production: now, when dealing with middlemen she only accepts orders against cheque. This strategy gives her more control over her finances but also reduces the number of potential buyers.

Concluding from this section, unreliable payment appears to be the striking reason why MSMEs avoid certain domestic buyers. Wholesalers and middlemen are embedded in traditional informal institutions that have been resistant to adapt to a dynamically growing and increasingly outward-oriented LGF sector. These MSMEs seek to minimise risk and turn to buyers whose terms and conditions differ from the traditional domestic market.

5.3.3.2 Coordination Between MSMEs and Large Domestic Companies

Large businesses ordering corporate gift items (e.g. folders, office bags, wallets) have turned out to be an important buyer for small leather goods producers. Contrary to cottage and micro industries, small manufacturers have certain market knowledge and usually draw on larger production capacities. Payment terms and conditions are favourable for the manufacturer's competitiveness; the bill is usually settled within one month of delivery and margins are exceptionally high:

> […] we have some buyers like corporate offices; we can gain 30–40 % of profit from working [with them; A. N.]. But the problem is they order like once or twice a year. That's why they are our second customers. But LGM G [a local large manufacturer; A. N.] is our first priority customer. (LGM E, English)

Such profit is only possible because local business corporations give these products to their clients as part of their promotional activities. They prioritise price over quality. As clients do not demand flawless quality, buyer pressure on suppliers is low. Consequently, manufacturers such as LGM E process low-quality raw material, accessories and chemicals and often subcontract production to even smaller low-skilled manufacturers (see Sect. 5.3.3.4). This means that corporate businesses allow the supplier to produce lower quality and achieve higher margins.

Sales to large local retailers are picking up among small manufacturers. Higher quality standards compared with smaller domestic buyers (wholesalers, retailers) and corporate businesses keep margins at a lower level (approx. 15 %). No down payment is given, so that the pressure on micro and small industries increases the larger the order. It is an advantage over other domestic buyers that the bill is usually settled after one month of delivery.

Despite favourable conditions provided by large companies, the seasonality of incoming orders exposes the small manufacturers interviewed to high risk (i.e. unreliable source of income) and forces them to diversify buyers.

5.3.3.3 Coordination Between Lead Firms and First-Tier Suppliers on the Domestic Market

Initial interviews with a number of MSMEs indicated that local large manufacturers play a critical role in coordinating the domestic market. The nature of the linkages between lead firms and micro, small and medium-sized producers helped establish a typology and refine the analysis (see Section "Magnitude, Characteristics and Importance of Subcontracting for MSMEs"). First, for both lead firms and MSMEs the extent, traits and impact of subcontracts on either competitiveness were scrutinised.

Magnitude, Characteristics and Importance of Subcontracting for Lead Firms

Subcontracts appear to be the dominant feature of Bangladesh's leather goods and footwear production network. The two large manufacturers interviewed outsource large quantities of their production to smaller producers.

The Social Enterprise

LGM G is owned by the country's largest NGO and calls itself a social enterprise. Being primarily a retailer of a variety of products (see below), it operated an in-house leather goods and footwear production until 2014. The firm offers a wide range of low to medium and higher value-added articles for the domestic market (e.g. jewellery boxes, purses, sandals, bags, jackets), whereas primarily low value-added product lines are eligible for exports (e.g. photo frames, card holders, pen holders, jewellery boxes, purses).

A look at LGM G's sales demonstrates impressively the extent of its reliance on external producers (Fig. 5.22).

In 2010, almost 90 % (on an average approx. 36,000 pc per month) of the production was managed by 45 subcontractors in Dhaka's leather clusters, among others Hazaribagh and Old Dhaka.[82] LGM G's own leather factory was just used as

[82]By March 31, 2011, LGM G maintained subcontracting relationships to 715 producers for all products. 45 of these produced leather goods and footwear.

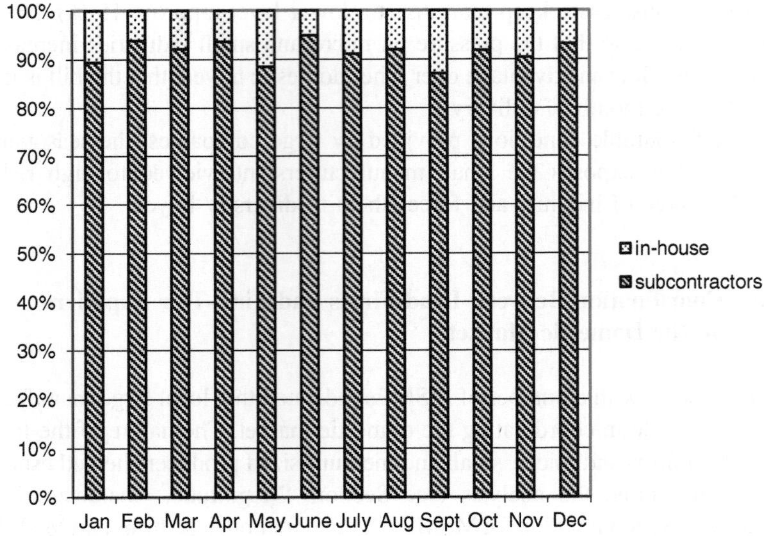

Fig. 5.22 Sales by LGM G's in-house and subcontracted production, 2010. *Source* Data provided by LGM G. Own illustration

a backup for supplier failure and utilised only 65 % of its capacity (3500 pieces). Exports from in-house production reduced from 11 % in 2010 to only 5 % in 2013. In the same year, the turnover attained in-house with leather products amounted to only 4 %. In 2014 the factory was closed for reasons that could not be verified anymore. This confirms that subcontracted producers are LGM G's mainstay of leather goods and footwear production.

Despite such large-scale production, LGM G has no set of criteria for selecting producers:

> We often like either needy people or we like people with very innovative thinking because even though we have designers here, we also like the fact of telling us what designs they can do. So there isn't really a standard criterion […]. (LGM G, English)

LGM G's producers range from a very basic skills and technology level (e.g. operations on the floor) with simple products (e.g. wallets, jewellery boxes) to well-organised semi-mechanised export-oriented factories that are capable of producing higher quality manufactured products (e.g. bags, jackets). Sample productions demonstrate the manufacturer's capabilities and the need for further development. Product quality from new producers is ensured in initial inspections and monitoring. After production processes have been routinized, LGM G controls the quality by the time of delivery. As LGM G markets consumer goods from 20 different industries with a strong focus on fabric and garments, leather goods and footwear play only a minor role in the company's total sales (less than 5 %). Hence, the lead firm's competences in leather manufacturing are limited, confirms the head of the Department of Social Compliance and Producers Relations (SCPR). This suggest that entry barriers for LGM G suppliers are low due to both the lower complexity of leather goods (in footwear only sandals are sold) and LGM G's nature as a social enterprise that advocates for the poor.

As conceptualised in Sect. 2.3, profit-seeking enterprises may outsource production for capacity constraints, access to specialised capabilities or cost reduction. LGM G, the social enterprise, says it is motivated by different reasons:

> Well, firstly, the reason is we believe in empowerment. So one of our main reasons for doing business is empowering people and developing them. […] So the idea of having these contractors are meeting our demand and at the same time empowering them. (LGM G, English)

LGM G's mission is to reduce poverty by commercialising art and crafts from all over Bangladesh (BRAC 2014). The enterprise employs more than 2300 people, 60 % of whom are female, and reinvests the earnings in development initiatives (BRAC 2014). LGM G offers a wide range of artisan products from clothing to toys and household items to leather products. It ensures the livelihoods of more than 65,000 artisans and craftspeople who are involved in manufacturing the final consumer goods on a subcontract basis. The Senior Manager of the SCPR Department sees subcontracting as a perfect fit for LGM G's plans to expand on the market:

> Well, it goes with our mission of empowering people, sustainable businesses, so it's… I mean LGM G ourselves we can't do it on our own. I mean the demand we have, we've got 11 outlets, we export a lot to … even though it's just 5 % of our local numbers, but still […] we do export also. (LGM G, English)

The narrative of empowering and developing unskilled producers is pivotal for the social enterprise's economic success. LGM G has been growing constantly since 1978 and has successively broadened its range of products. For garments and textile production the firm makes use of poor and mainly female producers in rural areas. Leather products are basically manufactured in and around Dhaka thanks to proximity to the tanning industry in Hazaribagh. The tannery estate and Old Dhaka are also home to a concentration of micro, small and medium-sized LGF-manufacturers. At the same time, the Senior Manager of SCPR unintentionally attenuates the empowerment argument by admitting that the firm's in-house production capacity of only 3500 pieces is unable to satisfy the rising demand. In-house production is only considered a backup in case of supplier failure. LGM G's benefits from subcontracting labour-intensive leather products on a very large scale are soberly embedded in the social enterprise discourse:

> […] we need producers because they make the products we sell to our customers, we need them to become sustainable businesses and be loyal to LGM G […]. That is also because, with us being a social enterprise, it's also very important for us to say that we have businesses who depend on us or who we help develop. So that's definitely very important. And the other thing is LGM G does intend to grow. So, at the moment we've got 11 stores, in the next five years we'll definitely have more. So, more means more products, more products mean more production for them. (LGM G, English)

The Senior Manager is keen to emphasise LGM G's sustainable business model that rests on developing socially compliant producers. When explaining the value of their suppliers to LGM G, she gets entangled with the social enterprise narrative despite obvious cost advantages in overhead and production. The lead firm's discourse of helping people to develop and to become sustainable businesses is opposed to the fact that LGM G keeps them 'dependent' so as to ensure supplies to meet an ever increasing demand. At the same time, the Senior Manager makes no secret of LGM G's intentions to grow at the expense of low-cost MSMEs. Whether these are allowed to grow with their lead firm and how they demand loyalty will be touched on in Sections "Coordination Through Selective and Mediated Market Access"–"Dependence Through Subcontracts".

The Profit-Seeking Enterprise

Things are different with the leather footwear manufacturer LFM D, a profit seeking enterprise which thanks to a joint venture with an Italian company in 2006, earns 80 % of its sales as an Original Equipment Manufacturer (OEM) for large global retailers. The firm operates two factories in a district near the capital city, each addressing either the domestic or the export market. The local factory was set up in 2010 to develop synthetic footwear, for which the skills and the market in Bangladesh are yet to be established, says the Managing Director of LFM D. With increasing market acceptance and decreasing costs he expects to better utilise the factory's capacity, which was then 40 % (November 2011). The lead firm outsources 40 % of its production to smaller producers, which testifies to its strong focus on subcontracting given that footwear manufacturing is its core business.[83] LFM D's distribution network comprises 240 outlets spread all over the country. Small leather footwear subcontractors manufacture rather basic final products such as sandals, whereas medium-sized enterprises qualify for more complex operations (e.g. low shoes, boots) for which more knowledge and technology (e.g. imported lasts) is required. Potential suppliers have to fulfil the following requirements:

- Manufacturers are expected to have a certain production capacity to supply sufficient quantities.
- The product range and capabilities of producers matter.
- Financial strength is necessary to cope with LFM D's terms of payment while serving own suppliers. The MSMEs are paid 90 days of delivery, that is, they have to endure a gap of at least four months between order placement and payment. Section "Coordination Through Payment Arrangements" enlarges upon the constraints and power asymmetries MSMEs are exposed to in payment arrangements.
- Suppliers need to comply with local regulation and adduce, for instance, a Tax Identification Number (TIN) and Value Added Tax (VAT) registration.

[83]Unfortunately, LFM D did not provide absolute numbers.

According to the Managing Director of LFM D, many MSMEs are unable to fulfil this requirement and are not eligible for subcontracts.

Subcontracting is vital for LFM D, one of the largest footwear manufacturers and retailers in Bangladesh. The lead firm sees several opportunities in sourcing final products from low-cost suppliers:

> On the local side about 40 % of what we sell is outsourced. Simply because […] there are small producers or very efficient [ones; A. N.] who are much more cost-competitive than us and who are specialised in products. So, for example, that sandal you are wearing is much better in a small factory; the detail is better, the quality is better. Also the big thing is that they can work on smaller quantities. So they don't need to get 1,000 pairs to start. So for us as a retailer sometimes we need to test the product. We can't afford to take a risk on 10,000 pairs, we test 500, 600 pairs. So here also we believe at LFM D very strongly that if we can bring these local SME producers into our supply chain, it helps them. It helps us be more flexible in our sourcing. (LFM D, English)

Cost reduction and flexibility through producing small runs production are the major reasons why LFM D subcontracts MSMEs. With small manufacturers producing small labour-intensive volumes the lead firm enhances its flexibility and reduces the risk that comes when launching new products on the market. Retail embraces the concept of less standardised and fewer products. Such market niches are very difficult for large companies to address. MSMEs offer capabilities to produce handmade quality footwear that are not available in-house. Moreover, subcontracting ensures cost-efficient production which is crucial for LFM D to compete in the medium and high-end domestic market with Bata, a global shoe company, and other few large local firms.

The labour-intensive production of barely standardisable consumer goods appears to be a profitable business for lead firms that, however, avoided providing exact figures. Small producers such as LFM A give an idea of their customers' financial benefit:

> […] the sandals I'm giving to LFM D for 475 Taka, they are selling it for 1,250 Taka. And in their factory it is not possible for them to make these sandals for 475 Taka. (LFM A, English)[84]

LFM D's in-house production cannot compete with low production costs of MSMEs. Costs for setting up contracts, monitoring production, quality control as well as marketing and distribution have to be added, but the mark-up of over 160 % implies that subcontracting is a lucrative deal. This means LFM D subcontracts MSMEs effectively to reduce costs and maximise margins.

To conclude, the two lead firms interviewed largely coordinate productive activities via subcontracting arrangements. Final products are supplied by MSMEs under very flexible and profitable terms. Entry barriers seem to be lower for LGM G's suppliers thanks to products with low complexity and the firm's character as a

[84]Currency converted as of February 12, 2011 (OANDA 2014): 475 BDT = US$6.81; 1,250 BDT = US$17.92.

Table 5.8 Traits of the leather goods and footwear lead firms interviewed, 2011

	Profit-seeking firm (LFM D)	Social enterprise (LGM G)
Primary competences	Manufacturing	Retail, manufacturing (garments)
Type of subcontracts	Full-assembly	Full-assembly
Subcontracting intensity	40 %	90–100 %
Entry barriers for suppliers	Financial strength; formal registration; production capacity	No selection criteria
Objective	Flexibility; cost reduction; niche markets	Social empowerment

Source Own composition

social enterprise. With the production, lead firms outsource risks. Subcontractors serve the purpose of testing niches cost-efficiently (Table 5.8).

The following section introduces the different types of MSMEs interviewed that have been identified as subcontractors of the two lead firms.

Magnitude, Characteristics and Importance of Subcontracting for MSMEs

The way large leather goods and footwear manufacturers coordinate their supply network through subcontracting translates into different dynamics within the heterogeneous group of suppliers. The following typology summarises and classifies briefly the characteristics of the MSMEs interviewed.

Low skilled exclusive suppliers (T1) produce low quantities of low value-added products (e.g. small lady's bags, purses, jewellery boxes) for only one lead firm. The micro producer LGM B failed to diversify buyers on the domestic market and his factory is underutilised.[85] His dependence on one lead firm makes him highly vulnerable as orders vary seasonally. Insufficient orders and the inability to fund from banks without taking high risks limit his opportunities to develop his business. Being neither in a position to receive funding from banks at interest rates of 15 %, nor able to improve the capacity utilisation, the goal of this type is to grow by order, not by loan. For T1 subcontracting is a strategy to get by but not a strategy for development.

Low skilled micro producers with export activity (T2) have capabilities that in principle qualify only for the domestic market. Thanks to a former official at LGM G, the micro producer LGM C liaised with an international buyer to whom he supplies low value-added, low-complex products such as business card holders and jewellery boxes. Domestic sales to LGM G are relatively low (20–25 %) but stable in absolute terms. This dependence on one single lead firm can only be partly

[85]Unfortunately, we were not provided with precise data.

compensated on the foreign market as exports are high but irregular. In 2011, exports dropped by 39 % and produced losses LGM C could not make up for on the domestic market. A capacity utilisation of 70 % leaves scope for growth but LGM G, his domestic lead firm, is reluctant to give orders beyond seasonal events:

> I need more orders. If the orders were more, profits would be more. [...] Then there would be no need to get loans from others. (LGM C, Bengali)

LGM C has started as a second-tier subcontractor of LGM G more than ten years ago and became a first-tier subcontractor more than six years ago. Transactions have become routinized; the lead firm's requirements of product quality are clear. Finding new buyers, however, is difficult and involves high transaction costs. For a long time, LGM C invested little in production facilities as handicraft products required low capital input. In 2014, he moved his factory from Ganaktuli to Hazaribagh, expanding production capacity by adding labour. This strategy works as long as orders from foreign buyers are stable. If exports decline, vulnerability increases and domestic subcontracts are insufficient for T2 to make progress.

Skilled export-oriented small manufacturers (T3) have been provided with excellent conditions to grow. This group consists of graduates from BCLT (LFM A, LGM D, LGM E) and international design schools (LGM F), where they acquired technological, design and management capabilities in leather product manufacturing. Two export strategies with implications for subcontracting have emerged:

First, manufacturers such as LGM E and LGM F have ambitions to export on a more regular basis, but still depend on subcontracts as export orders and earnings come in irregularly:

> If they [i.e. LGM G; A. N.] don't give me orders, I will have great problems running my factory. [...] Though I am getting 15 % profit but they provide the order regularly. (LGM E, English)

LGM E supplies small quantities to a small American buyer who aims to set up a distribution network. Orders fluctuate; in 2010, exports were nil, whereas in 2013 LGM E made 70 % of his earnings on the foreign market. The reducing intensity of subcontracts, however, does not reduce his dependence on his lead firm's order. He supplies LGM G on a regular basis and accepts margins (12–15 %) that are far lower than those for exports or corporate businesses (approx. 25–30 %). Regular subcontracts provide stability and order security, which irregular exports cannot ensure. These manufacturers within T3 seek to reconcile the two markets.

Another strategy is pursued by LFM A who is aware of current constraints to entering the export market:

> Of one design I gave them [i.e. LFM D; A. N.] almost 75,000 pairs of sandals in the last two years. Only one design! It's very good for me that my worker is habituated with the product and I don't have to make any changes in the production line. So that's why I always prefer LFM D than the local market, though there is twice profit than [with; A. N.] LFM D, but the credit system and the quantity of the order... A local purchaser never can give you an order of more than 50 pairs or 100 pairs of one design in one colour. But LFM D will give you minimum 1,000 pairs whenever they start to give order. (LFM A, English)

LFM A's major lead firm (LFM D) orders sufficiently large quantities that allow him to concentrate on few designs and to standardise production processes. Although other domestic buyers offer higher margins, lower volumes, late payment and infrequent orders make these sales less attractive. LFM D and LGM G place orders on a regular basis, thereby providing financial security to their regular suppliers. The requirements of foreign buyers on production facilities made LFM A rethink his strategy. Now he uses subcontracts to prepare for export market entry. Thanks to his ability to fund from different sources (family, bank loans) he invests in technological assets and in building up production capacity:

> […] my motto was just to make the entry because I want to set up a production line. If I go for LFM D, I can produce a huge quantity. [Currently; A. N.] I'm producing, but I have no market. I have to make my business grow [first; A. N.]. So I go for the production, not for the profit. (LFM A, English)

While other small producers with export ambitions take a two-pronged approach of supplying the domestic market and every so often catering small runs to global buyers, LFM A prefers to temporarily leave exports. His objective is to fill the gap to large export-oriented firms in terms of product quality by developing his workers' skills in producing demanding designs and using modern machinery. He prefers to professionalise production processes at the expense of higher profit rates and is gradually increasing his production capacity so that he is able to deliver larger volumes to international buyers. LFM A's strategy seems to work: in terms of production capacity, volume and turnover he has grown faster than any other small (leather goods) producer within T3.

To conclude, T3 consists of skilled small manufacturers that use subcontracting as a strategy to develop capabilities for the export market, though the emphasis within the group varies.

Export-oriented medium-sized manufacturers (T4) introduced standardised production processes based on division of labour and assembly line production. The dependence on lead firms was very high by the time of the first interview in 2011. Subcontracts (70; 90 %) are the financial backbone of this type of manufacturer. Large-scale orders of higher value-added products (e.g. lady's shoes, gent's closed shoes) on a regular basis ensure good revenues with relatively high capacity utilisation. Export activity is low as lacking technological requirements for more complex products (e.g. boots) are often an obstacle to market entry. Additionally, LFM B had difficulties exporting on a regular basis as he lacks language skills and therefore depends on buying houses. At the end of 2011, both manufacturers took pride in the long-term trustful relationship they had with their major lead firm LFM D, which had led to continuous growth. By 2014, default payment by foreign buyers (LFM C) and the lead firm (LFM B) had plunged both manufacturers into a financial crisis. Eventually, the lead firm LFM D took over LFM C by acquiring 76 % of the company's shares. The loss of LFM D as a main customer makes LGM G add up to 100 % of LFM B's billings; this is an untenably insecure position. This shows that T4 is highly vulnerable to power asymmetries on both

Table 5.9 Subcontracting typology of MSMEs interviewed

Determinants	Low skilled exclusive supplier (T1)	Low skilled supplier with export activity (T2)	Skilled export-oriented small manufacturers (T3)	Export-oriented medium-sized manufacturer (T4)
Skills level	Very low	Very low	Low	Low-medium
Subcontracted activity	Very high	Low	Low	High
Value-addition of subcontracted products	Very low	Very low	Low-medium	Medium-high
Customer diversification on domestic market	Nil	Nil	Medium	Very low
Dependency on one single lead firm	Very high	High	Medium-high	High
Export activity	Nil	High, irregular	Low, irregular	Low
Value addition of exported products	–	Very low	Low	Low-medium
Business strategy	Subcontracts to get by	Exports to reduce vulnerability from subcontracting	Subcontracts to develop export skills	Subcontracts as core business; against unreliable export market

Source Own composition

domestic and export market. Subcontracts are the core business as exports have not taken off yet.

Table 5.9 displays in compact form the characteristics according to the refined typology of the MSMEs interviewed.

With the typology of subcontractors in mind, I proceed to discuss how lead firms coordinate and control the LGF production network (research question 1/b/ii).

Coordination Through Selective and Mediated Market Access

All MSM producers lack a distribution network and depend on intermediaries to market their products in local retail. While wholesalers fulfil this function for the low-end domestic market (see Sect. 5.3.3.1), a few large manufacturers such as LFM D control the medium and upper market segment along with Bata, a global footwear manufacturer and retailer:

> Local market actually requires the biggest investment because you know in our market there are lots of big players […]. That's why if we want to enter this market, we have to be prepared well, otherwise it will be difficult […]. (LFM C, English)

MSM subcontractors are facilitated by being given mediated market access which they could not achieve by their own means. Large manufacturers and retailers control the medium-high-end domestic market where margins are higher than on the export market due to fewer requirements on product quality and social compliance. Smaller manufacturers cannot afford to invest in shops, especially not in affluent areas. Hence, particularly skilled export-oriented producers such as T3 and T4 benefit from the higher market segments they are able to target through their lead firms:

> When I went to LFM D, the […] general manager for marketing [and; A. N.] sales […] was not interested in buying my leather sole sandals. He told me, 'Liton[86]', he is one of my bosses, […] 'it is the product for the European market and the Japanese market, not for the Bangladeshi market. Do you think in the rainy season our people can use this type of product?' And what I told him, 'sir, this product is a costly item, leather soles are a posh item and the people who walk in the water in the rainy season, they will not wear my sandals. I target the people of the upper-middle class and you have this type of customers in your gallery. So I think you are my appropriate customer. If you think so […], then you can go for sample production'. […] And then he gave me [i.e. ordered; A. N.] only 600 pairs and I supplied it. And within two days it was sold out. Then he requested me to supply him with another 600 pairs and I supplied him. And for the next [order; A. N.] in 2010 I supplied 25,000 pairs of the same sandals of the same design. And my article was one of the bestsellers of LFM D. (LFM A, English)

LFM A started as a part-time leather technologist for LFM D's rented wet blue tanneries and used this connection to enter the leather footwear market. Leather sandals in the local MSME supply-based retail system rarely exceed US$15. Locally renowned companies such as LFM D or global brands such as Bata offer footwear from US$10 (sandals) to more than US$50 (low shoes). LFM A supplied an article with special characteristics that gave him room for negotiation. For climatic reasons leather outsoles for sandals are uncommon on the domestic market. Local large manufacturers such as LFM D like to add detailed labour-intensive products to their basic footwear. Such capabilities are neither available nor can they be produced cost-effectively in-house (see Section "Magnitude, Characteristics and Importance of Subcontracting for Lead Firms"). LFM A's preferential access to LFM D and his social and educational background as a graduate from BCLT enabled him to argue in favour of his products, so that he achieved market entry in the medium-high-end segments. But rather than the financial benefit of getting access to new market segments, it is the opportunities such market entry brings about. Producers learn from large manufacturers to increase their quality standards. In linkages to large firms they expect to improve the exportability of their products (see Section "Magnitude, Characteristics and Importance of Subcontracting for MSMEs").

---

[86]The name has been changed for reasons of data privacy.

By contrast, LGM G is not a market leader in leather goods and footwear but attracts a large number of consumers of medium to high-end products to its outlets. Although low-skilled manufacturers (T1, T2) produce only basic, low value-added products (e.g. jewellery boxes, photo frames), sales are guaranteed. This is a big advantage over other domestic buyers who order lower quantities on an irregular basis.

Subcontracts provide mediated market entry to MSMEs but exclude them systematically from direct sales. The suppliers are deprived of the opportunity to address customers with own brands:

> I have no identity, LGM E has no identity. […] But the customers who collect the products from LGM G, they actually think that they are purchasing LGM G's products. But they don't know the original scenario […]. But the main problem is the money. We don't have enough money, that's why we are selling our products to LGM G and LGM G is selling the product in whole Bangladesh and also in the foreign market. But they have money. They have outlets, so they are doing business. I have no money. (LGM E, English)

Subcontractors lack direct market access and thus cannot develop corporate identity, that is, market their products under their own brands. LGM G and LFM D integrate their suppliers' products in their widespread sales and retail network without informing their consumers about the real manufacturers. Taking deliberate advantage of the asymmetry in information, finances and marketing capabilities to their suppliers, the two lead firms feed subcontracted products into both the domestic and export markets (see Section "Subcontracting for the Export Market—Developing Capabilities or Becoming Invisible Exporters?"). In public LGM G enjoys prestige and recognition for giving support to primarily poor and female suppliers from rural areas. But with the exception of annual awards for specific products little is known about the production conditions of those craftspeople. To what extent consumers accept the practice of large renowned chains outsourcing the bulk of their production to low-skilled and under-resourced producers in workshops crammed with workers in the slums of Dhaka remains to be investigated.

In sum, lead firms provide entry to different market segments according to the manufacturers' skills levels. Skilled manufacturers (T3, T4) craft medium- to high-end products for the domestic market and approximate quality standards for low-end exports. T1 and T2 are exclusive suppliers of low value-added (basic) products for one single lead firm. The vulnerability to a buyer drop-out is accordingly high.

Coordination Through Costing and Price Setting

In costing and price setting, power imbalances between lead firms and subcontracted MSMEs come to the fore. Before the order is placed, lead firms compute the total cost per unit based on current material prices (raw material, accessories, inputs) and add a standard profit rate of 10–12 %.

With the exception of LFM C, whose products are exported by LFM D, all subcontractors criticise the little direct monetary benefit they obtain from their lead firms. The margins conceded undercut those of other domestic buyers (25–40 %) considerably. MSMEs have developed different strategies to adapt to such constraints.

Manufacturers with export ambitions (T3) complain about the tight costing that compromises their capacity for development but prove capable of negotiating prices:

> Actually I have a bar or a standard: I must earn at least 15 %, otherwise I will not take the order. For example, LGM G collects this bag from me. They provide me for this bag 1,100 taka. First they measure the leather, what square feet is needed, then the material costs, then making costs, then other costs like transportation, packing, tag. […] And then they provide 12 % profit. I said to you if I get 15 % profit, then I do the job. Then I have another area, factory overhead. I got the money from them. And it adjusts another 3 %. This 3 % comes from my factory overhead costs. And this 15 % I got from them as a profit. (LGM E, English)

LGM E successfully negotiated with his lead firm to cover his overhead costs which are usually excluded from costing. As a graduate from BCLT his social and educational background differs substantially from the more domestic-oriented producers (T1) or low-skilled exporters (T2). His export experience accounts for his ability to produce leather goods that meet international quality standards. More professional business management structures including, for instance, computerised accounting and access to (subsidised) loan programmes have contributed to his confidence and to his ability to negotiate acceptable terms and conditions. Export-oriented T3-producers appear to determine the strategy that serves their purpose most, that is, whether they focus on subcontracts or diversify buyers or try to export.

Contrary to the interview with LGM G, the lead firm seems to impose producers of very basic products (T1, T2) lower margins (10 %):

> They said that if the costing price and the market price do not diverge much, the number of customers will be more. […] They will get more customers if the cost is less. (LGM B, Bengali)

Unlike T3-producers, LGM B does not re-negotiate with or oppose his lead firm; he accepts the terms and adapts by cutting costs in other areas:

> LGM G gives me 500 Taka for leather. But I have to pay 450 Taka or 420 Taka for leather. So some money has been saved in this case. […] If the leather is cut nicely, then some leather can be saved. Although they give [a profit margin of; A. N.] 10 %, there is also room rent. In total, I can make 15 % profit. (LGM B, Bengali)

LGM B and LGM C (T1, T2) lack the knowledge and education to negotiate costing in their favour. Instead, like other manufacturers, they adapt by optimising the consumption of raw material and reducing overhead costs. Unlike small and medium-sized manufacturers, the extent of underage employment among cottage and micro industries is more widespread. LGM B and LGM C were seen to use child labour. New workers are often recruited as children between eight and

12 years from the owners' home districts to ensure reliability. Wages are extremely low and prone to be squeezed for the sake of the owner's profit.[87] The lead firm's low standard profit rates of 10 and 12 % respectively motivate the manufacturers to organise the production process more efficiently—or to resort to informal practices. The lead firm LGM G admits it is aware of producers quoting the nominal wages of trained adult workforce, which differ greatly from the real wages of child/untrained labour. Other (T3) producers also look to increase their margins:

> We naturally charge a little bit more in a different way to collect these things [i.e. for costing; A. N.]. You know this is hidden [interviewee laughs; A. N.]. (LGM F, English)

Both lead firms emphasise that their costing departments are well-informed about market rates for raw material and accessories. However, LGM G's core business is fabrics and garments, not leather. Producers may gain some percentages thanks to the lead firm's fewer competences in assessing raw material and inputs, the procurement of which subcontractors have to take care of:

> We don't have experience with non-textile goods. We don't want to take the liability for these products because we are not producing the raw material. (LGM G, English)

Instead, LGM G and LFM D give recommendations on how to increase efficiencies and encourage producers to join upgrading programmes (see Sect. 5.3.5.3). Such measures, however, primarily address quality assurance and contribute little to keeping producers from squeezing costs at the expense of labour conditions.

Export-oriented manufacturers (T3, T4) have the necessary knowledge and education to negotiate favourable terms and conditions. Although both types rely on one dominant customer, large-scale production (T4) and a more diversified customer structure (T3) allow them to deal with relatively low profit margins. Instead, low-skilled manufacturers (T1, T2) adapt to tight costing by optimising the consumption of materials and inputs and lowering labour costs. To what extent the lead firms' tight costing contributes to non-compliant practices will be discussed in Section "Assistance in Social Compliance".

Coordination Through Payment Arrangements

If a few lead firms direct a large number of suppliers, power can be exerted at different stages of the transaction. Like in the tanning industry, the way payment is arranged between lead firms and LGF-producers matters.

---

[87] Helpers start at an age of eight to 12 and learn for one year by observing and giving a hand to more experienced workers. Usually they stay at the factories and have Friday off to visit their family. Food and accommodation is provided by the owner; an additional allowance of approximately 200 BDT (US$2.85) per month is provided. In the same factory the salary of a 14 year old worker with work experience of three years amounts to: 3,000 BDT (US$42.80); a 15 year old worker with work experience of one and a half years: 1,500 BDT (US$21.40); an adult worker with work experience of eight years: 7,500 BDT (US$107) including overtime. All salaries are given as of March 3, 2011, and have been converted accordingly (OANDA 2014).

LGM G is an important domestic buyer for all micro, small and medium-sized leather goods manufacturers interviewed and offers monetary benefits that are exceptional on Bangladesh's domestic market. The firm outrivals other buyers through very attractive payment methods and loan facilities to suppliers. Producers do not enjoy advance payment facilities but are paid 100 % a few days after the delivery by cheque:

> So our main idea […] is to make sure that […] whoever gets us our product is paid immediately because I think that's the biggest financial help anyone can have. (LGM G, English)

Spot payment gives LGM G-suppliers a crucial advantage over domestic competitors who are usually paid in instalments until the bill is eventually settled before Eid-ul-Fitr (Ramadan). It ensures regular earnings from production and allows producers to reinvest in raw material and accessories. LGM G secures 5 % of every bill with their suppliers, thereby amassing savings that are used to assess the potential amount of credits producers can take with the parental company's bank. A deposit of 80,000 BDT (US$1,120) may result in a loan of 200,000 BDT (US$ 2,800),[88] explains the Senior Manager of the SCPR Department in March 2011. Terms and conditions state an interest rate of 15 % and repayment in ten instalments. According to the Head of the SCPR Department in April 2014, LGM G objects to the withdrawal of the deposit only if the subcontractors have been granted a loan by the parent company's bank. Only two of the producers interviewed have used this facility to date: one to keep production running (LGM F, T3); the other to manage a serious crisis when one major customer backed out (LFM B, T4). Particularly T1 and T2-producers are unaware of how to use this facility and are put off by the high interest rate. Their 'savings' are blocked, while LGM G's financial institute can work with that money.

To resume one of LGM G's objectives, the lead firm creates 'loyalty' (see Section "Magnitude, Characteristics and Importance of Subcontracting for Lead Firms") by very attractive payment arrangements and a sizable amount of money deposited at the parent company's bank.

LFM D's standard payment term is 90 days of delivery. Only a few trusted suppliers such as the medium-sized enterprise LFM C and producers of very desirable articles benefit from down payment. LFM D demands financial strength from suppliers to compensate payment shortfalls before, during and after production:

> […] if it's an old supplier there's always some payments that are coming mature and some payments that are coming new. If it's a new supplier, frankly, it depends on how much we want that product. […] Obviously we prefer not to [give any down payment; A. N.] because it blocks our finance. Our standard practice is not to make any down payments, we sign a contract and hopefully with that contract they can go to the bank and get some financing […]. (LFM D, English)

[88]Currency converted as of March 31, 2011 (OANDA 2014).

Two of LFM D's suppliers (LFM A, LFM B) complain about the lead firm's payment behaviour that often differs from the terms and conditions provided in the contract. They find it challenging to deal with delays and to produce on credit. The entire process, from the incoming order to the final payment, usually takes a minimum of four months, during which time suppliers need to finance raw material, inputs, accessories, and labour plus overhead expenses. MSMEs have no leverage over lead firms; they are bound to await payment and orders. Contrary to LFM D's expectations, high interest rates bar smaller manufacturers from applying for loans, while medium-sized enterprises have been able to fund from banks (see Section "Insufficient Access to Finances"). Low production volumes and irregular orders reduce their creditworthiness.

This section has shown that power asymmetry between lead firm and subcontractors materialises strikingly in payment methods. Down payments by lead firms, which have the important function of maintaining the manufacturer's solvency during production, are only given to very trusted suppliers. Without advance money, only order continuity and timely payment can ensure the subcontractor's competitiveness as exemplified by LGM G. Any interruption in the order-payment cycle increases the financial vulnerability of subcontractors. LGM G's financial benefits (spot payment) only partly empower MSMEs and partly create new dependency on the lead firm (e.g. 5 %-deposit with every bill). Despite considerable disadvantages the suppliers are exposed to in relationships to lead firms, MSMEs prioritise full payment and regular orders by large firms over higher profits (and more risk of outstanding payment) by other domestic buyers. This means that the payment arrangements of the two lead firms keep the suppliers captive.

Insufficient Access to Finances

As pointed out in Sect. 4.3, the institutional environment of the leather industry is deficient and hampers the competitiveness of the MSMEs interviewed in different ways. Financial stability and access to finance is essential to enhance the competitiveness and growth potential of MSMEs.

Interviews suggest that loan conditions of governmental and private banks are often inaccessible for micro and small manufacturers. High interest rates (12–17 %) act as a deterrent for many micro and small manufacturers that, moreover, are often unable to fulfil collateral requirements. The collateral-free sum is considered too low for substantial investments. Intermittent order inflow and low capacity utilisation discourage MSMEs from servicing loans in the low season. A high level of bureaucracy and corruption, particularly in governmental banks, involves huge transaction costs which micro and small industries cannot afford:

> You know in Bangladesh there is a huge corruption. […] Whenever small people [i.e. enterprises; A. N.] or the uneducated people go to the bank […] to get some loan, he has to pay some money to the officers. He has to make some extra costs. So it is not possible on his part to earn money from his business and make the instalment of the loans. (LFM A, English)

LFM A describes a common scenario for MSMEs that feel harassed by governmental banks. Particularly micro and small manufacturers (T1, T2, T3) are unable (and often unwilling) to strike this costly path. Private financial institutes are said to be less inclined to use illicit practices but usually charge higher interests. Some seek to extend loan facilities to MSMEs. For instance, LGM B (T1), an exclusive subcontractor of LGM G, has been offered loans by two private banks thanks to regular transactions with these:

> I am doing business with my own capital because if I pay their interest, my business will have to expand and their loan will have to be paid monthly or in due time. And to do this more benefit is needed. Why would I do that without a chance to earn profit and without getting enough buyers? The main issue is the buyer. (LGM B, Bengali)

Interest rates of approximately 15 % discourage cautious traditional manufacturers such as LGM B who prefers growing slowly by using his own capital. Although LGM G's facilities would yield a substantial amount of loan, he assumes the risk as too high, being that LGM G is his only buyer. A lack of knowledge and information about potential opportunities adds to the dearth of financial capital. As a result of missing buyers and a high seasonality of orders, LGM B refrains from necessary investments in machinery and production capacity to develop his business. Therefore, T1 gets by but cannot achieve growth.

LGM C's (T2) limitations in funding from banks are similar; he sees himself in no condition to take loans:

> No, I have never taken a loan. I am a small businessman. I live from hand to mouth. I earn 10,000 to 20,000 [Taka; A. N.] in a month. So I am not in the position to get a loan. (LGM C, Bengali)[89]

Both T1 and T2 relate their low revenues to the unstable order situation that has not been handled adequately. LGM C's irregular exports, though lucrative, provide no security to service a loan programme on a regular basis.

Small manufacturers (T3) that aim to export are also exposed to structural constraints in funding from banks, which is indispensable to make business thrive:

> So you can't enlarge your business every year, every year; it is not possible without any support from financial institutes or your family. (LFM A, English)

However, LFM A and other T3-producers appear to be more flexible in finding new funding opportunities. Their higher capabilities result from a better endowment of social, cultural and economic capital. As graduates from BCLT and international design schools, they proved eligible to participate in upgrading programmes. Thanks to PRICE (Poverty Reduction by Increasing the Competitiveness of Enterprises) which was funded by USAID (see Sect. 5.3.5.3), the Bangladesh Leather Service Centre (BLSC) which was financed by the International Trade Centre (ITC Geneva), and female entrepreneurship awards (for LGM D), this group

[89]Currency converted as of April 19, 2014 (OANDA 2014): 10,000 BDT = US$130.63; 20,000 BDT = US$261.27.

achieved preferential access to credit facilities by a governmental bank. Such loans, however, are usually only one-off opportunities. Regular funding from banks is very rare for that type of enterprise.

The medium-sized manufacturers (T4) interviewed have the capability to take loans and pay interest. High production capacity as well as high utilisation thereof (occasionally over 80 %) plus regular orders from either local large firms or global companies provide additional security to banks. LFM C can secure a bank loan with the L/C of an ongoing transaction. Long-term credits safeguarded by a mortgage on own property allowed LFM B to constantly develop his production capacity. Thus medium-sized manufacturers appear to have more opportunities than smaller industries to gain funding from banks.

Traditional investment finance seems to be accessible only to certain types of MSMEs (T4) or under specific circumstances (T3). Barriers to obtaining short-term finances within the formal banking system make manufacturers refer to two informal adaptation strategies:

First, funding from within one's own social network serves as a flexible source of capital. It is an effective means to adapt to structural constraints (e.g. high interests) and illegal practices (e.g. bribes) in formal financial institutions. Low entry barriers (no fees, no interests) make relatives and friends for the micro and small manufacturers interviewed (T1, T2, T3) the first choice. All manufacturing groups including medium-sized enterprises have been reported to occasionally take interest-free, short-term finance. Small amounts of capital are used to bridge bottlenecks in the off season or to purchase raw material and accessories. Collateral-free funding relies on the level of trust between the moneylender and the manufacturer. It provides flexibility which comes with a risk for the producer's effectiveness:

> Because you know, whenever you get loans from relatives, you have to pay them [at; A. N.] any time, he can ask for his money [at; A. N.] any time. So we are always in a tension for money. (LFM A, English)

Strong ties to peers that grant funds for a very limited time period (usually ten to 20 days) may exert pressure on the MSMEs. Terms on repayment are informally agreed and may be subject to change. Furthermore, delays in certain stages of a transaction (e.g. due payment by customers) may affect the timely repayment of informal loans and induce non-intended actions like purchasing raw material despite high prices or unsuitable quality. Consequently, informal funding is a flexible alternative to unattractive formal finance schemes but involves risks that may hamper the producer's competitiveness.

Very few enterprises are able to draw on family capital to the extent that investments in production facilities are realised and a long-term growth strategy is pursued:

> As I have got the support of my family, that's why I have enlarged my factory within two years by almost 20 times. I started my factory with five workers and now I have 36 workers. My working capital was only 3 lakhs [i.e. 300,000 Taka; A.N.] and my working capital is now almost 80 lakhs [i.e. 8,000,000 Taka; A.N.] because it is not from my profit. (LFM A, English)

LFM A had been able to mortgage parental land and secure 4 m BDT (approx. US$ 56,000) instead of the collateral-free maximum of 1 m BDT. This finance allowed him to set up a new and larger production site (from 1,000 to 2,500 ft^2) with new workers and increase production capacity substantially (from 2,000 to 4,000 pairs per month). LFM A's social background provided him with opportunities that other manufacturers lack. He was able to study Leather Technology at BCLT and started working as a leather technologist for the wet blue section of LFM D's tanning operations. Thanks to informal long-term financing, LFM A has been capable of investing in machinery to build up capacity and improve production processes.

Cooperatives are the second informal adaptation strategy. They act as savings groups and provide short-term collateral-free loans to their members who deposit a monthly fee. According to the manufacturers interviewed, loan conditions are unfavourable for MSMEs and thus not an option: interest rates may amount to 30 % and are collected on a daily basis; the repayment is arranged within a short time period and is ensured by pressure from peers. Cooperatives provide flexibility to underfunded MSMEs, while new dependencies emerge and undermine the manufacturer's competitiveness. It is assumed that only low-skilled producers who lack opportunities to gain funding from banks and relatives refer to such instantly available financial facilities.

In sum, the lack of down payments from lead firms reduces the manufacturer's solvency during production. The lead firms' terms of payment, particularly those of the profit-seeking LFM D, exert pressure on subcontractors. In view of the inadequate opportunities for MSMEs to get financing from banks, informal adaptation strategies have emerged. Low-skilled micro producers (T1, T2) draw on financial support from peers on a low scale. The export-oriented SMEs (T3, T4) proved more flexible in funding from both formal and informal sources, though only T4 can rely on permanent bank support.

Dependence Through Subcontracts

Subcontracts by nature imply an uneven relationship between the contracting body (local large firms) and the suppliers (MSMEs) of the final leather product. This section explores to what extent subcontracts make MSMEs dependent on dominant lead firms.

Both lead firms receive large supplies from subcontracted producers (see, for instance, Fig. 5.22) and the MSMEs realise a substantial part of their sales by subcontracts (see Table 5.7). Figures may well illustrate an interdependent relationship involving benefits for both but cannot hide the fact that lead firms strongly coordinate and control the supplies.

Decades of subcontracting have made LGM G experienced in addressing various market segments by producers with different skills. Very low value-added leather goods (e.g. purses, jewellery boxes, business cardholders, key rings) tend to be crafted by low-skilled producers (T1) that supply exclusively to LGM G. Their benefit of regular earnings comes with requirements that interfere with the producers' autonomy:

> Now, to be honest, [...] when we started, we always wanted our producers to be only producing or giving us products. But now [...] they're all becoming bigger and we're not able to give them a 100 % [of capacity utilisation; A. N.]. So, we always tell them, 'if you do subcontract to somebody else, fine', [...] but, you know they also need to survive and so do their workers, but we would still like to be first priority. We don't want our deliveries running late or we don't want our quality being compromised because of another buyer. So, we tell them and we make sure that they do that. Or you know I shouldn't say make sure because I don't know how we make sure but you know we tell them not to do that. (LGM G, English)

Even if LGM G lacked enforcement mechanisms, the firm presses its producers at least verbally grant it preferential treatment. Designs must not be used for other buyers; production and deliveries must not be hampered by other duties. The lead firm demands complete loyalty from its 'independent' producers which, in fact, are viewed as dependent (subcontractors). By regulating the order volume, lead firms have ways of controlling subcontractors. LGM B (T1), an exclusive supplier of LGM G for more than ten years, complains about insufficient and highly seasonal orders that have been constraining his ability to expand his business. While his factory is underutilised,[90] he lacks time and particularly the know-how to find new buyers:

> No, I have not found [other buyers; A. N.]. I am not educated, so I have not tried. I am going on with this small work." [...] I have not found a trustworthy person so I have not tried. Moreover, there is a need for some samples and measurements to try for new buyers. (LGM B, Bengali)

Low capabilities constrain LGM B's growth prospects and increase his dependence on the lead firm. In production peaks LGM B is tied to his lead firm and cannot build up trust to other customers. The off season, in principle, provides opportunities, but illiteracy and lacking knowledge in, for instance, using information technology (e.g. internet research) keep LGM B from looking for buyers or marketing his products at domestic trade fairs. In order to develop personal, trust-based relationships to potential buyers, manufacturers need to be embedded in corresponding social networks or have to incur high transaction costs (e.g. regular personal visits; several sample productions; initial small orders). Low design capabilities add to LGM B's cognitive limitations in diversifying buyers. The designs he manufactures for LGM G cannot be used for other buyers. In general, low-skilled manufacturers (T1, T2) are good at copying samples but have deficits in innovating, that is, they lack the knowledge and skills to research appropriate designs for copying in the way that, for instance, T3 and T4 do:

> We take these from the internet or there are some catalogues. Then we have a master, we sit together and then build up a face. If we don't like it, we make some changes or adjustments [...] (LFM B, Bengali)

---

[90]Unfortunately, the precise data could not be verified.

Although the design capabilities of all MSMEs are immature, export-oriented manufacturers (T3, T4) have learned by formal education or by interaction with foreign buyers to adopt and develop original designs from other markets. As pointed out in Section "Coordination Through Selective and Mediated Market Access", LFM A introduced buffalo leather outsoles for leather sandals in order to increase quality and to avoid imported plastic or low-quality local rubber soles.

Design variations are critical to buyer diversification. LGM B (T1) finds himself trapped between LGM G controlling his order situation and his desire to expand his business, which depends on the lead firm's appraisal of his capabilities:

> […] so somebody who is very skilled and maybe is an old producer has been with us for many years or somebody who actually has a very good factory and is able to understand design, they will get higher-end products, whereas the rest will probably get just very basic products […]. So, I'll be honest, we definitely make it a point to give them production and everyone production, but this might sometimes be more difficult in off-peak seasons. But I wouldn't say we make them sit. (LGM G, English)

The latter is, however, exactly what T1- and T2-producers of low value-added products complain about: their workers sit idle after Eid-ul-Fitr, the end of the high season. From an industrial management point of view, LGM G's classification in low-skilled and high-end product suppliers is absolutely justified. As with a social enterprise, however, questions remain over whether it suffices to incorporate low skilled producers in the supply chain. Real empowerment implies the lead firm's commitment to build up their suppliers' capabilities, for instance, in terms of design and organisation of the production process, thereby reducing the subcontractors' dependency. To what extent LGM G does justice to its responsibility to empower subcontractors will be discussed in Section "Assistance in Social Compliance".

The emerging T3-producers also rely on subcontracts but occasionally manage to export and sell to other local customers (e.g. corporate businesses; other large local retailers). Coming from a higher social stratus, they often criticise the lead firms' ignorance towards MSMEs:

> […] they are going for their facilities, their profit; they are not interested in the SMEs. They are not doing anything for the SMEs. […] What I've told, this was the first time that the SMEs took the opportunity to express their opinions.[91] And it happened because WE are the educated people, we are the technical people. Otherwise the people from Agamasi Lane [a leather cluster in Dhaka; A. N.] will not get the opportunity. (LFM A, English)

LFM A and other T3-producers demand more knowledge exchange with their lead firms to develop their businesses. Current profit margins leave them little room for investments. Many producers lack capital to finance modern technology and would appreciate a joint facility centre provided by their lead firm. T3's dependence on their lead firm is high, too. It remains to be seen whether this group's social,

[91]Industry leaders and SMEs spoke at the seminar on "Awareness Building on Product Standard and Environment of Leathergoods and Footwear Industry" organised by the business association LFMEAB on February 2, 2011.

technical and economic capabilities hold them well prepared for potential shocks, that is, in the event of payment default.

Such shocks happened to the two of the medium-sized footwear producers which initially had fulfilled all their lead firm's requirements: a large capacity, good skills and financial strength. LFM C was unable to sustain high overhead costs as particularly exports were not sufficiently picking up and buyers even dropped out of an ongoing transaction. In late 2013, LFM D took over LFM C by acquiring 24 % of the company's shares:

> It helped me survive. [...] Because sometimes it was difficult for me to pay salaries of my workers in time. So LFM D used to give me advance payment so I could give salaries. I was a permanent supplier and they trusted me as well; so they helped me in the time of needs. (LFM C, Bengali)

The acquisition saved LFM C's business but made him lose his independence. With LFM D being his only domestic buyer, LFM C had no backup when exports failed.

LFM B's dependence on his long-time lead firm has manifested in a different way. The footwear producer alleges to have been duped by LFM D which rejected an order of 500,000 BDT due to faulty outsoles. These, however, had been supplied by LFM D in bad shape, says LFM B. The business relationship broke; LFM B's turnover dropped by almost 80 % (see Table 5.7) in 2013, driving him into a serious financial crisis. Now he focuses on his other lead firm LGM G and started submitting samples to Bata, the largest footwear retailer in Bangladesh.

LGM G's approach of sourcing from low-skilled manufacturers without developing those appears to create highly dependent producers. T1 and partly T2 lack capabilities to diversify buyers. More outward-oriented suppliers (T3, T4) of both lead firms seem to be more successful in setting up trade relationships to other customers and markets. High competences, however, do not protect from the strong dependence engendered by subcontracts. Relatively low margins, little technical assistance and large volumes of subcontracted production tying resources appear to raise the suppliers' vulnerability to the extent that defaults in payment have posed a serious threat to their survival.

5.3.3.4 Coordination of Subcontracting Relationships Among MSMEs

The previous chapter highlighted coordination mechanisms between lead firms and first-tier suppliers. Pratim Sahu (2010) confirmed for Indian manufacturing industries that subcontracting systems are often multi-tiered. Interviews with leather goods and footwear manufacturers in Dhaka also suggest that subcontracting dynamics exist among MSMEs.

Only two of the MSMEs interviewed (LGM F, T3; LFM C, T4) declined to subcontract for quality reasons. Spatial distance to cheap suppliers, as their factories are remote from the leather clusters in Old Dhaka and Hazaribagh (see Fig. 5.21), was not mentioned. The rest of the interviewees (LGM B/C/D/E; LFM B) subcontracts for basically two reasons:

First, capacity constraints lead first-tier suppliers to subcontract parts of an order.

Second, producers look to reduce costs, while maintaining profits, in order to deal with the increasing competition among the MSME supply base. LGM D's order situation highlights these constraints:

> Sometimes I give some order to Bangshal [i.e. a leather cluster in Old Dhaka; A. N.]. […] they work just in one room; maybe ten or 15 people are working there. […] So their working costs are low and their wages are low […]. […] But when I go to Bangshal, I have different types of buyers, different types of costs. When a buyer gives me a wallet or belt at a low price, then I give it to Bangshal because if it is made by my factory, I can't profit. (LGM D, English)

LGM D's main domestic buyers are corporate businesses that place large orders of low value-added leather products at the turn of the year, confirming Holl (2008, p. 300) that "capacity subcontracting" fluctuates with the differing demand in the off season and peak season. If LGM D cannot produce low value-added small leather goods cost-effectively in-house, she resorts to cottage industries in Old Dhaka or to the plethora of home-based self-employed workers. The latter very often used to work for LGM D or have regular employment in the medium-sized leather goods factories of local tanneries during the day, while producing on a subcontract basis in night shifts. Given the abundance of low-cost cottage industries and homeworkers, subcontracts to second-tier suppliers still allow for profit. Customers are informed and decide whether to agree on subcontracts:

> […] so I told the buyer that I can make ten per a day with my regular workers and if you want more then I have to subcontract. […] if they don't want to do subcontract, they will give me ten and if they want more, then they know that I subcontract production. (LGM D, English)

This means that buyers are aware of the producer's/subcontractor's capacity and seem to accept second-tier subcontracting if price matters. Evidence from other studies (Holl 2008; Pratim Sahu 2010) suggests that locational factors such as agglomeration effects determine the dynamics of subcontracting, exerting downward pressure on costing. The small manufacturers LGM D and LGM E (T3) assure that they frequently monitor their subcontractors to ensure quality and lead time. Due to a lack of education, capabilities, adequate production conditions and production capacity, they cannot be considered a direct supplier to large manufacturers and firms.

Such asymmetry in capabilities and resources is reflected in (partly) informalised contract arrangements:

First, subcontracted cottage industries are expected to meet the lead time by adjusting the number of workers and working hours flexibly, including overtime and night shifts. Home-based self-employed workers often carry out job-work production after their regular working day. Normally, LGM D prefers to issue simple formal contracts, stating volume, costing, down payment and lead time. It states reference values without being a judicially binding contract. In the case of urgent orders, the transaction is agreed upon orally and the subcontractor has already been instructed about the product. Such weak formal contracts, however, exclude independent home-based workers from the privileges that permanent workers have (e.g. salary plus overtime, holidays), confirming their vulnerability (see Prügl and Tinker 1997; Webster et al. 1997).

Second, the payment is usually arranged on a per piece basis at the time of delivery. Down payments are only given in cases of large orders. These terms of payment involve risks for the contracting body, that is, for first-tier subcontractors: second-tier subcontractors are interested in maximising output for a higher profit, which is why they tend to care less about product quality. To avoid the quality being rejected first-tier subcontractors need to sensibly choose what products for what buyers can be subcontracted.

Corporate businesses (see Sect. 5.3.3.2) offer ideal conditions for subcontracting production to lower-tier producers, explains LGM E:

> Actually the main thing is they [i.e. corporate businesses; A. N.] are not worried about the quality, they are concerned about their price. (LGM E, English)

Corporate businesses mostly order price-sensitive leather goods (e.g. wallets, folders, diary covers) from mostly small manufacturers. They pander to their clients with gifts and thus pay little attention to quality issues. Low requirements regarding product quality allow the suppliers to save expenses for raw material and accessories, thereby gaining higher margins (30–40 %). Following Pratim Sahu (2010), multi-tiered subcontracting increases as the complexity of products and labour costs decrease.

Lead firms such as LGM G and LFM D order more value-added products (e.g. handbags, jackets, sandals, low shoes) which are subject to more rigorous quality control. Their suppliers (first-tier subcontractors) resort to a different informal network to increase their production capacity and meet their customers' quality standards.

Excursus: The Informal Network of Leather Goods and Footwear Manufacturers, LTSE

In 2009, a group of seven leather goods and footwear manufacturers who had graduated from Bangladesh College of Leather Technology (BCLT) founded the Leather Technologist SME Enterprises (LTSE).

The primary objective of LTSE is to develop their businesses along with the leather sector by providing support to each other. Members use this network to exchange knowledge and information, to share production facilities and to distribute subcontracts among each other. LTSE organises trainings jointly to save costs. Information on funding opportunities (e.g. international projects) is provided and, if possible, funds are acquired for other group members. In addition to information and knowledge, affiliates exchange machinery to deal with capacity constraints. LTSE serves as a platform to present ideas for joint facilities (e.g. facility centre for repair, maintenance and exchange of machinery) and pursue cooperative marketing strategies (e.g. tradeshows; showrooms) cost-efficiently. Interviews suggest that the nature of subcontracts within LTSE is different from outside the network. First-tier subcontractors of LTSE outsource more complex and higher value-added products (e.g. bags, jackets) to group members, while simple products (e.g. wallets, belts, key rings) are subcontracted to less-skilled manufacturers and home-based workers outside the network. Such cooperative processes contribute to raising competences among LTSE-producers that are excluded from direct transactions with local lead firms. The standards for product quality are passed on within the production network; the skills level is adjusted accordingly.

This self-help approach has contributed towards enhancing productive and marketing capabilities. Some members opened showrooms, although only in Hazaribagh and enlarged the group to 22 members in 2014. Having started as an informally organised network, LTSE registered as a cooperative society in 2012 and has received funds from Bangladesh Inspired, an international project that is funded by the European Union.

Source Data based on own interviews conducted in 2011–2014.

Producers can generate competitive advantages through joint activities within vertical (i.e. backward and forward) or horizontal linkages (Giuliani et al. 2005; Nadvi and Schmitz 1999). Producers of similar size and capabilities may share orders, market their products jointly or use machinery cooperatively (Giulani et al. 2005, p. 567). Subcontracts within the LTSE-network can be understood as joint activities within horizontal linkages, so as to ensure product quality and not to compromise the relationship to the lead firm. For instance, LGM E and LGM D have "a mutual understanding" (LGM D) about supporting each other by subcontracts. LGM E explains how production peaks make him informalise his production:

> […] now in my factory we produce the LGM G lady's bag. In this time I got the jacket order [for export; A. N.] and the delivery date is very soon. But we realised that the delivery for the LGM G lady's bag order and also the jacket delivery is possible for us. […] Then we calculated that we have 12 or 15 temporary workers, but we need 20 temporary workers [to realise both orders; A. N.]. […] So when we get more orders, we try to collect more people and engage more people in the work. Another way is we just exchange the work among our SMEs. Like LGM D's factory, XX factory, this type of factory we provide with subcontracts. 'You will do 100 pieces of bags and you will get this taka for one piece of bag. […]' This is the way we are working. (LGM E, English)

When production peaks, LGM E chooses to hire additional temporary workers or to subcontract a certain quantity to other skilled LTSE manufacturers such as LGM D. Temporary workers manufacture the products without receiving the benefits permanent workers are entitled to (e.g. monthly salary plus overtime; holidays; money for medical treatment). Occasionally, LGM E (i.e. first-tier subcontractor) subcontracts parts of an order for LGM G to LGM D (i.e. second-tier subcontractor). Conversely, LGM D asks LGM E to help out during production peaks. As subcontractor (LGM D) and contracting body (LGM E) share professional education, an informal network and technological capabilities, trust in product quality is ensured. Product specifications and transactions are agreed on orally. Relational governance keeps product specifications low and allows for simplified transactions with contracts often being concluded orally. Hence, strong informal ties in horizontal relationships turn out to be conducive to adapting to external constraints (i.e. tight costing) imposed by lead firms.

The low-skilled producers (T1, T2) interviewed produce only low value-added leather goods (e.g. jewellery boxes, purses). Temporary capacity constraints in LGM B's factory (T1) were considered the major motivation for subcontracting parts of LGM G's orders to former workers and family-related cottage manufacturers (LGM A). Oral agreements allow LGM B to flexibly react on festival-related production peaks. One of his subcontractors, his brother LGM A, only started becoming independent in 2010. Former work affiliations and family relations established trust in the producer's capabilities to ensure product quality. But the relationship is by no means equal. Despite the potential for development (e.g. improving product quality; increasing quantities), LGM A is highly dependent on his brother, a first-tier supplier of LGM G: the seasonality of orders LGM B's lead firm imposes also affects LGM A, making him sit idle during the off season. LGM A is provided with sewing machines and partly also with raw material. He is forbidden from dealing directly with LGM G, lacks market knowledge and has not established linkages to other buyers. Profit margins amount to 10 %. For the contracting body LGM B the risk of quality failure is relatively low as only low-complex leather goods are subcontracted for.

In some respects, lead firms direct subcontracting dynamics within the MSME sector. LGM G assures that orders are given according to the supplier's capacity. Contracts stipulate that producers are not entitled to subcontract. In cases of infringement, warnings are issued and suspensions imposed, although this has never actually happened. According to the Head of the SCPR Department, officers occasionally monitor production or follow the leads given by other producers. The producers interviewed seem to disagree as schedules are tight in practice. Large orders are given months ahead and may conflict with other customers:

> At present I'm doing work for "Pohela Boishakh" [i.e. the Bengal New Year; A. N.] and I'm also doing some work for Eid [Eid-ul-Fitr; A. N.]. I can't produce 50,000 pairs daily during Eid. In order to balance the work I don't wait for the order. Before taking their order my company starts to do some common work for the buyer like cutting, folding etc. But I don't do the work in full because if I do, it will be damaged. Then when they give order, we deliver them within a period of between three or six months. (LFM B, Bengali)

Until the breakup with his main lead firm LFM D in 2013, LFM B prefabricated individual components to be able to realise the final assembly on schedule and he subcontracts to his brothers. This practice indicates that lead firms cannot fully rule out further subcontracting. They seem to tacitly accept (or ignore) that parts of an order are supplied by others. Unannounced factory inspections to verify the real utilisation or close monitoring of the production have been reported as very rare. LGM B was the only manufacturer who mentioned LGM G officers paying him an unannounced visit once or twice a year. Unlike what LGM D does with corporate businesses (see above), LGM B avoids informing his lead firm about the fact that he subcontracts to his brother (LGM A):

> No, they don't know. LGM G only cares about the quality of my products. They will not take the products if minimum deviation is seen from their given sample. They will take only if it is 100 % accurate. (LGM B, Bengali)

LGM B suggests that LGM G's control mechanisms are weak. As long as product quality, which is LGM G's primary concern, is ensured, the lead firm refrains from further inquiries into potential non-contracted suppliers. Second-tier subcontractors seem to benefit from LGM G's negligent monitoring and auditing practices.

Dhaka's large MSME manufacturing basis provides excellent opportunities for the flexible and lean production of labour-intensive goods. Concluding from the analysis of subcontracting dynamics within the MSME sector, multi-tiered subcontracting has been identified as having substantial implications for product quality, power asymmetry and informal arrangements. Scarce capacity in peak season and rising competition among MSMEs are the driving forces for subcontracting of production activities. Product quality varies depending on the final customer and the complexity of the goods. Informal networks and trust seem to play a key role in subcontracting within the MSMEs interviewed. Horizontal subcontracts among peers (e.g. LTSE network) are characterised by a trustful and cooperative relationship. Here, differences in capabilities between first- and second-tier subcontractors are low; knowledge and partly also machinery are exchanged. Second-tier subcontractors attain additional income but depend little on the contracting first-tier supplier. Contract details are negotiated orally. This type of multi-tiered subcontracting corresponds to rather relational governance. In contrast, power asymmetry materialises more in subcontracts to less skilled producers and home-based workers (see Fig. 5.23). Here, second-tier subcontractors produce to the specifications that have been communicated on a low-formal level, that is, mostly in written form. Instructions are given and closer monitoring takes place to guarantee that minimum quality standards are complied with. Both the risk (e.g. quality differences) and vulnerability (e.g. insecure contracts; no benefits) increases. The core business of such second-tier suppliers is to produce on a subcontract basis for other MSMEs, so dependence on season-related excess orders from first-tier subcontractors and lead firms (and other customers) respectively is high. Asymmetries in capabilities (e.g. technological, design) and resources (e.g. knowledge, production facilities) to the contracting first-tier supplier seem to confine this type of second-tier subcontractors to merely surviving. While the former have ways to sell directly and can choose whether to make or to buy, the latter's opportunities to develop are poor and even blocked by first-tier suppliers

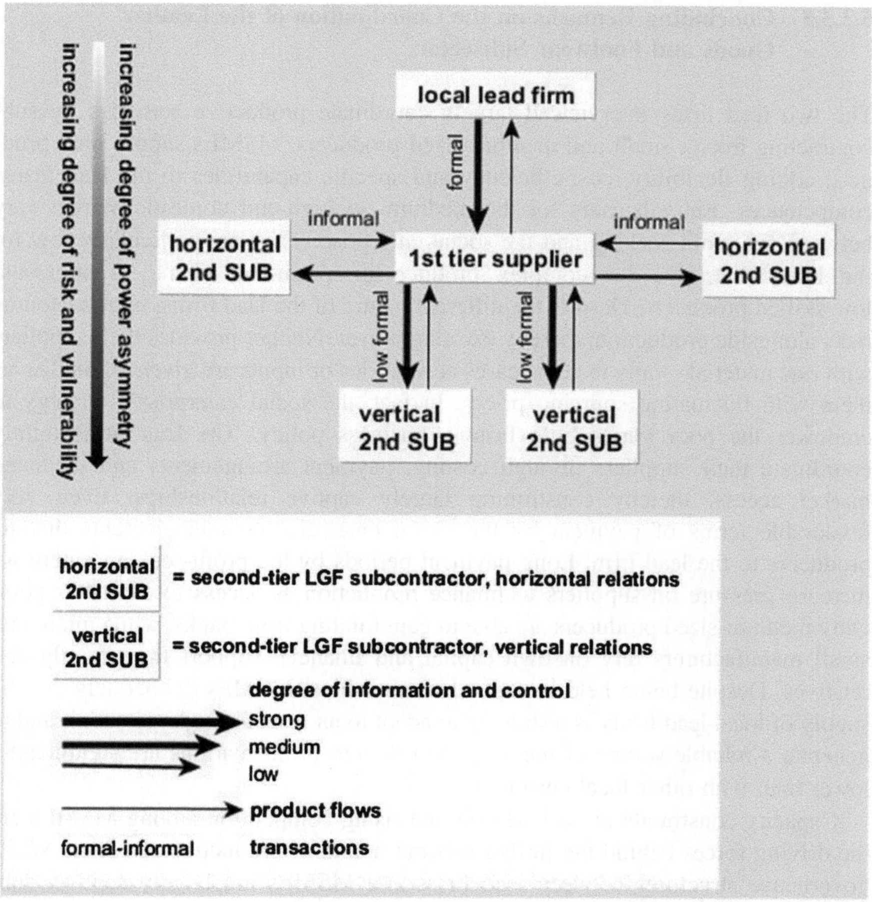

Fig. 5.23 Multi-tiered subcontracts in the leather goods and footwear industry. *Source* Data based on own interviews conducted from 2011–2014. Own illustration

who aim to maintain their privileged position to lead firms. In this case, first-tier suppliers keep second-tier subcontractors captive.

In a nutshell, subcontracts are multi-tiered and feature both relational and captive governance elements among MSMEs with differing potential for development for second-tier subcontractors.

Before I proceed to the MSME's integration into the foreign market, the coordination of the leather goods and footwear production network will be summarised in brief.

5.3.3.5 Concluding Remarks on the Coordination of the Leather Goods and Footwear Subsector

The two lead firms interviewed largely coordinate productive activities by subcontracting micro, small and medium-sized producers. MSMEs supply final products, adding flexibility, cost-efficiency and specific capabilities to the lead firms' competences. Entry barriers for the medium- to high-end domestic market vary between the profit-seeking and the social enterprise. They are particularly low for the latter that give low-complex product lines, among others, to poor and low-skilled producers. Despite the different nature of the lead firms, both outsource risks alongside production, thereby exerting power. Neither provides their suppliers with raw material—only in some cases accessories or inputs are given—, but leaves them with fluctuating sourcing prices. In fact, the social enterprise's strategy to empower the poor varies little from a business policy. The lead firms tightly coordinate their suppliers through costing, payment arrangements and mediated market access, thereby constituting largely captive relationships. Even very favourable terms of payment by the social enterprise contain elements that tie producers to the lead firm. Long payment periods by the profit-seeking enterprise increase pressure on suppliers to finance production as access to capital is poor. Only medium-sized producers are able to gain funding from banks, while micro and small manufacturers rely on own capital and financial support from family and relatives. Despite being held in captive relationships, MSMEs deliberately use the supply of local lead firms as a strategy to adapt to an insecure order situation and to generate a reliable source of income, even though profit margins are significantly lower than with other local customers.

Capacity constraints in peak season and rising competition among MSMEs are the driving forces behind the further subcontracting of productive activities. While governance structures between lead firms and MSMEs are largely captive, subcontracting among MSMEs may also contain relational elements. Multi-tiered subcontracting has been found in horizontal and vertical relations. The final customer and the complexity of the goods determine the type of subcontracts. Low requirements for product quality allow for the verticalising of subcontracts to cottage industries or home-based self-employed workers. Here, coordinating activities are just to ensure minimum quality standards in reliable response time (e.g. weak formal contracts). For medium- to high-end domestic buyers, production is outsourced to producers of similar skills and knowledge (e.g. LTSE network). Horizontal relations are characterised by trustful and cooperative relationships that are informally negotiated. Joint actions within horizontal networks enable knowledge transfer and increase competences.

To what extent the lead firms provide their producers with opportunities to develop their capabilities will be discussed in Sect. 5.3.5.1 on upgrading and learning from local large manufacturers. Prior to this, I will look into the MSMEs' integration into the foreign market.

5.3.4 *Integration of Micro, Small and Medium-Sized Leather Goods and Footwear Manufacturers in the Global Market*

This section takes a look at how MSMEs achieve global market entry, the way the buyer-supplier linkage is coordinated, and the strategies MSMEs use to overcome barriers in supplying foreign buyers.

In contrast to an early outward-looking tanning industry, Bangladesh's leather goods and footwear manufacturers have long been producing only for the domestic market only (Ahmed 2002; GTZ 2006; GTZ-PROGRESS 2006). In 2012–2013, exports amounted to 18.7 and 35.2 % respectively and for the first time exceeded the exports of crust and finished leather (see Fig. 5.24).[92]

Growth rates are highly dynamic in both manufacturing subsectors (30 % for leather footwear; 62 % for leather goods).[93] Despite this favourable performance, market access is unevenly distributed within the leather manufacturing industry. Interviews with upgrading organisations and manufacturers indicate that MSMEs in particular are struggling for market entry.

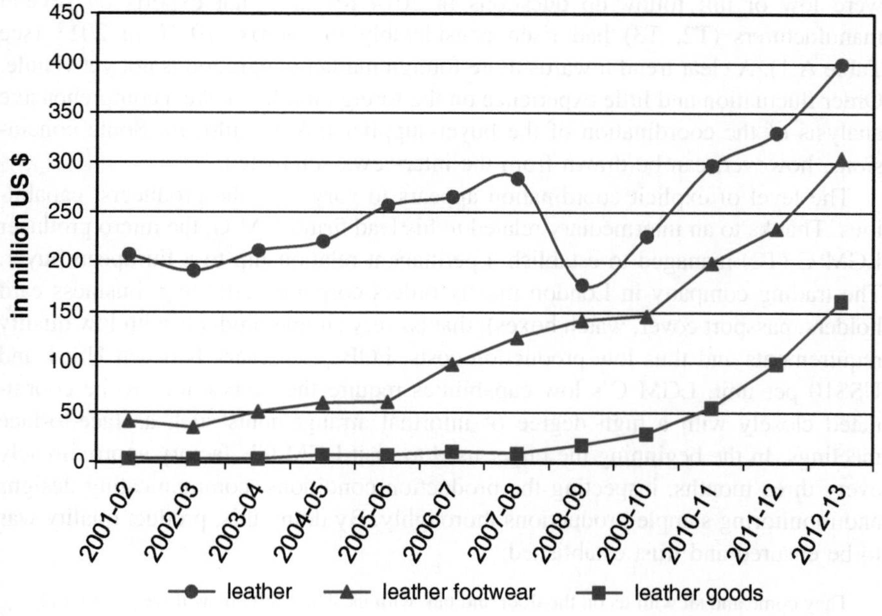

Fig. 5.24 Subsectoral export performance, 2001–2013. *Source* Export Promotion Bureau (2014). Own illustration

[92]Figure 5.24 is identical to Fig. 5.7.

[93]Interviews suggest that cost inflation caused by substantial increases in prices for raw material may have driven growth rates.

Both leather goods and footwear subsectors compensate for the low technology level by high labour-intensity. Mechanisation in the leather goods manufacturing industry started in the late 1980s, 20 years after footwear had gone for a technological upgrading (Ahmed 2002). This technological gap is visibly reflected in export charts. Only in the 1990s did the Bangladeshi government start considering fiscal and financial incentives for leather goods and footwear, thereby stimulating the subsectoral development (see Section "Institutional Framework"). Since 1997, export promotion strategies have been aiming at higher value addition within Bangladesh, demanding a stronger vertical integration of leather processing and manufacturing to take advantage of the favourable factor availability (e.g. raw material, cheap labour force) on the local market (interview EPB). Export subsidies on the net FOB value of 15 % are granted to help the LGF industries mature and provide incentives for stronger market integration (BOI 2011, p. 61).

5.3.4.1 Coordination of Producer-Foreign Buyer Linkage

Export activities of the MSMEs interviewed are either not existent or highly irregular. At the time the first interviews were taken (April/November 2011) exports were low or nil; follow-up questions in 2014 revealed that exports by several manufacturers (T2, T3) had risen considerably to approx. 70 % in 2013 (see Table A.1). A clear trend towards more foreign market integration is not yet visible. Order fluctuation and little experience on the foreign market make a comprehensive analysis of the coordination of the buyer-supplier linkage difficult. Some conclusions, however, can be drawn from the interviews conducted.

The level of explicit coordination appears to vary with the producers' capabilities. Thanks to an intermediary related to his lead firm LGM G, the micro producer LGM C (T2) managed to establish a permanent relationship to a European buyer. The trading company in London mostly orders corporate gifts (e.g. business card holders, passport cover, watch boxes); that is, very simple products with low quality requirements and thus low production costs. FOB prices vary between US$1 and US$10 per unit. LGM C's low capabilities require the transactions to be coordinated closely with a high degree of informal arrangements such as face-to-face meetings. In the beginning the buyer used to visit LGM C's factory approximately every three months, inspecting the production conditions, communicating designs and monitoring sample productions thoroughly. By doing this, product quality was to be ensured and trust established:

> They come and sit with us on the floor and talk with us. They sit here as if we were family members. They come with chocolates and give it to us. They have given a dress to my younger sister. (LGM C, Bengali)

The way this buyer seeks confidence with the producer is unusual, if not disturbing, considering LGM C's production conditions: a small workshop with 20 permanent workers; several workers are under both age limits 18 and 14; the mechanisation level is very low and workers operate on the floor. LGM C's net profit is above local rates, ranging between 15 and 20 %, but below other (T3-) producers (see below), which is down to the 10 % commission rate his intermediary charges. His buyer wants to relocate production from China to Bangladesh and has to adjust to the producer's low capabilities. Codification is accordingly very low. Product specifications for simple leather goods are communicated in person, including illustrative instructions that correspond to LGM C's cognitive capabilities:

> Once, a big buyer came. We took with us ten or 12 pieces of different items and then they selected two items. They told me that these two items were good, but some modification and changes were needed. Then I asked them 'where will the modification be?' They answered me by drawing. (LGM C, Bengali)

A lack of language and communication skills makes LGM C rely on a close guidance from buyers and buying houses. Once trust in LGM C's product quality has been established, transactions are coordinated through the buying house that is responsible for the final quality control, packing and shipment. Payment is settled three days of delivery by T/T, a convenient but risky payment method for MSMEs as we saw in Section "Enhancing the Security of Payment Methods and Reducing the Tanneries' Vulnerability to Informal Arrangements in Trade Transactions" on tanneries. Meanwhile, LGM C manages to send two shipments per month, which indicates a high export activity and would yield substantial export earnings if he were aware of the export subsidies of 15 % he is entitled to. This lack of knowledge weighs on LGM C's competitiveness.

The capabilities of more skilled export-oriented producers (T3, T4) producers allow for more value-added products and a higher degree of codification. Personal visits precede any new buyer-supplier relationship, but later direct transactions allow designs to be communicated by email. Production is not as intensively monitored as with T2. Instead, power asymmetries may manifest themselves in payment arrangements, though apparently to a far lesser extent than in the tanning industry. All SMEs interviewed favour either at-sight-L/Cs, which guarantee timely payment but are costly compared to the low-value transactions of small quantities, or T/T which is preferred over L/C because of the lower export charges and more capital during the production process. In fact, most of the T3-producers' last transactions were settled by T/T. There, the buyer advances approximately 50 %, which enables the producers to invest in raw material and finance overhead costs during production. The remainder is paid at the time of delivery after successful quality control. Among small manufacturers, even those who deal with buying houses, no payment defaults have been reported. Trusting relationships to known buyers (and buying houses) regulate the risk of T/T-transactions with respect to the final payment. Low buyer fluctuation stabilises buyer-supplier relationships. LFM E, for instance, did not export in 2010 and 2011, but has managed to sustain a direct relationship to two small buyers (USA, Japan) from before that. Thanks to a loan at an interest rate of 15 %, he was able to invest in machinery, hire workers and dedicate more time to developing samples. With a two-and-a-half-times increase of the production capacity in 2012 (see Table 5.7), he paved the way for resuming exports with his former buyers, boosting sales to 70 %. Higher profit margins (20–30 %) in comparison to LGM C (15–20 %) are a result of direct buyer-supplier linkages, subsidies and more value-added products; the FOB value varies between US$4–10 for wallets and US$25–40 for bags. Export subsidies are complex to apply for and according to LGM E only granted for direct exports. Small producers with few exports desist from applying:

> Yes, yes. When I export, I may get some incentives, but I don't take them because […] they require so many papers and each desk along the way means I lose money [laughing, alluding to bribes; A. N.). If I give money, then they clear the papers. I need 25 papers, so I haven't been taken the incentives yet. (LGM D, English)

As T3-producers already surrender to cumbersome bureaucracy and corrupt government officials, export subsidies are rendered an ineffective tool for boosting exports among low-skilled MSMEs. By all means, regular domestic orders by lead firms are the financial backbone of their business. It is yet unclear whether the higher export ratio in 2013 is the result of an upward trend of market integration or just the outlier of irregular export activity.

Medium-sized companies transact larger quantities of more value-added products (e.g. closed shoes, boots) thanks to the standardised production process. Although (technological) competences are higher compared to T2- and T3-manufacturers, export activity is quite low, amounting to only one to two orders per year. The T4-producers interviewed have difficulties meeting the buyers' requirements on product quality, technology and lead time. Very few designs as well as time-consuming sample production deter foreign buyers from placing orders. Normally, they transact using the more secure L/C which, however, is not devoid of risks for the seller. LFM C was approached by the intermediary of a South Korean buyer who issued the L/C. The buyer delayed the payment thanks to an amendment he had made and eventually let the L/C expire without taking LFM C's footwear (ladies' shoes). LFM C had neither a personal relationship to the buyer nor was he able to claim the money; after the expiration of an L/C, the seller is left with no protection (Investopedia 2014). Even irrevocable L/Cs cannot eliminate every risk. Hence, the FOB value of US$100,000 compelled LFM C to internalise costs in domestic sales. Thanks to his close subcontracting relationship with LFM D, LFM C was able to sell the footwear under his lead firm's brand at domestic market rates, thereby minimising losses to less than 20 %. Other local retailers, that are smaller in size, would have had difficulties to market such quantities and quality.

Foreign buyers may take strategic advantage of their downstream position; they can put producers under pressure by letting the L/C expire or concede to amendments only if the seller agrees to price reductions:

> The foreign buyer said they would amend the L/C if I decreased the value of my goods by 10 %. (LFM B, Bengali)

Producers who have not been able to establish trusting relationships with foreign customers or buying houses are especially exposed to buyers misusing their power:

> No, the buying house did not [sue the buyer; A. N.]. The buying house was new and the foreign buyer was also new to me as well as to the buying house. (LFM B, Bengali)

New business relationships increase the vulnerability of medium-sized enterprises to defaults in payment and pressure on prices. Unlike assumed, rising supplier competences do not prevent them from risks. Looking forward to export earnings, the medium-sized producers forgot about taking necessary precautions to secure the transactions:

> The inspection was to assess the quality of my products and the buyers were supposed to come just before shipment. But they did not come. Then they told me 'you had missed the shipment and there was no evidence that we had not come to see your goods.' They also told me that there was no evidence that I had finished production in time. According to them, the main reason was that I had missed their shipment. So neither I nor the buying house was able to take any legal action against them. (LFM B, Bengali)

Despite a valid irrevocable L/C, LFM B had no choice but to give into the buyer's demands. He was forced to accept the price reduction of 10 % as sales on the domestic market are even less profitable (see LFM C). Bad experiences with foreign buyers have made him increasingly distrustful towards foreign buyers, even more so as he lacks the support of a reliable and experienced buying house:

> Generally, I get buyers who are hardly known to me. […] I do not have enough knowledge to check their quality and authenticity. I cannot identify whether they are good or bad. (LFM B, Bengali)

As a result of lacking language skills, LFM B cannot search for and deal with foreign buyers directly; dependency on buying houses is high. These, however, appear to lack competences in market and buyer research. Regardless of his manufacturing capabilities, entering the foreign market has been tiresome for LFM B. Buyer requirements for more value-added shoe and boot production are high; lacking technology (e.g. clamping machine; lasting machine) makes potential customers back out, distrusting the supplier's ability to meet product quality and delivery time with manufacturing production techniques. Costly sample productions and small orders discourage LFM B to engage more in export activities. The fact that his major domestic customer (LFM D) dropped out in November 2011 put him in a critical financial situation, making him highly vulnerable.

These cases from T4-producers confirm what has already been suggested with regards to the tanning industry: even secure and formalised transactions require a great deal of trust in order to handle transaction risks and reduce power asymmetries. Direct and long-term relationships seem to contribute towards increasing resilience and building up confidence between the transacting parties. MSMEs adapt to transaction failures (e.g. payment default, quality rejection) as a consequence of power asymmetries through local sales. This, however, requires a network of potential local buyers and the readiness to accept poorer terms and conditions.

Conclusions from the MSMEs' low market integration and little export experience have to be drawn with caution. Coordination appears to vary with the capabilities of the supplier. T2- and T3-manufacturers prioritise financial capital provided through T/T over payment security (L/C), though risk cannot be totally offset (see T4). Direct relationships to buyers seem to increase resilience to less secure payment methods (T/T). More in-depth studies are needed to draw relevant conclusions from the nature and duration of buyer-supplier relationships for the vulnerability of MSMEs in the export market.

5.3.4.2 Constraints to Market Integration: Low Competences in the Supply Base

This chapter delves into the low capabilities in the supply base, which are regarded as the major impediment to foreign market integration.

The production facilities of MSMEs in developing countries often fall short of the expectations of foreign buyers due to the low requirements of their primary (domestic) market. With the exception of T2, who was luckily introduced to a permanent buyer by a local agent, but who in fact lacks export requirements, all small export-oriented manufacturers (T3) are aware of their individual constraints. Several attempts to export always yielded the same result for T3-manufacturers: buyers appreciate the detailed products but have serious doubts about the reliability of the production process.

The first reason for buyers to not source from the MSMEs interviewed is the low production capacity that cannot ensure sufficient quantities and timely delivery:

> […] I have exported only […] two shipments [of handmade sandals; A. N.]. The first one was 200 pairs and the second one was 600 pairs. But if I go for a regular order, then I have to maintain [i.e. fill; A. N.] a minimum of one container of footwear. That requires almost 4,000 pairs. (LFM A, English)

Then LFM A was unable to meet those quantities. High shipment costs make small volumes (below 1,000–2,000 pairs) of low value-added articles unprofitable; these are usually only used to assess the producer's capabilities. If LFM A succeeds in meeting the requirements on lead time and product quality, bigger orders follow, but MSMEs face huge challenges in supplying these:

> He [i.e. the buyer; A. N.] gave us [i.e. asked for; A. N.] 10,000 pairs a month. At that time we were producing only 1,000 pairs. (LFM A, English)

Small producers lacking sufficient capacity often have to turn down large orders. Given the substantial differences in the requirements between the export and the domestic market, subcontracts to other factories are out of the question. The producers interviewed prefer not to compromise their reputation and the trust of their customers. Besides, foreign buyers would not place orders that exceed the factory's capacity.

Second, the low skills level and low division of labour, which characterise T2 and T3 in particular, weigh on their potential for global market entry. Workers are trained on-the-job to operate in all sections (e.g. cutting, sewing, finishing). Only medium-sized factories (T4) partly use a conveyor belt system and assign workers to specific activities. For T2 and T3 applies: the wider the product range the lower the productivity. Decreasing efficiencies due to all-rounders are a common drawback among micro and small industries:

> Sometimes I do bags, sometimes I do wallets and sometimes I do belts. So that affects the productivity because if the workers are always doing bags, bags, bags, their productivity is improving. So I want a small set up when we go to Savar [i.e. the new tannery site; A. N.], with three types of products, three types of workers. (LGM D, English)

More specialisation and a more efficient organisation of production processes would enable MSMEs to respond better to the buyers' needs. By now, financial constraints stand in the way of a major reorganisation of production facilities. Outdated technology and unskilled labour force keep the labour productivity low. Very often producers criticise the quantity and quality of their machinery. Simple machines (e.g. sewing, cutting) are available, though often second-hand and in small number. The MSMEs interviewed lack modern technology for finishing activities (e.g. spray/skiving/glazing machines):

> It is the confidence of the buyers with the working environment and also with the machineries. I don't have enough machinery. (LFM A, English)

The lack of adequate technology is a development constraint to all micro, small and partly also medium-sized manufacturers. Only one medium-sized manufacturer (LFM C) that supplied LFM D with footwear for the export market (see Section "Subcontracting for the Export Market—Developing Capabilities or Becoming Invisible Exporters?") had been temporarily provided with specific machinery by his lead firm. The very low mechanisation level is compensated by labour intensity, though those T3-manufacturers who invested in modern machinery (LFM A, LGM E, LGM F) complain about the lacking skills of their workers to handle these:

> I have money, I bought the machines, but I don't have any skilled people to handle the machines. (LGM E, English)

Skilled labour is a rare commodity in Bangladesh's leather industry; systematic training is lacking. BCLT only offers graduate courses for leather technologists. Floor-level workers are trained on the job. They start as helpers to become familiar with the raw material and different machinery. After several months they begin to work on their own. Salaries are adjusted depending on practical knowledge and output (see Footnote 87; Section "Coordination Through Costing and Price Setting"). The structural dearth of skilled labour affects both foreign and domestic markets. Many MSMEs work below their capacity because the technology and skills level are insufficient to meet the demand from local and foreign customers with varying requirements on product quality. All LGF-manufacturers stress that Bangladesh's leather industry is going to need a trained labour force to succeed on the export market. The development of vocational training systems is a new approach to enhance the skills level among leather goods and footwear operators (see excursus).

Excursus: Vocational Training—The Example of COEL
In 2011, the Centre of Excellence for Leather Skill Bangladesh Limited (COEL) was established to provide skill development programmes to supervisors and floor-level workers. It has been common practice in the leather industry to train workers on the job. COEL's objective is to enhance the skills level in the leather-related labour force by systematically providing training programmes. After a three-month free-of-charge apprenticeship course, workers are certified by the leather association LFMEAB, the Government of Bangladesh, and ILO.

Large local manufacturers and international partner organisations (Footwear Design and Development Institute India, Swiss Development Cooperation, EU, USAID PRICE, International Labour Organization) have been supporting and funding the initiative. As a member of LFMEAB, the local footwear company LFM D was one of the driving forces behind setting up the first vocational institute for the leather industry. Large manufacturers donated machinery and raw material, among other resources. They expect to see their investment reimbursed by increased efficiencies and more value-added products.

COEL strives to connect firms, labour, the state and international organisations to create a dynamic industrial environment. It is a promising initiative to provide a labour pool for all leather-related manufacturing enterprises, satisfying the needs of a developing industry. Questions remain as to whether subcontractors and non-linked MSMEs also benefit. COEL is a unique opportunity to raise competitiveness and truly reduce inequalities within the industry if MSMEs are adequately involved.

Source COEL (2014), Own interviews with LFM D.

At the time of the last interviews on the ground (November 2012), it was too early to assess COEL's impact on the MSMEs. By then, only one supplier, the medium-sized footwear manufacturer LFM C, had been able to make use of the vocational institute thanks to his privileged partnership with LFM D:

> Sometimes they [i.e. COEL; A. N.] send us an instructor, […]. We have a place where we put some machines and give trainings of 15 days, two months, one month; then they come. But they do mainly supervisor training, not that much worker training. But they said we [i.e. they; A. N.] are planning to do worker training. (LGM C, English)

COEL can be effectively used to increase the skill level of the existent workforce on specific machinery. The institute, however, was primarily devised to feed new, skilled workers into the industry. Setting up new production lines often requires 70–90 workers, says LFM C. COEL can help medium-sized and large factories minimise losses in productivity. Skill development programmes for floor-level workers have to take into account that a large percentage of the workforce is barely educated or even illiterate:

> Those who are not literate you cannot work with them easily because you need to [make them; A. N.] understand: 'These are the things you are doing; if you do it in this way, it is wrong.' So we need to motivate them all the time, you know, 'don't go now, go later, work a little more, you will have some more money.' (LGM F, English)

LGM F complains about the difficulty to qualify illiterate workers and illustrates that power is negotiated in social interaction irrespective of the actors' positions in the chain. Generally, MSMEs invest over a year in making a worker become skilled and versatile, turning him/her into a valuable asset. Large factories give less time and often recruit from smaller manufacturers, making their operators replaceable. MSME workers are able to resist overtime, thereby putting the owner under pressure and reversing power asymmetries in MSMEs. They are aware of their value and are unlikely to be dismissed.

A major deficit in the GVC literature is that production networks or chains are not understood to be operating within cultural, institutional and socio-political environments (COE et al. 2008, p. 279). The environment the MSMEs interviewed operate within opposes greater market integration. Education is low and not adjusted to the industry's needs. The striking dominance of the garment industry promoted by the political-economic complex leaves little scope for the needs of other industries. Structural and regulatory constraints have not been addressed adequately to establish a competitive mix of MSMEs and large firms. At the moment few large export-oriented manufacturers stand out in a widely underdeveloped and unregulated MSME basis that does not raise the confidence of foreign companies in sourcing from Bangladesh:

> Now there are only three or five export level factories and that's why the customers are not coming to Bangladesh. They are coming to India, they are coming to Pakistan, they are coming to Sri Lanka, China, but they are not coming to Bangladesh. (LGM E, English).

Two years and a successful export record (2013) later, LGM E has seen greater interest among foreign buyers. In any case, particularly export-oriented small manufacturers (T3) seek to overcome structural constraints to market entry by connecting to and learning from local large export-oriented firms (see Sect. 5.3.4.3). They strive to become a member of the local leather association LFMEAB that provides knowledge and important export-related services (e.g. export certificate; certificate for tax rebate against capital machinery import). With the association dominated by few large manufacturers, the requirements are not adjusted to the needs and concerns of MSMEs, many of which can neither afford admission fees and annual subscriptions nor register with the Board of Investment. The Managing Director of LFM D understands that the firm's success on the export market depends on a competitive MSME basis that is capable of meeting international standards; the lack of organisation in MSMEs, however, impedes closer cooperation. MSMEs are an important constituent of Bangladesh's leather industry. To create more innovation and competitiveness among LGF producers a platform is needed where practitioners and advocates can meet and exchange ideas to do better.

Third, MSMEs struggle with international regulatory requirements that allow foreign buyers to raise pressure:

> In the beginning buyers wanted to talk about the quality and the design, but now they are asking about the environment as well. 'Where do you collect the leather, which chemicals are in the leather, and […] do they have an ETP [i.e. effluent treatment plant; A. N.] where you collect the leather?' If they don't, then they [i.e. the buyers; A. N.] are quite unhappy. (LGM D, English)

Regulation of northern markets brought up environmental and health issues that have long been ignored in a low-cost country such as Bangladesh (see Hesselberg and Knutsen 2002). The introduction of codifiable standards provides security to buyers and consumers. Bangladesh's leather industry is unable to meet international standards on environmental compliance yet. The new tannery site is to provide an environmentally compliant infrastructure; until it is specified whether and how many LGF enterprises will be able to relocate, at least those in Hazaribagh will have to deal with the locational disadvantage of the repelling environmental conditions on the tannery estate.

Environmental compliance still has a long way to go in Bangladesh. International regulations on product safety standards appear to be more effective in changing non-compliant practices in low-cost producer countries. The main markets of the MSMEs interviewed are Europe, Japan, and the United States, with the EU having the most rigorous regulations concerning restricted substances (Wilson and Schwarzman 2009). All leather goods and footwear manufacturers exporting to the EU have to make sure that their leather is devoid of restricted substances, complying with REACH. However, small buyers and particularly those from rather weakly regulated markets appear to impose laxer requirements when it comes to evidencing the restricted substances in leather products:

> There are some chemical testing facilities, but I don't have this type of buyers yet. (LGM E, English)

LGM E's buyer is from the United States, whose chemicals policy is considered to have failed to protect public health and the environment (Wilson and Schwarzman 2009, p. 1202). The 'type of buyer' he refers to orders only small quantities and demands no tests on sample products. The medium-sized manufacturer LFM C specifies on this matter:

> […] because the Japanese orders are very small. That's why they are not very much serious regarding tests. They can control this because […] we have the certificates […] from the tanneries also. Then there is no need to test. Ok, and European buyers, they are very much serious because they have to face, I think, all this media attack and their orders are bigger than for the Japanese market. (LFM C, English)

Consumer awareness and the REACH regulation in the EU market appear to have sensitised the buyers for more rigorous requirements. The clearance certificate provided by the tanneries only guarantees that the chemicals used are devoid of restricted substances; it does not provide any information about the way the leather has been processed. Buyers can ensure full compliance only by requesting chemical tests from independent certification bodies (e.g. SGS, Bureau Veritas), thereby limiting the financial risk of warnings or product withdrawals from the market. Weak regulation and small order sizes seem to discourage buyers to pressure producers in ensuring product safety. For only several hundred pieces of bags or pairs of footwear foreign customers prefer to avoid additional costs and rely on less reliable clearance certificates instead. This means that micro and small enterprises (T2, T3) are able to evade international standards with the help of foreign buyers, thereby offsetting tight governance. More disturbingly, the discrepancy of global and domestic market requirements is huge. All manufacturers interviewed apply double standards as for the use of chemicals for the local and the global market. This is not only unfair as workers and consumers of domestic products are exposed to harmful substances, while consumers in the North (most likely) are not. It is also unsustainable and inefficient as clean practices are not continuously applied throughout the production process. Aligning domestic to export standards could increase efficiencies, improve product safety and public health, and enhance the workers' skills level.

Weak marketing is a fourth constraint to market integration. Transactions with foreign customers are usually mediated by buying houses like in the leather processing subsector. Local buying agents figure out the producer's capabilities, submit designs and samples; they get quotes from potential suppliers, request sample production runs, place the order, and are responsible for packaging, shipment and negotiating the terms of payment. Technical assistance and monitoring during production is rather low, except for new production lines with low-skilled producers (T2; Sect. 5.3.4.1). For micro and small producers (T2, T3) intermediaries and buying houses are pivotal to market entry. Export market research requires capabilities (e.g. language, market knowledge) and resources (e.g. time, money) that many owners of micro and small enterprises lack as they are in charge of all activities prior, during and after production (e.g. design; procurement of raw material; market research; bank transactions). Buying houses allow them to centre on core competences, that is, on inbound logistics and production. For domestic-oriented manufacturing businesses such as LGM B (T1) buying houses are still out of reach:

> I don't know the location of the buying houses. I don't know where they are. [...] I get along well with this. It's not so good, not so bad. So I didn't try [to find buying houses; A. N.]. The major factor is since I don't know English I don't go and try. (LGM B, Bengali)

LGM B started his business from scratch, developing gradually from being a helper in his relative's workshop to a subcontractor of LGM G. Being illiterate, he lacks knowledge and access to networks to improve his marketing activities. His lack of language skills makes him wary of seeking opportunities in exports. His primary objective is to reduce the dependency on his lead firm and to diversify to local buyers.

The larger and more educated manufacturers are, the more buying houses limit their assistance to negotiating terms and conditions with buyers. The brokers secure transactions and control business risks (e.g. in terms of delays) by communicating with the customers. Unlike in the tanning industry, where buying houses employ leather technologists to supervise the production process, they seem to be less involved in monitoring leather goods and footwear production. Buying houses charge a regular commission of 5 % for their services and are often considered an additional cost factor. As we saw in Sect. 5.3.4.1, coordination and power asymmetry appear to be strongest among low-skilled suppliers. LGM C, for instance, is closely monitored and controlled by his intermediary who deducts a commission rate of even 10 %. The buying house's competences, however, determine market entry and the quality of buyers. If transactions fail or buyers drop out, they are expected to mediate in the seller's favour, which they are often not capable of (see LFM B's case in Sect. 5.3.4.1). Above all, buying houses exclude MSMEs from dealing directly with foreign customers:

> No, no, no, we don't know. They don't let us know, buying houses don't let us know to whom they sell. (LFM B, Bengali)

Buying houses control the linkage to buyers by knowledge and information. If MSMEs wanted to access foreign buyers directly, a different marketing strategy that relies on distinct capabilities and resources would be required.

Fifth, tradeshow marketing is a strategy to promote products in foreign markets that is still underrepresented among the MSMEs interviewed. Here, goods are introduced to a large group of potential customers. Tradeshows play an important role in gathering information about competitors and markets. They serve the purpose of approaching new buyers without the help of costly intermediaries and of strengthening business relationships with regular customers. Several T3-producers from the LTSE network participated a few times in Dhaka Trade Fair with the help of USAID PRICE, an international development project (see Sect. 5.3.5.3). International trade fairs are more difficult to attend. All export-oriented producers agree on the advantage of face-to-face contact to buyers. Informal exchange is considered critical to the company's success given Bangladesh's image as a garment-exporting nation and as a haven for polluters in the leather industry:

> LGM D went to the Italian fair and the experience is that if you want to gain the buyer's confidence, then you have to attend two or three times because the buyer has to become habituated with you. (LFM A, English)

Trade fairs provide an opportunity to showcase the latest products, assure potential customers about the quality and build up trust with one another. High transaction costs, however, put underfunded micro and small manufacturers at a disadvantage. Travel expenses and booth rates exceed the financial capabilities of T2- and T3-producers. To boost the national economy and promote exports, SMEs are given the opportunity to apply to the Export Promotion Bureau (EPB) for financial support. As an award-winning female entrepreneur, LGM D was granted participations in Indian and Italian trade fairs, from which resulted in a relationship to a European buyer who she managed to supply once. It was not possible to continue this relationship due to capacity constraints. Producers prioritise direct sales not just to cut out middlemen, but also to establish continuity in buyer-supplier relations. Permanent customers allow for productivity increases as quality requirements rarely change and manufacturers can adapt their production process to product lines that are in high demand.

Medium-sized companies (T4) also rely on buying houses; like LFM B, for instance, who lacks sufficient knowledge of English and whose primary market is the domestic one, as exports have not picked up yet (see Sect. 5.3.4.1). These producers, however, have more (financial) opportunities to invest in marketing and attend international trade fairs more often. LFM B was able to accompany his buying agent to trade fairs in Singapore in 2008 where he learned about communication with buyers and their requirements. However, no transactions resulted from this trip due to his limited production capacity. LFM C markets his footwear on business-to-business web portals and has already participated in tradeshows in Europe (Italy, Germany) and China from where he started transacting directly with European and Japanese buyers. This investment enabled him to achieve irregular direct sales to foreign customers and thus higher margins.

Among the promotional tools of MSMEs, advertising and online marketing play a minor or no role at all yet. Buying houses prepare the acquisition of new transactions and provide guidance according to the manufacturer's skills level. They are particularly important for micro and small manufacturers (T2, T3) that lack financial resources to participate in international trade fairs. Medium-sized manufacturers (T4) are able to invest more in direct distribution channels but have difficulties finding reliable buyers. Despite providing essential services for market entry, buying houses obstruct a long-term development strategy, keeping their suppliers captive.

Interviews revealed that low competences weigh on the MSMEs' chances of succeeding in the export market. While some constraints call for individual investments and capacity building (e.g. production capacity, marketing), others (e.g. environmental regulation, compliance with international standards, skill development) require institutional changes at the national level and increasing pressure from international markets.

In response to institutional constraints and low capabilities, the MSMEs have developed different adaptation strategies as will be set out in the following section.

5.3.4.3 Strategies to Adapt to Constraints in Market Integration

Unlike the tanning industry, leather goods and footwear manufacturers have developed only few strategies to adapt to constraints in foreign market integration (research question 3).

The manufacturers interviewed avoid referring to informal or illicit practices to achieve market entry (research question 2b). They rule out subcontracting to other MSMEs to compensate capacity constraints for two reasons:

- They are concerned about not being able to guarantee consistent quality.
- Buyers would not place orders that exceed the producer's capacity. Unlike in the tanning industry, tight coordination and control mechanisms leave no room for

informal cooperative production but confine MSMEs to exports of small order sizes (see Table A.1).[94]

In view of their low capabilities, most of the manufacturers interviewed look for order stability on the domestic market, while they cater to international buyers every so often. They gradually adjust their production facilities to export market requirements (see the expansion of production capacity in Table 5.7). Domestic market activities ensure their earnings; a deliberate export strategy is lacking.

Some T3-manufacturers have consciously chosen a different way to adapt to limited capabilities. Aware of their limitations, they have been temporarily pursuing a more domestic-oriented approach (see Section "Magnitude, Characteristics and Importance of Subcontracting for MSMEs"). Particularly LFM A rigorously seized the opportunities he was provided with by his local lead firm and revisited his export strategy:

> And that's why I have increased my capacity and I have bought some machines, sewing machines, some cutting machines and some [inc.] and roughing machines also. Now I'm capable of producing 4,000 pairs a month in my factory […] this year we don't have the target to export. We are working with the [domestic; A. N.] buyers and we are developing the product. (LFM A, English)

LFM A opted to focus on the domestic market to reduce internal shortcomings and adjust his production conditions to international requirements. Subcontracts for LFM D help him increase his production capacity, develop products and enhance his workers' manufacturing skills. Thanks to a family mortgage, he was able to enlarge his production site, invest in working capital and technology (e.g. hydraulic cutting, embossing, lasting machine), and expand his capacity from 1,000 pairs of sandals per month to 3,000 in 2011 and 4,000 in 2013. Innovative design (e.g. buffalo leather soles for leather sandals) ensures large orders on a regular basis from his lead firm. His long-term goal is an assembly line production of 10,000 pairs per month, which will allow him to meet the buyers' demands he used to refuse.

This strategy of adapting to lacking export requirements appears to work for LFM A: in 2011, subcontracts were the major sources of his earnings (see Table A.1). He maintained weak linkages to (small) foreign buyers by delivering small quantities every so often. In 2013, exports picked up to 70 % thanks to the increase in capacity he had realised. This producer enhanced his competitiveness by dissociating temporarily from the export market and focusing on subcontracts for large local manufacturers. Regular orders stabilise sales and help workers adopt routinised practices in the production process. Intense inter-linkages to large export-oriented firms the quality standards of which outreach other local buyers are expected to contribute to develop production capabilities.

To put it in a broader perspective, the buyers' requirements for market entry made producers invest in production facilities and link up with local lead firms to

[94] Export activity among the MSMEs interviewed appears to be volatile. In 2010/2011, the export activity ranges between 5 and 25 %. In 2013, some producers realised even 70 % of their sales by exports.

increase the skills level. MSMEs have learned from foreign buyers despite the little interaction to date. The domestic market provides opportunities for MSMEs; whether knowledge can be transferred here that serves to establish foreign market activities will be explored in the next chapter.

5.3.4.4 Concluding Remarks on the Coordination of Foreign Buyers and Leather Goods and Footwear Manufacturers

Although exports have been picking up dynamically in recent years (see Fig. 5.24), the MSMEs interviewed struggle for market entry. Incipient and fluctuating export activity makes drawing conclusions possible only to a limited extent.

MSMEs have difficulties meeting the requirements of production capacity, technology and product quality imposed by potential customers. Low competences tie them to small foreign buyers who coordinate them either directly or through buying houses. The size of buyers and weakly regulated consumer markets provide MSMEs with opportunities to produce cost-efficiently, giving less importance to product safety. Monitoring and control varies with the suppliers' capabilities; particularly low-skilled producers (T2) are under tight supervision. Power imbalances between buyers and suppliers are also manifest in payment arrangements. As MSMEs suffer from insufficient resources to finance production (see Section "Insufficient Access to Finances"), they prioritise risky but capital-providing terms of payment (T/T) over more payment security (L/C). In one-off mediated transactions the risk of reductions in prices and payment defaults increases; here, buyers tend to take advantage of their power, putting pressure on prices. Even in captive relationships, some MSMEs have been able to lower the risk of payment default inherent in both payment methods through direct transactions.

Some (T3) producers adapt to the high entry barriers imposed by foreign buyers by temporarily desisting from the foreign market and strengthening ties to local large manufacturers instead. In so doing, they have been able to raise quality standards and improve production conditions. Power asymmetries, however, are also dominant on the domestic market as shown in Sect. 5.3.3. How MSMEs can improve their conditions to do better on both domestic and global markets will be presented in the next chapter.

5.3.5 Upgrading in the Leather Goods and Footwear Manufacturing Industry

This analysis of the leather goods and footwear production network indicates a widespread practice of tying MSMEs as subcontractors to larger and more mature firms. Recent studies on upgrading in India (Reps and Braun 2012; Bettiol et al. 2011) argued that local lead firms can be the driving force towards (environmental) upgrading. Results from this study's interviews suggest that the dynamics in Bangladesh's leather goods and footwear industry are different, although large firms play a critical role in developing low-skilled suppliers. The way local lead firms coordinate the supply chain determines the MSMEs' competitiveness on domestic and export markets as well as their potential for upgrading. This study conceptualises upgrading as learning from buyers and external stakeholders (development organisations) in order to produce more efficiently (process upgrading), to make better products (product upgrading) or to move to other activities that increase the value-added (functional upgrading).

The following section explores the extent to which the MSMEs interviewed learn and receive assistance to upgrade from local lead firms. In Sect. 5.3.5.2 learning effects by foreign market integration will be examined. How far MSMEs have benefited from external development projects will be discussed in Sect. 5.3.5.3.

5.3.5.1 Learning from Local Large Manufacturers

The literature on upgrading in global value chains suggests that the way a value chain is governed determines upgrading trajectories (e.g. Humphrey 2004; Humphrey and Schmitz 2002; Gereffi 2005). Local lead firms coordinate and control the manufacturing segment of the chain by incorporating the MSME supply base in their sourcing strategies. While these are strongly integrated into the local production network, they have difficulties achieving exports on a regular basis (see Sect. 5.3.4; Table A.1). Hence, rather than with international companies, MSMEs maintain enduring business relationships with local lead firms. These have an interest in improving their suppliers' capabilities and thus are the reference for upgrading processes.

This section is expected to show in how far lead firms share information and knowledge with their suppliers (Bettiol et al. 2011). It will fathom the extent to which the assistance that lead firms provide to their suppliers translates into process, product and functional upgrading.

Technical Assistance

The MSMEs interviewed are full-assembly suppliers, that is, they perform the entire production process. Lead firms are interested in making their supply base comply with their requirements. Particularly export-oriented small manufacturers (T3) emphasise their shortcomings and the importance of technical assistance by their lead firms:

> […] because the quality of their products and the quality of our product is a little bit different. We are not to the point in our product. That's why we need to meet them […]. We need to visit their factories, see how they work, how they do the total work, how they manage the people or what type of machines they are using. (LGM E, English)

T3-producers such as LGM E know about the limitations that prevent them from catering to the foreign market on a more regular basis. Domestic supplies to local large manufacturers are expected to gradually enhance quality management, increase efficiencies in the use of technology, and improve the organisation of production processes, among others. Even though they miss out on higher margins from other buyers, a linkage to local lead firms is expected to yield more than monetary returns.

The assistance of the two large firms interviewed differs from the strategies of multinational corporations that closely coordinate their suppliers in developing countries. Unlike the GVC perspective, this study's analysis of subcontracting dynamics revealed that local lead firms are not yet the "primary sources of material input, technology transfer, and knowledge" (Gereffi 1999, p. 38). MSMEs only receive information on the requirements for raw material and accessories; procurement is up to them. LFM D seems to provide technical assistance to trusted suppliers of critical products. Only LFM C had occasionally been lent specific machinery (e.g. embossing as he used to produce on subcontract for the export market before he was taken over by his lead firm after a financial crisis in 2013 (see Section "Subcontracting for the Export Market—Developing Capabilities or Becoming Invisible Exporters?").

All other suppliers interviewed care for their own raw material and inputs. In general, lead firms give only suggestions as to the use of specific technology that increases product quality and efficiencies. They do not provide advisory services on funding sophisticated machinery, which could help MSMEs better assess the risk and benefits of such investments.

The way knowledge is transferred tells much about the low extent of codification in the leather goods and footwear production network. Designs and quality standards are communicated orally. Micro producers frequent their lead firm on a regular basis, taking samples and presenting countersamples:

> There is a coming and going for designs, colour, meetings and also for any objection. (LGM B, Bengali)

The low level of skills forces LGM B to see his lead firm's different departments (design; raw material and accessories; costing; quality control) on a regular basis. There, he is instructed on the use of the design and raw material, and how to maintain quality. Skilled small and medium-sized manufacturers (T3, T4) already command email communication and require less control. LGM E, for instance, sees his lead firm only once a month. LGM G trusts in his capabilities to produce the products as per contract requirements. All manufacturers copy the designs from a catalogue or a sample provided by the lead firm which then assesses the product quality and issues its approval. After initial test runs lead firms limit quality control to the final product. LFM D checks quality three times (at the factory; in the lead firm's central depot; before delivery to retailers) in order to avoid faulty footwear being fed into the retail network. LGM G only controls once after completion of production. The rejection rate has been confirmed by both lead firms and producers to be between 5 and 10 %, so payment default is low. The low complexity of LGM G's products seems to exempt producers from abiding by strict requirements:

> The kind of leather products we have… so boxes usually don't get rejected because you know it's a friendly production technique, […]. […] Sandals get rejected a little bit more than others but not a lot. It's not even significant enough. (LGM G, English)

A "friendly production technique" refers to low-complex, labour-intensive production processes that are easy to carry out. None of the products of the two lead firms are subject to chemical or physical tests by independent organisations. Moreover, assistance in increasing efficiencies during production is lacking. Instead, an international development project (PRICE) intervened for the interests of both lead firms and subcontractors (see Sect. 5.3.5.3).

MSMEs perform all manufacturing-related activities (sourcing; sample production; production). Unlike the GVC perspective, lead firms at the local level catering to the domestic market are not yet the primary source of raw material, inputs and machinery. Thanks to the low complexity of the products and the low market requirements, they only provide the design and specify quality standards that are ensured by weak monitoring and the final control. There is also a lack of advice about the risks of investments in new technology and funding options. Only one producer who was subcontracted for the export market (and was bought over by his lead firm in 2013) received technical assistance.

There are different ways to learn from more competitive companies. Assisting suppliers in the adoption of socially compliant practices may reveal a great deal about the lead firms' understanding of their producers and power asymmetries involved.

Assistance in Social Compliance

Social compliance is contextualised within social upgrading and thus was not supposed to be a part of this study. As, however, both lead firms brought up compliance issues themselves, relating it to a constraint for subcontracting for the export market, more relevance was given to it during the interviews.

Both lead firms refer to different strategies to deal with compliance issues on the domestic and export market. For local suppliers LFM D refuses to apply standards that go beyond local regulation:

> Our position on compliance is very simple: the first compliance has to be with the laws of Bangladesh. I'm not so much interested in what is the standard of XYZ buyer where we are complying. (LFM D, English)

Standards set by global buyers made LFM D join the Business Social Compliance Initiative (BSCI), a corporation-driven code of conduct, which is monitored by external auditors (Egels-Zandén and Wahlqvist 2007, p. 180). MSMEs that are subcontracted for the domestic market are excluded from these international guidelines; they are expected to abide by local laws and regulation.

Local laws differ from international regulation and are less rigorously enforced, so that vulnerability rises for domestic market producers. LFM D is particularly concerned about child labour and occupational health and safety (OHS), which, however, appears to be weakly enforced:

> Do we actually give them an audit? The answer is: No. Because I think if we gave them an audit, nobody would pass. (LFM D, English)

Inappropriate production conditions as for instance, such as employing underage workers or people working on the floor have been spotted during the interviews at least at one of his suppliers' factories (LFM A). For the managing director of LFM D non-compliant practices are not a reason to terminate subcontracts. He emphasises the challenge of implementing and enforcing compliant conditions in a highly unorganised MSME sector. According to him, compliance with local regulation is a matter of finance; stopping production would harm the producers even more. Instead, LFM D pays their subcontractors visits and gives suggestions:

> That's one of the things we do, we bring them to our factories. And this is what a factory can be. […] We don't expect you to have all these million dollar machines, but can we have straight lines? Can we have people working off the floor? Can we have electrical wire not on the floor but above? Can we not have naked flame? […] So, we try for the basics. We show them our good practices and encourage them to follow the same. (LFM D, English)

By showing good practices LFM D guides MSMEs in managing health and safety in their workplace. MSMEs learn how to organise the production process adequately by avoiding hazardous substances, removing dangerous electricity lines, or ensuring proper housekeeping, among others. Doubts remain as to whether this approach can induce change. Follow-up visits are rare and effective enforcement is not in place. LFM D refrains from subjecting MSMEs to audits that examine the compliance with the national regulation and the company's requirements. The way practices are implemented suggests that quality management and cost-effective production are prioritised over compliance issues. It would compromise the firm's objective of a cost-effective and flexible production if non-compliant subcontractors were excluded from the supply chain. A business association representing the interests of MSMEs could facilitate communication with lead firms and promote compliance among its members.

By contrast, LGM G is a social enterprise and a certified member of the World Fair Trade Organization (WFTO). Since LGM G joined WFTO in 2007 a separate set of producers caters to the export market:

> We've got two to three producers who are our export producers. So we work with WFTO, World Fair Trade Organisation, in the Netherlands. They come here twice a year and they […] meet our producers […]. So the buyers have come, showed them, seen their place, understood them, and that's how they [i.e. the producers; A. N.] understand what export quality is. And these are the three producers who basically work with leather and export outside. There is nobody else. So we make sure the quality and the standards are right. (LGM G, English)

Compliance with a set of requirements based on the “10 principles of Fair Trade”, one of which is to ensure no child labour and no forced labour, is a prerequisite for becoming a WFTO member (2014). WFTO is a global network of organisations (producers, exporters, importers, retailers, wholesalers) that are committed to implementing a fair trade supply chain from production to sales (ibid.). It monitors and audits the use of Fair Trade principles in private enterprises, usually in developing countries. Given its nature as a process standard, practices and (production) processes across the supply chain are being checked for environmental and social compliance (ibid.). Unfortunately the three export producers could not be included in the study any more.[95] However, interviews with LGM G and its suppliers exposed a blatant discrepancy between the lead firm’s discourse of empowering poor people and the reality in the producers’ workshops. Similarly to the profit-seeking LFM D, LGM G’s standard of social compliance for export producers differs substantially from its requirements for local suppliers. In visits to production sites several LGM G producers were found employing children as low-paid helpers and low-skilled workers (e.g. LGM B, LGM C, LFM A, LFM B). Hazardous practices such as the application of glue by fingers or without wearing protective clothing were observed. In this regard, there is no need to refer to international standards as the national law is already very clear, for instance, about child labour. Bangladesh enacted the Labour Act in 2006, which prohibits employment of children aged under 14 and “hazardous forms of child labour for persons under age 18” (UNICEF 2010). The National Child Labour Elimination Policy 2010 seeks to eliminate all forms of child labour by 2015 (UNICEF 2010). Both lead firms tie weak enforcement to the highly unorganised MSMEs. LGM G’s senior manager of the SCPR Department emphasises that the wide range of MSMEs of differing social, educational and technological capabilities make it difficult to implement a social compliance policy at domestic level. In fact, rather than local lead firms, the requirements of foreign buyers have raised the skilled export-oriented producers’ (T3, T4) awareness of compliance issues (see Sect. 5.3.4.2), though adoption is still slow. According to the Senior Manager of SCPR, low-skilled producers are more reluctant to adopt new practices. Although this can be confirmed for T1 and T2 which are more concerned about a regular order inflow, the lead firm barely enforces transgressions. By the time of the first interview and personal visits (2011), clear guidelines for dealing with child labour were still lacking. LGM G’s position seems undefined and partly contradictory. The producers were given recommendations about non-compliant practices to be followed up without questioning the subcontracting relationship:

> Termination is not a possibility because that also doesn’t fit within our mission. (LGM G, English)

[95]The late interview with LGM G (March 31, 2011) made additional producer interviews impossible.

The mission is to empower low-skilled and poor producers by integrating them into the supply chain. Termination cannot be an option because LGM G's in-house production amounted to only 6 % of the monthly production volume in 2010 and was ultimately even closed in June 2014. A loss of production cannot be compensated that quickly by other or new subcontractors. LGM G's business logic is built on external producers; but does the lead firm need them to be compliant? Convincing micro and small manufacturers to stop child labour is a challenge, particularly as many of LGM G's producers started as child workers themselves (e.g. LGM B). The Senior Manager of the SCPR Department sees the responsibility with the producers to provide opportunities for child workers, implicitly accepting this practice:

> So our idea is here, 'well, enough understood, but have him [i.e. the child worker; A. N.] as a part-time worker, but also invest in him so that he can study'. So we're kind of making him understand this. And the two producers who I have encountered who had child labour before, who we told they can't have, we went back and haven't actually seen them. And we were told that 'we've sent them back to the village' […]. (LGM G, English)

Against the backdrop of the author's visits to production sites, it seems questionable whether low-skilled producers adhere to weak recommendations. Neither supplier made efforts to hide child workers; two refused pictures being taken or questions being asked of under-aged employees (LGM B, LGM C). For LGM G it seems quite convenient to believe that the problem is solved as the children are gone. Usually it is not.[96] When the Senior Manager points to the parent company's education and health programme in which child workers of LGF producers are expected to be integrated in the future it becomes clear that LGM G is well aware of child labour among its producers. It just seems not to know how to handle this problem. In the end of the interview, she purported a much more prohibitive attitude than in the beginning:

> So we always tell our producers this, that, you know, if you continue, we can't work with you. And it's because of us. And, you know, so one child in the whole of LGM G it's just going to be very difficult. (LGM G, English)

Child labour is a very sensitive issue that draws western societies' attention. The interview with the author of a European background may have given reason for the Senior Manager of the SCPR Department to intensify and eventually rectify her initially rather approving position towards child labour. It can be also assumed that the global WFTO standard, though only applicable for export producers, seems to have sensitised LGM G about potential sanctions because of irregular production conditions ("it's because of us"). In 2011, four years after LGM G became a member of WFTO, a social compliance policy for producers for the domestic market had not yet been established:

---

[96]There are grounds to assume that the lead firm's tight costing may foster non-compliant practices of subcontractors (see Section "Coordination Through Costing and Price Setting").

> […] our social compliance policy is in process. We haven't finalised it yet, but it's the same… it's almost the same as the 10 Fair Trade principles. We've also had a look at the ETI [i.e. Ethical Trading Initiative; A. N.] based code and also we've had a look at the SA 8000. They're pretty much similar. (LGM G, English)

In fact, there are differences between the international standards, though the criteria for compliance may not differ substantially. Social Accountability 8000, an auditable certification standard that is based on the conventions of the International Labour Organisation (ILO), international human rights norms and national law (Social Accountability International 2013), and WFTO are voluntary standards that are certified by independent certification bodies. By contrast, the Ethical Trading Initiative (ETI) emerged as an alliance of private companies, trade unions and voluntary organisations to promote ethical labour conditions. Contrary to SA8000 and WFTO, ETI neither audits nor issues certificates, though members are requested to subject themselves to audits by third-party organisations. It considers itself a learning organisation and believes that ethical trade is a constant process of improvement (ETI 2014). This way, however, effective sanctions for non-compliance cannot be applied. According to the latest information by the Head of the SCPR Department (April 2014), LGM G has been conducting announced audits on an annual basis since 2012.[97] This means that independent third-party controls are lacking and producers have the chance to prepare their production site to pass the audits.[98] All suppliers emphasise that LGM G's main concern is quality, whereas little attention is paid to social principles.

To conclude, the two lead firms interviewed apply different standards of social compliance for the domestic and the export market. Child labour and unsafe workplaces dominate the lead firms' discourse of social compliance. Enforcement, however, is weak; third-party audits do not take place. LGM G's participation in international standards (WFTO) initiated a process of developing a social compliance policy also for domestic market suppliers, which cannot be assessed yet. Its discourse of social empowerment, however, does not match the actual efforts that have been made to date. Double standards and negligent enforcement practices among domestic market producers undermine the firm's credibility as a social enterprise.

The local production network is determined by subcontracted relationships between large local manufacturers and MSMEs. The following section explores whether subcontracts for the export market provide learning opportunities for the MSMEs.

[97]Unfortunately, it was not possible to verify the final content of the social compliance policy.

[98]The latest follow-up questions (April 2014) with MSMEs revealed that two subcontractors (LFM B, LGM F) had been audited on production and working conditions.

Subcontracting for the Export Market—Developing Capabilities or Becoming Invisible Exporters?

Based on the extent of subcontracting for the domestic market it was assumed that lead firms also use MSMEs for the cost-efficient production of export ware. Only one manufacturer, the medium-sized footwear company LFM C, was found producing on subcontract for the foreign market. The others denied both active and passive subcontracting linkages in exports.

In line with Pratim Sahu (2010), the incidence of multi-tiered subcontracting for the export market seems to be low. The two of the lead firms interviewed ruled out local SMEs being qualified for producing export quality on subcontract. As an OEM, LFM D produces brands for other companies. Supported by its Italian counterpart, LFM D has expanded production and improved product quality to meet international standards. SMEs still have limitations that disqualify them for subcontracts for the export market managing director of LFM D:

> […] the first thing is they won't pass compliance, the social compliance, that is, by the big buyers in Europe, Germany and UK. If they come and see the conditions where they are working, they can't pass. […] Second issue: like I said, tax, VAT [i.e. Value Added Tax; A. N.]. Third issue: […] As you know we import components duty free as long as we re-export. Let's say we get all the components duty free to our factory, we find a great small SME who can do it, we want to sell the components to them; we can't! They don't have a bonded warehouse license. (LFM D, English)

LFM D sees two main barriers to taking advantage of MSMEs in the export market: the requirements of foreign buyers and compliance with local laws and regulation.

First, LFM D's buyers operate on a global scale; one of them is the largest European footwear retailer. With growing consumer awareness international buyers of this kind have become very sensitive to corporate social responsibility. Laws and ethical standards are communicated as being met by subjecting the company and its producers to third-party audited compliance initiatives (e.g. BSCI) or by establishing internal codes of conducts (Deichmann 2014). The production conditions (e.g. operation on the floor; some under-age workers) of at least two footwear manufacturers interviewed (LFM A, LFM B) would fall short of the requirements of Europe's biggest shoe monger. Deichmann (2014) sources large quantities directly from producers of, for instance, LFM D's size and guarantees its customers low prices. The low capacity of MSMEs opposes a formal supply relationship.

As for the second limitation, LFM D insinuates that MSMEs tend to infringe upon local laws and regulation. In fact, many of them produce in residential areas and are said to evade taxes and licenses. Large buyers are exposed to public attention and thus cannot afford the risk of having non-compliant suppliers. Furthermore, the bonded warehouse system denies large export-oriented firms from letting subcontractors benefit from duty-free imported accessories. Here, LFM D implies that it applies standards that differ from the leather processing industry where large tanneries have institutionalised illicit practices of misusing bonded licenses.

As opposed to LFM D's discourse, the medium-sized producer LFM C claimed that he supplied the lead firm with footwear for the export market:

> Now we are doing LFM D only [for the; A. N.] export [market; A. N.]. […] Two years ago we were doing work for their local market [inc]. But now we are doing all for export. (LFM C, English)

Before LFM C sold 76 % of his company's shares to LFM D, he was a regular supplier of LFM D and achieved 20 % of own exports (see Table A.1). A production capacity of 1,400 pairs daily, an organised and standardised production process (e.g. conveyor belt; labour division; six production lines), a bonded warehouse license,[99] and export experience qualified LFM C to be subcontracted for the export market. Unlike subcontractors for the local market, LFM C received technical assistance at all stages of the transaction; he was supplied with raw material, received advance payment and was occasionally provided with machinery. Close monitoring throughout the entire production process was necessary to ensure product quality, unlike with domestic market producers whose goods are only checked at the time of delivery:

> They had a person in my factory and he used to check everything related to production. He was appointed by LFM D and used to stay at my factory. […] They used to check everything like: production process, materials, […] the quality of my products, etc. (LFM C, Bengali)

Even if only few SMEs produce for LFM D's foreign customers, LFM C's case allows for differentiation between subcontractors for the export and the domestic market. Despite tighter supervision, export producers enjoy more technical support and thus have more opportunities to learn, which is why they are less exposed to power asymmetries than domestic market producers (see Fig. 5.25).

Though recognising great opportunities for cost reduction, LFM D's official discourse is that the SME supply base is not ready yet for subcontracts to the export market. But pressure on prices is high and opportunities abound, given the large MSME supply base. LFM D's managing director referred to the production strategy of one Indian sandal exporter, which is informative concerning the firm's export ambitions:

> So what we did is: adapt something that is very hand-made, you can't produce in factories like ours. It needs hand-made technicians there, craftsmen to do it. So what they [i.e. the Indian firm; A. N.] did is: these big factories took lots of orders and then they job-worked it out to the small guys. They made all the production, they made all the quality, brought it back 'cause the small guys didn't have the paper work license that people need to do export. So they collected back and they exported that. I think that… that's a great way [excited]. I…I…I dream of that possibility […]! Today, a lot of retailers want to do small quantities, they don't want to have big 10,000 pair, 15,000 pair orders. They want to do 200 pairs of this style, 300 pairs of this style. Very difficult to do for us because our factories are too big. So FLEXIBLE production is what we are missing. If we could access these SMEs, we could use them as our flexible production unit. (LFM D, English)

[99]Unfortunately, it was not possible to clarify how LFM C managed to get this license despite not meeting the requirements (e.g. 100 % export-oriented).

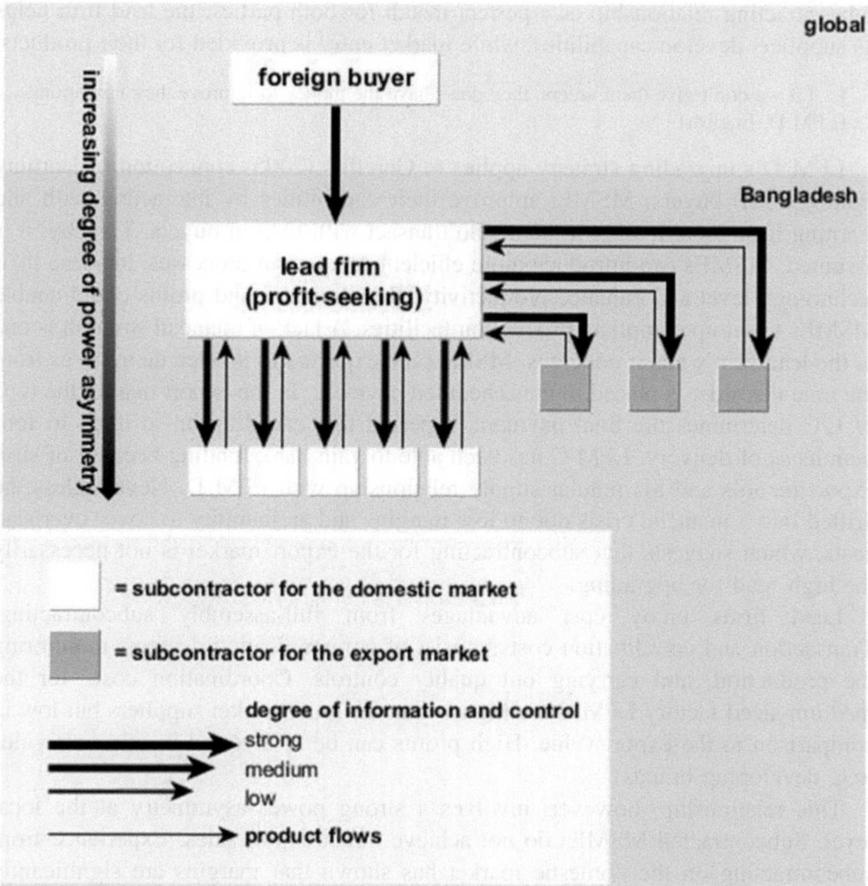

Fig. 5.25 Coordination of subcontractors for the domestic and the export market. *Source* Own illustration

The opportunities LFM D expects from subcontracting MSMEs are flexibility, low-cost production and a broad range of products. MSMEs have the ability to produce small quantities of labour-intensive handmade products cost-efficiently. They satisfy market needs as retailers aim at reducing the risk of product failure. Low runs of low-standardised products target market niches that large factories such as LFM D's cannot get into. This would oppose to the sourcing strategy of one of LFM D's major buyers (see above) who advertises with low prices thanks to economies of scale in production. To meet the retailers' new demands, the capabilities of MSMEs would have to be raised to the export level. LFM D sees a subcontracting relationship as a perfect match for both parties: the lead firm helps its suppliers develop capabilities, while market entry is provided for their products:

> […] if we don't give them orders, they don't have the money to improve their conditions. (LFM D, English)

LFM D's upgrading strategy applies to Gereffi's (2005) conception of learning from (global) buyers. MSMEs improve their capabilities by interacting with and learning from local market leaders who transact with foreign buyers. Thereby, it is assumed, MSMEs can introduce more efficient production processes, increase their technology level and enhance productivity. Regular sales and profits could enable MSMEs to set up compliant production facilities. A lack of financial strength is one of the lead firm's major concerns. MSMEs are expected to finance themselves from the time the order is placed to the scheduled payment. In the export market the type of L/C determines the final payment, a period that can drag on to three to four months as of delivery. LFM C has been able to gain bank funding because of size, export records and his regular supply relationship with LFM D. Nevertheless, he drifted into a financial crisis due to low margins and an inability to cover overhead costs, which suggests that subcontracting for the export market is not necessarily the high road for upgrading.

Lead firms enjoy cost advantages from full-assembly subcontracting. Transaction and coordination costs consist of communicating designs, monitoring the production, and carrying out quality controls. Coordination costs for the medium-sized factory LFM C are higher than for local market suppliers but low in comparison to the export value. High profits can be re-invested in other activities (e.g. developing brands).

This relationship, however, involves a strong power asymmetry at the local level. Subcontracted MSMEs do not achieve direct export sales. Experience from subcontracting on the domestic market has shown that margins are significantly lower where intermediaries (i.e. lead firms, buying houses) are involved. Production risks are outsourced to the MSMEs who usually need to deal with fluctuating raw material prices and quality differences (e.g. rejects). The mediated market entry comes at the expense of the MSME's corporate identity. Their products cannot be traded under the producer's name in international transactions. So, subcontracting for the global market turns local MSMEs into *invisible exporters*.

While LFM D dreams of expanding subcontracts of low-cost footwear producers to international markets, some leather goods suppliers assumed that their lead firm exported some of their products, but were not certain about it. LGM G's export activities in leather products are very low; only 1 % are sold abroad. The structure within which it exports deserves attention (see Section "Assistance in Social Compliance"):

> […] the other thing is we have a separate set of producers who only export, who only do export production because we have to be socially compliant because we are a member of Fair Trade. So, all the products we sell to our buyers are usually a member of Fair Trade, so that…I mean they are our main buyers, so we have to ensure that those factories are good factories. (LGM G, English)

LGM G has subcontracted three manufacturers for export production. As LGM G's products are marketed by the World Fair Trade Organisation (WFTO), the Senior Manager of SCPR places emphasis on compliant factories. Unfortunately, the export producers could not be included in this study, so conclusions with regard to differences in dependency and power asymmetry compared to local suppliers cannot be drawn. But according to WFTO, LGM G has fulfilled all requirements to become a member of the organisation. In a next step LGM G has to submit a self-assessment report to start the first WFTO Guarantee System cycle, at the end of which the firm is assigned low, medium or high risk, according to which audits are conducted every six, four or two years. The fact that WFTO suppliers are subject to audits indicates that export producers are tightly supervised and controlled by the lead firm and the organisation to meet its requirements. Domestic market producers are less embedded within monitoring and control schemes concerning issues of social compliance. Only quality and delivery are (relatively) strictly ensured (see Sect. 5.3.3.3). LGM G's double standard of compliant producers for the export market and subcontractors that lack comparable standards on the domestic market is reflected in Fig. 5.26.

To conclude, according to the lead firms' discourse, their MSME suppliers lack compliance for the export market. Given a dearth of data, subcontracting for the export market could not be examined as an appropriate upgrading strategy for MSMEs. The social enterprise LGM G applies double standards to subcontractors for the domestic and export market, thereby ignoring its mandate of empowering low-skilled producers in implementing compliant conditions. The profit-seeking lead firm LFM D was found to be subcontracting to one medium-sized footwear manufacturer (apparently informally) who was strictly monitored and controlled. Benefits and drawbacks resemble those in domestic subcontracts. MSMEs are excluded from direct transactions with foreign buyers and turn into invisible exporters. The lead firm assumes the role of a coordinating intermediary, thereby legitimising higher prices for consumers. These results indicate that standards in the foreign market force lead firms to coordinate their supply chain more strictly than they do for the domestic market. More research is needed to define the impact of export subcontracts on the productive and financial capabilities of MSMEs.

Concluding Remarks on Learning from Local Large Manufacturers

Local lead firms have induced limited learning processes for MSME suppliers through an exchange of information and knowledge as well as by providing raw material, inputs and machinery. Instead, they outsource risks in procurement and product quality to their full-assembly suppliers. Double standards of social compliance for the domestic and export market as well as negligent enforcement practices exclude domestic market producers from sustained learning. LGM G's discourse of social empowerment concentrates merely on the numerical integration of low-skilled suppliers. Little importance has been given to qualifying suppliers through assistance during the production process and reducing their vulnerability to

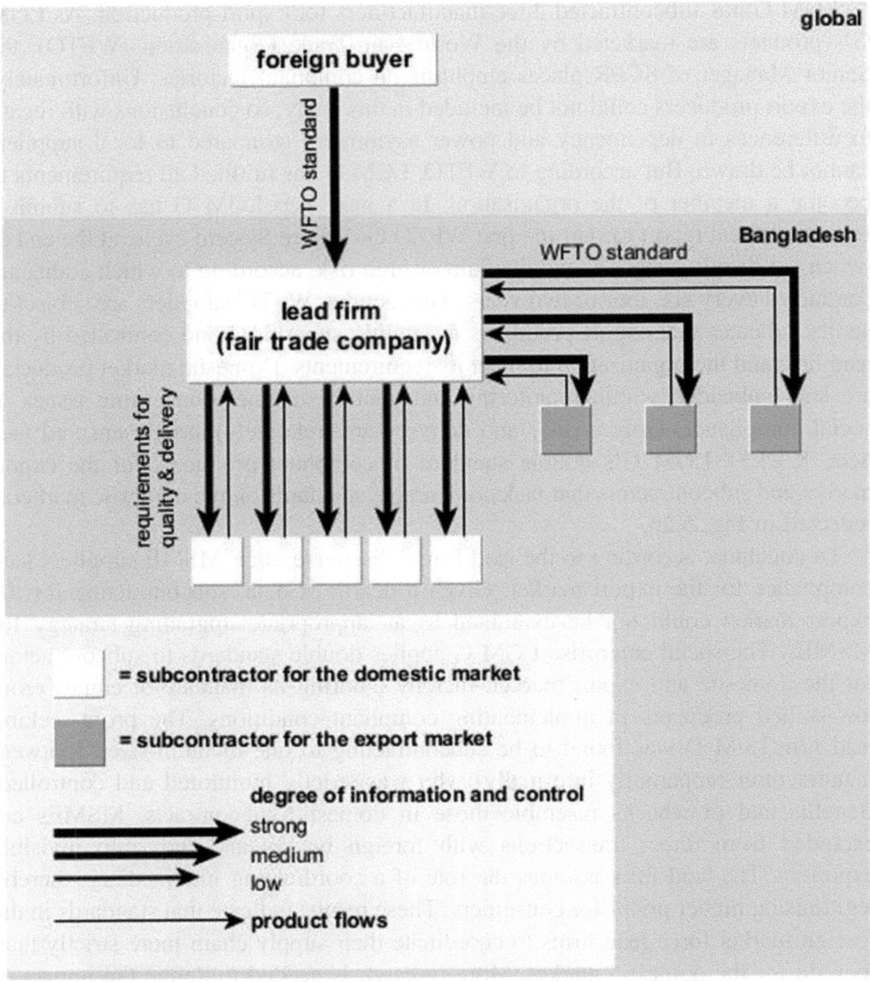

Fig. 5.26 Coordination of producers for the domestic and the export market by the social enterprise. *Source* Own illustration

fluctuation in prices and orders. On the one hand, this is due to LGM G's lacking competences in leather manufacturing, so knowledge can hardly be imparted to their external producers. Interviews, on the other hand, suggest that the strategy of both lead firms is to take advantage of low-cost suppliers while guaranteeing minimum quality standards. LFM D, an OEM that entered a joint venture with an Italian company, appears to be interested in subcontracting MSMEs for the export market and sees a great need for raising domestic suppliers to the export level.

In this regard, it is noteworthy that the two of the lead firms started participating in the development project USAID PRICE in 2010 to induce more sustained learning processes through upgrading activities for a selected number of supplying

MSMEs. In what way the interviewed MSMEs were embedded within such upgrading strategies to overcome their manifold shortcomings will be presented in Sect. 5.3.5.3. First, it will be examined whether foreign market integration contributes to moving the producers up the value chain.

5.3.5.2 Learning from Foreign Buyers

The global value chain perspective considers learning from global lead firms as crucial for emerging markets. Gereffi et al. (2005) conceptualise lead firms in captive value chains as multi-national corporations that exercise power through information and control over suppliers. In this view, foreign buyers transfer knowledge, material, and technology to suppliers in developing countries. This abstraction misses complexity: only large producers have the capabilities to supply global lead firms and thus the opportunity to learn from them. MSMEs are either loosely linked to small foreign buyers and/or are strongly embedded in local production networks that are governed by those large manufacturers. Hence, the suppliers' competences seem to influence learning and upgrading trajectories.

The leather goods and footwear industry is still in its infancy. Fluctuations in export activity (see Sect. 5.3.4) by the time of the main interviews made it difficult to draw conclusions as to what extent MSMEs learn from foreign customers.

Buyers transfer knowledge and information mainly to ensure product quality the requirements of which vary strongly between the domestic and the export market. LGM C (T2), a very low-skilled supplier who de facto lacks export capabilities, has been trained by his buyer and buying house to make his products reach export quality:

> Because at LGM G different controllers checked our products on different days. So they were not real experts in understanding all the flaws. If one person checks it regularly, then he will be expert about it. But in exports only two or three persons are involved with quality control. This means good leather is needed, so the sewing will be smoother. That means they make me understand every part of the product, although I knew it before. But they make it clearer to me and suggest how I can do better. (LGM C, Bengali)

LGM C instructively explains that the competences of his local lead firm to assess quality, in principle specialised in fabrics and garments, are below export requirements. Tight supervision and direct support (see Sect. 5.3.4.1) allows his British buyer to intervene and teach him specific steps in the production process to increase product quality. LGM C needs to be sure to purchase raw material of adequate quality (e.g. tanning), whereas on the local market he generally looks for the best price, even though his lead firm sets benchmarks in terms of quality. As long as domestic market requirements differ so enormously from international standards, there are no incentives for LGM C to apply better, though often more expensive practices continuously throughout the production process.

Export-oriented T3-producers took their buyers' criticism on the environment and production capacity to heart (see Sect. 5.3.4.2). While operating in small workshops in residential areas of Hazaribagh and Old Dhaka, they had difficulties attracting foreign buyers given the substandard environmental and production conditions:

> Several times, several times it happened. The buyer came to my factory because first time he gave me the pictures; I made the product, he said the product is ok; 'very nice. I want to visit your factory'. Whenever he came to my factory, 'aaah no, residential area and it is a very small factory.' Then he asked me, 'have you made it by yourself?' Then I show him my other products, I'm making this type of product. Ooh, he doesn't get the confidence to give me the order. (LFM A, English)

As a result of reiterative buyer complaints, in 2011 LFM A (as well as LGM D and LGM E) decided to move his factory within Hazaribagh from a residential to a more industrial zone. He enlarged the production area, invested in simple machinery, improved occupational health and safety standards (e.g. storerooms for materials; ventilation), and changed the household line for an industrial electrical line (see Photos 10 and 11). Workers are partly sitting on the floor, partly operating at the table.

Photo 10 Old workshop LFM A, February 2011. *Source* Own photo

Photo 11 New workshop LFM A, November 2012. *Source* Own photo

Photo 12 Factory LGM F, Keraniganj/Dhaka district, 2014. *Source* Own photo

LGM F had left bustling Old Dhaka already in 2010 for a multi-story production site on the outskirts of Dhaka (see Fig. 5.21). He considered a clean and neat environment that attracts foreign buyers more important than the spatial proximity to the leather suppliers in Hazaribagh. His production site is well-organised with workers operating at the table (see Photo 12).

All these suppliers have been able to enlarge their production capacity significantly (see Table 5.7), though mostly supported by labour and to a lesser extent by technology. The export-oriented T3-manufacturers who are aware of their limitations after being admonished by foreign buyers expand on their own or using family capital, thereby gradually improving their conditions to qualify for future international buyers.

Surprisingly, LGM C (T2) followed suit by moving to the same premises as LFM A and LGM D, a former tannery, in 2014. He managed to sell parts of his father's properties, augmented the production area significantly and increased the capacity by adding workers. Unlike T3-producers, he sees no need to invest in machinery and equipment:

> I do not need many types of machinery as what I do is related to handicrafts. (LGM C, Bengali)

LGM C's buyer orders low value-added leather goods (e.g. business card holders, key rings) for corporate gifts. Given LGM C's limited production capabilities (see Photo 13), she is unlikely to extend LGM C's product lines to include more sophisticated articles. LGM C, in turn, relies on only one intermediary and has failed to acquire new buyers.

LFM C's (T4) case is different from other manufacturers. Coming from the garment industry, he first built up product lines for a known French buyer. His experience on the foreign market qualified him for subcontracts with LFM D. He starts from a higher level of competence: the production process has been industrialised; the production site is spacious and well-organised (see Photo 14); and the

Photo 13 Old workshop LGM C, Ganaktuli/Dhaka, 2011. *Source* Own photo

Photo 14 Factory LFM C, Gazipur district, 2014. *Source* Own photo

capacity meets the requirements of rather smaller buyers. His customers suggest achieving increases in efficiencies by investing in technology, for instance, by purchasing an insole machine which produces better quality and renders costly imports unnecessary. This is a road that LFM C cannot yet go down. Such investments amortise only in large quantities and require better market integration.

Derived from the investigation of learning effects by interaction with foreign buyers, producers focus on constraints that affect their export ability most. Export-oriented, skilled T3-producers primarily invest in the production site and capacity, while the low-skilled T2-manufacturer is assisted in bringing product quality up to international standards. T4-producers still have difficulties moving from labour-intensive to more technology-intensive production. These results seem to confirm what has been widely acknowledged in the literature: buyers support manufacturers in increasing product quality and productivity, but avoid enhancing other capabilities that might reduce the power asymmetry.

5.3.5.3 Learning from External Development Projects

Thanks to foreign development projects such as PRICE or GTZ-PROGRESS, some of the manufacturers were embedded in activities to increase efficiencies in the production process, improve product quality and enhance marketing skills.

Against the backdrop of foreign companies moving production to Bangladesh, USAID launched PRICE (2009–2013) to respond to the lack of skilled workforce to satisfy export-oriented firms (USAID 2010, p. 34). The objective was to increase the competitiveness of underperforming MSMEs by "establishing and strengthening linkages to large manufacturers" (Head of PRICE) with the assistance of the local leather association LFMEAB. This approach implies that linkages between MSMEs and large manufacturers such as LGM G and LFM D were weak by the time the programme started. Interviews provide evidence that they were not (see Section "Magnitude, Characteristics and Importance of Subcontracting for Lead Firms"). Several manufacturers interviewed had been tied to LGM G and LFM D as subcontractors before PRICE started (e.g. LGM B/C/F; LFM B/C).

PRICE centred its strategy on more educated manufacturers to reduce the large firms' distrust towards SMEs.[100] According to the head of the development project, lead firms suspect that SMEs use substandard material, are unreliable in meeting the buyers' requirements, and lack literacy. Hence, few representative SMEs, most of them with an educational background from BCLT, were initially incorporated in upgrading programmes to develop good practices that can be followed by other (less skilled) enterprises. PRICE identified LTSE (Leather Technologist SME Entrepreneurs), a group of leather technologists engaged in manufacturing (see Sect. 5.3.3.4), to qualify for subcontractors for large export-oriented companies.

[100] After pilot projects with the most capable producers the initiative was to be extended to less skilled manufacturers. Due to time constraints results of the last phase could not be collected.

The pilot project included seven enterprises in process and product upgrading activities, five of which were part of this study (LFM A, LFM B, LGM D, LGM E, LGM F). The objective was to reduce inefficient operations, to increase product quality and to cut down waste. Trainers from large local and global manufacturers (e.g. Bata, LFM D) were hired to address efficiency increases in production processes (production planning, organising labour force), housekeeping, quality development, and costing (USAID 2010).

Process Upgrading

As regards improving processes, participants were taught to use inputs and raw material more efficiently. According to PRICE, waste in adhesive application was reduced at least by 15 %. The productivity increase was striking for LGM E:

> […] out of three litres of adhesive we produced 20 to 25 bags. Now it's almost 40 bags we are able to produce with this adhesive. (LGM E, English)

Small changes in inputs such as solvent-free water-based adhesives establish clean technology and help perform operations more cost-efficiently. This gives participants of PRICE a competitive advantage over producers that lack such knowledge or are excluded from this programme. The medium-sized footwear producer LFM B enlarged his capacity and hired more workers thanks to a productivity increase initiated by PRICE:

> Like, they showed us how to make a shoe in one hour instead of two hours. The labour cost for two hour is 120 taka […] so 60 taka is already in my pocket. In our country, the local producers produce their shoes at a cost of 100 taka per pair. But I can produce the shoes with 20 taka only. So 80 % is in my pocket. I have learned these things from the seminars and workshops. (LFM B, Bengali)[101]

Low-skilled cottage, micro and small producers prevail in Dhaka's leather goods and footwear industry. Most of them lack access to modern technology and only use sewing machines (GTZ 2006). The rest of the production process is done manually. They compensate for their low mechanisation level by low labour costs so they are cost competitive on labour-intensive consumer goods (e.g. sandals, slippers), provided that semi-industrial manufacturers such as LFM B have not introduced standardised processes based on the division of labour and more efficient technology.

New inputs (e.g. adhesives, chemicals) require few changes in the production process but achieve huge effects on costs and even health. The introduction of technology is a matter of finance. Simple machinery can increase productivity enormously, emphasises LFM A:

[101]Currency converted as of February 9, 2011 (OANDA 2014): 20 BDT = US$0.29; 60 BDT = US$0.86; 100 BDT = US$1.43; 120 BDT = US$1.72.

> [...] small machines [...] can make a huge difference in the production line. PRICE has introduced some training by the local expert Mr. XX; he was technical manager of Bata and he suggested some handmade machines to us and other factories. And it has hugely reduced working time! What ten people can do in one day, one person can do in four hours! (LFM A, English)

LFM A's case is instructive for upgrading MSMEs in the global South. Trainings and workshops need to be adjusted to the producers' capabilities. Instead of expensive, sophisticated technology, simple low-cost machinery may help small manufacturers achieve a great leap forward in competitiveness. Productivity increases release resources that can be reinvested. The risk of layoffs is low at this stage. With the support of PRICE LFM A has been able to build up workforce, constantly adding employees from approximately 30 in 2011 to over 50 at the end of 2012. PRICE conducted a workforce development programme to increase skills at the operator level. Floor-level workers of selected companies were qualified in using machines and inputs properly before they were re-integrated into their factories. 30 of LFM A's permanent workers and potential future workers from his home district participated. PRICE covered 50 % of the workers' salaries for three months to compensate for low output and productivity in the early stage. Such trainings are intended to develop skills that increase productivity, ensure quality and reduce waste. However, it requires financial strength and a regular order inflow to sustain increasing overhead costs, which LFM A was able to provide.

Upgrading encompasses activities that offer higher returns (Memedovic and Mattila 2008, p. 492). To secure participation the MSMEs had to be assured that the adoption of new practices would translate into monetary benefit, explains the Head of PRICE. LGM E's initial reluctance on the significance of housekeeping issues changed when he realised about the impact on costs and product quality alike:

> This type of thing [i.e. the training on housekeeping; A. N.] makes us protect the product or the leather or the accessories from wastage because we just dump our leather. Last time you saw my sofa. But after we came back from the training we started preserving [i.e. we stored] the leather in a good way; and this type of small things make some difference. And it is helpful for our factory because it saves money. (LGM E, English)

In practice, process and product upgrading are often interrelated and sometimes difficult to discern (Ponte and Ewert 2009, p. 1638). Quality management is lacking among the MSMEs interviewed (see Sect. 5.3.4.2). Micro and small manufacturers in particular were seen as careless, with raw material, accessories, and instruments scattered on the floor. Producers were trained in ISO 9001:2008 to meet the requirements of a quality management system that ensures product quality according to customer, statutory and regulatory standards (ISO 2014). ISO 9001:2008 is a voluntary standard that is certified by third party organisations. Seminars on housekeeping teach producers how to effectively organise production in order to reduce costs and ensure consistent quality for their customers. They also aimed to reduce the fire incidence that is particularly high in residential areas with manufacturing activities, where many of the beneficiary producers are located (Hazaribagh, Ganaktuli/Old Dhaka). Nevertheless, in factory visits by the author old patterns were often seen to re-emerge (e.g. LGM E, LFM A). According to PRICE, impact assessment surveys were carried out; the producers interviewed, however, saw their factories checked only once after the trainings. Consistent improvement and sustained learning processes require follow-up trainings and monitoring. Questions remain concerning the real impact of PRICE after the project phased out in 2013. A first report on the pilot project recognised deficits in adopting the processes learned; out of seven enterprises only three were able to implement several of the recommendations given by PRICE (USAID 2010). Unfortunately, the report did not go into practicable outcomes in more detail.

PRICE extended the pilot to 20 of LGM G's old suppliers which were "continuously not very profitable" (Senior Manager of SCPR). Among the participants was a growing sense of frustration and disillusion after the trainings ended:

> But I think the thing was having spent six sessions outside, six half days outside, they probably expected something immediate which we couldn't give them. […] And also it wouldn't depend on us, it would depend on them how they change their practices. So after we finished those trainings they were like 'so what happens now'? […] And the other thing was expectation of more work from us. […] So we were like, 'no, these are not to give you more orders, these are to help you organise your existent production. If you do this better, […] maybe if we have more demand, we'll give it to you'. (LGM G, English)

Cost reductions release resources that can be valorised in additional orders or with new buyers. Both ways are unlikely as many of these underperforming producers are exclusive suppliers of LGM G and lack marketing skills. The trainings on housekeeping and production planning were intended to place neither more nor higher value-added products. They managed, however, to reduce lead times and lower costs. In so doing, LGM G benefits most as the costing is adjusted, while the profit margin of 10–12 % remains the same. It is difficult for MSMEs to change persistent, inefficient practices that have been learned by experience and have been passed on without being questioned. Time and close assistance by the lead firm is needed; otherwise the positive effect of the trainings will be wasted. Incentives such as order increases could drive LGM G's producers towards better performance.

Interviews suggest that MSMEs are more willing to adopt new techniques if benefits are reflected in product improvements or cost reductions. Low-skilled micro producers (T1, T2) were especially critical about the meaning and purpose of trainings:

> I need orders to improve my business. Improvement to me means orders. (LGM C, Bengali)

By the time the main interviews were taken (February–April/November 2011), low-skilled long-term suppliers had received little (LGM B) or no training (LGM C) and thus were less aware of potential opportunities.[102] To them, the only benefit is to augment orders and buyers. LGM C's (quantitative) understanding of

[102]Only LGM B participated in upgrading seminars by PRICE. Unfortunately, due to time constraints, he was unable (and unwilling) to answer questions about the impact of trainings and seminars on production processes.

improvement may be founded in his seasonally varying capacity utilisation and the few requirements both global and local buyers place on technology. Buyer pressure on cleaner and more efficient production technology appears to be low.

The practices PRICE teaches correspond to international standards that many domestic-oriented producers are not ready for yet. For instance, workers of LGM B were seen applying adhesive with their fingers, while PRICE-trained manufacturers (e.g. LFM A, LGM D, LGM E) already use brushes. Neither uses masks against toxic fumes. Awareness about the impact of clean technology on environment and health is increasing only slowly. Better-educated manufacturers (T3) are more concerned about cleaner production conditions. Thanks to PRICE, LGM D learned that locally available adhesive is carcinogenic:

> I attended some workshops and I came to know that this is not good. […] No buyer asked for this, but it is my concern that I came to know that this is dangerous. It is not hygienic, so I want to do this. (LGM D, English)

Only 5 % of LGM D's annual sales are directed to European (UK, Italy) and Asian (Japan, Cambodia) buyers who purchase only small quantities of leather bags and small garments (e.g. wallets); they do not ask for chemical tests yet. Changing inputs and making processes cleaner does not increase the value added but has beneficial effects for the workers' health. Clean practices that harm neither workers nor the environment and that ensure safe products for consumers may give LGM D competitive advantages in attaining very specific customers.

In sum, the more skilled and export-oriented producers (T3, T4) benefited widely from process upgrading implemented by PRICE. T1- and T2-producers are neither included in upgrading activities nor aware of potential improvements. With the practices taught to raise productivity, augment workforce, and use raw material and inputs more efficiently, the small and medium-sized manufacturers interviewed may aim to better organise the production process and attract new buyers.

Product Upgrading

The development of more value-added products requires extension services, for instance, in research and technology or cooperation within horizontal or vertical linkages (see Giuliani et al. 2005). While the former is virtually absent except for LSBPC, a governmental agency that organises technical assistance for leather manufacturers to enhance their competitiveness (see Sect. 4.2), joint actions among the MSMEs interviewed are largely lacking, unless to increase efficiencies (see LTSE network).

PRICE focused on skills development which is an effective means to improve both productivity and product quality. A higher skills level is expected to yield more value-added products in less response time. PRICE trained producers on giving care to accessories and inputs, which are usually neglected:

> We learnt […] where we can get the good materials like thread, adhesive and also some ornaments. (LGM E, English)

The general practice of the local lead firms interviewed is to take no liability for raw material, accessories or inputs. MSMEs, however, often lack information as to from where to source adequate quality, which deteriorates their capacity to negotiate better terms. Given the lead firms' tight coordination (e.g. costing), subcontractors often end up purchasing low-cost material. PRICE raises awareness of quality material that reduces not just exposure to toxins (e.g. carcinogenic adhesive), but also allows producers to enhance the properties of products (e.g. better adhesion) to realise higher returns. Moreover, lasting methods have been trained to footwear manufacturers, such as moulding the upper leather to the last and gluing it properly. Operations inaccurately performed can deteriorate product quality significantly.

Such small changes of this kind require few financial resources and can be implemented easily. Investments in technology are more delicate:

> And the other thing was that […] quality will be improved if they buy those machineries. So that was a concern for us because we didn't know if we were actually able to give them that much money to buy all that machinery because they're very expensive. (LGM G, English)

As to the author's knowledge, no MSME interviewed received financial assistance in purchasing machinery. Even good performers are reluctant to draw on own funds if the return on investment is insecure:

> To buy a [hydraulic cutting; A. N.] machine I need 10 lakh taka [i.e. 1,000,000 BDT; A. N.]. [They say; A. N.] if I do the work with this machine it will last more, the durability of the product would be better, but [inc.] 10 lakh taka is needed for that. They tell me if I do this, they are going to take more of these products, but I can't do that because of the money. (LFM B, Bengali)[103]

Before MSMEs can move into "more sophisticated product lines" (Humphrey and Schmitz 2002, p. 1020), lead firms want their suppliers to improve the quality of existing products. The use of specific machinery increases the unit value and, additionally, makes it possible to produce goods at shorter notice. Among the MSMEs interviewed, not even T4-manufacturers have qualified to invest in specific technology (e.g. finishing). Though LFM B already managed bank loans, he is unable to import high-quality machinery from Europe. Instead, he purchases the machine second-hand for only 150,000 BDT (approx. US$2,000) either from other large manufacturers or imported from China. Micro and small manufacturers cannot pay heed to such suggestions yet. They lack solid funding from banks to finance machinery of that scale. Moreover, producers are wary of investing in modern technology as workers are often unskilled at handling sophisticated technology, lack knowledge of proper repair and maintenance or spare material has to be imported at high cost.

Trainings and suggestions make low-skilled producers aware of the importance of higher quality materials and modern technology for product properties. Apart

[103]Currency converted as of November 17, 2011 (OANDA 2014): 1,000,000 BDT = US$13,300.

from PRICE, little initiative comes from within the MSMEs, although there are opportunities also for small manufacturers with limited resources. LFM A's case is again instructive for how to succeed in crafting more sophisticated products:

> If you observe […] the local footwear industry, the SME like us, then you will find that they all are producing the sandals with polyurethane [rubber; A. N.] soles, imported from China or [from; A. N.] the local market. But I think it is not fashionable. If I go for a different design with leather soles, I can earn some more profit. […] The same kind of sandals with polyurethane soles, the next shop sells it in 500 or 600 Taka and with leather soles I sell this type of sandals in 900 or 1,000 Taka. (LFM A, English)[104]

As already outlined in Section "Coordination Through Selective and Mediated Market Access", LFM A took ideas from the foreign market, researched samples online, implemented them and eventually introduced leather sandals of buffalo leather outsoles into the domestic market. Locally available raw material outweighs costly imports and increases the unit value considerably.

The producers interviewed received assistance in product upgrading but only have the resources to implement small changes, for instance, in procurement or housekeeping. Without access to loan programmes, the producers are excluded from more sophisticated technology. Neither the lead firms nor PRICE engaged in product development. Joint actions with other producers in this regards were lacking. More research institutes and own market research is necessary to share knowledge and develop own products.

Functional Upgrading

It has been widely acknowledged that lead firms in the North allow their suppliers to develop capabilities to produce more efficiently and make better products, but are reluctant to let them operate more value-added activities prior or after production (e.g. Ponte and Ewert 2009; Giuliani et al. 2005; Humphrey 2004; Humphrey and Sturgeon 2002). The two local lead firms interviewed coordinate MSME suppliers embedded within the leather goods and footwear production network in a similar way (see Sect. 5.3.3.3). One component of PRICE was to strengthen functions other than production.

Because of a lack of finances and marketing knowledge most of the MSMEs are dissociated from lucrative distribution channels. A buyer-supplier meeting in 2009 between the retailer LGM G and several MSMEs resulted for the LTSE members LFM A and LGM E in mediated access to the medium-high-end domestic market.[105] The subcontracting relationship has been ongoing since and helped the small manufacturers to significantly increase order stability and product quality as has been shown in Section "Magnitude, Characteristics and Importance of Subcontracting for

---

[104]Currency converted as of February 12, 2011 (OANDA 2014): 500 BDT = US$7.17; 600 BDT = US$8.60; 900 BDT = US$12.90; 1,000 BDT = US$14.34.

[105]LGM D participated too, but did not pass.

MSMEs". This market entry, however, came at the expense of power asymmetries between the lead firm and the suppliers (see Sections "Coordination Through Selective and Mediated Market Access"–"Dependence Through Subcontracts").

To strengthen marketing activities and reduce dependency on one dominant lead firm, PRICE supported several LTSE-manufacturers in participating in Dhaka International Trade Fair (DITF):

> The main benefit is that we are so weak in marketing and if we want to attend DITF, then our financial stability is not too strong to attend all the technologies, but PRICE helps me for that and also helps us to create a catalogue. That is very helpful for our marketing and for the workers. (LGM D, English)

The T3-manufacturers LFM A, LGM D and LGM E received subsidies for the stall rent to jointly present their goods to national and international buyers at DITF. A catalogue displayed all products and supplier details. Direct marketing requires funds to which particularly micro and small industries have no access. As a female entrepreneur, LGM D was enabled by EPB and SME Foundation to participate in Lineappelle in 2008, an important leather fair in Bologna/Italy, where she established contact to her first buyer. Such financial assistance is essential for small producers to build up linkages to the foreign market:

> We are not participating in the fair at this moment. Without the support of organisations such as World Bank, GTZ [i.e. German Technical Cooperation; A. N.] or other organisations we cannot just participate every year in the fair. And being an exporter you have to participate in the fair. (LGM F, English)

Financial assistance in direct marketing temporarily helps connect buyers and suppliers but is insufficient in sustainably improving access to other markets. Hence, it is necessary to establish enduring linkages to financial institutions and export promotion organisations (e.g. EPB, SME Foundation). Temporary loan programmes with reduced interest rates for some small manufacturers provided assistance in financing production, machinery, and tradeshow participations (see Section "Insufficient Access to Finances"). However, without permanent access to capital, small producers will have enormous difficulties reducing their dependencies from buying houses and attending international trade fairs on their own account.

In 2006, LGM F and LGM D took part in an upgrading project directed by GTZ-PROGRESS which developed design and marketing functions in SMEs. The German development organisation gave only little importance to the project, dismissing it as a "waste-product" (director GTZ-PROGRESS) of its design activities in the garment industry. Leather goods manufacturers were trained in developing design skills, getting away from copy and paste. A product line of hand bags that combined jute and leather was developed to be presented to large European retailers (e.g. H&M; Mark & Spencer) in tradeshows. As GTZ-PROGRESS was unable to ensure compliance (e.g. labour conditions; leather free of chromium VI), the retailers backed out and the project was abandoned. GTZ's critical position towards the leather sector is founded on its reputation of being traditional and not very innovative. Despite some achievements (e.g. capacity building in designing;

catalogue of final jute-leather products), this 'by-product' turned out to be of limited scope. It is vital for the success of such development projects to impart knowledge and implement good practices that persist after funds run dry. Unfortunately, PRICE did not follow-up on GTZ's approach, although former participants demand these capabilities be reinforced:

> I think that in my sense I need some training on design. [...] If I attend some international fairs with totally new designs, then maybe it's better [...]. And I also wanted to combine some local products, some gloves, hand stitched, and also jute with leather. [...] [These are; A. N.] the uncommon things for the buyers because the jute we produce, the hand work we stitch, maybe [...] this is our speciality. [...] If I combine it with jute, then maybe...this is my strength to improve my design. (LGM D, English)

LGM D expresses her need to enhance her design capabilities in order to reduce her dependency on local designs that are simple and not suitable for the foreign market. Bangladesh is one of the major producers of jute and the leading exporter of raw jute (ITC 2006b). Designs that combine jute and leather or draw on skills that are only available locally increase value addition within the country and may provide opportunities in marketing *deshi* (local) products abroad. LGM G and other larger retailers already market jute-leather bags produced by subcontractors on the domestic market. It requires external assistance to empower MSMEs to supply such products also to foreign buyers.

Functional upgrading reduces the producers' vulnerability (Giuliani et al. 2005). PRICE and GTZ-PROGRESS initiated a number of promising activities, of which the most striking and enduring has been the linkage to large local manufacturers (and retailers). Thanks to these, some of the MSMEs interviewed were able to expand their business and increase their competitiveness.

Subcontracting, however, involves a variety of power asymmetries which were not sufficiently approached by PRICE. Attempts to improve design, product innovation and marketing were not forcefully pursued. LFM D's terms of payment make suppliers produce on credit for at least four months; advance payment could soften the hardship. LGM G's costing and mandatory deposit of 5 % blocks suppliers' finance and creates new dependency. Despite the positive impact of linking buyers and suppliers, PRICE failed to improve the latter's position to negotiate with powerful lead firms.

Table 5.10 summarises the impact of the upgrading interventions the four types of producers received.

The strong focus on process-related activities tested by more skilled manufacturers has to be shifted towards low-skilled suppliers who are in need of technical assistance. Although the gap between T3- and T4-producers and large manufacturers has reduced in terms of quality, it widened at least within the small range of MSMEs interviewed. T1 and T2, both long-term suppliers of LGM G, received little or no assistance with PRICE, which points to the challenge of disseminating good practices among low-skilled MSMEs. Only at the end of the project were 50 MSMEs introduced to the lessons learnt from the five-year development project. Other organisations offering capacity-building programmes to MSMEs (e.g. SME Foundation,

Table 5.10 Impact of upgrading interventions on MSMEs interviewed

	Low-skilled exclusive supplier (T1)	Low-skilled supplier with export activity (T2)	Skilled export-oriented small manufacturers (T3)	Export-oriented medium-sized manufacturer (T4)
Process upgrading	Very low	Nil	High	High
Product upgrading	Nil	Nil	Low	Low
Functional upgrading	Nil	Nil	Low	Nil

Source Own illustration

COEL) were provided training materials developed by PRICE. These, however, often tend to target educated and skilled producers as these have the knowledge to cooperate adequately. A stronger interaction between governmental agencies and private vocational institutes in combination with adequate financial programmes is necessary to create the institutional environment for a more competitive MSME supply base in Bangladesh. If MSMEs were to adopt and pursue specific strategies, they need to be better organised (e.g. business associations) and more closely linked to such institutes that can be learned from. The scope of the interventions in product and functional upgrading has been too small to enhance the producers' capabilities significantly. Structural constraints such as the lack of knowledge and access to finances are the major barrier to implement long-term strategies. A five-year development project can only start initiatives and raise potentials among MSMEs. If MSMEs are really to be qualified and their dependency to be reduced, they need more assistance that sustainably alters their approach towards designing, product development, management, capital, and marketing. In the long run, this might enable them to encroach in their lead firms' core competences.

5.3.5.4 Concluding Remarks on Upgrading

There is broad consensus in the GVC literature that governance structures determine upgrading trajectories, with global lead firms as the key drivers (Gereffi 2005; Humphrey 2004; Humphrey and Schmitz 2002). This study showed that export-oriented micro, small and medium-sized manufacturing units are struggling for market entry which is reflected in faltering export activity. Instead, they are strongly embedded as subcontractors in local production networks which are dominated by local lead firms that prevent them from getting access to specific market segments. Direct access to both the domestic and foreign markets is required to start upgrading trajectories as suggested in Table 2.4. Both local and foreign customers hold MSME suppliers captive, while subcontracting among MSMEs may also contain relational elements. This opens up different opportunities for learning as illustrated in Table 5.11 and explained below:

Table 5.11 Governance and opportunities for learning for MSMEs

Governance	Type of relationship	Driver	Type of learning	Type of upgrading
Captive	Vertical	Lead firm; contracting MSME	Learning from contracting/lead firm → knowledge transfer	Process, product
Relational	Horizontal	MSME	Peer learning → knowledge exchange	Process, product, functional

Source Own illustration

As shown in Sect. 5.3.3, local lead firms are regular customers of MSMEs and thus were assumed to qualify for key drivers of upgrading processes. While one is a profit-seeking OEM and the other a social enterprise with corresponding objectives, both exert power over full-assembly MSME subcontractors. They outsource risk and impose on subcontractors the liability for fluctuations in sourcing prices and product quality. Assistance is confined to enforcing quality requirements; a real exchange of knowledge and information is lacking. MSMEs are used as a flexible, cost-efficient production unit that allows for testing niche markets. Attractive payment arrangements offered by the social enterprise create "loyal" (Senior Manager SCPR), in fact, dependent producers. The lead firm's discourse of social empowerment has not translated into adequate actions to reduce their suppliers' dependence. Low-skilled exclusive suppliers have received little assistance to date. More importantly, both lead firms apply a double standard of social compliance for the local and the export market. Despite power asymmetries, MSMEs look for order stability and, if export-oriented, for improvements in product quality that only large manufacturers/retailers can guarantee on the local market.

In multi-tiered supply systems, joint actions within horizontal linkages tend to be relationally governed. Here, second-tier producers share skills, knowledge, for instance, about marketing or financing opportunities, and often also machinery. They learn indirectly, through their contracting body (first-tier supplier), from the lead firms' requirements. As these producers operate within similar structures, they exchange knowledge among peers rather than have it imposed. By contrast, vertical subcontracts to cottage industries and home-based self-employed workers comprise mostly low-value articles that meet only minimum quality standards. Accordingly, learning is limited.

Foreign buyers tightly coordinate export-oriented producers to rise to international quality standards. As only small buyers source from MSMEs, knowledge transfer addresses only very basic requirements. However, minimum requirements on production capacity, production conditions, quality management and environmental conditions have induced changes which could not have come from local lead firms. Meeting these requirements is a condition of market entry that most of the MSMEs interviewed have been struggling for. With the relationships to foreign buyers being captive (see Gereffi et al. 2005), MSMEs cannot develop capabilities in designing, branding or marketing. Direct sales to smaller buyers as achieved by some small and medium-sized producers may provide opportunities in this regard (see Ponte and Ewert 2009, p. 1638).

Knowledge transmission from buyers to suppliers is useful but not sufficient to achieve sustained competitiveness, particularly when buyers are small (see Ponte and Ewert 2009). In view of a dynamically growing LGF industry and more exports looming, development projects such as USAID PRICE add extra resources to upgrading activities. They have more opportunities to systematically reduce shortcomings in the supply base. Bringing in local lead firms has improved the knowledge transfer to low-skilled suppliers, thereby strengthening the local LGF production network. While local and foreign customers assist in process and product upgrading, PRICE also engaged in expanding MSMEs' range of functions. Some activities provide temporary support (e.g. participation in trade fairs and loan programmes) and may even enable some producers to take that path further. However, questions remain as to whether practices can be consolidated after projects phase out. Moreover, PRICE endorses the lead firms' argumentation about the benefits from linking buyers and suppliers. There is little awareness of how lead firms actually wield power over their suppliers (e.g. through payment arrangements) and to what extent this can be softened.

MSMEs choose to improve their capabilities by supplying local lead firms. Despite a small number of participants in the study, it is fair to say that upgrading processes induced by local lead firms only have a limited impact on their competitiveness. As MSMEs are at the very beginning of market integration, foreign customers can stimulate considerable process and product upgrading. However, if power asymmetries are to change at both domestic and global levels, more (external) assistance is needed to develop functions other than production.

5.4 Discussion of the Results in View of the Conceptual Framework

This study aimed to comprehend the leather production network in Bangladesh, within which a myriad of actors engage in productive and trading activities. The leather value chain was differentiated into two strands of distinct dynamics and strategies to feed into the global economy: the tanning industry exporting crust and finished leather; and the leather goods and footwear subsectors. An understanding of the chain's complex structure was essential in order to explore the nature of the interactions and processes between the dominant actors, thereby identifying development constraints and power asymmetries. Chain segments that were critical to the overall industry's competitiveness were analysed for specific characteristics, drawbacks and opportunities. This approach made it possible to draw conclusions on the governance forms at specific nodes of the value chain and identify opportunities for upgrading. The results point to seven major findings with respect to the conceptual framework of this study:

1. **Different chain segments can have different governance structures**, corroborating Talbot (2009). The complexity of the leather value chain goes beyond a merely captive governance scheme that is typically analysed for labour-intensive industries in low-cost countries. Gereffi et al. (2005) conceptualise governance for the linkages of global lead firms and local large producers, ignoring the variety of buyer-supplier relationships at the producer level and other stages along the chain. Beyond the customer-producer nexus, different actors (e.g. state, standard-setting organisations, consumers) can engage in governance activities (see Coe et al. 2008). With an increasing range of actors involved in chain governance, the complexity of the governance schemes rises. Section 5.2.2 testifies to the importance of socio-cultural institutions for chain governance (see below). New actors (e.g. temporary intermediaries, families, Madrassas) join in the supply segment and temporarily modify governance. This gives reason to argue that power asymmetry is not limited to the varying value of the three key variables, but also shaped by institutional dynamics. As opposed to Gereffi et al.'s (2005) supposition, power may well be played detached from resources and capabilities.
2. **Institutions matter in the leather value chain**, subscribing to Palpacuer's (2008) and Gibbon et al.'s (2008) notion of GVC analysis. This study revealed that informal institutions are an essential part of interactions at different nodes of the value chain; they are not just positioned at the lowest end. Dysfunctional and powerful formal institutions (e.g. import policies, regulations, buying houses) are systematically evaded and superseded by institutionalised informal and illicit practices. The state-tolerated non-compliance with existing environmental regulation has been formalised, imposing a de facto informal regulatory regime, which supports the global buyers' low-cost sourcing strategy and upholds the local industry's price competitiveness. Informal institutions provide resourceful strategies for procurement (e.g. raw material on seasonal occasions; under-invoicing of chemicals)—systemic trust on Eid-ul-Azha even levels power imbalances—, and help adapt to overcome power asymmetries in market entry. Their impact, however, is ambiguous as they often provide temporary benefits that do not translate into sustained competitiveness. The GVC framework lacks analytical categories to conceptualise institutional constraints. Bringing in institutions might enhance the GVC framework's conceptual clarity about informality in governance.
3. **The leather value chain is vertically and horizontally segmented**, supporting Talbot's (2009, p. 102) criticism of the GVC analysis. Both the leather and leather goods/footwear value chains are characterised by a complex network of suppliers of varying capabilities. Low competences tie MSMEs only loosely to rather small foreign buyers. MSMEs do not qualify for first-tier suppliers of large global brands and retailers that source large quantities from local large manufacturers or from middlemen (buying houses). As the latter tend to

(informally) forward orders to MSMEs, pressure from global buyers and standard-setting organisations fails to address the real producers. Hence, multi-tiered supply networks disguise competences and responsibilities.

4. **Multi-tiered vertical supply networks constrain learning processes.** Requirements for quality appear to be only passed on if MSMEs are subcontracted for exports. With the domestic market often lacking regulation and enforcement even more so, standards in social and environmental compliance are low or not existent. Pressure from actors other than global buyers is low. Supplies that are mediated either by lead firms or by buying houses prevent MSMEs from exchanging knowledge with foreign buyers. Learning is confined to basic improvements in production processes and product quality. Only manufacturers of a higher competence level (e.g. high level of skills and technology; export-oriented; access to finances) are able to generate conditions for endogenous growth, although a high level of vulnerability remains. Intermediaries per se have no interest in suppliers developing competences other than production. The literature on upgrading in GVCs is unspecific as to the increasing importance of mediated supply relationships.
5. **Multi-tiered supply networks in labour-intensive low-cost industries also unfold in captive relationships**; they are not confined to relational and modular value chains as suggested by Gereffi et al. (2005). MSMEs are tied as full-assembly suppliers to local lead firms with varying degrees of dependency. New power imbalances emerging from this have implications for their competitiveness. Subcontracts among MSMEs due to cost or capacity constraints often entail relational and captive governance patterns depending on the customer's requirements and the supplier's competence level.
6. **Subcontracting as a means of empowering poor producers** has, to the author's knowledge, not been contemplated conceptually in the literature. However, the social enterprise in this case study has grown enormously by using external producers of leather and several other commodities, drawing on the same motivation as profit-oriented enterprises do. Suppliers are largely held captive (see above) and have had few opportunities for social and economic improvement.
7. **Local lead firms may qualify as key drivers of upgrading processes**, but only under specific circumstances, following Bettiol et al. (2011). Local lead firms can improve the knowledge transfer to low-skilled suppliers, thereby strengthening the local leather goods and footwear production network. Captive relationships give account of a still widespread distrust which has to be dismantled first. Assistance from external organisations is needed to improve the suppliers' reliability and steer upgrading towards more functional activities (e.g. design, management, marketing). This allows for a systematic reduction of shortcomings in the supply base and increases the producers' independence. Suppliers for the export market receive more assistance and are subject to closer monitoring and control.

These findings highlight research needs to fill conceptual voids. By unpacking the complex network and interdependencies within the Bangladeshi leather industry, the importance of institutions as a conceptual category within the GVC framework was shown. Production networks or chains are operating within cultural, institutional and socio-political environments (see Coe et al. 2008). Informal institutions in particular shape the nature and quality of formal institutions, and determine in co-evolution the ways of development (North 1990). The role of local lead firms in governance and upgrading trajectories require a critical examination, in particular to discern dynamics in developing countries such as Bangladesh and emerging economies such as India in the South. Further studies are needed to understand how multi-tiered supply networks including subcontracting dynamics at local level impact on chain governance and influence risk.

In sum, more research in countries with specific socio-cultural institutions is necessary to bring the findings of this case study to an abstraction that may have implications for theory and policies alike.

References

Ahmed, K. A. (2002). *A comprehensive study on leather sector industries of Bangladesh.* Dhaka: Bangladesh Finished Leather, Leather Goods & Footwear Exporters' Association.

Alsayyad, N., & Roy, A. (2004). Urban informality: Crossing borders. In A. Roy & N. Alsayyad (Eds.), *Urban informality: Transnational perspectives from the Middle East, Latin America, and South Asia.* Oxford: Lexington Books.

Azom, M. R., Mahmud, K., Yahya, S. M., Sontu, A., & Himon, S. B. (2012). Environmental impact assessment of tanneries: A case study of Hazaribag in Bangladesh. *International Journal of Environmental Science and Development, 3*(2), 152–156.

Baksi, S., & Bose, P. (2007). Credence goods, efficient labelling policies, and regulatory enforcement. *Environmental & Resource Economics, 37*(2), 411–430.

Bangladesh Meteorological Department (2014). *Temperature data.* Retrieved from: http://www.bmd.gov.bd/Files/16012014011427pmMnlyTempWeb.pdf. Accessed March 13, 2014.

Bathelt, H., & Glückler, J. (2012). *Wirtschaftsgeographie*. Stuttgart: UTB.

Bettiol, M., De Marchi, V., Di Maria, E., & Micelli, S. (2011). Economic, social and environmental upgrading in value chains: Social entrepreneurship and the role of emerging economy lead firms. *Working Paper 4*, School of Environment and Development/University of Manchester, Manchester.

BLSC—Bangladesh Leather Service Centre (2009). *The baseline survey on small, micro enterprises & artisans of footwear & leather goods sub-sector in Bangladesh*, Dhaka.

BOI—Board of Investment (2010). *Foreign direct investment in Bangladesh (1971–2010)*, Dhaka.

BOI—Board of Investment (2011). *Investing in Bangladesh: Handbook & guidelines*, Dhaka.

BPC—Business Promotion Council (2014). *An abridged overview of Bangladesh leather sector.* Retrieved from: http://www.bpc.org.bd/lsbpc_bridge_overview.php. Accessed June 24, 2014.

BRAC (2014). *Aarong*. Retrieved from: http://enterprises.brac.net/aarong. Accessed August 17, 2014.

Brooke, C. (1987). Sacred slaughter: The sacrificing of animals at the Hajj and Id al-Adha. *Journal of Cultural Geography, 7*(2), 67–88.

BSCI—Business Social Compliance Initiative (2014). *The BSCI code of conduct.* Retrieved from: http://www.bsci-intl.org/our-work/bsci-code-conduct. Accessed January 10, 2014.

Buehn, A., & Eichler, S. (2011). Trade misinvoicing: The dark side of world trade. *World Development, 34*(8), 1263–1287.

Burke, J. (2013). Bangladesh factory tragedy gives hope to leather workers. *The Guardian,* July 7, 2013.

Business Dictionary (2013). *Letter of credit (L/C).* Retrieved from: http://www.businessdictionary.com/definition/letter-of-credit-L-C.html. Accessed December 19, 2013.

Business Dictionary (2014). *Telegraphic transfer.* Retrieved from: http://www.businessdictionary.com/definition/telegraphic-transfer.html. Accessed January 7, 2014.

Cattaneo, O., Gereffi, G., Miroudot, S., & Taglioni, D. (2013). Joining, upgrading and being competitive in global value chains. A strategic framework. *World Bank,* Policy Research Working Paper 6406, April.

CIA (2013). *The World factbook.* Retrieved from: https://www.cia.gov/library/publications/the-world-factbook/geos/bg.html. Accessed January 25, 2013.

Coe, N., Dicken, P., & Hess, M. (2008). Global production networks: Realizing the potential. *Journal of Economic Geography, 8*(3), 271–295.

COEL—Center of Excellence for Leather Skill Bangladesh Limited (2014). *COEL.* Retrieved from: http://www.coelbd.org/index.php. Accessed May 15, 2014.

Dannenberg, P. (2012). *Standards in internationalen Wertschöpfungsketten: Akteure, Ziele und Governance in der Obst- und Gemüse-Wertekette Kenia – EU.* Münster: Lit Verlag.

Deichmann (2014). *Global business stay fair.* Retrieved from: https://www.deichmann.com/DE/en/corp/globaler_handel.jsp. Accessed April 9, 2014.

Dietsche, C. (2011). *Umweltgovernance in globalen Wertschöpfungsketten: Umweltschutz und Qualitätssicherung im Handel mit tropischen Garnelen und Ledererzeugnissen.* Münster: Lit Verlag.

Egels-Zandén, N., & Wahlqvist, E. (2007). Post-partnership strategies for defining corporate responsibility: The business social compliance initiative. *Journal of Business Ethics, 70*(2), 175–189.

EPA—Environmental Protection Agency (1998). *Toxicological review of trivalent chromium: In support of summary information on the integrated risk information system (IRIS).* Retrieved from: http://www.epa.gov/iris/toxreviews/0028tr.pdf. Accessed June 13, 2014.

ETI—Ethical Trading Initiative (2014). *About ETI.* Retrieved from: http://www.ethicaltrade.org/about-eti. Accessed March 17, 2014.

Etzold, B., Bohle, H.-G., Keck, M., & Zingel, W.-P. (2009). Informality as agency—Negotiating food security in Dhaka. *Die Erde, 140*(1), 3–24.

European Commission—Enterprise and Industry (2013). *REACH—Registration, evaluation, authorisation and restriction of chemicals.* Retrieved from: http://ec.europa.eu/enterprise/sectors/chemicals/reach/index_en.htm. Accessed November 17, 2013.

European Commission—Health and Consumers (2013). *Consumers.* Retrieved from: http://ec.europa.eu/consumers/safety/prod_legis/. Accessed November 17, 2013.

European Commission—Trade (2013). *Generalised scheme of preferences (GSP).* Retrieved from: http://ec.europa.eu/trade/policy/countries-and-regions/development/generalised-scheme-of-preferences/index_en.htm. Accessed May 3, 2013.

EPB—Export Promotion Bureau Bangladesh (2014). Statistics details. Retrieved from: http://www.epb.gov.bd/detailsexportdata.php. Accessed August 9, 2014.

Fattahul Alim, S. (2010). Why this recurrent impasse in rawhide market? *The Daily Star,* November 22, Dhaka.

FAO—Food and Agriculture Organization of the United Nations (2009). The State of Food and Agriculture 2009—Livestock in the balance. Rome.

FAO—Food and Agriculture Organization of the United Nations. (2014). *Data.* Retrieved from: http://data.fao.org/dataset-data-filter?entryId=c70af091-56be-41cc-8535-92c2ae460943&tab=data&type=Measure&uuidResource=7b5f0d07-896a-4c2e-9be5-fa0726635fb7. Accessed June 26, 2014.

Fernandez-Stark, K., Frederick, S., & Gereffi, G. (2011). *The apparel global value chain: Economic upgrading and workforce development*, Center on Globalization, Governance & Competitiveness, Duke University.

Fleury, A., & Fleury, M. T. (2001). Alternatives for industrial upgrading in global value chains: The case of the plastics industry in Brazil. *IDS Bulletin, 32*(3), 116–126.

Fox, A. (1974). *Beyond contract: Work, power and trust relations*. London: Faber & Faber.

Gereffi, G. (1999). International trade and industrial up-grading in the apparel commodity chain. *Journal of International Economics, 48*(1), 37–70.

Gereffi, G. (2005). The global economy: Organisation, governance and development. In N. J. Smelser & R. Swedberg (Eds.), *Handbook of economic sociology* (pp. 160–182). Princeton, NJ: Princeton University Press and Russell Sage Foundation.

Gereffi, G., Humphrey, J., & Sturgeon, T. (2005). The governance of global value chains. *Review of International Political Economy, 12*(1), 78–104.

Gibbon, P., Bair, J., & Ponte, S. (2008). Governing global value chains: An introduction. *Economy and Society, 37*(3), 315–338.

Giuliani, E., Pietrobelli, C., & Rabellotti, R. (2005). Upgrading in global value chains: Lessons from Latin American clusters. *World Development, 33*(4), 549–573.

GME, COTANCE, UECBV, & Collagen Industry (2006). *European guidance note on the safe handling of raw hides and skins throughout the whole value chain in the community.* Retrieved from: http://www.food.gov.uk/multimedia/pdfs/euguidehidesandskins.pdf. Accessed July 2, 2012.

Green Cross Switzerland (2013). *The world's ten most polluted places of 2013.* Retrieved from: http://www.greencross.ch/en/news-info-en/case-studies/environmental-reports/ten-most-polluted-places-2013.html. Accessed November 5, 2013.

GTZ—Gesellschaft für Technische Zusammenarbeit (2006). *Value chain assessment of the leather sector in Bangladesh,* Dhaka.

GTZ-PROGRESS (2006). *A census study on leather sector in Bangladesh & a desk study on status/strategies of the leather sector of the competing countries*, Dhaka.

Hasan, G. M. J., & Chowdhury, M. A. I. (2005). Municipal waste management and environmental hazards in Bangladesh. *Pakistan Journal of Biological Sciences, 8*(6), 921–928.

Hassler, M. (2004). Raw material procurement, industrial upgrading and labour recruitment: Intermediaries in Indonesia's clothing industry. *Geoforum, 35*(4), 441–451.

Heinen, L. (2014). *Production.* Retrieved from: http://www.heinen-leather.de/3-1-produktion.html. Accessed January 31, 2013.

Hesselberg, J., & Knutsen, H. M. (2002). Leather tanning: Environmental regulations, competitiveness and locational shifts. In Jenkins, R., Barton, J., Bartzokas, A., Hesselberg, J., & Knutsen, H. M. (Eds.), *Environmental regulation in the new global economy: The impact on industry and competitiveness* (pp. 155–219). Northampton: Edward Elgar Publishing.

Holl, A. (2008). Production subcontracting and location. *Regional Science and Urban Economics, 38*(3), 299–309.

Hoque, A., & Clarke, A. (2013). Greening of industries in Bangladesh: pollution prevention practices. *Journal of Cleaner Production, 51*, 47–56.

Hossain, I. (2012). Prices of raw hides, skin lower than last year's, traders say. *The Financial Express*, October 30, Dhaka.

Hossain, I. (2013). Govt, tanners sign MoU for tannery relocation Sunday. *The Financial Express*, October 12, Dhaka.

Hossain, A. M. M. M., Monir, T., Ul-Haque, A. M. R., Islam Kazi, M. A., Islam, M. S., & Elahi, S. F. (2007). Heavy metal concentration in tannery solid wastes used as poultry feed and the ecotoxicological consequences. *Bangladesh Journal of Scientific and Industrial Research, 42* (4), 397–416.

Human Rights Watch (2012). *Toxic tanneries—The health repercussions of Bangladesh's Hazaribagh leather.* Retrieved from: http://www.hrw.org/sites/default/files/reports/bangladesh1012webwcover.pdf. Accessed January 18, 2013.

Humphrey, J. (2004). *Upgrading in global value chains.* ILO Policy Integration Department, Working Paper No. 28.

Humphrey, J., & Schmitz, H. (2000). Governance and upgrading: Linking industrial cluster and global value chain research. *IDS Working Paper, 120*, University of Sussex, Brighton.

Humphrey, J., & Schmitz, H. (2002). How does insertion in global value chains affect upgrading in industrial clusters? *Regional Studies, 36*(9), 1022–1027.

Imamul Huq, S. M. (2000). Critical environmental issues relating to tanning industries in Bangladesh. In: Naidu, R., Willet, I. R., Mahimairajah, S., Kookana, R., & Ramasamy, K. (Eds.), *Towards better management of soils contaminated with tannery waste: Proceedings of a workshop held at the Tamil Nadu Agricultural University* (pp. 22–28), Coimbatore, India, January 31 to February 4, 1998. ACIAR Proceedings No. 88, Canberra.

Investopedia (2014). *Irrevocable letter of credit—ILOC.* Retrieved from: http://www.investopedia.com/terms/i/iloc.asp. Accessed August 17, 2014.

ISO—International Organization for Standardization (2014). *ISO 9001:2008. Quality management systems. Requirements.* Retrieved from: http://www.iso.org/iso/catalogue_detail?csnumber=46486. Accessed July 28, 2014.

ITC—International Trade Centre (2006a). *Leatherline—Leather guidebook.* Retrieved from: http://legacy.intracen.org/leatherline/leather_guide.htm. Accessed May 29, 2014.

ITC—International Trade Centre (2006b). *A road map for jute.* Retrieved from: http://www.intracen.org/uploadedFiles/intracenorg/Content/Exporters/Sectoral_Information/Agricultural_Products/Fibres/jute_roadmap-1.pdf. Accessed July 28, 2014.

ITC—International Trade Centre (2014). *Trade competitiveness map.* Retrieved from: http://legacy.intracen.org/appli1/TradeCom/TPIC.aspx?RP=050&YR=2012. Accessed July 18, 2014.

Jabbar, M. A., Kiruthu, S., Gebremedhin, B., & Ehui, S. (2002). *Essential actions to meet quality requirements of hides, skins and semi-processed leather from Africa.* Retrieved from: http://www.unido.org/fileadmin/import/10197_Jabbar.2.pdf. Accessed July 16, 2014.

Kaplinsky, R. (2010). *The role of standards in global value chains and their impact on economic and social upgrading.* World Bank.

Kulke, E. (2009). *Wirtschaftsgeographie. Grundriss Allgemeine Geographie* (Vol. 4). Stuttgart: Auflage, Ulmer.

Kumar Bhowmik, A. (2013). Industries' location as jeopardy for sustainable urban development in Asia: A review of the Bangladesh Leather Processing Industry Relocation Plan. *Environment and Urbanization Asia, 4*(1), 93–119.

Kumar Gupta, P., Roy, D., & Ahmad, K. (2012). Close eye or closed eye: The case of export misinvoicing in Bangladesh. *IFPRI discussion paper 0115.*

LANDac—Land Governance for Equitable and Sustainable Development (2012). *Bangladesh: Food security and land governance factsheet.* Retrieved from: http://www.landgovernance.org/system/files/Bangladesh%20Factsheet%20-%202012.pdf. Accessed June 7, 2014.

Leather International (2002). *Feeling weak?* April 24, 2002. Retrieved from: http://www.leathermag.com/features/featurefeeling-weak/. Accessed December 16, 2013.

Leather International (2004). *Influences of hides on upholstery sector?* November 16, 2004. Retrieved from: http://www.leathermag.com/features/featureinfluence-of-hides-on-upholstery-sector/. Accessed December 16, 2013.

Leather International (2006). *Process control*, November 20, 2006. Retrieved from: http://www.leathermag.com/features/featureprocess-control/. Accessed December 16, 2014.

Leather Working Group (2013). *Leather Working Group: Improving environmental stewardship.* Retrieved from: http://www.leatherworkinggroup.com/index.htm. Accessed January 10, 2014.

Li, P. P. (2007). Social tie, social capital, and social behaviour: Toward an integrative model of informal exchange. *Asia Pacific Journal of Management, 24*(2), 227–246.

Lund-Thomson, P. (2009). Assessing the impact of public-private partnerships in the global south: The case of the Kasur Tanneries Pollution Control Project. *Journal of Business Ethics, 90*(1), 57–78.

Masri, B. A. (1989). *Animals in Islam.* Wiltshire: The Crowood Press.

Memedovic, O., & Mattila, H. (2008). The global leather value chain: The industries, the main actors and prospects for upgrading in LDCs. *Technological Learning, Innovation and Development, 1*(4), 482–519.

Meyer, S. (2011). *Informal modes of governance in customer producer relations. The electronic industry in the Greater Pearl River Delta (China).* Stuttgart: Steiner.

Ministry of Agriculture of the Government of the People's Republic of Bangladesh (2013). *MoA agencies.* Retrieved from: http://www.moa.gov.bd/about_MoA.htm#DAM. Accessed December 6, 2013.

Ministry of Commerce of the Government of the People's Republic of Bangladesh (2007). Export Policy 2006–2009, Non-published English version.

Nadvi, K. (2008). Global standards, global governance and the organization of global value chains. *Journal of Economic Geography, 8*(3), 323–343.

Nadvi, K., & Schmitz, H. (1999). Clustering and industrialization: introduction. *World Development, 27*(9), 1503–1514.

Navas-Alemán, L. (2011). The impact of operating in multiple value chains for upgrading: The case of the Brazilian furniture and footwear industries. *World Development, 39*(8), 1386–1397.

North, D. C. (1990). *Institutions, institutional change and economic performance.* New York: Cambridge University Press.

OANDA (2014). *Forex trading and exchange rates service.* Retrieved from: http://www.oanda.com/. Accessed June 14, 2014.

Oguoma, O., Nkwocha, V., & Ibeawuchi, I. (2010). Implications of middlemen in the supply chain of agricultural products. *Journal of Agriculture and Social Research, 10*(2), 77–83.

Ortolano, L., Sanchez-Triana, E., Afzal, J., Ali, C. L., & Rebellón, S. A. (2014). Cleaner production in Pakistan's leather and textile sectors. *Journal of Cleaner Production, 68*, 121–129.

Palpacuer, F. (2008). Bringing the social context back in: Governance and wealth distribution in global commodity chains. *Economy and Society, 37*(3), 393–419.

Ponte, S., & Ewert, J. (2009). Which way is "Up" in upgrading? Trajectories of change in the value chain for South African wine. *World Development, 37*(10), 1637–1650.

Ponte, S., & Gibbon, P. (2005). Quality standards, conventions and the governance of global value chains. *Economy and Society, 34*(1), 1–31.

Pratim Sahu, P. (2010). Subcontracting in India's unorganised manufacturing sector: A mode of adoption or exploitation? *Journal of South Asian Development, 5*(1), 53–83.

Prügl, E., & Tinker, I. (1997). Microentrepreneurs and homeworkers: Convergent categories. *World Development, 25*(9), 1471–1482.

Reeves, P. (2002). Regional diversity in South Asian Inland fisheries: Colonial Bengal and Uttar Pradesh compared. *South Asia: Journal of South Asian Studies, 25*(2), 121–135.

Reich, G. (2009). *Ökologische Aspekte wichtiger Gerbverfahren.* Frankfurt.

Renton, A. (2012). Bangladesh's toxic tanneries turning a profit at an intolerable human price. *The Guardian*, December 13, Dhaka.

Reps, N. (2008). *Lokale Auswirkungen globaler Wertschöpfungsketten: Leder- und Lederwarenproduktion in Kanpur und Agra, Indien.* Diplomarbeit (unpublished).

Reps, N., & Braun, B. (2012). Going Green: Ökologische Aufwertungsprozesse und Koordinationsstrukturen in den Wertschöpfungsketten der indischen Kraftfahrzeugsindustrie. *Zeitschrift für Wirtschaftsgeographie, 56*(4), 226–243.

Rodríguez, A., Ali, I., Afzal, M., & Shah, N. A. (1993). Marketing of goat and sheep skins in highland Balochistan, Pakistan. *Small Ruminant Research, 12*(3), 259–270.

Schjolden, A. (2000). Leather tanning in India: Environmental regulations and firms' compliance. *FIL Working Papers, 21*.

SEHD—Society for Environment and Human Development (1998). *Leather Industry: Environmental pollution and mitigation measures.* Dhaka: SEHD.

SGS Bangladesh Limited (2011). Awareness building on environment in leather and footwear industry. *Seminar on "Awareness Building on Product Standard and Environment of Leathergoods and Footwear Industry"*, January 31, 2011, Dhaka.

Shapiro, S. P. (1987). The social control of impersonal trust. *American Journal of Sociology, 93* (3), 623–658.
Silvateam (2013). *Quebracho extracts.* Retrieved from: http://en.silvateam.com/Products-Services/Leather/Vegetable-extracts/Quebracho-extracts. Accessed November 11, 2013.
Social Accountability International (2013). *SA8000 Standard.* Retrieved from: http://www.sa-intl.org/index.cfm?fuseaction=Page.ViewPage&PageID=937. Accessed December 15, 2013.
Steer, L., & Sen, K. (2010). Formal and informal institutions in a transition economy: The case of Vietnam. *World Development, 38*(11), 1603–1615.
Strasser, J., Dannenberg, P., & Kulke, E. (2013). Temporary resource availability and quality constraints in the global leather value chain—The impact of the festival of sacrifice on the leather industry in Bangladesh. *Applied Geography, 45*, 410–419.
Sturgeon, T. J. (2002). Modular production networks. A new American model of industrial organisation. *Industrial and Corporate Change, 11*(3), 451–496.
Sturgeon, T. J. (2009). From commodity chains to value chains: Interdisciplinary theory building in an age of globalization. In J. Bair (Ed.), *Frontiers of Commodity Chain Research* (pp. 110–135). Stanford: Stanford University Press.
Switch-Asia (2013). *Re-Tie: Reduction of environmental threats and increase of exportability of Bangladeshi leather products.* Retrieved from: http://www.switch-asia.eu/projects/re-tie-bangladesh/. Accessed April 26, 2013.
Talbot, J. M. (2009). The comparative advantages of tropical commodity chain analysis. In J. Bair (Ed.), *Frontiers of commodity chain research* (pp. 93–109). Stanford: Stanford University Press.
Tewari, M., & Pillai, P. (2005). Global standards and the dynamics of environmental compliance in India's leather industry. *Oxford Development Studies, 33*(2), 245–267.
Todaro, M. P., & Smith, S. C. (2011). *Economic development* (11th ed.). Pearson: Addison-Wesley.
Tran, N., Bailey, C., Wilson, N., & Phillips, P. (2013). Governance of global value chains in response to food safety and certification standards: The case of shrimp from Vietnam. *World Development, 45*, 325–336.
Triple Line Consulting Ltd (2002). *Study 1: Market requirements for importers of African hides and skins. The hides, skins and leather sector in Africa—Essential actions to meet quality requirements of importers.* Retrieved from: http://www.unido.org/fileadmin/import/10211_triplebottom.2.pdf. Accessed June 9, 2014.
Ullah Mirdha, R., & Saha, S. (2012). Supply glut keeps hide prices low. *The Daily Star*, October 30, Dhaka.
Umweltbundesamt (2003). *Integrierte Vermeidung und Verminderung der Umweltverschmutzung (IVU). Referenzdokument über die Besten Verfügbaren Techniken für die Lederindustrie.* Retrieved from: http://www.bvt.umweltbundesamt.de/archiv/bvt_lederindustrie_vv.pdf. Accessed April 15, 2013.
UNICEF—United Nations International Children's Emergency Fund (2010). *Factsheet: Child labour in Bangladesh.* Retrieved from: www.unicef.org/bangladesh/Child_labour.pdf. Accessed March 11, 2014.
UNIDO—United Nations Development Organization (1997). *Regional Africa Leather and Footwear Industry programme. Report of the programme evaluation.* Retrieved from: https://www.unido.org/fileadmin/import/43198_FINAL_EVAL_REPORT_19970221_USRAF92200.pdf. Accessed July 17, 2014.
UNIDO—United Nations Development Organization (2012). *Re-Tie Bangladesh: Reduction of environmental threats and increase of exportability of Bangladeshi leather products.* Technical report: Abridged. Prepared for the Government of Bangladesh (unpublished).
US CPSC—United States Consumer Product Safety Commission (2013). *About CPSC.* Retrieved from: http://www.cpsc.gov/en/About-CPSC/. Accessed November 17, 2013.
USAID (2010). Bangladesh poverty reduction by increasing the competitiveness of enterprises (PRICE). Annual report October 2009–September 2010 (no place).

Verband der Deutschen Lederindustrie (2014). *Die wichtigsten Stationen der Lederherstellung.* Retrieved from: http://vdl-web.de/leder-infos/herstellungsschritte/. Accessed March 28, 2014.

Wayua, F. O., & Kagunyu, A. (2012). Constraints and opportunities in the hides and skins value chain in pastoral areas of northern Kenya. *Livestock Research for Rural Development, 24*(8). Retrieved from: http://www.lrrd.org/lrrd24/8/wayu24135.htm. Accessed July 17, 2014.

Webster, M., Alder, C., & Muhlemann, A. P. (1997). Subcontracting within the supply chain for electronics assembly manufacture. *International Journal of Operations and Production Management, 17*(9), 827–841.

WFTO—World Fair Trade Organization (2014). *WFTO guarantee system handbook.* Retrieved from: http://www.wfto.com/index.php?option=com_content&task=view&id=2005&Itemid=413. Accessed April 28, 2014.

Wikipedia (2014). *Administrative geography of Bangladesh.* Retrieved from: http://en.wikipedia.org/wiki/Administrative_geography_of_Bangladesh. Accessed June 7, 2014.

Wilson, M. P., & Schwarzman, M. R. (2009). Toward a new U.S. chemicals policy: Rebuilding the foundation to advance new science, green chemistry, and environmental health. *Environmental Health Perspectives, 117*(8), 1202–1209.

Wirtschaftslexikon (2013). *Dokumenteninkasso.* Retrieved from: http://www.wirtschaftslexikon24.com/d/dokumenteninkasso/dokumenteninkasso.htm. Accessed November 28, 2013.

Your Commonwealth (2011). *Bangladesh, women and the distribution of inherited property.* Retrieved from: http://www.yourcommonwealth.org/2011/07/25/bangladesh-women-and-the-equal-distribution-of-inherited-property/. Accessed June 7, 2014.

ZDF (2013). *Gift auf unserer Haut: Leder und Pelze für Deutschland.* Retrieved from: http://www.zdf.de/37-Grad/Gift-auf-unserer-Haut-29878404.html. Accessed October 10, 2013.

Zuther, F., & Marschner, B. (n.d.). *Qualitätssicherung in der Lederherstellung: Der Gerbstoff Chrom.* Retrieved from: http://www.feldtmann.de/docs/lexikon/2004-09-24%20Gesamtbericht%20Chrom.pdf. Accessed July 16, 2014.

Chapter 6
Conclusion

Abstract The last section synthesises core results by relating to the research questions this work has drawn on. It gives account of what has been brought to light, shows where more research is needed and suggests what lessons can be learned. It concludes that the discussion of the research questions revealed a number of specific phenomena and strongly interwoven dynamics in Bangladesh's leather industry that ensure price competitiveness on the international market but impinge on sustained competitiveness. Other countries' strategies to improve the competitiveness of MSME suppliers cannot be taken prescriptively. The author suggests an individual but holistic approach that takes into account the role of informal institutions for the industry's competitiveness. Much of the future of Bangladesh's leather industry depends on the relocation of the tanning estate to Hemayetpur/Savar.

While a great deal of research has been done on the implications of globalisation for cross-border customer-producer relations, little is known about the dynamics and power relations in local production networks. This study examined the structure of the Bangladeshi leather processing and leather goods/footwear industry and shed light on the interactions and processes therein with regard to institutional dysfunctions and power asymmetries at the nodes of the value chain. Constraints in different chain segments responsible for the leather sector's low performance led different, often weaker actors to adapt by drawing on informal and even illicit practices in order to remain competitive. This work has aimed to define the deficiencies and opportunities along the value chain to highlight the potential for upgrading, which comprises a broad range of activities for both leather and leather goods/footwear subsectors.

In the following, I briefly relate to the research questions this work has drawn on to give account of what has been brought to light, to show where more research is needed, and to suggest what lessons can be learned. I discuss the organisation, formal and informal market integration, and adaptation strategies (research questions 1–3) for the leather and leather goods/footwear subsector separately, before bringing together both strands in an elaboration on the potential for upgrading

J. Strasser, *Bangladesh's Leather Industry*,
Springer Geography, DOI 10.1007/978-3-319-22548-7_6

(research question 4). I conclude with some general remarks about the specificity of this case study and prospects for the Bangladeshi leather industry.

1. How is the Bangladeshi leather value chain organised?
    (a) How is the Bangladeshi leather processing industry organised?
        (i) Who are the actors and what are the commodity and information flows in the leather processing industry?
        (ii) How is the leather processing chain segment governed?

A number of different traders, tanners, leather goods/footwear manufacturers as well as buying houses constitute and organise the complex leather value chain. GVC analysis is said to bring advantages and disadvantages at the producer level to the fore, whereas services are rather neglected (Ballard 2001). In this work the supply of raw hides and skins proved particularly instructive in understanding sourcing dynamics that have repercussions for the competitiveness of downstream actors. Trust is the dominant mechanism that trade in raw material relies on. The tanneries' sourcing strategies in the off season comprise personal trust-based and long-term firm-to-firm relationships. Thanks to systemic trust in festival hides and skins, patterns of relational governance in the off season are superimposed by more market-based governance in the peak season. Institutions matter in the leather value chain (Finding 2; see Sect. 5.4) and trust, an informal institution, redefines power relations. During the Festival of Sacrifice, institutional constraints such as the religious requirements for sacrificial animals impact on the multifaceted coordination at just one stage of the chain, with consequences for the competitiveness of downstream actors. This indicates a rather fragmented coordination of business relations at the lower end of the value chain. Even at the same linkage different ways of exerting and receiving power exist, contravening Gereffi et al.'s (2005) orthodox understanding of linear power asymmetry and explicit coordination (Finding 1). Power is not just a matter of resources but also contested in social interaction (see Coe et al. 2008).

Policy changes in the 1990s (e.g. ban on wet blue exports) laid the foundations for a restructuring process within the tanning industry, which is ongoing and has been affecting its integration into the world market (research questions 1a). Many tanneries have either been driven to rent out their production facilities to commercial leather exporters or have ended up supplying low value-added wet blue to leather processors of a higher competence level (research questions 1ai). Limited production capabilities confine the tanneries interviewed largely to exporting lower value-added, semi-finished crust leather. Within a diverse network of leather processors, confirming the leather value chain's vertical and horizontal segmentation (Finding 3), few large tanneries concentrate market power and control input prices (e.g. chemical), but are increasingly defied by non-tannery owning leather exporters (research question 1aii). The export-oriented tanning industry relies strongly on brokering buying houses that compensate the tanners' lacking ability to codify complex transactions (see also research question 2).

2. How is the Bangladeshi leather industry integrated into the global market?
   (a) What formal institutional framework does Bangladesh's leather (processing) industry rely on to join in the global leather value chain?
   (b) To what extent are informal arrangements understood as institutions, practices and strategies conducive to global market entry?
   (c) What is the impact of informal institutional arrangements on power relations?

As a Least Developed Country (LDC), Bangladesh's tanning industry benefits from the Generalised Scheme of Preferences (GSP), which has made the EU the most important market for leather products from Bangladesh (research question 2a). However, the tanners interviewed see China on the rise as an export destination since these buyers grant higher margins and impose fewer requirements for social and environmental compliance than EU customers. The tanneries' export activity was fuelled by subsidies that were significantly lower than those for the more value-added leather goods and footwear industry before they ultimately phased out in 2012. Buying houses assume a strategic position in compensating the tanneries' lack of ability to produce to the buyers' detailed specifications and to handle complex (payment) transactions.

The tanneries' differing capabilities determine power asymmetries and informal dynamics within the industry. Three areas have been identified as having strategic importance for leather processors to turn to informal practices and strategies to counteract dysfunctional institutions and power asymmetries on the way to global market entry (research question 2b): chemical imports, environmental regulation, and leather exports.

The state-tolerated non-compliance with existing environmental regulation has de facto established an informal regulatory regime or organising logic (see Alsayyad and Roy 2004) which allows for cost-efficient production and keeps the tanneries in the low-end market.

The (medium-sized and large) tanneries' strategic use of bonded-licenses to control chemical imports and to strengthen their price competitiveness in international markets has led to institutionalised (adaptive) practices of importing chemicals under-invoice, establishing an informal regulatory regime (research questions 2b/2c).

Moreover, the tanneries have informalised solid waste management, shirking their responsibilities and bolstering practices that are utterly harmful to public health. Mostly medium-sized and large tanneries have made solid waste a profitable business, reinforcing their power (research question 2c).

3. How do export-oriented tanneries adapt to power asymmetries in the global leather value chain?

Despite providing important services to the tanneries (e.g. monitoring, negotiating), buying houses keep their suppliers highly dependent. Indirect export relations reduce margins and exclude tanners from learning from buyers (Finding 4); only large tanneries are capable of cooperating closely with their customers to achieve better quality. Enduring relationships create trust and allow for a more flexible interpretation of business transactions. As a result of structural limitations, few tanneries have been able to benefit from long-term relationships to foreign buyers. Those who have transact with their buyers rather relationally; power seems to play no role. More secure payment methods, which means a higher degree of formalisation (e.g. L/C), cannot resolve power asymmetries but may prevent weaker parties from being taken advantage of in informal practices. More capacity building in payment methods is needed to reduce the tanneries' vulnerability in international transactions.

By exporting leather under-invoice, local leather processors adapt either to unfavourable power relations at the local level or to critical conditions in the international market, thereby exposing themselves to high levels of risk (see also research question 2b). In both cases of under-invoicing (i.e. chemical imports, leather exports) close cooperation and trust with international partners are indispensable for risk control. These results signalise that more research is needed to analyse the role of global companies (e.g. chemical firms, leather importers) in handling misinvoicing practices and the conditions under which the transactions are initiated.

When exporting, low-skilled tanners often draw on informal institutions to adapt to entry barriers and bypass powerful gatekeepers such as buying houses. Multi-tiered informal subcontracts allow tanneries of a low competence level (e.g. low production capacity) to cater to foreign markets but increase the risk of transaction failure and confine their benefits to export revenues. As the transactions are mediated, tanneries are excluded from learning from buyers. Hence, informal adaptation strategies temporarily increase individual benefits and overcome asymmetric power relations in market entry but impinge on sustained competitiveness.

The informal institutions identified are essential for the tanneries' price competitiveness in the international market (Finding 2). They are persistent and systemic and expose the firms as the entire sector to high risk, undermining corporate integrity and reliability in the market. While informal practices in chemical imports (e.g. under-invoicing), leather exports (e.g. under-invoicing) and environmental regulation are destructive for society at large, informal subcontracts are an important and legitimate strategy for low-capable tanneries to cater to the foreign market. However, these need to be better coordinated to minimise the risk of supplier failure. Future research will have to look into the way informal tannery networks manage risk (for Vietnam, see Steer and Sen 2010).

1. How is the Bangladeshi leather value chain organised?
   (a) How is the Bangladeshi leather goods and footwear industry organised?
      (i) Who are the actors and what are the commodity and information flows in the leather goods and footwear industry?
      (ii) How is the leather goods and footwear chain segment governed?

The dynamics in the leather goods and footwear industry are different. A large number of MSME-suppliers oppose a few large manufacturers, all of whom have a strong focus on the domestic market (research question 1bi). The two lead firms interviewed, one a profit-seeking and the other a social enterprise, coordinate the local production network by subcontracting micro, small and medium-sized producers according to their skills level for different market segments. These MSMEs supply entire products, adding flexibility, cost-efficiency and specific capabilities to the lead firms' competences, which market them on their own. Despite the different nature of the lead firms, both outsource risks alongside production, thereby exerting power (research question 1bii). Neither provides their suppliers with raw material—only in some cases are accessories or inputs given—, but leaves them with fluctuating sourcing prices. The terms of payment proved to be essential for keeping producers captive: while the profit-seeking company drags on payment periods up to four months and longer, the social enterprise creates 'loyalty' by spot payment and a sizable amount of money deposited at the parent company's bank. As loan conditions are unfavourable for many MSMEs, money for investment is blocked. Hence, the social enterprise's strategy to empower poor producers by subcontracting them (Finding 6) differs little from a business policy. The two lead firms tightly coordinate their suppliers through costing, payment arrangements and mediated market access. Despite being held in captive relationships, MSMEs deliberately use the supply of local lead firms as a strategy to adapt to an insecure order situation and to generate a reliable source of income, even though profit margins are significantly lower than with other local customers. MSMEs pass on pressure on prices or capacity by further subcontracting to peers or even less-skilled manufacturers, governing them either relationally or rather captively depending on their skills level and customer requirements. This means that multi-tiered supply networks unfold also in captive relationships (Finding 5).

2. How is the leather goods and footwear industry integrated into the global market?
   (a) What formal institutional framework does the leather goods and footwear industry rely on to join in the global leather value chain?
   (b) To what extent are informal arrangements understood as institutions, practices and strategies conducive to global market entry?
   (c) What is the impact of informal institutional arrangements on power relations?

Although high export subsidies (15 %) aim to increase value-added leather goods and footwear exports (research question 2a), the entry into foreign markets is still a challenge for the MSMEs interviewed. They have difficulties meeting the buyers' requirements of production capacity, technology and skills level, and product quality. Low competences tie them to small foreign buyers who coordinate them either directly or through buying houses. Order size and weakly regulated consumer markets (e.g. USA, Japan) allow the MSMEs to produce cost-efficiently, giving less importance to product safety. Monitoring and control varies with the suppliers' capabilities; low-skilled producers in particular are under tight supervision to meet standards in product quality and lead time. As with the tanneries, power imbalances between buyers and suppliers are manifest in payment arrangements. MSMEs prioritise risky but capital-providing transactions (T/T) over more payment security (L/C). Despite operating in captive relationships, direct transactions allow MSMEs to control the risk of payment default inherent in both payment methods. New buyers in mediated transactions, however, are more likely to take advantage of their power by putting pressure on prices.

Both lead firms were found to use MSMEs to a low extent to feed to the global market. The lack of data did not allow for a detailed analysis; however, both firms subject their export producers to tighter monitoring and control schemes to meet the foreign customers' requirements. The social enterprise applies double standards to subcontractors for the domestic market and those who export by the Fair Trade standard of WFTO, ignoring its mandate of empowering poor producers. Benefits and drawbacks resemble those in domestic subcontracts and turn MSMEs into invisible exporters. More research is needed to understand to what extent producers supplying compliant with WFTO requirements and those exporting without heeding standards differ from domestic subcontractors in their potential for growth and development.

Unlike the tanneries, MSMEs seem not to resort to illicit practices to supply to the global market (research question 2b). Some small producers have adapted to foreign market requirements by temporarily dissociating from exports and strengthening ties to local large manufacturers instead. They have created an informal network to exchange knowledge, facilities, and domestic orders, which might eventually also lead to sharing experiences on the foreign market. Multi-tiered (informal) subcontracts yet seem to be a strategy only for the domestic market. Future studies need to address to what extent local lead firms work on improving the MSME's capabilities in order to link them (informally) to global value chains and whether such relationships may provide the MSMEs with conditions for endogenous growth as suggested by Bettiol et al. (2011).

3. How do export-oriented leather goods and footwear producers adapt to power asymmetries in the global leather value chain?

As the integration into the world market of the MSMEs interviewed is unstable and irregular, conclusions have to be drawn with caution. Like in the tanning industry, even more secure and formalised transactions require a great deal of trust in order to handle transaction risks and reduce power asymmetries. Direct and long-term relationships seem to contribute towards increasing resilience and building up confidence between the transacting parties. Some better-skilled producers adapted to transaction failures (e.g. payment default, quality rejection) as a consequence of power asymmetries by selling their products on the domestic market. This, however, requires a network of potential large local buyers and the readiness to accept poorer terms and conditions. More in-depth studies are needed to draw relevant conclusions from the nature and duration of buyer-supplier relationships for the vulnerability of MSMEs in the export market. The risk of payment in international business transactions has a huge impact on the power balance in producer-customer relationships and appears to be widely under-researched for GVCs.

4. What upgrading strategies are conducive to improving the competitiveness of Bangladesh's leather industry?

   (a) What upgrading strategies does the leather industry require to address weaknesses and seize opportunities in the global leather value chain?

Governance structures determine upgrading trajectories. The captive value chains both tanners and leather goods/footwear producers are operating within are supportive of process and product upgrading but create barriers to functional upgrading. Unlike in the GVC analysis, global lead firms are not necessarily the key drivers (see Bettiol et al. 2011). Despite the tanneries' strong reliance on the foreign market, pressure from global buyers to upgrade is low and only addresses improvements in production processes (e.g. technology, chemicals, productivity) that impact product quality, too. Upgrading through adherence to private standards (e.g. Leather Working Group, BSCI) is unrealistic under the current environmental and labour conditions in Hazaribagh. Mandatory standards such as REACH have proven effective in restricting the use of harmful chemicals in products entering the EU market. Tewari and Pillai (2005) demonstrated for the Indian leather industry that it is critical to compliance to get the state involved. Regarding the environmental compliance in Hazaribagh, Bangladesh's government lacks this commitment to regulation and enforcement. Standards on leather that has been produced in a socially and environmentally compliant way can provide a competitive edge, but Bangladesh's leather industry still has a long way to go to qualify for these. In the long run, private standards might provide an opportunity for few large tanneries to produce compliant high-quality leather.

Though the strategy of organising the production process more efficiently is insufficient to reposition a firm in a GVC, it is a *conditio sine qua non* to develop its competitiveness. The heterogeneous tanning industry requires strategies that are devised to the group-specific needs of the tanneries. In view of the relocation to come, small and very small tanneries are given few chances to survive; cooperative tanning facilities might provide opportunities for a few of them. Medium-sized and large tanneries need to be encouraged to invest in technology and skills development to rise to international quality standards. Investment in technology and improving the skills level for operators and technicians are pivotal for the industry to abandon its race to the bottom. Vocational institutes can complement the extant graduate courses in leather technology already started in the leather goods and footwear industry.

There, upgrading processes are different. As ties to foreign buyers had not stabilised by the time this study started, local lead firms as regular customers of MSMEs were assumed to qualify for driving upgrading activities (for India, see Bettiol et al. 2011). However, the lead firms only provided as much technical assistance as to guarantee product quality and lead time. Both lead firms apply a double standard of social compliance for the local and the export market. The social enterprise fails in truly empowering its subcontractors and reducing their dependence. Low-skilled exclusive suppliers in particular have received little assistance to date, while more proficient producers were improving by being linked to upgrading programmes. This indicates that local lead firms may qualify for key drivers of upgrading processes, but only under specific circumstances (Finding 7). Bettiol et al. (2011) show for India that a large local company well-linked with fair trade organisations can improve the social and economic conditions of their low-skilled suppliers. Long-term relationships and investment in functional activities (e.g. design; management competences) increase suppliers' competitiveness and reduce their dependency. Hence, when buyers are small or not interested in seeing their suppliers grow, external organisations (e.g. development projects such as USAID PRICE and Re-Tie Bangladesh) can add extra resources to upgrading activities such as developing competences other than production. As for this study, USAID PRICE and Re-Tie Bangladesh initiated valuable processes that increased the productivity and product quality of a number of suppliers. However, they did little to reduce the suppliers' dependency on powerful downstream players (e.g. buying houses, lead firms); functional upgrading was barely considered. A sustainable effect is likely to arise only if assistance can be established for a longer period so shortcomings in the supply base can be systematically reduced.

The findings from this study suggest that lead firms are still very powerful in coordinating the local production network. With more integration into the foreign market, subcontracting for exports might expand and more cooperative structures between lead firms and MSME-suppliers might develop. However, the focus on the conditions for global market entry tends to overlook the huge potential of the domestic market, where margins are higher and pressure for compliance is non-existent. Capacity building for MSMEs (e.g. marketing initiatives, joint labels) is necessary to improve their direct access to the medium- and high-end segment without compromising the company's responsibility for a socially and environmentally compliant production.

(b) How are upgrading strategies to be devised that cater to the reality of informal dynamics in a GVC in order to improve the local producers' competitiveness?

If public and private actors manage to cooperate with each other, the relocation to the new tannery site may offer a unique opportunity to set up an environmentally compliant industry, liberating it from many burdens of the past. Process (or in this case rather locational) upgrading can be conducive to eliminating destructive institutionalised informal practices (e.g. solid/liquid waste management). By re-introducing regulation and enforcement, trust with new buyers can be established. Upgrading strategies need to take account of formal and informal institutions that interfere in the industry's competitiveness and exacerbate power asymmetries.

Formal institutional constraints such as international terms of payment or import duty on chemicals may reinforce power asymmetries at both global and local scales within the leather production network. Adaptation strategies often contain a high level of risk for the producers. The trade-off between formalising practices and price competitiveness is high and has to be approached institutionally (e.g. regulation, law enforcement). One of the most pressing issues is to restructure the chemical market by, for instance, reconsidering the rates of import duty and the allocation of bonded licenses, among others. Investment in R&D and an own chemical industry may foster indigenous innovation processes in tanning and finishing operations. It requires a comprehensive overhaul of the institutional framework (e.g. fiscal and financial incentives) to encourage the tanning and the leather goods/footwear industry to invest in their facilities, enhancing and capturing the value added within Bangladesh. In view of Bangladesh's dependency on the garment industry, only comprehensive, long-term strategies qualify for building up a sustainable leather sector, paying heed to power asymmetries and informal institutions the leather production network is embedded within. In this regard, it will be vital to reconsider the organisation of the Festival of Sacrifice (e.g. mass sacrifice) and to develop strategies that take into account both the importance of the religious side of the festival and the economic impact for the leather industry.

The discussion of the research questions revealed a number of specific phenomena and strongly interwoven dynamics in the Bangladeshi industry that to some extent ensure its price competitiveness on the international market but impinge on sustained competitiveness. Cultural-religious constraints, for instance, also exist in other countries with a strong leather industry (e.g. India, Pakistan); but there, the incidence appears to be either irrelevant or the ability to adapt is higher. The Indian leather industry, for instance, though also affected by a "structural lock-in" (for Kanpur, see Dietsche 2011, p. 111), has a higher level of competences that allow for the production of more-value added articles (e.g. safety shoes, saddles) by using buffalo instead of cattle or imported hides and skins. Other studies (e.g. Triple Line Consulting Ltd. 2002; Wayua and Kagunyu 2012; Jabbar et al. 2002) have analysed the indigenous supply of raw material, also in countries with Muslim population, but did not bring to attention a potential impact of the Festival of Sacrifice, let alone the dimension of such cultural-religious institutions. Hence, other countries' strategies to improve the competitiveness of MSME suppliers cannot be taken prescriptively. As seen in this study, what is needed is an individual but holistic approach that takes into account the role of informal institutions for the industry's competitiveness.

Much of the future of Bangladesh's leather industry depends on the relocation of the tanning estate to Hemayetpur/Savar. Removing Hazaribagh, long since considered a trade barrier, is expected to initiate a profound restructuring process and likely to boost the sector's competitiveness. This process has to be accompanied wisely to steer it in the right direction.

References

Alsayyad, N., & Roy, A. (2004). Urban informality: Crossing borders. In A. Roy & N. Alsayyad (Eds.), *Urban informality: Transnational perspectives from the middle east, latin America, and South Asia.* Oxford: Lexington Books.

Ballard, R. (2001). *A preliminary study on the bovine leather value chain in South Africa.* CSDS Research Report No. 40, University of Natal, Durban.

Bettiol, M., De Marchi, V., Di Maria, E., & Micelli, S. (2011). Economic, social and environmental upgrading in value chains: Social entrepreneurship and the role of emerging economy lead firms. *School of Environment and Development/University of Manchester, Working Paper 4*, Manchester.

Coe, N., Dicken, P., & Hess, M. (2008). Global production networks: Realizing the potential. *Journal of Economic Geography, 8*(3), 271–295.

Dietsche, C. (2011). *Umweltgovernance in globalen Wertschöpfungsketten: Umweltschutz und Qualitätssicherung im Handel mit tropischen Garnelen und Ledererzeugnissen.* Lit Verlag, Münster.

Gereffi, G. (2005). The global economy: Organisation, governance and development. In N. J. Smelser & R. Swedberg (Eds.), *Handbook of economic sociology* (2nd ed., pp. 160–182). Princeton, NJ: Princeton University Press and Russell Sage Foundation.

Jabbar, M. A., Kiruthu, S., Gebremedhin, B., & Ehui, S. (2002). *Essential actions to meet quality requirements of hides, skins and semi-processed leather from Africa.* Retrieved from: http://www.unido.org/fileadmin/import/10197_Jabbar.2.pdf. Accessed July 16, 2014.

Steer, L., & Sen, K. (2010). Formal and informal institutions in a transition economy: The case of Vietnam. *World Development, 38*(11), 1603–1615.

Tewari, M., & Pillai, P. (2005). Global standards and the dynamics of environmental compliance in India's leather industry. *Oxford Development Studies, 33*(2), 245–267.

Triple Line Consulting Ltd. (2002). *Study 1: Market requirements for importers of African hides and skins. The Hides, Skins and leather sector in Africa—Essential actions to meet quality requirements of importers.* Retrieved from: http://www.unido.org/fileadmin/import/10211_triplebottom.2.pdf. Accessed June 9, 2014.

Wayua, F. O., & Kagunyu, A. (2012). Constraints and opportunities in the hides and skins value chain in pastoral areas of northern Kenya. *Livestock Research for Rural Development 24*(8). Retrieved from: http://www.lrrd.org/lrrd24/8/wayu24135.htm. Accessed July 17, 2014.

Appendix

See Table A.1.

A.1 Selected Interview Guidelines—Producers

A.1.1 Tanneries and Commercial Leather Exporters

General information

- What does your company produce?
  - If you produce crust leather only, why is this the case?
- Where do you operate your production?
  - If you are not the owner, why do you rent tanneries/machinery?
- How do you source raw hides and skins?
  - What criteria are important for you when procuring raw hides and skins?
  - How does the price vary with the condition (*dried/salted/green*) of hides and skins?
  - What problems do you face in preserving the raw hides and skins?
  - To what extent do quality defects of hides and skins affect your business?
  - What do you do to ensure the quality of hides and skins?
  - How and after which processing stage do you grade the leather?
  - How do you transact with your suppliers of raw hides and skins?

    How do you agree on prices?
    What type of payment is arranged?
    What are the advantages/disadvantages of this type of payment?

  - How do you deal with the seasonal demand of raw hides and skins?
  - Have you ever considered importing raw hides?

J. Strasser, *Bangladesh's Leather Industry*,
Springer Geography, DOI 10.1007/978-3-319-22548-7

Table A.1 Traits of leather goods and footwear manufacturers interviewed

Acronym	Type	Class	Product complexity	Education	Type of dependency	Intensity of subcontracts (in %)	Export activity (in % of sales)	Type of export relations
LGM A	n.a.	Cottage	Very low	Illiterate	Second-tier subcontractor	100 %	0 %	None
LGM B	T1	Micro	Very low	Illiterate	First-tier subcontractor; further subcontracting	2010: 100 %	2010: 0 %	None
						2013: m.v.	2013: m.v.	
LGM C	T2	Micro	Very low–low	Junior secondary	First-tier subcontractor; further subcontracting	2010: 10 %	2010: 90 %	Mediated
						2013: 20 %	2013: 75–80 %	
LGM D	T3	Small	Very low–low-medium	Leather technologist	First-tier and second-tier subcontractor; further subcontracting	2010: 5 %	2010: 5 %	Mediated
						2013: 5 %	2013: 5 %	
LGM E	T3	Small	Very low–low-medium	Leather technologist	First-tier subcontractor; further subcontracting	2010: 40–50 %	2010: 0 %	Direct
						2013: 25 %	2013: 70 %	
LGM F	T3	Small	Low–medium	Diploma in designing	First-tier subcontractor; not subcontracting to others	2010: 25 %	2010: 75 %	Mediated
						2013: 25 %	2013: 75 %	
LFM A	T3	Small	Low–medium	Leather technologist	First-tier subcontractor; not subcontracting to others	2011: 95 %	2011: 5 %	Mediated
						2013: 25–30 %	2013: 70 %	
LFM B	T4	Medium-sized	Low–medium–medium-high	Higher secondary	First-tier subcontractor; further subcontracting	2010: 90 %	2010: 10 %	Mediated
						2013: 100 %	2013: 0 %	
LFM C	T4	Medium-sized	Medium–high	University	First-tier subcontractor; not subcontracting to others	2011: 80 %	2011: 20 %	Direct; mediated
						2013: 60–70 %	2013: 30–40 %	

(continued)

Table A.1 (continued)

Acronym	Type	Class	Product complexity	Education	Type of dependency	Intensity of subcontracts (in %)	Export activity (in % of sales)	Type of export relations
LGM G[a]	Lead firm	Large	Medium–high	n.a.	Lead firm; subcontracting	2010: 80–90 %	2010: 11 %	Direct; mediated
						Since 06/2014: 100 %	2013: 5 %	
LFM D[a]	Lead firm	Large	Medium–high	n.a.	Lead firm; subcontracting	2011: 40 %	2011: 80 %	OEM (joint venture)
						2013: m.v.	2013: m.v.	

[a]Data applies only to in-house production
Source Data based on interviews conducted in 2010–2014. Own composition

- What input components do you use to produce leather?
  - How do you source chemicals for leather processing?

    What problems do you face in sourcing chemicals?
  - How do you source your machines and accessories?

    What problems do you face in sourcing machines/accessories?
  - How do you maintain your machines?

    What problems do you face in maintaining your machines?
  - How do you cope with high prices of raw material and inputs?

Costs and financial subsidies

- What expenditures affect your business most at present?
- What kind of financial subsidies or incentives do you get from the government?
  - How important are these subsidies and incentives for your business?
- How do you get access to financial capital?
  - What problems do you face in getting access to financial capital?
  - When do you usually need financial capital?

Integration in the global market

- What is the advantage/disadvantage of having your tannery in Hazaribagh?
  - How do you cooperate with other tanneries?
- What is the demand for leather in the foreign market currently like?
  - How satisfied are you about your supply and sales performance?
- Why do you prioritise exporting over the domestic market?
  - What capabilities are required to produce leather for the domestic and/or export market?
  - How does export leather quality vary from that of the local market?
  - What are the advantages or disadvantages of the export market in comparison to the local market?

Buyer-supplier relationships

- Where/who do you supply your leather to?
  - How many buyers do you supply directly or via buying agents?
  - What is the benefit of a long-term relationship to foreign buyers and/or buying agents?
  - What is the risk of working with new buyers/buying agents?

- How do you communicate with them?
- How do you agree on prices with your customers?
- What impact does this method of setting prices have on your business?

- What kinds of requirements do buyers/buying agents impose on your production?
  - How do they ensure you produce according to their requirements?
  - What do you do if you see you may have difficulties meeting these requirements?
  - How have the requirements of international buyers changed during the last two decades?
  - What have you learned from doing business with international buyers/exporters?
  - What do you need to improve your negotiating position towards your foreign buyer?
- What other options do you have to market your leather?
  - Why do you not market and export your leather yourself?
  - How do you inform yourself about access to (new) markets?
  - Why do you do business with buying agents?
- How do you handle large order quantities?
  - What are the consequences for you if you exceed the agreed lead time?

Potential for improvements

- What problems do you face most in your business at the present time?
- What needs to be improved in the production process to increase your output per worker?
  - What investments are urgently needed in your tannery?
- What do you do to ensure your leather has export quality?
  - What quality tests for wet blue, crust and finished leather is your company subject to?
  - What testing facilities for chemical and physical tests do you use?
  - What does it depend on that buyers require you to submit chemical tests?
  - How do you inform yourself about e.g. modern tanning methods, machinery maintenance, clean technologies, and effluent treatment?
- Have you ever thought about linking leather processing with the production of leather footwear or leather goods? Why/not?
- What kind of waste does your tannery produce?
  - What do you do with solid and liquid tanned waste?
  - How and after what production steps do you recover solid and liquid tanned waste?

- If you were operating before 1990, please think back to the export ban on wet blue. How did it affect your business?
  - How did you manage to re-enter the export market?
  - What changes in the production process did your buyers ask you to make?
  - Why do you think the buyers chose you as a supplying company?

Labour

- What criteria are important for you to hire a leather worker?
  - How do you adjust your workforce to seasonally varying production volume?
  - What kind of contract do you conclude with your workers?
  - How do you train your workers?
  - What specialisation level do you expect them to acquire (i.e. how many operations do they usually carry out)?
  - How do you provide safety and occupational health to your workers?
  - How do your workers represent their interests towards you?

Assistance

- How do you get access to advisory service or technical assistance for your tannery?
  - What trainings or programmes have you already attended?
  - What impact have these trainings and programmes had on your business?
  - What kind of quality tests (chemical and physical quality) do you subject your leather to?
  - Do you know about the Bangladesh Leather Service Centre (BLSC)?
  - What services provided by BLSC have you already used?
  - What trainings and advice do you need to improve the production process?
- How do the leather/tannery associations support you?
  - Are you satisfied with them?
  - What could they do better?

Formality

- If applicable, please recall when you started out in business. What registration procedure did you go through before you started processing hides and skins?
  - What licences and registration do you have for running this business?
- To what extent are you subject to controls by governmental agencies?
  - What impact do these controls have on your business?
  - How often do you have to renew registration and licenses?

Outlook

- What challenges and opportunities do you see for your business in the next five years?

A.1.2 Tanneries—Eid-ul-Azha

- Did you buy Qurbani hides during Eid days? Why/not?
  - How many Qurbani hides and skins did you buy during Eid days?
  - What is the average size of a cow hide or a goat skin on Qurbani?
- How long are Qurbani hides and skins usually available in the market?
  - Given this time period how do prices develop after Eid?
- When do you usually purchase the bulk amount of Qurbani hides? Why?
- How long do you buy Qurbani hides and skins? Why?
- How many pieces/ft^2 of cow hides/goat skins did you target to buy this Qurbani?
  - How many pieces did you eventually buy?

    If so, why didn't you achieve your target?
  - What was your target price for cow hides/goat skins this Qurbani?

    At what price did you eventually buy?
- How many ft^2 of hides and skins do you usually purchase over a year?
- How many ft^2 of cow and goat leather do you export annually?
- How many Qurbani hides and skins did you buy in 2011?
  - What quantity of hides and skins did you purchase during Qurbani 2011 in relation to your annual collection (in %)?
- How many losses do you suffer due to unprofessional handling in slaughtering and trading the Qurbani hides?
- At which time do you start salting the hides and skins coming in on the first Eid day?
- Who supplies (i.e. what type of suppliers) you with Qurbani hides?
  - How do you pay your suppliers of Qurbani hides?
- How many months of your annual production do the Qurbani hides cover?
- How do you finance the purchase of your Qurbani hides?
  - At what interest rates are you funded by banks or other financial institutions (friends, family)?
  - By when are you requested to repay the loan?

- What difficulties do you face in processing large quantities of raw hides to wet blue in such a short time?
  - Where do you process the Qurbani hides to wet blue?
  - How many pieces of cow hides and goat skins can you process per day in your tannery (i.e. capacity)?
  - Do you rent other facilities or do you need to do job work to process the hides and skins on time?
- How many additional workers do you hire for processing Qurbani hides?
  - For how long do you employ these workers?
  - How do you hire these workers?

A.1.3 Leather Goods and Footwear Manufacturers (MSMEs)

General information

- What does your company produce?
- What production steps do you carry out in your workshop?
- Why did you choose to produce these leather goods?
- What market segment do you target?
- How do you source raw material?
  - Have you ever considered importing crust/finished leather for further processing?
  - What is the difference in imported tanned leather and locally produced leather?
- How do you transact with tanneries?
  - How do you agree on prices?
  - What type of payment is arranged?
  - What are the advantages/disadvantages of this type of payment?
- What type of inputs do you use to produce a leather product?
  - How do you source your accessories?
  - What problems do you face in the supply of accessories?
  - What chemicals do you need to produce leather goods/footwear?

    How do you source your chemicals?
    What problems do you face in the supply of chemicals?

  - How do you source machines?

    What problems do you face in the supply of machinery?

Costs and financial subsidies

- What costs affect you most? Why?
  - How do you cope with current prices of raw material and other inputs?
- What kind of financial subsidies or incentives do you get from the government?
  - How important are these subsidies/incentives for your business?
- How do you get access to financial capital?
  - What problems do you face in getting access to financial capital?

Integration into global market

- How satisfied are you about your present sales performance?
- What are your reasons for producing for the export market (instead of the domestic market)?
  - How do the requirements for exported leather goods/footwear differ from those for the local market?
  - What are the (dis-)advantages of the export market in comparison to the local market?
- How did you manage to enter the export market?
  - When did you start doing business with buyers/buying agents? Why?
  - Why do you think the foreign buyer chose you as a supplier?
  - What changes in the production process were you asked to make in order to supply to foreign buyers?
  - What kind of assistance did the foreign buyers provide you with?

Buyer-supplier relationship

- Where/who do you supply your leather to?
  - How many buyers do you supply directly or via buying agents?
  - What is the benefit of a long-term relationship to foreign buyers and/or buying agents?
  - What is the risk of working with new buyers/buying agents?
  - How do you communicate/keep contact with your buyer/buying agent?
  - If market entry was achieved recently: How did the relationship to your first foreign buyer develop after the first deal?
- What kind of requirements do foreign buyers impose on you?
  - How do they ensure you meet these requirements?
  - What do you do if you realise you might have difficulties meeting these requirements?
  - To what extent have the requirements of foreign buyers changed over the last two decades? Why?

- How do your buyers involve you in the design development process?
- How do you market your products? Why not by yourself?
  - Why do you not deal directly with the buyer?
  - How do you inform yourself about international market trends?
- What would help you improve your negotiating position towards your foreign buyer?
- How do you deal with seasonal demand of leather goods/footwear?
- How do you deal with large order quantities?
- What are the consequences if you exceed the agreed lead time?
- How do you cooperate with other subcontracting leather goods/footwear producers?
- What has changed for your enterprise since you have been supplying to the export market?
- What have you learned for your own business from supplying to foreign buyers?

Potential for improvements

- How important is it for you to have your factory/workshop located in …?
  - What sites as workplace would be more convenient for you?
- What problems do you face currently most in your business?
  - What needs to be done to solve these problems?
  - What is to be improved in the production process to increase your output per worker?
  - What do you need to invest in most?
- Have you ever considered extending your product line to other leather goods/footwear? Why/ not?
- How do you ensure your leather products have export quality?
- What facilities for quality control do you use?
- What type of quality tests do you subject your leather products to?

Labour conditions

- What criteria are important for you to hire a leather goods operator?
- What kind of contract do you conclude with your workers (operators, supervisors)?
- How do you train your operators?
  - How specialised do you want them to become?
- How do you provide safety and occupational health to your workers?
- How do your workers represent their interests towards you?
- How do you adjust your workforce to seasonally varying production volumes?

Assistance and advisory service

- How do you inform yourself about modern production methods, clean technologies, and machinery maintenance?
- How do you get access to advisory services or technical assistance for your business?
  - How useful has this assistance been to you?
  - What trainings have you already attended?
  - What impact have these trainings had on your business?
  - What kind of certification tests do you subject your leather goods to?
  - Do you know about the Bangladesh Leather Service Centre (BLSC)?
  - What trainings and advisory services do you need to improve the production process?
- To what extent have leather associations proven helpful (for your business) in representing your interests?

Formality

- Please think back to when you started your business. What registration procedure di you go through before you were allowed to open your workshop/factory?
- What kind of licences and registration do you need now to run this business?
- To what extent are you subject to controls by governmental agencies?
  - What impact do these controls have on your business?
  - How regularly do you have to renew registration and licenses?

Outlook

- What challenges and opportunities is your business likely to face within the next 5 years?

A.1.4 Local Lead Firms

Background

- How did your company come into being as a footwear producer/manufacturer (and retailer) of traditional Bangladeshi products and design?
- How did you manage to set up this retail network in the local market?
- Can you give me an idea about the monthly production capacity and the actual production volume of your own factories?
  - What is the reason for underutilising your production capacity?

Outsourcing practices

- What is the production volume you outsource to other companies?
- How much of your monthly production do you outsource to other enterprises?
- Which criteria do you apply to enterprises that qualify for being subcontracted?
  - What kind of enterprise do you entrust with the production for XX?
- How many producers are involved in producing leather goods/footwear?
- How much of your outsourced production goes to the domestic market?
  - How much feeds into the export market?
- What are the reasons why XX outsources production to local SMEs?
- How do you guarantee quality when outsourcing production to SMEs?
- What kind of training do you give to your suppliers?
- What are your opportunities/benefits in subcontracting local SMEs?

Buyer-supplier relations

- How do you communicate with your subcontracted enterprises?
  - How often do you pay them a visit?
  - What do you check when visiting them?
- How do you make your suppliers commit themselves to your company?
- What is your company's benefit from a long-term relationship to its suppliers?
- What are the benefits in subcontracting for your suppliers?
- How do you carry out transactions (contract, payment) with your suppliers?
- You advertise with spot payment on delivery. What is the reason for these (at least locally) unusual terms of payment?

Global integration

- How does XX market its footwear/*deshi* handicrafts abroad?
- How do you investigate international market trends?
- How much of your overall production is destined for the export market?
  - Which production facilities do you use for supplying the export market?
  - Do you also subcontract for the export market?

Requirements and standards

- When supplying to the export market what difficulties do you face meeting international requirements for product quality?
- How do you enforce the requirements for product quality at the supplier level?
  - How do you ensure your suppliers keep the lead time?
  - How do you monitor the performance of your suppliers in meeting these quality standards?

- What does corporate social responsibility mean to your company?
- What does your company to ensure that labour standards are met in your subcontracted companies?
- What does your company do to provide its workers and the workers of their subcontracted companies with a healthy and safe working environment?

Upgrading

- What upgrading initiatives have you started with local SMEs?
  - What were the reasons for starting these initiatives?
  - What impact has this had on your suppliers and on your company?
  - On what basis did you select the SMEs in the PRICE upgrading programme?
  - What difficulties did you face in implementing these upgrading programmes?
  - What does your company expect from these upgrading initiatives for future cooperation with local SME?

A.2 Selected Interview Guidelines—Traders

A.2.1 Traders of Raw Hides and Skins

General information

- How did you come to trade raw hides and skins?
- What type of hides and skins do you mostly trade with?
- What operations do you carry out in your warehouse/godown?
- What amount of cow/buffalo hides and goat/sheep skins (in pc or ft^2) do you trade monthly (season, off-season)?
- How has the price of each changed in comparison to 2009?
  - What are the main reasons for this change/price difference compared with 2009?
  - What impact has this increase/decrease had on your business?
- How do you get access to financial capital?
  - What problems do you face in getting access to financial capital?

Buyer-supplier relationships

- Where do you preferably source your raw hides and skins?
  - From which type of suppliers do you usually buy raw hides and skins?
  - What problems do you face with unauthorised hide and skin dealers?

- How do you transact with your suppliers (collectors/butchers)?
  - How do you agree on prices?
  - What type of contract and payment is arranged?
  - What are the advantages/disadvantages of this type of payment?
- What criteria are important for you when you source raw hides and skins?
  - What grade, size and thickness do you usually trade with?
- When do you prefer to purchase and sell raw hides and skins?
- How do you transact with the tanneries in Hazaribagh?
  - How do you agree on prices?
  - What type of contract and payment is arranged?
  - What are the advantages/disadvantages of this type of payment?
  - What kind of problems do you face with your business partners in Dhaka?
- How do you cope with outstanding payments from customers?
  - What do you do to prevent such problems?
  - Where do you get support from when you face such problems with your customers?
- To what extent have associations proven useful in representing your interests?
- How do you get advice or technical assistance for your business?

Potential for improvements

- What are the main problems you face in your business?
- What problems do you face with non-professional butchers flaying hides and skins?
  - What impact do they have on your business?
- What should be done to solve these problems?
- What are the criteria for good quality cow hides and goat skins?
- What kind of quality problems do you face with raw hides and skins?
  - What problems in preserving hides and skins after slaughtering do you face?
  - What kind of diseases do you encounter among cattle, goat and sheep livestock?
  - What is the impact of these quality defects on your business?
  - How do you cope with quality defects?
- How do you ensure the quality of hides and skins?
  - What happens if your customers in Hazaribagh are not satisfied with the supplied quality?
  - What measures are required to improve the quality of raw hides and skins in Bangladesh?

- What tools/machines would you need to facilitate your work and increase your productivity (i.e. output per worker)?
- Have you ever thought of processing raw hides and skins yourself?
  - What are the main reasons for not linking trading with processing?

Labour

- What criteria are important for you to hire a worker?
- What kind of contract do you conclude with your workers?
- How do you train your workers?
  - What specialisation level do you expect them to acquire?
- How do you adjust your demand for workforce to seasonally varying production volumes?
- What do you do to provide your workers with a safe and healthy working environment?
- How do your workers represent their interests towards you?

Formality

- If applicable/possible, please think back to when you started your business. What documents did you have to submit to trade with hides and skins?
  - What kind of licences and registration do you need now to run this business?
  - How regularly do you have to renew registration and licenses?
- To what extent are you subject to controls by regulatory agencies?
  - What impact do these controls have on your business?

Outlook

- What challenges and opportunities do you expect for your business within the next 5 years?

A.2.2 Traders of Raw Hides and Skins on Eid-ul-Azha

General information

- How much did you pay for these hides/skins?
- Where did you get these hides/skins from?
  - Where do you buy hides and skins during Eid days (in general)?
- At what price do you want to sell it on?
- Where do you want to sell the hides and skins? Why?
  - Do you already know to whom you want to sell the hides/skins?

- How many hides and skins have you already bought today?
- How many Qurbani hides and skins do you target to buy?
  - Over which time period do you want to buy this amount of hides and skins?
  - Over which time period do you want to sell this amount of hides and skins?
- How many days/weeks/months do you usually deal with Qurbani hides and skins?
  - If so, why don't you also deal with hides and skins after Eid?

Experience and motivation

- Did you already buy and sell hides last year on Qurbani?
  - For how long have you been dealing with hides and skins on Qurbani?
- Why do you deal with hides and skins on Qurbani?
- Do you have a license to trade hides and skins?

Training and capabilities

- How do you assess the quality of the hides and skins?
- How do you measure the size of the hides and skins?
- How do you know about the current price rate?
- Do you apply salt to the hides and skins?
  - If so, when?
- How many people do you employ to achieve your collection target?
- What costs (employees, transportation, etc.) do you have to bear for collecting hides and skins on Eid?

MIX
Papier aus verantwortungsvollen Quellen
Paper from responsible sources
FSC® C105338

If you have any concerns about our products,
you can contact us on
ProductSafety@springernature.com

In case Publisher is established outside the EU,
the EU authorized representative is:
Springer Nature Customer Service Center GmbH
Europaplatz 3, 69115 Heidelberg, Germany

Printed by Libri Plureos GmbH
in Hamburg, Germany